✖ INSIGHT GUIDES

THE GAMBIA
& SENEGAL

● Discovery
CHANNEL

APA PUBLICATIONS L

Part of the Langenscheidt Publishing Group

INSIGHT GUIDE

THE GAMBIA & SENEGAL

Editorial
Managing Editor
Carine Tracanelli
Art Director
Ian Spick
Picture Manager
Steven Lawrence
Series Editor
Dorothy Stannard

Distribution

UK & Ireland
GeoCenter International Ltd
Meridian House, Churchill Way West
Basingstoke, Hampshire RG21 6YR
Fax: (44) 1256 817988

United States
Langenscheidt Publishers, Inc.
36–36 33rd Street 4th Floor
Long Island City, NY 11106
Fax: 1 (718) 784 0640

Australia
Universal Publishers
1 Waterloo Road
Macquarie Park, NSW 2113
Fax: (61) 2 9888 9074

New Zealand
Hema Maps New Zealand Ltd (HNZ)
Unit 2, 10 Cryers Road
East Tamaki, Auckland 2013
Tel: (64) 9 273 6459. Fax: (64) 9 273 6479

Worldwide
Apa Publications GmbH & Co.
Verlag KG (Singapore branch)
38 Joo Koon Road, Singapore 628990
Tel: (65) 6865 1600. Fax: (65) 6861 6438

Printing

Insight Print Services (Pte) Ltd
38 Joo Koon Road, Singapore 628990
Tel: (65) 6865 1600. Fax: (65) 6861 6438

©2009 Apa Publications GmbH & Co.
Verlag KG (Singapore branch)
All Rights Reserved

Second Edition 2009

ABOUT THIS BOOK

The first Insight Guide pioneered the use of creative full-colour photography in travel guides in 1970. Since then, we have expanded our range to cater for our readers' need not only for reliable information about their chosen destination but also for a real understanding of the culture and workings of that destination. Now, when the internet can supply inexhaustible (but not always reliable) facts, our books marry text and pictures to provide those much more elusive qualities: knowledge and discernment. To achieve this, they rely heavily on the authority of locally based writers and photographers.

How to use this book

This book is structured to convey an understanding of The Gambia's and Senegal's culture and people, and guides readers through its cities, national parks and traditional villages.

◆ The **Features** section, indicated by a pink bar at the top of each page, covers the cultural history of both countries as well as illuminating essays on Peoples of The Gambia and Senegal, their cuisines, festivals and art scene.

◆ The main **Places** section, indicated by a blue bar, is a complete guide to all the sights and areas worth visiting. Places of special interest are coordinated by number with the maps.

◆ The **Travel Tips** listings section, with a yellow bar, provides full information on transport, accommodation, activities ranging from culture to shopping to sports, an A–Z section of essential practical information, as well as two handy French and Wolof phrasebooks. An easy-to-find contents list for Travel Tips is printed on the back flap, which also serves as a bookmark.

LEFT: a fisherman mending his nets on Tanji Beach, The Gambia.

extensively. Also working within the music and arts scene, she has been involved in projects and collaborations with many Gambian artists with the focus on uplifting and promoting West African culture worldwide.

This new edition builds on a previous edition written by **Andy Gravette**, **Amadou Moctar Gueye**, **Kaye Whiteman**, **Nim Caswell**, and **Michael** and **Elizabeth Kelly**.

Insight Guides and Philip Briggs would also like to thank the team at **The Gambia Experience** for their invaluable help organising his trip and on-the-ground guidance.

The majority of the photographs were taken especially for this edition by **Sylvaine Poitau**. Poitau grew up in North Africa and this early experience of the continent helped her capture the beauty of the region and its people. Poitau has worked for numerous English newspapers, including the **Financial Times** and **The Independent**. Most of the wildlife pictures are from South Africa-based **Ariadne Van Zandbergen**, who has photographed African wildlife extensively.

This book was proofread by **Neil Titman** and indexed by **Helen Peters**. Thanks also go to **Lesley Gordon** as well as **Paula Soper** and **Rachel Fox** for their editorial help.

The contributors

This new edition was commissioned and edited by French-born, bilingual editor **Carine Tracanelli** and builds on an earlier edition produced by **Philip Sweeney** and **Dorothy Stannard**.

The majority of the update and footwork – or, in this case, bush taxi work – was done by **Philip Briggs**, an acknowledged expert on African travel who regularly contributes articles to a variety of travel magazines. He also wrote other Insight Guides on *Tanzania* and *East African Wildlife*. Briggs was also responsible for updating the history and the restaurant listings throughout the book, as well as The Gambia Travel Tips.

The features on Food and Drink, Arts and Crafts, as well as the photo feature on festivals were updated by **Lena Nian**. A photographer/designer with family in The Gambia and Senegal, she has travelled both countries

Map Legend

—— - -	International Boundary
— — —	Region/District Boundary
—•—	National Park/Reserve
— — —	Ferry Route
⊖	Border Crossing
✈ ✈	Airport: International/Regional
🚌	Bus Station
✉	Post Office
ℹ	Tourist Information
✝ † ⚔	Church/Ruins
∴	Archaeological Site
☪	Mosque
∩	Cave
1	Statue/Monument
★	Place of Interest
⌐	Beach
⌐⌐	Lighthouse

The main places of interest in the Places section are coordinated by number with a full-colour map (e.g. ❶), and a symbol at the top of every right-hand page tells you where to find the map.

BELOW: making his way through the delta waters.

Contents

LEFT: brightly painted
fishing pirogues.

Travel Tips

THE BEST OF THE GAMBIA & SENEGAL: TOP SIGHTS

The Atlantic coast may be the biggest draw for sun-starved visitors, but both countries also offer great wildlife-viewing, and attractions providing insight into traditional and colonial history

△ West Africa's scaled-down answer to Stonehenge, the mysterious **Senegambian Stone Circles** at Wassu (The Gambia) and Siné Ngayène (Senegal) were erected as grave markers by an unknown civilisation in early medieval times and accorded Unesco World Heritage Site status in 2006. *Page 128*

▽ One of the world's most thrilling avian spectacles, the **Parc National des Oiseaux du Djoudj**, perched at the southern end of the Sahara, is descended upon by up to 3 million thirsty migrants at the start of the European winter, and supports remarkable concentrations of pelicans, flamingos and other aquatic species throughout the year. *Page 218*

△ Be it the bustling resort atmosphere of Kololi or Saly Portugal, or the untouched swathes of sand that hem in Gunjur or Kafountine, the **Atlantic beaches** of Senegal and The Gambia offer a perfect blue-skied seaside escape from the northern hemisphere winter. *Pages 93–109, 169–185 & 271–285*

△ Starting at the city of Saint-Louis, the off-the-beaten-track **Senegal River Route** arcs for hundreds of kilometres inland along West Africa's second-largest waterway, whose banks support numerous crumbling relics of the early colonial era alongside absorbing traditional cultures and architecture. *Pages 217–31*

◁ A wildlife sanctuary the size of a small European country, the **Parc National de Niokolo-Koba**, despite heavy poaching, retains a compelling wilderness atmosphere, a wealth of ungulates and birds, and Senegal's last remaining free-ranging populations of lion, chimpanzee, buffalo and wild dog. *Page 259*

△ A short ferry ride from the bustle of Dakar, the tiny **Île de Gorée** – at various times Portuguese, Dutch, British and French-occupied – boasts a unique concentration of colonial architecture and sleepy backwater demeanour, belying its association with the horrors of the transatlantic slave trade. *Pages 163–7*

△ Fringed by tall palms and sweaty jungle, the pristine stretch of tropical waterway protected within the **River Gambia National Park** comes across as a transplant from the Congo Basin, complete with chattering monkeys, colourful birds, and easily observed chimpanzees on three of its five islands. *Page 129*

△ Home to Mandina Lodge, the region's most exclusive and luxurious bush retreat, **Makasutu Culture Forest** also offers a fascinating cultural programme to day visitors, blissful dugout trips into mangrove-lined creeks, and close-up encounters with baboons and innumerable birds. *Page 101*

◁ Now reopened to tourism after a long civil war, the **Casamance**, with its wealth of traditional Diola architecture and rustic camps, offers endless opportunities for low-key exploration, not to mention superb beaches. *Pages 271–87*

▷ A small conservation area, the **Abuko Nature Reserve** nevertheless protects a stunning wealth of wildlife, including 300 bird species and a variety of forest antelope and monkeys. *Page 100*

THE BEST OF THE GAMBIA & SENEGAL: EDITOR'S CHOICE

Old colonial splendour, sandy beaches, lush mangrove creeks and wonderful wildlife are all waiting to be experienced in The Gambia and Senegal. Here are the editor's top tips for making the most of it

BEST WILDLIFE EXPERIENCES

● **Abuko Nature Reserve** Forest footpaths, varied birds, and a hide at a pool where crocs lurk and antelope drink. *See page 100.*

● **River Gambia National Park** The most beautiful stretch of the Gambia River, good for hippos, chimps and monkeys. *See page 129.*

● **Parc National de Niokolo-Koba** The most biodiverse park in Senegal, with plenty of antelope and four of the Big Five. *See page 259.*

● **Réserve de Bandia** Rhinos, giraffe and impala in baobab-studded savannah, a short distance from the Petite Côte. *See page 172.*

● **Réserve de Fathala** The Siné-Saloum's answer to Bandia, protecting the rare Derby's eland. *See page 202.*

● **Réserve de Guembeul** Reintroduced breeding herds of the endangered scimitar-horned oryx and Dama gazelle. *See page 211.*

BEST BEACH HANGOUTS

● **Gunjur and Kartong** These pristine beaches in southern Gambia are studded with eco-retreats. *See pages 105 & 106.*

● **Kotu** The best beach along the main Gambian resort strip from Bakau to Kololi. *See page 97.*

● **Cap Skirring** Arguably the region's best compromise between resort facilities and pristine beachfront. *See page 281.*

● **Kafountine** Beautiful beach and

laidback resorts catering to a youngish crowd. *See page 284.*

● **Saly** The most built-up resort in Senegal has excellent facilities, including dozens of great eateries and bars, and the beach is just fine too. *See page 176.*

● **La Somone** Quieter northern counterpart to Saly, with good facilities and a lovely beach terminating at a bird-filled lagoon. *See page 175.*

ABOVE LEFT: the horned African forest buffalo.
ABOVE: sandy beach at the foot of Ngala Lodge.
LEFT: the distinctive Diana monkey.

BEST BIRDWATCHING

- **Parc National des Oiseaux du Djoudj**
Resident pelicans by the thousand, plus millions of trans-Sahara migrants in season. *See page 218.*

- **Kiang West National Park**
Top raptor viewing, with the mighty bateleur above and secretary birds stalking the grass. *See page 121.*

- **Parc National de Niokolo-Koba**
Key sanctuary for large woodland birds such as Abyssinian ground hornbill, as well as Egyptian plover. *See page 259.*

- **Tanji River Bird Reserve**
Fabulous marine birdlife south of The Gambia's main resort strip with over 300 bird species. *See page 104.*

- **Siné-Saloum Delta**
Mangrove ecosystem harbouring immense breeding colonies of herons, gulls, spoonbills and terns. *See page 191.*

BEST CULTURAL EXPERIENCES

- **Dakar nightlife**
The nightclubs and bars of the Senegalese capital reverberate with contemporary African sounds. Be prepared to start late. *See page 330.*

- **Tanji**
Insanely chaotic fishing beach where colourful pirogues land the day's catch. *See page 103.*

- **Abbaye de Keur Moussa**
Pop in for Sunday Mass, when the Benedictine monks chant Gregorian to a backing of traditional African instruments. *See page 158.*

- **Bassari Country**
Animist beliefs and vibrant traditional ceremonies are main-tained in Senegal's remote southwest. *See page 266.*

- **Matam old town**
Welcoming maze of curvaceous adobe architecture on the remote banks of the Senegal. *See page 227.*

BEST MUSEUMS AND HISTORICAL SITES

- **Wassu**
The most accessible of the mysterious megalithic circles in the Gambia/Saloum basin. *See page 127.*

- **National Museum of Gambia**, Banjul
Its local and regional history displays are a highlight of The Gambia's capital. *See page 82.*

- **Musée Théodore Monod d'Art Africain**, Dakar
Ethnographic displays and traditional artefacts from various West African animist cultures. *See page 150.*

- **Saint James and Related Sites**
Seven sites on the North Bank linked with slave trade out of The Gambia and the later enforcement of abolition, including James Island, Juffureh and the Museum of the North Bank. *See page 89.*

- **Île de Karabane**
Former French trade outpost and present-day backwater steeped in history. *See page 279.*

ABOVE: Kankurang dance costumes in Banjul.
BELOW: initiation ceremony of the Bedik tribe in Iwol.

BEST ARCHITECTURE

ABOVE: a selection of Gambian crafts.

● **Île de Gorée**
Dense with pre-20th century colonial relics including the notorious Maison des Esclaves. *See page 163.*

● **Saint-Louis**
A wealth of colonial and Creole architecture complemented by an enchanting contemporary buzz. *See page 205.*

● **Mlomp**
Superb examples of the traditional two-storied houses built in the Casamance. *See page 278.*

● **Île à Morfil**
This island, which lies between the Senegal River and the Doué River, houses several good examples of adobe mosques. *See page 223.*

● **Touba Mosque**
Africa's tallest mosque dominates the skyline of the Mouride holy city of Touba. *See page 246.*

ABOVE: the colourful streets of Île de Gorée.
BELOW: Touba mosque.

BEST MARKETS

● **Marché Sandaga**
The chaotic commercial hub of downtown Dakar, not aimed primarily (or even secondarily) at tourists. *See page 148.*

● **Albert Market**
The main market in central Banjul, very down to earth but with a good crafts section. *See page 83.*

● **Kaolack**
All roads lead to this pivotal junction town, which comes across as one giant open-air market. *See page 248.*

● **Marché Saint-Maur-des-Fossés**
The most important market in Ziguinchor, hassle-free and totally authentic. *See page 275.*

● **Marché de Touba**
West Africa's most important contraband market, overshadowed by the great Mouride mosque. *See page 246.*

BEST SCENERY

● **Lac Rose**
Bizarre and compelling saline lake, seasonally given a pink hue by its unusual chemical content. *See page 158.*

● **Îles de la Madeleine**
Craggy cliffs, sandy coves and plentiful birds distinguish these tall volcanic outcrops offshore of Dakar. *See page 154.*

● **Siné-Saloum Delta**
Monotonous this vast mangrove-lined delta south of Dakar may be,

but the effect is hypnotic rather than soporific. *See page 191.*

● **Lompoul Desert**
An isolated Sahara-esque landscape of tall dunes inland of the coast dividing Dakar from Saint-Louis. *See page 254.*

● **River Gambia National Park**
The most haunting riverine vegetation in the region, like the setting for *Heart of Darkness*. *See page 129.*

ABOVE: the pink-tinged Lac Rose.

BEST BUSH GETAWAYS

● **Badi Mayo**
Superb tented camp on a cliff above the Gambia River; daily chimp visits are part of the package. *See page 301.*

● **Mandina River Lodge**
Floating and stilted wooden cabins on a mangrove-lined tributary of the Gambia. *See page 299.*

● **Tendaba Camp**
The Gambia's oldest upriver camp provides a thoroughly rewarding – and agreeably affordable – break from the coastal resort. *See page 300.*

● **Bird Safari Camp**
Overgrown riverside camp on the west end of MacCarthy Island, within walking distance of historic Janjanbureh (often referred to as Georgetown). *See page 301.*

● **Hôtel Simenti**
The architecture lacks inspiration, but the setting – overlooking the Gambia River in the heart of Niokolo-Koba – is simply stunning, and a great location for viewing wildlife too. *See page 327.*

ABOVE: sunset over a riverside lodge.

BEST FOR CHILDREN

● **Coastal resorts**
The sea may be a little rough for toddlers, but the best resort hotels all have children's pools, and offer a range of activities suitable for youngsters.

● **Réserve de Bandia**
The ideal mini-safari for short attention spans, lining up rhinos, giraffe, monkeys and several antelope species in a 90-minute drive. *See page 172.*

● **Football**
Bring one with you, and your children will attract plenty of playmates in these football-obsessed countries. *See page 304.*

● **Kachikally Crocodile Pool**
This is a thrilling face-to-face experience with sacred crocodiles basking by the dozen in a fenced pool in suburban Bakau. The

crocodiles are said to have mystical powers. *See page 95.*

● **Dream Park**
This new amusement park in Kololi has dodgems, carousels and a host of other rides suitable to children. *See page 305.*

CLOSE – AND DISTANT TOO

Exotic and redolent of the dark age of the
slave trade and of the trans-Saharan camel
caravans, The Gambia and Senegal also
make for a thoroughly practical and
convenient holiday destination

For most visitors, it starts with the beaches. You can opt for the plush transatlantic five-star retreat sampling every creature comfort imaginable, or choose a busy (but not overcrowded) Mediterranean-style resort zone spilling over with cheap and cheerful bars, restaurants and nightclubs. Or if you just want to while away the days reading, swimming and walking along a pristine stretch of palm-lined sand, then the lush Atlantic coastline of Senegal and The Gambia has something to suit almost all tastes and budgets.

Logistically, both countries have a lot going for them too. Boasting the most northerly beach frontage in sub-Saharan Africa, francophone Senegal and anglophone Gambia lie less than six hours from Europe by air, and the absence of a significant time difference means there is no risk of the jetlag associated with more far-flung tropical beach destinations. Moreover, the long West African dry season, when sunny skies, warm day temperatures and pleasant nights are all but guaranteed, runs from November to May, making for an ideal winter break.

A major draw is undoubtedly the African setting. Venture into the dry interior and you'll be swept up in the warmth and bustle of this exciting continent. Also, lots of day tours venture beyond the tourist zones, whether it be a birding trip to Abuko or half-day safari to Bandia, a visit to the heaving Mbour fish market or sacred crocodile pool of Kachikally. More darkly, a "Roots Tour" to Juffureh and James Island or ferry trip to Gorée Island provide a sobering insight into how West Africa was exploited by the transatlantic slave trade.

Longer excursions, taking you deeper into the interior, might include a luxury cruise past the time-worn ports of the Senegal River, a boat trip to see chimps and hippos in River Gambia National Park, or a hot and dusty safari into the remote savannah of Niokolo-Koba. And while Senegal and The Gambia both cater mainly to the beach package market, these most approachable of African countries also offer unlimited scope to independent travellers, ranging from the contemporary urban buzz of Dakar or Saint-Louis to the more traditionalist mood that infuses the hinterland of the Casamance and Gambia River. ❏

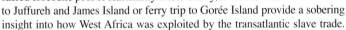

PRECEDING PAGES: pirogues lining the beach at Cap Skirring, Senegal; checking
the winning lottery numbers in Banjul, The Gambia; market vendors in Brikama,
The Gambia. **LEFT:** shell-pickers making their way home, Siné-Saloum delta, Senegal.
ABOVE: Gambian smile. **RIGHT:** palm-fringed beach at the Atlantic Hotel, Banjul.

TWO COUNTRIES, ONE ETHNIC MIX

Though they speak different languages,
anglophone Gambians and francophone Senegalese
share a great number of ethnic similarities

The many ethnic groups that inhabit Senegal and The Gambia all have a unique history, set of customs, language and cultural identity. However, the traditional boundaries recognised by these cultural groups were largely ignored by the European bureaucrats who delineated most of the continent's international boundaries. As a result, throughout Africa today, many people still share a deeper cultural heritage and linguistic bond with affiliates in neighbouring countries than with the bulk of their modern countrymen.

Senegal and The Gambia are no exception. Many ethnic groups are common to both countries, while others have territories extending into neighbouring Mali, Guinea or Mauritania. Unlike in many other African countries, however, ethnicity was not exploited on a divide-and-rule basis by the colonisers of Senegal and The Gambia, nor has it played a disproportionate role in post-independence politics, and both countries tend to embrace cultural diversity rather than seeing it as a force for fractiousness.

One reason for this is a long West African philosophical tradition of cultural cousinship, which stresses connections between people rather than

Many subtleties are lost on outsiders, but one West African will recognise another's ethnic group almost unconsciously, thanks to a complex set of social, linguistic and behavioural clues.

differences, and encourages good neighbourliness except in times of overt conflict. Paradoxically, while Senegalese and Gambians are both proud of their national identity and conscious of the links

between different groups, individuals are always acutely aware of each other's backgrounds.

Humour, as always, is a great intermediary: a form of tongue-in-cheek ritualised abuse has come to play a strong role in enforcing the tradition of cultural cousinship, possibly because it subverts cultural stereotypes with open laughter. It might not strike us as very funny for a Serer to remind a Tukulor that he would have been his slave in days gone by, but that sort of banter reliably tickles the Senegalese funny bone. Family names and histories are also subjects for fun. When a Seck meets a Gueye, one of them will soon refer to the other's excessive appetite for rice. This is taken in good part – it's better to be greeted warmly with a joke, even at your own expense, than coldly or distantly.

LEFT: Gambian cajun nut-sellers.
RIGHT: Senegalese artist, Dakar.

Islam in West Africa

Although the teachings of Islam are broadly universal, the branch of Sufism practised in West Africa has developed several unique features

One particularity of Islam in this area is the significance of the marabout, a name that derives from the Arabic for "one who is attached" and might refer to any Islamic leader, scholar or mystic. Some marabouts have led jihads or founded million-

strong brotherhoods, others are teachers or imams, and others still live as vagrants, but all are viewed as mystics and sages and possess attributes that Christians might associate with saints.

The defining feature of Islam in Senegal and The Gambia is the brotherhoods that dominate every facet of daily life. Many males are inducted into these brotherhoods as pre-teen *talibés* ("students"), who are attached to specific marabouts and often earn their keep as beggars. Adult followers pay tribute in money, goods or land; if they cannot afford any of these, they can work the brotherhood's land for free. As with most religious sects, there is a strong regional or hereditary aspect to membership of a brotherhood, but anybody is free to join, including Europeans who embrace the institution's beliefs.

The Mouride, Senegal's largest and most influential brotherhood, was founded in 1883 by Cheikh Amadou Bamba, whose opposition to colonial rule led to his exile to Gabon in 1894 and house arrest after his return. The Mouride emphasis on hard work is not dissimilar to the Protestant work ethic. Traditionally farmers, the Mouride played a large role in the creation of the groundnut industry, though declines in production have forced many into the towns to work as small traders, often sponsored and protected by larger retailers and suppliers of the same fraternity.

The country's greatest annual pilgrimage is the Mouride Magal, when over a million pilgrims descend on the holy city of Touba. Magal (literally "return voyage") celebrates the return from exile of Bamba to Touba. Like other Islamic feasts, Magal is movable, falling between the 10th and 11th days of the 11th month of the Muslim calendar. It peaks with a night of prayer in Touba Mosque or among the followings of individual marabouts.

A sub-branch of the Mourides, the Baye Fall – named after Cheikh Ibrahim Fall, a disciple of Bamba – can be recognised by their dreadlocks, colourful tunics, clubs, calabashes (used for drinking and collecting coins) and often rather wild-eyed appearance. It is said that Ibrahim Fall and his followers were excused observance of traditional Islamic obligations because of their extraordinary zeal. The movement mostly attracts younger men, who work the fields or walk the town streets chanting prayers and begging.

The country's oldest and second-largest brotherhood, the Tidjiane was founded in Algeria by Cheikh Ahmed El Tidjiane in the early 19th century. It was brought to prominence by El Hadj Malick Sy, who lived in Tivaouane, the movement's spiritual headquarters, in 1902. The Tidjiane also prevails in the Kaolack region. The smaller Layène brotherhood, centred on Yoff on the Cap Vert peninsula, are noted for their all-white attire and mass marriage ceremonies. Most followers adopt the name Laye, synonymous with the name of God, after their family name. The Cap Vert peninsula is studded with sites linked with the Layène founder Seydina Limamou Laye. ❏

LEFT AND ABOVE: two facets of Islam in West Africa, the marabout and the mosque.

The Wolof

The most numerically significant group in Senegal, occupying most of the coastal belt and western interior north of Kaolack, is the Wolof, who number about 5 million and comprise some 43 percent of the total population. By contrast, the 250,000 Wolof who live in The Gambia represent just 15 percent of the national population, though their pre-eminence around Banjul and high profile in neighbouring Senegal mean that Wolof has become the lingua franca of both countries, spoken by more than 90 percent of people as a first or second language.

The Wolof are believed to have entered central Senegal in the 12th century, possibly a little later. They were early converts to Islam, and remain almost exclusively Islamic today, forming the backbone of the Mouride brotherhood. They are also sometimes referred to as the Jollof, in reference to the Djolof Empire, which thrived as a single entity ruled from Linguère and comprised several vassal states in medieval times, but broke into six autonomous states in the early days of coastal trade with the Portuguese.

Traditionally, the Wolof have a clearly defined hierarchical caste system, which persists in diluted form today. At the top are the *geer* (nobles) and *badolo* (ranking somewhere between free peasants and gentry). Lower down the social scale are the

GREETINGS

Extended greetings are crucial social lubricants in Africa. When acquaintances meet, they shake hands, then spend several minutes, hands loosely clasped, exchanging mutual interrogations – how are you, how's the wife, how are the children, how are the cattle? The detail of such greetings need not concern the casual visitor, but it does serve to remind that human – particularly family – relationships are accorded greater weight here than in Europe or North America. Introduce your elderly parents to a local and it will be seen as a great honour. And any contact, however casual, will go more smoothly if you greet properly before starting a conversation: even the most mispronounced *"Nanga'def"* or *"Kassoumaye"* will set the right tone.

artisans, whose crafts were hereditary; this group included blacksmiths, tailors and the minstrel-historians known as *griots*. At the bottom are the *jaam*, or slaves, and the outcast *neeno*. Marriage between castes was once forbidden, a prohibition that has relaxed somewhat today, though families still sometimes argue about such matches.

In recent times, the Wolof have excelled at farming and agriculture, having been instrumental in the development of groundnut cultivation (unfortunately sometimes to the exclusion of other, equally necessary, crops). Unusually for West Africa, the men work the fields, while the women take care of the home, kitchen and children. Prominent Wolof

ABOVE: warm welcome at Banjul International Airport.

figures in modern Senegal include all the Mouride caliphs such as the incumbent Cheikh Bara Mbake, President Abdoulaye Wade (also a highly active member of the Mouride brotherhood), the recently deceased "father of African film" director and novelist Ousmane Sembène, and the legendary Dakarois singer Youssou N'Dour.

The Fula and Tukulor

Sometimes referred to collectively as the Halpulaar or Haalpulaaren (literally "Pulaar-speakers"), the Fula and Tukulor are a diverse group of traditional pastoralists linked by their common Pulaar language. Also known as the Fulani, Peul and Fulbe, the Fula are the most widespread of West African people, with a presence in 19 countries ranging eastwards from Mauritania and Guinea to Niger, Central African Republic and parts of Sudan. Pulaar-speakers, including the Tukulor subgroup, comprise 25 percent of the total Senegalese population, and around 15 percent of The Gambia's, where they dominate in the east.

Lighter-skinned than other Senegalese, the Fula are semi-nomadic pastoralists by tradition, herding cattle, goats and other livestock in parts of West Africa too dry to support agriculture, where their traditional dress of green, yellow and other brightly coloured wraps enlivens an otherwise rather

THE LAND OF HOSPITALITY

The Senegalese and Gambian people place great importance on manners, and are very welcoming – indeed, Senegal has been dubbed the *Pays de la Teranga* ("Land of Hospitality"). Local manners may require minor adjustments, but your hosts will know a great deal more about your ways than you about theirs, and an inadvertent unintended faux pas will most certainly quickly be forgotten. Contrary to the spirit of *teranga*, begging, though much decried by older Senegalese and Gambians, is common in parts of the region,

and the best response to a request for your money or possessions is a laughing "It's not mine" *("Ce n'est pas à moi")* or "Next time" *("La prochaine fois")*. And abuse of *teranga* is the stock in trade of those persistent strangers who latch on to tourists, claiming to work at their hotel or spinning sob stories, characters who may occasionally require a firmer "No" *("Non")*. Outside the big cities, however, most approaches by locals reflect the genuine hospitality and friendliness of which locals are rightly proud.

parched and hazy landscape. Their trademark herds of hump-necked zebu are of immense cultural importance. As with the Maasai of East Africa, the Fula regard the size of a family's herd to mark its social prestige and represent its wealth, and cattle are seldom killed to eat. Great efforts are therefore made to build up and conserve herds, and marriages between rich families usually involve the exchange of large numbers of animals in dowry.

Within Senegal, the Fula are mainly distributed in the dry north and east, an area they have inhabited for centuries, but which has recently been battered by the conflicting problems of desertification and high population growth, so that many individuals are now dependent on trade or other income sources, and poverty is rife. The origin of the Fula is unknown: one hypothesis traces them back east, to Sudan or Ethiopia, but linguistic evidence suggests that they have inhabited West Africa at least since AD 500.

The most historically influential subgroup of the Fula is the Tukulor of the Senegal River region. The name Tukulor derives from Takrur, an empire founded c. AD 800 along the Senegal River, west of the contemporaneous Ghana Empire. Takrur peaked during the 12th century after Ghana was captured by the Almoravids, but it collapsed following the rise of ancient Mali. More recently, in the mid-19th century, the Tukulor – almost certainly the descendants of the people of Takrur – forged a vast but short-lived empire under the charismatic leadership of El Hadj Oumar Tall *(see page 46)*.

Today, the Tukulor are the most overtly traditionalist of Senegal's major cultural groups, with a more sedentary society than the nomadic Fula, and a strictly defined social hierarchy comprising three classes divided into a dozen castes, of which the highest are the religious leaders and marabouts of the Toorobbê. Born in Podor, the singer, guitarist and UNDP Youth Emissary Baaba Maal is probably the most internationally renowned Pulaar-speaker of Senegalese origin *(see page 225)*.

Other Islamic peoples

The Mandinka (or Mandingo) inhabit nine countries in West Africa, and account for 42 percent of the population of The Gambia. Upper-caste families are said to descend from warriors who swept into The Gambia after the break-up of the Mali

Empire, and were probably already converted to Islam. However, the greater majority of Mandinka are converted from animism under the influence of the Fula in the 18th century. They suffered heavy losses to the Djolof and Fula during the slave-raiding era, and a significant proportion of Afro-Americans are of Mandinka origin. Mainly farmers today, the Mandinka are known for the rich oral literary tradition of the *griot* musician caste, whose unique harp-lute – known as the kora – has made regular appearances in European concert halls in the hands of popular musicians such as Mory Kante.

The Soninké (also known as Serahuli or Sarakholé), reputedly the descendants of the founders

of the ancient Ghana Empire, are relatively pale-skinned people whose Mandé tongue is not too dissimilar to Wolof and whose traditional homeland is centred on the upper Senegal south of Bakel. Known for their solidarity, military skill and readiness to travel, the Soninké constitute one of the main groups of Senegalese living in France, where they stick close together in tight communities that help out new arrivals.

Sometimes described as a subgroup of the Wolof, the Lébou are concentrated in the Cap Vert region, where they arrived from the north four centuries ago. Renowned as farmers and fishermen, they formerly had a strong sideline as ship-wreckers and looters. The Lébou are unique in operating their own mini-government, which is recognised by cen-

---

FAR LEFT: Gambian drummer. **LEFT:** family values are inherent to both Gambian and Senegalese societies. **RIGHT:** the younger generation.

tral government, the continuation of a tradition founded in the early 19th century, when the French colonists recognised the legitimacy of a fledging Lébou "republic" before the existence of Dakar.

The most prominent outsider Islamic community consists of Mauritanians, who are also known as Moors. The Mauritanian presence in Senegal is not what it used to be, following the riots of 1989, though you do see quite a few in Saint-Louis, and there are a great many living in The Gambia, especially Banjul. Of Berber stock, Mauritanians tend to be pale-skinned with finely chiselled features; they wear voluminous pale-blue robes and mostly operate as shopkeepers and craftsmen, particularly

silversmiths. The Gambia and to a lesser extent Senegal also have small populations of Lebanese, who are invariably involved in commerce, whether it be high finance or operating one of Banjul's ubiquitous schwarma restaurants.

Animism

Animism is a term used to describe a pantheistic belief system that considers all or most earthly things to possess a spirit or soul, whether it be a tree, an animal or even an inanimate object such as a stone. Most animist systems are strongly fetishist, imbuing certain creatures or objects with a particular spiritual force or significance. In the Kaolack region, for example, the lizard is particularly revered and people would never harm one of these reptiles. Similarly, the crocodile is revered all over the region, as evidenced by the number of sacred crocodile pools in the region. Animism often goes together with ancestor worship, and homage is paid to ancestral spirits, usually in the form of an offering or sacrifice, during times of crisis such as drought or illness.

Animism as a formal and principal belief has been replaced by imported monotheistic religions such as Islam and, more recently, Christianity in most parts of Senegal and The Gambia, obvious exceptions being parts of Casamance and the Bassari Country in the southeast. However, residual animist traits often underpin the beliefs of local Muslims and Christians, and they may come to the fore when modern medicine, prayer and the semi-magical remedies of marabouts fail to cure an illness. In some cases Christian or Muslim saints become identified with older deities, allowing the two to be worshipped simultaneously.

A WOMAN'S PLACE

Senegalese and Gambian societies present an unexpected mix of strength and oppression among women. Marriage can be legally enforced or more informal, and it is common for a man to have more than one wife, especially in the countryside, where sharing a husband may be the only way to balance almost constant pregnancy and childbirth with the demands of farming and family. Women remain very much members of their own families, even after marriage, and often retain their maiden name, or use both family names interchangeably. In a traditional milieu, marriages are organised, though rarely against the wishes of the couple, and the wife's family is paid a dowry. In rural areas, early marriage is often seen as the only way to avoid pre-

marital sex and pregnancy, so girls as young as 12 are often married off, and might be "promised" at half that age.

Despite the Islamic influence, few women cover their faces and many have a good deal of economic independence. This makes travel for a single woman very hassle-free compared to Mediterranean countries. Where clothing is concerned, there are no taboos about arms or shoulders, but it is frowned on for women to expose their legs above the knee. A woman moving around on her own can expect to be propositioned every now and then. Seldom meant aggressively, this is best brushed off as a joke; invent a husband, if you haven't got one already. The best answer to the question *"I ke malee?"* (Where is your husband?) is probably *"A bi dje"* (He's here).

Animists and Christian cultures

Before the arrival of Islam in the 8th century, and for centuries afterwards, most West Africans were animists. Today, animist cultures are restricted to a few remaining pockets, most famously the Dogon of Mali's Bandiagara Escarpment, whose closest Sene-

The Lébou ceremony known as Ndeup is a mystical therapy, often conducted by women, that aims to extract the evil spirit from a patient through animist sacrifices, dancing and drumming.

galese counterpart is the Bassari and Bedik of the remote hills bordering Guinea near Niokolo-Koba National Park. Comprising 1 percent of the national population, the Bassari and Bedik live as subsistence farmers in small mud-and-thatch villages, and their annual initiation rites are among the most colourful animist ceremonies held in Africa.

The Diola or Jola, who make up 10 percent of Gambians and dominate the Casamance region of Senegal (though they count for only 5 percent of the national population), also have a strong tradition of animism, though this is less obvious to outsiders than in Bassari Country due to a greater level of westernisation and the growing influence of Christianity. Generally smaller in stature than the region's other darker-skinned peoples, the Diola are fishermen and subsistence farmers who grow rice and other tropical crops. Over recent centuries, they have often been under siege: from neighbouring ethnic groups, from the Portuguese founders of Ziguinchor and from French colonists. As a result they have developed a fiercely independent spirit that goes a long way to explaining the region's violent separatist campaign in the 1990s. Diola villages still have animist shrines, whether it be a giant kapok tree or a crocodile pool. The animist culture of the Casamance truly comes to the fore during the Bukut initiation ceremonies held once every generation.

The Serer, who account for 14 percent of Senegal's population and a tiny minority in The Gambia, live in the Siné-Saloum region, and were the primary movers for the two eponymous ancient empires. Animists by tradition, they have been converted to Christianity after centuries of interaction with Europeans along the coast. However, their brand of Christianity is underpinned by a fetishism epitomised by the "black Madonna" grottoes and

icon at Popenguine. The Serer ceremony of Pangal, which venerates the souls of ancestors, is one of the most distinctive of animist rituals still practised, albeit with increasingly scarcity. The poet-politician Léopold Sédar Senghor was a Serer from Joal.

A small but influential group in The Gambia are the Kriol or Aku, descendants of former slaves from Sierra Leone who speak a form of pidgin English known as Krio or Creole. Kriol is also the name for the pidgin Portuguese that is the lingua franca of Guinea-Bissau and is still spoken by Christian minorities in Ziguinchor and Kolda in the Casamance. There are also a few French, English and other Europeans settled in Senegal and The Gambia.

Christian influences

Christianity reached West Africa with the Portuguese, but was for a long time confined to European trading and military settlements. It was resisted by the indigenous people due to its association with invading Europeans and the strong existing influence of Islam. Only when Lat Dior was defeated by the French in 1886 did the Catholic Church establish itself in the Senegalese interior. Today, adherents to Christianity represent around 5 percent of the population, with Catholicism predominant in Senegal and Anglicism in The Gambia. Services are often adapted linguistically and musically to African practice, most notably at the Abbaye de Keur Moussa near Dakar, where the mass is backed by traditional instruments such as the kora and balafon. ❑

LEFT AND RIGHT: friendly Gambian faces.
FOLLOWING PAGES: a Dakar mosque.

DECISIVE DATES

5000–2000 BC
Agriculture and pastoralism arrive in West Africa from across the Sahara.

6th Century BC
Euthymenes sails down the African coast to a great river, the Senegal or Gambia.

5th Century BC
Trans-Sahara trade established by Berbers from North Africa. Hanno the Navigator sails down the African coast as far as the Gambia mouth.

3rd Century AD
Earliest known Iron Age societies in Senegal settle on Île à Morfil, Senegal River.

7th Century
Ghana (Ouagadou) Empire founded in present-day Mali and Mauritania.

8th Century
The Trans-Sahara trade route introduces Islam to West Africa within 100 years of its foundation. Unknown Stone Age culture erects megalithic circles as burial markers at many sites along the Gambia and Saloum rivers.

9th Century
Tukulor Empire founded in the Senegal River Valley.

1076
Almoravid army, supported by Tukulor allies, captures Kumbi Saleh, capital of Ghana, and the empire splits into several smaller states.

1200
Mansa Uli, ruler of emergent Mali Empire, undertakes Hajj (pilgrimage to Mecca).

1230–55
Mali Empire moulded into the dominant regional power by Mansa Sundiata.

1324–6
Mansa Musa of Mali undertakes Hajj, flooding Mediterranean market with gold.

1330–50
Timbuktu emerges as main regional centre of Islamic scholarship and trade.

1415
Portuguese capture Moroccan port of Ceuta.

1434
First Portuguese consignment of African slaves captured in Western Sahara.

1443
Portuguese navigator Nuno Tristão docks on Arguim Island in Mauritania. Two years later it is a Portuguese trading post exporting 800 slaves annually.

1444
Dinas Diaz sails up Senegal River and south to "Cabo Verde" (Cap Vert).

1450
Djolof, tributary of Mali Empire, expands across much of present-day Senegal. Venetian Alvise Cadamosto opens Senegal and Gambia rivers to Portuguese trade.

1468
Timbuktu captured by Songhai Empire, eclipsing Mali as dominant regional power.

1490s
Songhai ruler Askia Mohammed undertakes Hajj from imperial capital of Gao.

1510
First Portuguese slave ship sails from West Africa to the Americas.

1550–1600
Portuguese maritime trade sparks dissolution of Djolof

into constituent states of Walo, Cayor, Baol, Siné and Saloum. Songhai collapses after a Berber attack on Gao.

1617
Dutch trade outpost founded at Gorée.

1619
George Thompson charts Gambia River's course 100km (60 miles) inland.

1645
Portuguese establish Ziguinchor as trade outpost on Casamance River.

1659
French found colonial capital of Saint-Louis at mouth of Senegal River.

1677
French take over Gorée.

1745
British military expedition establishes fort at Podor on Senegal River.

1756
Britain captures all France's West African outposts during Seven Years War.

1763
Gorée returned to France.

1775
France regains its other outposts during American Revolution.

1783
France loses Gorée to Britain.

1795
Mungo Park travels inland from Gambia to Ségou, the first European to reach the Niger River.

1803–15
Britain captures all French West African outposts during Napoleonic Wars and returns them in 1815.

1807
Britain abolishes the slave trade, followed by France in 1814. A clandestine slave trade out of West Africa lasts until the French abolition of slave ownership in 1848.

1816
Captain Alexander Grant establishes Bathurst (Banjul) at mouth of Gambia

River to block slave ships from heading upriver.

1828
René Caillié becomes first European to reach Timbuktu and return home alive.

1830s
French trade outposts established at Karabane and Sédhiou in Casamance.

1848
The Tukulor leader El Hadj Oumar Tall starts a jihad to forge an empire that extends over much of present-day Senegal, Guinea and Mali at its 1860s peak.

1848–52
Saint-Louis and Gorée allowed to elect a deputy to the National Assembly in Paris.

1854–65
Governor Louis Faidherbe extends French influence along Senegal River, captures Lébou, Walo and Cayor empires, and founds Dakar.

1876
"Scramble for Africa" initiated by Belgian King Leopold II's annexation of The Congo.

1884–5
Berlin Conference formalises borders of many modern African states.

1888
Portugal cedes the Casamance region to France.

1889
The Gambia, partly under British protectorateship since the 1820s, is made a crown colony.

1895
Senegal is incorporated into the Afrique Occidentale Française (AOF) colony, together with present-day Mali, Niger, Benin, Chad, Côte d'Ivoire, Guinea, Burkina Faso and Mauritania, with Saint-Louis as administrative capital.

1902
Dakar made capital of AOF (though Saint-Louis remains capital of Senegal).

1939–45
Senegalese and Gambian recruits fight for allies during World War II.

1946
French colonies become overseas territories. Léopold Senghor is the first African to sit in French National Assembly.

1947
Separatist forces form the Movement of Democratic Forces of Casamance (MFDC).

1956
Universal suffrage established in Senegal.

1958
AOF disbanded following referendum in which constituent territories all vote in favour of autonomy.

1960
Senegal and Mali gain independence as the Mali Federation, but split into separate republics by the year's end, with Léopold Senghor as president of Senegal.

1961
First universal franchise in Gambia elects Dawda Jawara and People's Progressive Party (PPP) to power.

1962
President Senghor of Senegal abolishes the position of prime minister and dismisses then jails the incumbent Mamadou Dia for treason.

1965
The Gambia attains independence with Dawda Jawara as prime minister.

1966
Prime Minister Dawda Jawara of Gambia is knighted.

1970
Sir Dawda Jawara proclaims The Gambia as a republic with himself as president. Abdou Diouf is appointed prime minister of Senegal when this post is reinstated.

1975
Senegal and The Gambia are among 15 founder states of the Economic Community of West African States (ECOWAS).

1980
Senghor retires and is replaced by Abdou Diouf.

1981
An attempted coup against Jawara in Banjul leaves 500 people dead.

1982
Jawara and Diouf form the Confederation of Senegambia, which will hold common policies on key matters.

1983
President Diouf wins multi-party presidential election amid allegations of vote rigging. Police kill 25 protesters during an MFDC separatist rally in Ziguinchor.

1985
Abdou Diouf elected president of the Organisation of African Unity (OAU).

1989
Confederation of Senegambia dissolved by Diouf in

FAR LEFT TOP: the French enter Timbuktu, Mali. **LEFT BOTTOM:** Gambian identity cards. **LEFT MIDDLE:** first Senegalese president Léopold Senghor. **ABOVE:** Yahya Jammeh asking for votes. **RIGHT:** President Abdoulaye Wade of Senegal.

response to a critical speech by Jawara.

1990
The MFDC, seeking independence for the Casamance, launches a formal armed struggle that results in thousands of deaths over the next decade.

1993
Diouf returned to power after beating Abdoulaye Wade in presidential elections. Wade is later charged with complicity in the murder of Babacar Sèye, but charges are dropped a year later. Senegal closes land borders with The Gambia.

1994
Lieutenant Yahya Jammeh ousts President Jawara in a bloodless military coup and appoints himself the new head of state.

1996
Jammeh holds (and wins) presidential election, restoring civil rule to The Gambia.

2000
Wade defeats Diouf in a landmark presidential election that marks the first real power shift since independence 40 years earlier.

2001
Jammeh is returned to power in presidential elections. The opposition United Democratic Party (UDP) boycotts subsequent legislative elections in protest at alleged vote rigging.

2004
President Wade fires Prime Minister Idrissa Seck in

connection with charges of corruption. An MFDC treaty with the Senegalese government restores the Casamance to something approaching full peace. In The Gambia, Jammeh introduces a set of laws inhibiting press freedom. Days later, prominent press freedom advocate and journalist Deyda Hydara is murdered in suspicious circumstances.

2006
Jammeh is re-elected as president. In the electoral build-up, an alleged military coup against his regime is foiled by security forces.

2007
The 80-year-old Abdoulaye Wade defeats Idrissa Seck in presidential elections by a margin of 40 percent. President Jammeh announces that he has developed a cure for Aids and forcibly expels a UNDEP country representative who contends this claim.

2008
President Jammeh announces that homosexuals in The Gambia will be punished by forced expulsion or decapitation.

AFRI CAE TA BVLA NOVA

AFRICAM GRAECI LIBYAM APP.

EDITA ANT. VERPIAE 1570

EARLY HISTORY

It would be misleading to talk of either
Senegal or The Gambia as an isolated historical
unit prior to the colonial era, and the area's
early history is best understood in the broader
context of West Africa as a whole

Senegal and The Gambia are essentially modern political entities. Their borders, like those of most other African countries, date to the late 19th century "Scramble for Africa", when various European powers – most significantly England, France and Germany, but also Portugal, Belgium, Spain and Italy – carved the entire continent (with the exception of Liberia and Ethiopia) into a patchwork of somewhat arbitrarily delineated colonial territories and protectorates.

The beginnings of civilisation

It is impossible to say when humans first inhabited Senegal and The Gambia. The palaeontological record dates back only a few millennia, but our current knowledge of early human evolution and movement patterns – based on a wealth of discoveries in eastern and southern Africa, which offer more favourable conditions for the recovery of suitable fossils – makes it more than likely that the region was inhabited by our hominid ancestors for millions of years. These early inhabitants would have been nomadic hunter-gatherers, but agriculture probably arrived from across the Sahara as early as 5000 BC, and cattle-herding and other forms of pastoralism were being practised in much of West Africa by around 2000 BC. The presence of around 1,000 megalithic stone circles erected along the Gambia and Saloum rivers from the 8th century AD onwards, along with the discovery of metal tools and pottery in tumuli of similar vintage along the Senegal River, point to the emergence of a more urbanised and complex society during the 1st millennium AD.

LEFT: map of the African continent, 1570.
RIGHT: bronze plaque from the royal palace of the Oba, Benin, West Africa.

Medieval West Africa

Medieval West Africa consisted of four broad economic units. The coastal belt of present-day Morocco, Algeria and Tunisia, sometimes referred to as the Maghreb, had enjoyed direct links with other Mediterranean civilisations since ancient times, and assimilated a strong Islamic influence by the 8th century AD. South of the Mediterranean zone, the Sahara Desert, a waterless expanse almost as large as Europe, was then as it is now practically devoid of human settlement. Below the Sahara, present-day Senegal and The Gambia both form part of the Sahel, a belt of dry savannah whose population is concentrated along the coast and the banks of major rivers such as the Niger, Volta, Senegal and Gambia. Further south still, nudging into the Casamance region of Senegal, is the moist Guinean rainforest and savannah belt, which follows the Atlantic coastline eastwards from Guinea-Bissau to Togo.

These four regions have been economically linked since the 5th century BC, when Berber merchants conquered the formidable physical obstacle presented by the Sahara on camelback to pioneer a trade caravan route with the Sahel. The Berbers carried salt, fine cloth and other luxury items on the southward leg across the Sahara and traded them for items such as gold, ivory and kola nuts, which were generally sourced in the lush Guinean rainforest belt and transported north

powerful centralised trade empire that acted as an intermediary between the trans-Sahara caravans and mines of the Guinean coastal belt. This ancient empire, founded by Mandé-speakers before the 7th century AD, was known to outsiders as Ghana, in fact the name of its monarch, and to its own citizens as Ouagadou, literally "Land of Herds". At its peak, the Ghana Empire extended over some 150,000 sq km (58,000 sq miles) of present-day Mali and Mauritania between the rivers Niger and Senegal (an area, incidentally, that has no territorial overlap with the modern state of Ghana, whose name was chosen by President Nkrumah for symbolic reasons when it gained independence in 1957).

along rivers such as the Niger and Volta. The specifics of the trans-Sahara trade prior to the 8th century AD are largely a matter of conjecture, but the main routes almost certainly terminated in present-day Mali and Niger, to the east of Senegal and The Gambia. Nevertheless, the entire region was strongly influenced by the caravan trade, which was probably responsible for the introduction of Iron Age technology to the Sahel, and was instrumental in the spread of Islam.

Medieval empires

The first written record of the Sahelian interior dates to the 8th century AD, when an unknown Arabic writer alluded to the sub-Saharan region as a "Land of Gold" and reported that it had long supported a

The capital of ancient Ghana was Kumbi Saleh, a city of 30,000 souls whose wealthier merchants lived in stone houses, and whose emperor was able to muster an army numbering 200,000 at the empire's 10th-century peak. At around the same time, an important local rival to ancient Ghana emerged in the form of the Tukulor Empire, founded in the 9th century by the Fula of the Senegal River Valley. By the early 11th century, the dense population of Kumbi Saleh had started to place unrealistic demands on its Sahelian surrounds, which were also affected by creeping desertification. In 1076, the Almoravid army, led by the Moroccan Abu-Bakr Ibn-Umar and supported by its Islamic Tukulor allies, captured Kumbi Saleh, with the dual aim of taking total control over the trans-Saharan trade and furthering the spread of Islam into western Africa. Although the Almoravid hold on the ancient Ghanaian capital endured for little more than a decade, it undoubtedly catalysed the empire's dissolution into several smaller and less powerful states in the 12th century.

A clear successor to ancient Ghana eventually emerged in the form of the Mali Empire, which was founded by the Mandinka people in the late 12th century, and moulded into a regional superpower over AD 1230–55 under the expansionist rule of Mansa Sundiata. The rulers of ancient Mali were Islamic converts from the start. As early as AD 1200, Mansa Uli undertook a pilgrimage to Mecca, a rather low-key affair compared to the legendary trans-Saharan journey undertaken by Mansa Musa at the empire's prime in 1324–6. According to contemporary records, Mansa Musa distributed gold gifts so liberally that the Mediterranean market for the metal was undermined for several years afterwards. As a result of Mansa Musa's pilgrimage, Mali first appeared by name on an Arabic map dating to 1339. The Islamic scholars with whom he returned to Mali are credited with inventing the unique mud-and-stick style of mosque construction associated with the Senegal River Valley and various other sites in West Africa.

The rise of Timbuktu

It was also in the mid-14th century that Timbuktu emerged as the most important regional centre of Islamic scholarship and trade, thanks to its strategic location alongside the Niger River as it arcs to its most northerly point on the southern verge of the Sahara. At around the same time, the part of

The name Senegal derives from Zenaga, the name of a powerful medieval Berber tribe whose unique tongue was still spoken widely along the north bank of the Senegal River until the mid-19th century.

present-day Senegal north of the Saloum River saw the emergence of the Djolof (or Wolof) Empire, which started life as a vassal state of Mali but emerged as a distinct political entity in the

FAR LEFT: stone handmill from the National Museum of Gambia in Banjul. **LEFT:** this prince in chainmail was introduced in Benin, West Africa, in the 15th century by the Portuguese. **RIGHT:** Mansa Musa, king of the Islamic Mali Empire, holding a gold nugget in his hand.

mid-15th century. Djolof itself was a relatively small landlocked state ruled by a *Bourba* (king) from Linguère (in the northern interior of Senegal), but its sovereignty extended over the coastal tributary states of Walo, Cayor, Baol, Siné and Saloum, each of which was governed by its own hereditary ruler.

In 1468, Timbuktu was captured by the Songhai Empire, which broke away from ancient Mali under the leadership of Sunni Ali and soon replaced it as the dominant Sahelian state. In the 1490s, Askia Mohammed, one of the most powerful of Songhai rulers, made the pilgrimage from the imperial capital of Gao (on the Niger River

east of Timbuktu) to Mecca. At its early 16th-century peak, Songhai extended its rule over much of present-day Gambia and southern Senegal, leading to the widespread adoption of Islam in this region. Songhai collapsed in 1591, leading to a centuries-long period of economic stagnation in the West African interior, one whose primary cause was the radical reorientation of trade patterns that followed the arrival of the Portuguese at the Atlantic coast.

European settlement and the associated growth of the slave trade originating out of West Africa was also instrumental in the simultaneous dissolution of Djolof into its six constituent states, all of which retained a certain degree of autonomy into the colonial era.

Ancient forays to Senegal and The Gambia

The first recorded voyage along the west coast of Africa was undertaken in the 6th century by the Greek explorer Euthymenes of Marseille, who sailed as far south as a great river with a brackish outflow, assumed at the time to be the Nile, but more likely the Senegal or Gambia. Euthymenes was followed c.470 BC by the Persian navigator Sataspes, who was charged by King Xerxes I with the punitive task of circumnavigating Africa. Sataspes sailed south along the coast for several months, encountering "a dwarfish race, who wore a dress made from the palm tree" before he opted to turn back (only to be executed by King Xerxes for failing in his task).

A few years either side of this, the Carthaginian Hanno the Navigator sailed partway down the West African coast, relaying encounters with elephants and hippopotami along the rivers he named "Chertes" and "Bambotus" – again, quite possibly the Senegal and Gambia rivers, though nobody knows for sure. These ancient journeys inform the second-hand accounts of Africa included in the writings of Herodotus and Ptolemy, but no other first-hand accounts of the Atlantic coastline survive from that era, and the first Arabic description of the interior dates from the 8th century AD.

Portuguese exploration

The first serious post-medieval attempt to map the region was the *Catalan Atlas* produced in 1375 by the Jewish cartographer Abraham Cresques and his son Jehuda. These and other contemporary cartographic efforts were based as much on mariners' tall tales as on any factual evidence, but they nevertheless inspired Portugal's Prince Henry the Navigator to commission a series of exploratory trips down the west coast of Africa, and to appoint Jehuda Cresques to coordinate the naval school he established at Sagres.

The Portuguese presence in Africa started modestly enough in 1415, with the capture of the Moroccan port of Ceuta, the first small step in an era of naval exploration that would lead to the first southern circumnavigation of the continent almost a century later. In 1443, Nuno Tristão became the first Portuguese emissary to sail almost as far south as the Senegal River when he docked on Arguim Island in the south of what is now Mauritania. In

NOT SO HIDDEN AGENDA

Several motives lay behind the Portuguese forays into Africa. Religion was a key factor, in that the Portuguese crown was eager to forge links with the legendary Christian kingdom of Prester John (Ethiopia) and to spread its faith into the heathen and Islamic lands south of the Sahara. The Portuguese had strong economic motives, as they hoped to wrest control of the lucrative Indian Ocean spice trade and to find a sea route to the source of the ample gold that they knew was arriving at Ceuta via the Sahara. To some extent, the Portuguese succeeded in all of these goals, but the most immediately prof- itable form of commerce they undertook in Africa was the capture and sale of slaves. As early as 1434, the first consignment of African slaves, captured in the vicinity of the western Sahara, was brought to Lisbon. Setting an ominous trend, Tristão captured 28 slaves when he landed on Arguim in 1443; only two years later the island was settled as a Portuguese trading post, exporting gum arabic and up to 800 slaves annually. It was this early trade in Mauritanian captives that led to the notion of using West Africa as a pool for slave labour to work the cane fields and other plantations of the Americas and Caribbean.

1444, Dinas Diaz leapfrogged Tristão into present-day Senegal, where he sailed some distance up the Senegal River, before continuing south to the peninsula that he named Cabo Verde (Green Cape) and which is still known as Cap Vert today. In 1446, Tristão sailed past the southern border of present-day Senegal to the site of Bissau, while later the same year Álvaro Fernandes pushed on almost as far as Sierra Leone, which is probably the most southerly point reached by any Portuguese sailor prior to the death of Henry the Navigator in 1460. Shortly before this, in the late 1550s, the Venetian explorer Alvise Cadamosto undertook a lengthy voyage for the Portuguese crown, opening up the

because it was so ruthlessly organised and so broad-ranging in its effects. At least 10 million African captives were shipped across the Atlantic over the 16th–19th centuries, a five-week voyage in conditions so cramped and unhygienic that half the human cargo frequently died in transit.

The trade was devastating to the West African interior, which became literally flooded with European firearms – Britain alone traded up to 100,000 guns annually against fresh captives – and rapidly deteriorated into a hunting ground where village after comparatively defenceless village was subjected to armed slave raids led by more powerful neighbouring tribes. And for every

Senegal and Gambia rivers for trade (the word Gambia is thought to come from *Cambio*, meaning exchange in Spanish), and noting cotton, rice, wild animals and golden jewellery along their banks.

Transatlantic slave trade

Slavery in some form has been a feature of most human societies prior to the 20th century. Nevertheless, the transatlantic slave trade is a singular event in human history, not simply because it operated on an unprecedented scale, but also

LEFT: West African slaves milling sugar cane in the windmill of a plantation on the Caribbean island of Antigua (West Indies). **ABOVE LEFT:** Henry the Navigator. **ABOVE RIGHT:** map of West Africa, *c.*1575–84.

able-bodied African captured during these violent raids, several more – infants, the elderly, the infirm – were killed on the spot.

The first Portuguese slave ship to leave West Africa for the Americas sailed as early as 1510. Soon after, the slave trade formed part of a triangle involving most of the major European powers and linking three continents. Trinkets were shipped from Europe and exchanged for African captives, who were sold to Caribbean producers of sugar, rum and tobacco destined for the markets of Europe. The business depended on easy access to the sea from harbours and ports on the West African coast. Each settlement in the 1600s had its own "factory" or collecting station where slaves would be gathered to wait for the trading ships. Although the English were comparatively late arrivals on the scene – Captain John Hawkins took the first English slave ship to the West Indies in 1562 – Elizabethan mariners made up for lost time by organising trading expeditions backed by military force. Towards the end of the 16th century, the Portuguese lost interest in the slave trade, preferring to deal in Far Eastern spices, and from then on control of the slave trade alternated between French, Dutch and English entrepreneurs.

In 1617, the first permanent European trading settlement was founded by the Dutch West India Company at Gorée. By 1621 the French had dug in on the Senegalese coast at Saint-Louis, and built a French built a strategic outpost called Albreda, which they fortified in 1681 and held until 1857. Just behind this French enclave in English territory, an English trading post was built at neighbouring Juffureh in 1680.

Further north, in Senegal, the Swedes had taken the island of Gorée in 1655, the Dutch having retired to Rufisque a few miles away. The Dutch had also constructed a "factory" at Arguim Island north of the Senegal River and the French had, by 1659, fortified their base at Saint-Louis in the far north of Senegal. Skirmishes over trade and territory occurred almost monthly during these times until, in 1677, the French Admiral d'Estrées drove the Dutch

fort there. France also built a slave factory on the island of Bocos off the Cape Verde peninsula. French expansion was stimulated when Cardinal Richelieu commissioned the Senegal Company in 1633. Meanwhile, Charles II of England, fuelled by legends of El Dorado, the fabled gold lands of West Africa, sent the like-minded Prince Rupert to explore the Gambian coast in 1652, leading to the foundation of the Royal Adventurers Trading in Africa Company, which set up stall on James Island in 1661. The Dutch ousted the English from the island the following year, but the English then made a deal over Gorée Island with the Dutch that enabled them to keep a platoon at James Island until the French conquered it in 1695. In 1670, on the northern river bank opposite James Island, the from the region by capturing Gorée Island. The British Royal African Company was chartered in 1684 and the Royal Senegal Company was founded by 1696. By this time there were more then 10 main slave trading posts and forts in Senegal and The Gambia, including Saint-Louis, Gorée, Rufisque, Portudal, Joal, Albreda, James Island, Juffureh, Podor, Matam and Bakel, most of which stayed active throughout the 18th century, occasionally changing hands between the French and the English.

ABOVE: a European buying slaves on the West African coast. **RIGHT:** Britain's brig *Acorn* in pursuit of the slave-ship *Gabriel* in July 1841. **BOTTOM RIGHT:** plan of a slave ship showing the cramped conditions as the slavers made most use of available room on board.

Early exploration of the interior

One of the first men to follow the Gambia River inland was George Thompson, who charted its course for about 100km (60 miles) into the interior in 1619. A year later, Richard Jobson followed the river even further inland, a journey recalled in fascinating detail in his book *The Golden Trade*, which includes lengthy descriptions of Mandinka culture and riverine wildlife such as hippos and crocodiles. Over the next century, few Europeans ventured further inland than the slave-trading stations located near the estuaries of the Senegal and Gambia rivers, partly because exploration was deterred by territorial squabbles between France and Britain.

The early 18th century saw renewed interest in the West African interior, particularly among the English. Some, such as Captain Bartholomew Stibbs, who sailed up the Gambia River in 1723, came in search of the legendary mines that had once supplied gold to the trans-Sahara caravans. Others, like Francis Moore, who published an account of his time in The Gambia in *Travels in the Inland Part of Africa, 1735*, were driven primarily by scientific curiosity. And it was almost certainly the desire to assert greater control over the slave trade that led a 1745 British military expedition up the Senegal River as far as Podor, where they constructed the precursor to the fort that stands there today.

ANTI-SLAVERY

The advent of the 19th century should have brought relief for West Africa, as international opinion rallied around calls for abolition, leading to a British ban on slavery throughout its territories in 1807, followed by the US in 1808, and then Holland, France, Portugal and Spain between 1814 and 1817. Also in 1817, several of the above nations signed a Reciprocal Search Treaty, which in effect allowed Britain to search boats captained by people of other nationalities. As a result, the slave trade was subdued, but it was by no means halted – during the first few years of

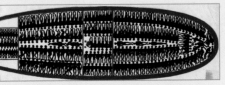

Britain's anti-slavery policy, more than 100 slave vessels were captured off the Gambian coast, bound either for Cuba or Brazil, and it became common practice among slavers to throw all their human cargo overboard at the approach of a British naval patrol. Britain soon recognised that it would take nothing less than the abolition of slavery to end the trade, and therefore decided to ban slavery throughout its entire colonial empire in 1833, followed by France in 1848, the US in 1865 (after a bloody civil war dominated by the issue) and finally Brazil in 1888.

Exploration of the interior

Although Portugal and various other European powers maintained a strong presence along the Atlantic coastline from the 16th century onwards, the West African interior remained largely *terra incognita* prior to the 19th century. The main catalyst for exploration deeper inland was the formation of the ponderously entitled Association for Promoting the Discovery of the Interior Parts of Africa (often abbreviated to the African Association) in London in 1788. An aristocratic club chaired by Sir Joseph Banks, the Africa Association was particularly concerned with determining the source and course of the Niger River and the

crossing the Senegal River and proceeding into the Sahara, where he was robbed and killed at the village of Simbing in September 1791.

The Africa Association's next recruit was the Scottish doctor Mungo Park, who followed Houghton's route up the Gambia as far as Pisania

> *Upon returning to his native Scotland in 1797, Mungo Park wrote the account of his adventures entitled* Travels in the Interior Districts of Africa, *which was published in 1799 to considerable public acclaim.*

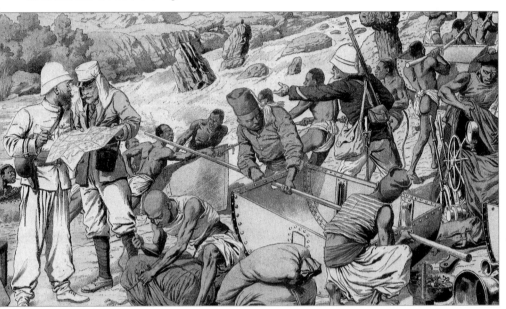

location of the legendary lost city of Timbuktu, and it funded several noteworthy expeditions into the African interior.

The earliest expeditions sponsored by the African Association met with limited success. An American recruit called John Ledyard made it as far as Cairo in August 1788, then accidentally poisoned himself with sulphuric acid, while Simon Lucas's simultaneous attempt to cross the Libyan desert was aborted when he was abandoned by his guides and had to return on foot to Tripoli. Rather more successful was the Irishman Major Daniel Houghton, who was commissioned to find the source of the Niger in 1790. Houghton penetrated deeper into the interior than any European had before, following the Gambia upriver to its last navigable point, then

(Karantaba) in 1795, and spent five months there learning the Mandingo language. Park continued eastwards in early December, reaching Ségou (in present-day Mali) in July of that year, where he became the first European to set eyes on the Niger River, and to discover that, unlike any other West African river, it flows in an easterly direction. Park followed it downstream for 150km (90 miles) as far as Silla, but ill health and a lack of essential supplies prevented him from pressing onward to Timbuktu. Nevertheless, Park did at least make it back home alive, returning to Pisania in June 1797

ABOVE: members of an expedition transport provisions during their journey along the River Niger through Mali.
RIGHT: German explorer Heinrich Barth reaches Timbuktu.

and Scotland in December. In 1805, Park led a second and much larger expedition in search of the source of the Niger, one that ended in disaster when he and all the surviving members of his party were ambushed and killed on the river.

The quest to locate Timbuktu reached new heights in 1824, when the Paris-based Société de Géographie offered a massive cash reward to the first non-Muslim to reach the town and return to tell the tale. This lured a succession of explorers inland, including Major Gordon Laing, who reached Timbuktu in 1826 but was murdered on leaving the city on 26 September. Laing was followed by René Caillié, who first visited Senegal aged 16 in 1815

sions in the area between 1849 and 1855, the French explorer Henri Duveyrier travelled inland during the 1850s, followed by another German, Gustav Nachtigal, from 1869 to 1874. Gerhard Rohlfs pursued a number of ancient trade routes from 1862 to 1878, and Oskar Lenz entered the headwaters of the Senegal River in 1879–80, tracing it down its estuary. By this time, most of the interior of Senegal and The Gambia had been mapped, and as the "Scramble for Africa" intensified, the arrival of river steamers and the construction of railways – the first of which was the Dakar to Saint-Louis line in 1886 – brought an end to the period of discovery. ❏

and returned in 1824 to spend eight months learning the local Arabic dialect and Islamic customs at a village to the north of the Senegal River. In 1827, disguised as an Egyptian Arab, Caillié set out from the mountainous Fouta Djalon region of Guinea and followed the Niger eastwards, reaching Djenné in January 1828 and Timbuktu in April of the same year, then joining a trans-Sahara caravan to Morocco, from where he returned to France.

Timbuktu was firmly on the map, but ambitious adventurers still set out into the interior in search of the source of the Niger, or elusive gold mines, or the fame attached to making a fresh discovery in a region Sir Richard Burton – who visited The Gambia in 1863 – referred to as the "White Man's Grave". The German Heinrich Barth made excur-

A LOT OF MAMBO JUMBO

The story of the "Mambo Jambo" talisman has long been associated with Park's journey through eastern Senegal. Thought to be an idol in the shape of a grotesque snake, the talisman was used by the Woolli River people to solve village disputes by making sacrifices to the image. Park found a mask of the Mambo Jambo spirit near Tambacounda. His story of the rituals associated with the fetish so confused his listeners back in Britain that the phrase mumbo jumbo was introduced to the English language.

MODERN HISTORY

Both Senegal and The Gambia gained their independence in the 1960s. After a period of prosperity, Senegal faced a series of territorial conflicts and electoral fraud, while The Gambia suffered a military coup which would see the rise of a repressive regime

Starting in the mid-15th century, the Portuguese and other European powers established a network of trade outposts along the West African coast without initially displaying any inclination to extend their direct sphere of influence beyond those isolated settlements. Many of these outposts changed hands repeatedly over the centuries – Gorée Island, for instance, was occupied twice by the Portuguese, twice by the Dutch and once by the British between 1444 and 1677, when it became a French possession – but for a full 400 years the core relationship between the European settlers and the surrounding indigenous cultures was commercial rather than colonial.

The build-up to colonisation

That relationship underwent a gradual change during the 19th century, a shift attributable to a variety of factors, many of which – ironically – can be traced to the abolition of the selfsame slave trade that Europe had instituted 350 years earlier. By the time of abolition, the West African interior supported a patchwork of powerful empires whose economies were intrinsically linked to the insatiable demand for slave labour on the opposite side of the Atlantic, and whose estimable firepower had been gained in exchange for meeting that demand. Abolition, as instituted by Britain in 1807 and France in 1814, thus had a huge impact on the economy of the interior, where a substantial clandestine traffic in slaves persisted until France finally illegalised the actual ownership of slaves in 1848.

LEFT: *"Nos soldats d'Afrique – le tirailleur sénégalais"* ("Our African soldiers – the Senegalese marksman"), cover picture from *Le Petit Journal*, 16 March 1913.
RIGHT: strategically located Gorée Island changed hands repeatedly over the centuries.

Colonial acquisitiveness was thus a less significant factor in early European attempts to exert control over the West African interior than the desire to stamp out the slave trade at its source and replace it with more benign forms of commerce. This is especially true of The Gambia.

The founding of Bathurst

Banjul (formerly Bathurst) was founded at the river mouth in 1816 to blockade slave ships from heading upriver, while Janjanbureh (Georgetown), the oldest inland British settlement, was established for the British crown in 1823 as a settlement for freed slaves. Britain also encouraged groundnut cultivation along the river as a form of legitimate trade, and exports of this product to the European market stimulated a fresh economic boom. And while the establishment of British protectorateship over Bathurst and Georgetown in the 1820s proved to be the path to eventual colonisation, that path was initially paved with the most altruistic of intentions.

The French take Senegal

Questions of motive aside, any hint of European interference or expansion inland was bound to be greeted with less than wholehearted enthusiasm by the region's existing inhabitants. Particularly so in Senegal, where half a dozen fiercely autonomous centralised empires were long accustomed to dealing with the European settlements along the coast

as partners in trade rather than political or military opponents. The political upheaval that characterised the Senegal and Niger river basins in the mid-19th century, though rooted in an expansionist religious jihad initiated in 1848 by the Tukulor marabout El Hadj Oumar Tall *(see panel below)*, must also be seen as a response to the collapse of existing trade patterns following abolition, and growing outside interest in the interior following the pioneering journeys undertaken by Mungo Park, René Caillié and others in the early decades of the century.

The pivotal figure in French expansionism inland was Louis Faidherbe, Governor of Senegal – which then amounted to little more than the islands of

Notre Domaine Colonial

LE SÉNÉGAL

EL HADJ OUMAR TALL

The driving figure behind the 19th century expansion of Islam in Senegal was El Hadj Oumar Tall, a Tukulor leader born on Morfil Island in 1797. Tall returned from a youthful pilgrimage to Mecca in the 1820s fired with a zealous desire to convert all and sundry to Islam. In 1848, his Tukulor army launched a jihad against the non-Islamic Malinké, in the process founding an empire that comprised parts of Mali and Guinea by the time Faidherbe built his forts along the Senegal River. In April 1857, Tall led an attack on the French fort at Medina. The siege lasted for almost two months before Faidherbe arrived with relief troops and drove the Tukulor away.

After this defeat, Tall focused his expansionist aspirations on the Bambara kingdoms in the Niger River region of present-day Mali. The Tukulor captured the ports of Ségou and Hamdalaye in 1861 and 1862, the latter with immense loss of life (some estimates are as high as 100,000). Tall overstretched himself in 1863, however, when an aborted attack on Timbuktu led to his expulsion from Hamdalaye and death in a gunpowder explosion a year later. Oumar Tall is remembered as a legendary figure of anti-colonial resistance in his home country of Senegal, but from a Malian perspective his bloody jihad achieved little more than to pave the way for the arrival of the French a few years later.

Saint-Louis and Gorée and the mainland town of Rufisque – from 1854 to 1865. Faidherbe was charged with implementing a government directive to open up the West African interior to free trade, a policy motivated at least as much by parochial French economic interests as any other factor. Following the Senegal River inland from Saint-Louis, Faidherbe constructed a series of a dozen forts running as far upriver as Bakel between 1854 and 1860, leading to a victorious clash with the Tukulor army at Medina in 1857. Further south, Faidherbe ordered the seizure of the Lébou Republic – the strip of coastal land between Saint-Louis and Gorée – with the intention of running rail, road and telegraph links between the Lébou capital, Ndakarou (which the French renamed Dakar in 1857), and Saint-Louis. Faidherbe was also responsible for promoting the growth of groundnuts as a cash crop in the 1850s.

The French takeover of the rest of present-day Senegal was a gradual process and one that met with mixed levels of resistance. Walo, the closest of the inland empires to Saint-Louis, was conquered in 1855 without much of a struggle, after Faidherbe chose to ignore a longstanding treaty it had held with its French neighbours. By contrast, the Cayor Empire was swallowed into the French colony only after some 25 years of bloody clashes with its leader, Lat Dior Ngoné Latyr Diop, who died under French fire in the 1886 Battle of Dékhélé. Neighbouring Baol was annexed more gradually, with some parts falling as early as 1859 and others holding out until 1895. Further south, the Serer kingdoms of Siné and Saloum entered into a colonial relationship more willingly, and as a result their leaders were recognised by the French throughout the colonial era.

Colonisation

It is difficult to overstate the transformation wrought by the "Scramble for Africa". In 1875, more than 90 percent of Africa remained autonomous, few formal international borders were recognised, and the most territorially significant alien power was Turkey, which controlled present-day Egypt, Libya and Sudan. Twenty years later, the entire continent (with the exception of Ethiopia and Liberia) had been carved up into colonies: northwest Africa was dominated by France, the south and east were mostly British, while lesser stake-

holders included Germany, Portugal, Belgium, Italy and Spain, and Turkey was out of the frame completely. This hastily executed colonial carve-up was entered into with little premeditation and mixed enthusiasm by France and Britain, the dominant regional powers, and it was catalysed by a pair of countries whose prior involvement in Africa had been minimal. These were Belgium, where the ambitious King Leopold II charged the explorer Henry Stanley with annexing the Congo Basin in 1876, and Germany, whose sudden interest in Africa was cultivated in order to acquire overseas pawns to use in European territorial negotiations with Britain and France.

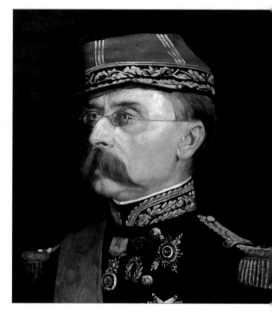

The scramble climaxed at the Berlin Conference of 1884–5, wherein a long list of issues between France, Britain and Germany was settled by diplomats whose scant knowledge of the African interior was matched only by their disregard for the existing territorial boundaries of its indigenous inhabitants. Overall, Senegal and The Gambia, whose modern borders took shape at the Berlin Conference, were less arbitrary creations than many other African colonies. Much of The Gambia had been a British protectorate since the 1820s, while France's oldest and largest African colony had been centred on present-day Senegal even before the scramble. By contrast, the Casamance, to the south of The Gambia, shared strong pre-colonial links with neighbouring Portuguese Guinea (now Guinea-Bissau) and

---

LEFT: advertisement from the chocolate-maker Poulain praising its colonies, here Senegal.
RIGHT: Louis Faidherbe, Governor of Senegal.

was ceded to Senegal only in 1888. Seven years later, the Senegalese capital of Saint-Louis was made administrative capital of the Afrique Occidentale Française (AOF), a vast French colonial federation comprising present-day Senegal, Mali, Niger, Benin, Chad, Côte d'Ivoire, Guinea, Burkina Faso and Mauritania. In 1902, the AOF capital shifted south to Dakar, though Saint-Louis would remain capital of Senegal itself until 1960.

Franco-Senegalese relations

From the mid-19th century, France had granted unusual privileges to Senegal, decreeing that any person born in Saint-Louis, Gorée, Rufisque or

and extended the offer of French citizenship to all who lived there. Ten years later, in 1956, universal suffrage was established in Senegal under the *loi-cadre* reforms, which aimed eventually to create an independent government. Because Dakar had been the capital of the AOF, it had infant industries that needed the wider hinterland the federation offered, and it housed a large bureaucracy designed for the federation. Most Senegalese political leaders thus favoured maintaining the AOF in some form, and Senegal was never expected to enter independence as a single country.

Charles de Gaulle's proposed Franco-African community was dealt a fatal blow in a September

Dakar was automatically a French citizen. In addition, these regions were each entitled elect a local representative in the French parliament. As part of the process of assimilating its African subjects into French society and politics, the first Senegalese deputy was elected to French parliament in 1848, serving until 1852. It was not until 1914, however, that the first Senegalese of non-European ancestry was elected to deputise. His name was Blaise Diagne, and he held the post for 20 years until 1934. By 1920, the communes of Dakar, Gorée, Saint-Louis and Rufisque boasted a "colonial council" which consisted not just of local dignitaries and representatives but also chiefs from the interior.

In 1946, a year after World War II ended, France restyled all its colonies as full overseas territories

> In 1946, Léopold Senghor, aged 40, became the first African to sit in the French National Assembly as a representative of Senegal.

1958 referendum wherein all but one of the AOF constituent territories voted for autonomy, the odd man out being Guinea, which voted for full independence. The AOF was dissolved shortly afterwards. Côte d'Ivoire, Niger, Burkina Faso and Benin formed the short-lived Sahel-Benin Union, while Senegal and the French Soudan gained independence on 4 April 1960 as the Mali Federation (Fédération du Mali), named after the ancient African empire. Modelled on de Gaulle's 1958 Constitution of the Fifth Republic, the Mali Federation provided for a president, prime minister and a national assembly elected by universal suffrage. By the end of the year, however, internal stresses had caused it to split into the separate republics of Senegal and Mali.

Anglo-Gambian relations

The Gambia, as a British protectorate, was often granted privileges denied to crown colonies, though to a less significant extent than Senegal. The Gambian parliament, established in 1852, offered ministers of both local and foreign descent an administrative role over the protectorate. By the time of the "Scramble for Africa", however,

protectorate into the 1920s. Britain retained a somewhat non-committal attitude to The Gambia throughout the colonial era. Economic and educational development was largely restricted to Bathurst and its environs, and access to the interior was limited by a lack of paved roads or public ferries along the river.

As was the case in several other British colonies, the drive for Gambian independence gained ground after World War II, when Africans recruited to fight for the British against Nazi tyranny returned home to find they were still second-class citizens in their own country. Two sets of constitutional changes were implemented

Britain had come to regard this tiny and unproductive protectorate in the heart of French West Africa as something of a liability, and it held onto The Gambia somewhat reluctantly, only after failing to persuade France – or anybody else, for that matter – to trade it against a more advantageous territory. After the Scramble, Bathurst (Banjul) and its immediate environs became a crown colony, while the rest of the country remained a

LEFT: Senegalese tribesmen and French colonial troops land on the beaches of southern France from coastguard-manned invasion transports and landing barges, September 1944. **ABOVE LEFT:** King Archibong II of The Gambia in 1922. **ABOVE RIGHT:** French President Charles de Gaulle visits Dakar in 1958.

in the 1950s, both aimed at granting greater representation to upcountry and other local leaders. In 1961, the first universal franchise elections were held, resulting in victory for Dawda Jawara (a trained veterinary surgeon) and his People's Progressive Party (PPP). The Gambia was the last of Britain's West African colonies to attain full independence, mainly because it was so poor and small that the administration had doubts about its economic viability. The option of closer links with Senegal – even a merger – was mooted, but contacts foundered when it came to working out power-sharing arrangements. Thus The Gambia became an independent sovereign state on 18 February 1965, with Dawda Jawara as its first prime minister.

The Poet-Politician

Senghor's place in history comes from the way he managed to combine the role of writer and poet with that of practical politician and statesman

Léopold Sédar Senghor enjoyed a special position among the African leaders of the independence generation: a successful intellectual in politics. Born in Joal in 1906, Senghor took delight in his mixed ancestry of a Serer businessman father, an

Islamic Fula mother and a surname derived from the Creole culture of Casamance (Senghor is a bastard-isation of the Portuguese *Senhor*). It was the perfect expression of his notion of cultural *métissage* (cross-breeding), a recurrent idea in his writing and thinking.

His education, with the Holy Fathers in Senegal then, after 1928, as a student of literature at the Sorbonne in Paris, instilled a profound appreciation of French culture. Critics who have singled him out as a black Frenchman have failed to appreciate his basic duality. The philosophical and literary movement *Négritude*, which he helped to launch in Paris, was a reaction to the weight of the French culture he had experienced. And, although an uncompromising theory of the assertion of black African values, *Négritude* still bore the mark of a Parisian literary movement.

Much of Senghor's intellectual, literary and even polit-ical career revolved around promoting and redefin-ing *Négritude* – an expression which, although he did not invent it, will always be linked to him.

After graduating from the Sorbonne in 1935, where he was the first African to achieve the Agrégation in French grammar, Senghor stayed in France to teach. A supporter of de Gaulle, he was taken prisoner of war in 1940. With the Liberation he entered politics, build-ing on his academic prestige. In 1946 he was elected a deputy of Senegal in the French National Assembly, from where it was a short step to ascendancy in Senegal's politics. He was also leader of one of two groups of Africans in the Assembly in Paris, and was a minister in the 1955 government of Edgar Faure.

When Senegal achieved independence in 1960, Senghor became its first president. After some initial crises he established confident supremacy over the political scene. The high level of political conscious-ness among Senegal's diverse, numerous and vola-tile educated elite made it a difficult country to run.

Senghor used his own intellectual reputation and access to French political circles, but also became a master of Machiavellian manoeuvre, the *politique politicienne* he affected to despise. While the support of the French was crucial at key moments, he knew he needed to retain the support of the marabouts, the leaders of the Islamic brotherhoods dominant in rural areas. Although for a time he alienated the mara-bouts over problems with groundnut production, he used his Catholic faith to present himself as a neutral force between the different powerful brotherhoods.

Senghor stressed the importance of culture as the basis of politics, and the vibrancy of Senegal's culture owes much to his patronage – as seen in the first World Festival of Black Arts, held in Dakar in 1966, arguably Africa's most successful large-scale arts festival. At times his intoxication with ideas made him seem remote, especially when he took up with the "universal civilisation" idea of Father Teilhard de Chardin. His advocacy of *la francophonie* (a colonial language, after all) was questioned. His rationale was, in part, that it was a way of tying Europe to Africa, fit-ting in with another concept he advocated – Eur-Africa, two continents tied together in symbolic relationship.

After retiring in 1980 he became the first black member of the French Academy in 1984. His poetry ranges from lyrical evocations of an idealised Africa (*Songs of the Shade*, 1945) to themes of cultural conflict in *Ethiopiques* (1956). He died in Normandy in 2001, and a state funeral was held in Dakar. ❑

LEFT: Senghor spent his last years in France.

Senegal's first president

Following the dissolution of the Mali Federation, Léopold Senghor, the first president of the Senegal Republic, came to power in a political crisis. He experienced several more over the first decade of independence, although in the end his position was consolidated. In December 1962, Senghor faced a major challenge to his authority from his prime minister, Mamadou Dia. Senghor dismissed Dia, who claimed the party had sovereignty over the state, and then tried and jailed him for treason. Soon afterwards, the constitution was changed by referendum to abolish the position of prime minister and transfer full exec-

prime minister was reinstated in 1970 in order to free him to concentrate on affairs of state and foreign policy, most notably the foundation of the Economic Community of West African States (ECOWAS) in 1975. By 1974, having beaten back organised political opposition either by assimilating or banning other parties, Senghor was strong enough to permit one legal opposition party, then two, and finally three while trying to dominate the centre-left by changing the name of the ruling party to Parti Socialiste (PS). Nevertheless, the education sector – the teachers' union, the University of Dakar in particular, and even the schools – continued to be a focus for discontent. In 1980,

utive powers to the president. The next significant challenge to Senghor's leadership occurred in May 1968 when a combination of student-worker demonstrations (echoing those in Paris of the same month) paralysed the government. Senghor depended on the armed forces to stay in power, and also drew strength from the endorsement of the Islamic brotherhoods, especially the Mourides, who mobilised their rural supporters to rally behind Senghor against what was primarily an urban disaffection.

After the turbulent 1960s, the 1970s were a period of consolidation for Senghor. The post of

Senghor's sense of historical perspective made him see the need to withdraw from political power in good order and prepare his succession.

Senghor announced his retirement, stabilising what had at times appeared to be a highly volatile political situation. Predictions of the regime's violent demise proved unfounded, and Senghor's voluntary retirement created a favourable climate for his chosen successor, Abdou Diouf, a highly experienced politician who had formerly served as secretary-general of the president (1964–8), minister of planning and industry (1968–70) and prime minister (1970–80).

ABOVE: Léopold Senghor becomes newly independent Senegal's first president in 1960.

Enter Diouf

Diouf enjoyed a two-year political honeymoon. He was helped by Senghor's complete withdrawal from politics, and by the presence at his side of Secretary-General Jean Collin, a French-born Senegalese with vast experience of both administration and politics. Diouf lifted Senghor's restriction on a maximum of three political parties to make Senegal a true multi-party democracy, but his image was tarnished by allegations of vote rigging in the 1983 elections. In 1985, Diouf was elected president of the Organisation of African Unity (OAU) and used this platform to encourage President Mitterrand of France to speak out in

was detained on a charge of incitement and handed a suspended sentence upon his release in May 1988. In April 1991, Diouf offered Wade and four other PDS members the opportunity to join a Government of National Unity (GNU). Wade served under Diouf as minister of state without portfolio for 18 months before he and the other four PDS members resigned from government. However, as part of the GNU, the PDS did manage to pressure the PS into granting opposition parties access to the state-owned media, and it negotiated a new constitutional ruling that limited the president to two terms in office, but extended the presidential term from five to seven years.

favour of sanctions against apartheid South Africa. In 1986, Diouf had the foresight to embark on an anti-HIV programme that encouraged the media, schools and religious organisations to advocate safe sex; as a result the HIV infection rate for Senegal never rose above 2 percent, one of the lowest anywhere in Africa.

Diouf vs Wade

Student unrest marked the build-up to the 1988 election, where Diouf received 72 percent of the vote against the 25 percent garnered by Abdoulaye Wade, leader of the opposition Parti Démocratique Sénégalais (PDS). When fresh allegations of electoral fraud in the wake of Diouf's victory stimulated widespread strikes, Abdoulaye Wade

Diouf was returned to power in 1993 with 58.4 percent of the vote as compared to Wade's 32 percent. Shortly afterwards, he set about trying to reduce the budget deficit with a series of stringent and unpopular austerity measures that included a 15 percent cut in the wages of public sector workers, docking one day's pay per month from private sector workers, and devaluing the currency by 50 percent. These measures provoked widespread demonstrations and were eventually revoked a year later. On 15 May 1993, the day after the National Assembly elections results were announced, the

ABOVE: Senegal's second president, Abdou Diouf, was in power for 20 years. **RIGHT:** Mauritanians being deported after race riots in Senegal.

vice-president of the Constitutional Council, Babacar Sèye, was assassinated in mysterious circumstances. Five months later, Abdoulaye Wade, his wife Viviane, and two other prominent PDS members were charged with complicity in Sèye's murder. Wade and several other PDS leaders were arrested as a threat to state security following fresh rioting in February 1994, and although the murder charge was dismissed in May, Wade was only released in July after he and his co-defendants went on hunger strike. As a measure of the disruption caused by student unrest during this period, Dakar University was forced to declare invalid the 1993/4 academic year. Meanwhile, the PDS rejoined the GNU in March 1995, with Wade serving as minister of state, but the GNU dissolved again in the build-up to the presidential elections scheduled for 2000.

Wade takes charge

The 2000 election was arguably the most momentous in Senegalese history. Initially, it looked like Diouf would hold on to power, garnering 41 percent of the first-round vote as opposed to Wade's 31 percent. However, without a clear first-round majority, Diouf was forced to stand against his nearest opponent on a one-to-one basis in the second round. The other opposition candidates,

THE SENEGAL-MAURITANIA CONFLICT

Senegal's tensest international dispute since independence was a border war that flared up with Mauritania in 1989. It started as a simple dispute over dry-season grazing rights along the Senegal River near Bakel, but escalated in April 1989 when a riot broke out along the river bank after Mauritanian border guards shot dead two Senegalese farmers. As news spread, Mauritanian-owned shops were looted in retribution for the killings, and Mauritanians resident in Senegal were forced to return home.

The Mauritanian authorities retaliated by forcing some thousands of their southern countrymen – who are still today routinely denigrated as "Black Africans" by the paler northerners – into exile in either Senegal or Mali.

As cross-border tensions grew, a series of low-key military raids resulted in hundreds of deaths on both sides of the border, and some 250,000 Senegalese and Mauritanian farmers were impelled to abandon their homes in fear of their lives.

Diplomatic relations were eventually restored between the two countries and the border reopened in 1992 after President Abdou Diouf signed a treaty with his Mauritanian counterpart Ould Taya. According to the UN High Commission for Refugees, however, more than 25,000 "black" Mauritanians were still living as refugees in Senegal or Mali as of June 2007, when their government finally instigated moves to repatriate them.

including third-placed Moustapha Niasse, opted to rally behind Wade, who then went on to win the second round with 58.5 percent of the vote.

This was the first time in the first 40 years of Senegalese independence that an opposition leader was voted into power, and it also put an end to Diouf's 36 years in high office, a run that included 10 years as prime minister and 20 as president. In what was then something of rarity for Africa, Diouf accepted the election result gracefully and stood down to make way for Wade, who proceeded to appoint Niasse as his prime minister. In April 2001, Wade followed up his personal presidential triumph by leading the PDS-dominated Sopi Coalition (*sopi* being the Wolof word for "change") to victory in the parliamentary election.

Following a national referendum, a new constitution was adopted in 2001, one that increased the importance and power of the prime minister's role, and cut the presidential term back to five years as of 2007.

In 2002, the septuagenarian Wade appointed his younger protégé Idrissa Seck as prime minister. In September of the same year, shockwaves were felt throughout the country when the government ferry MV *Le Joola* tragically sank in a storm, killing more than 1,800 passengers off the Gambian coast

THE CASAMANCE CONFLICT

Throughout the 1990s, the Casamance experienced a low-level civil war pitting the independence-seeking Movement of Democratic Forces of Casamance (MFDC) against the Senegalese government. This conflict is rooted in the arbitrary drawing of borders that characterised the "Scramble for Africa", linking the Diola people of the Casamance to the near-disjunct north of Senegal rather than the more closely affiliated people of The Gambia or Guinea-Bissau. Regular Diola uprisings occurred during the colonial era, leading to the formation in 1947 of the MFDC, demanding complete independence both from France and the rest of Senegal.

In 1960, Senghor promised the MFDC that Casamance would be independent within 20 years if it remained part of Senegal for the time being. Two decades later, that promise remained unfulfilled, and a series of MFDC rallies in Ziguinchor culminated in the death of 25 demonstrators in a clash with armed police in 1983. The MFDC launched an armed struggle in 1990, and although it signed several ceasefires later in the decade, none lasted for very long as Senegal refused to countenance the possibility of independence.

By 2000, thousands of non-combatants had been killed in Casamance. In December 2004 the MFDC signed a more enduring peace treaty with Wade's government. Although a brief spate of renewed fighting in 2006 forced thousands of civilians to take temporary refuge in The Gambia, the Casamance has been reasonably calm ever since.

en route between Ziguinchor and Dakar. The ferry was carrying nearly four times as many people as it should have been when it went down. In 2004, Wade fired Seck and in July 2005 the disgraced former prime minister was detained and charged for corruption in connection with a road project at Thiès, as well as for threatening state security. The charges were eventually dropped in 2006, and Seck – forcibly expelled from the PDS – started his own party Rewmi (Wolof for "Country") and announced he would run against Wade in 2007.

In the end, Wade won the 2007 presidential election with a comfortable 55.9 percent of votes, despite having turned 80 the previous year,

The Gambia since 1960

The immediate post-independence era brought hope and relative prosperity to the smallest country on mainland Africa. The global price of groundnuts – the country's main crop – increased steadily through the first decade of independence, and the country also experienced a remarkable surge in package tourism, from a few hundred visitors per annum at the time of independence to almost 30,000 by the late 1970s. As a consequence of the two trends, the country maintained an average economic growth of around 10 percent between 1966 and 1980, and the per capita income increased by a remarkable 25 percent in

while Seck was the closest runner-up with 14.9 percent. Although there is doubtless some substance to opposition complaints that the Wade regime is marred by corruption and constraints on civil liberties, Senegal under his leadership has also come to be perceived as one of the most stable, progressive and economically viable countries in the whole of Africa.

FAR LEFT: a Senegalese army tank drives through the border between Guinea-Bissau and Senegal during the Casamance conflict. **LEFT:** a woman walks near a billboard warning of possible landmines in Zinguichor, Casamance. **ABOVE:** meeting between French president Nicolas Sarkozy, then minister of the interior, and Abdoulaye Wade, Senegal's president, in Dakar in 2006.

the 1970s. Prosperity was matched by political stability, and the first 15 years under Dawda Jawara – who was knighted in 1966 – were largely uneventful, though Jawara did cut all formal ties with Britain by proclaiming The Gambia as a republic, with himself as president, in 1970.

Sir Dawda faced his first major crisis on 29 July 1981, when elements in the Field Force, the paramilitary arm of the police (until 1981 The Gambia had no army), attempted a coup, which left 500 dead and was accompanied by ransacking and looting. The coup attempt was quelled with the assistance of Senegalese troops, invited in under a defence and cooperation treaty. But the violence of the event produced a reaction in favour of established authority, and dented Jawara's image.

Although the PPP was able to resume its dominance and continue winning elections, the shadow of 1981 lingered. In its wake came the formation of the Confederation of Senegambia in 1982. For the next three years, protocols were agreed on common policies in the field of defence and security, external relations, communication and information. The protocol of defence was particularly significant for The Gambia, providing the country with its own armed forces, a small gendarmerie equipped by France and trained by the Senegalese. The confederation made great economic sense, and it came as a surprise when President Diouf summarily dissolved it as "a waste of time and money"

many observers, noticed by few until after it happened, and welcomed enthusiastically by most Gambians, who believed the Jawara administration to be irretrievably corrupt. The man behind the military takeover was 29-year-old Lieutenant Yahya Jammeh, who claimed the coup had been organised in less than 24 hours and just as quickly banned all political activity and pronounced himself the new head of state. Unfortunately, the coup led to a sharp economic downturn as the all-important tourism industry collapsed and several Western governments denounced the military takeover and withdrew aid in line with their policy of not supporting military governments. Tourism and aid started to flow back

in response to a critical speech by Jawara in 1989. Deteriorating relations between the countries, focused on the problem of cross-border smuggling, culminated in Senegal's unilateral closure of all land borders with The Gambia in 1993, thus blocking Gambian land trade with all neighbouring countries. Although the borders were subsequently reopened, relations between the two countries remained wary.

Jammeh's coup

After independence, The Gambia conducted freely contested elections every five years, and by the early 1990s it ranked as one of the oldest multi-party democracies in Africa. In July 1994, however, President Jawara was ousted from power in a bloodless military coup that came as a complete surprise to

> In 2004, Jammeh called on journalists to obey his government "or go to hell". In 2005, he stated on radio and television that he had allowed "too much expression" in the country.

into The Gambia after March 1995, when Jammeh announced plans to hold a presidential election and draft a new constitution allowing for civil rule.

True to his word, Jammeh held a presidential election in September 1996, a four-horse race that saw him returned to power with 56 percent of the vote, representing the newly formed Alliance for Patriotic Reorientation and Construction (APRC). Jammeh introduced a new civil constitution the next year, and also appointed an Independent

Electoral Commission (IEC) to take responsibility for the registration of voters and other electoral matters. A full cycle of presidential, legislative and local elections were finally held in 2001, and Jammeh was retuned to power with 53 percent of the vote as against the 33 percent won by the opposition United Democratic Party (UDP) candidate Ousainou Darboe. The election was generally held to be free and fair by foreign observers, but the UDP accused the APRC of electoral fraud and vote rigging, and boycotted the subsequent legislative elections in protest, ensuring that the APRC maintained its strong majority in the National Assembly.

after further legislation restricting press freedom was enacted, Deyda Hydara, the editor of independent newspaper *The Point*, and a strong advocate of press freedom and critic of the Jammeh regime, was assassinated in his car by unidentified gunmen.

In the tense build-up to the presidential elections of March 2006, security forces announced the discovery and disarmament of a planned military coup, an event that led to the arrest of several army officers and the cross-border flight of many others, including the military chief of staff. Three Gambian journalists were arrested shortly afterwards, and some sceptics have claimed that the entire thing was a presidential fabrication to consolidate support

A new repressive regime

Since 2001, The Gambia has enjoyed a relatively high level of economic growth, and tourism in particular has boomed in an atmosphere of apparent political stability. At the same time, the Jammeh regime has become increasingly repressive, and many observers regard it as bordering on a police state. Never very tolerant of criticism, Jammeh cracked down on press freedom in 2002, passing a law that allowed for journalists to be imprisoned at the whim of the security forces. In 2004, only days

LEFT: President Jammeh addresses his people. **ABOVE:** the newspaper headlines after Jammeh's coup. **RIGHT:** Jammeh promises peace and prosperity but is getting increasingly repressive.

shortly before the election, which Jammeh won comfortably, and was reported to be free and fair.

Recent proclamations by Jammeh demonstrate a worrying disconnection from reality. In January 2007, he announced that he had developed a three-day cure for HIV/Aids using a secret bouquet of medicinal herbs and fruits. Days later, Fadzai Gwaradzimba, the Zimbabwe-born country representative of the UN Development Programme (UNDEP) for The Gambia, voiced concerns that this claim might encourage risky sexual behaviour, and was expelled from the country. In May 2008, Jammeh again made international headlines with an announcement that homosexuals of both genders had 24 hours to get out of The Gambia, or risked being beheaded as punishment. ❏

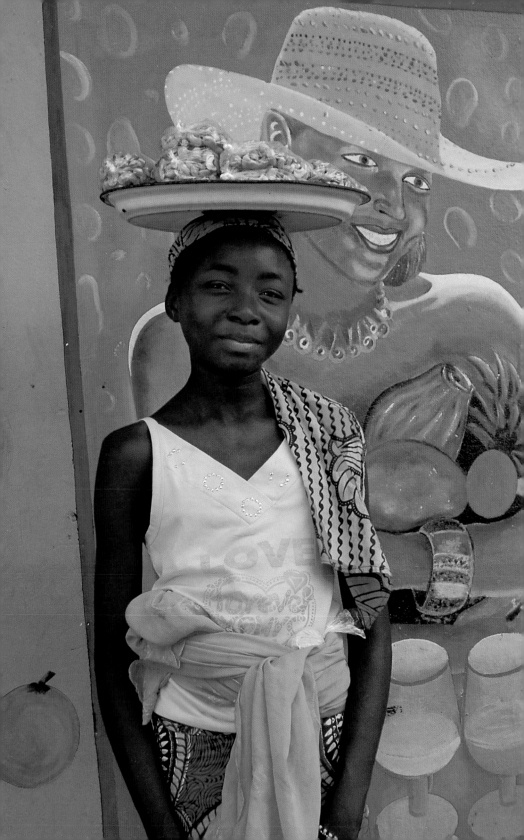

FOOD AND DRINK

From rich rice dishes to elegantly presented nouvelle cuisine, Senegal and The Gambia offer a wide range of choices for food connoisseurs

I n Dakar and on the Atlantic coast of The Gambia, strings of high-quality restaurants invite hungry visitors to their tables. Local cooking, however, is best sampled in inconspicuous eating houses and at family celebrations – so make sure you get yourself invited, don your most elegant clothes and prepare to sample delicious *cheb* (rice), fried doughnuts and sweetened baobab porridge.

Food and its preparation are essential to a country's culture. Conditioned by geography and shaped by history and traditions, they reflect a nation's soul. This is particularly true of Senegalese cooking. The Senegalese have used great imagination and style to create an eclectic cuisine, drawing on Arabic, French, Portuguese, Antillean and, more recently, Vietnamese influences, as well as on the rich and complex history of their own country.

Rice is by far the most popular grain in Senegal, though the country itself cultivates only a small percentage of its own supplies. Also grown in the country are sorghum and millet, the latter being the main ingredient for couscous, the classic meal of Senegal's Fula population.

Couscous, originally from North Africa and made with wheat, is made with millet in Senegal and, with local additions such as baobab leaf (lalo) in the stew, has become a standard dish.

Senegal's national dish is *cheb-ou-jen* (*thiébou-dienne* in the French transliteration) – which literally means rice and fish, and refers to a delicious meal of rice cooked in tomato sauce and served with chunks of fried fish and vegetables.

LEFT: cajun nut-sellers are ubiquitous.
RIGHT: corn for sale at The Gambia's Brikama market.

Millet is the essential ingredient in festive dishes such as *ngalakh*, a type of porridge made of ground millet, groundnut paste and baobab cream, and *lakh*, a version of *ngalakh* served with soured milk. It's also used for the popular dessert *chakri* (steamed millet with sweetened yoghurt) that you can buy on any street corner. In the markets, you can sometimes see an array of bowls containing different types of millet – half-steamed millet, millet meal, millet flour, unpounded millet, de-husked millet – for the connoisseur housewife.

Fish is the base to many dishes, and particularly popular as well as cheap in the areas near the Atlantic coast. The most common fish are barracuda, tuna, groupers (sea bass, the Senegalese *thiof*), mullet (*dem*), Nile perch (*capitaine*), swordfish (*espadon*), monkfish (*lotte*) and sole. Make sure you visit at least one of the large fish markets of Dakar or The Gambia's Atlantic coast as the boats draw in from the sea in the early evening – even if you're not buying, it's a feast for the eyes.

And don't forget to sample the delicious local shellfish. There are enormous prawns, crabs, lobsters, crayfish, sea urchins and oysters (grown on mangrove roots in the creeks but taken to oyster beds off the Pointe des Almadies to be washed clean by the Atlantic tides and thus made safe for eating). They should be tried by the discerning visitor, whether freshly grilled over an open fire, deep-fried, sautéed, boiled in stews,

baked in foil with herbs, or stuffed à la Saint-Louisienne. Dried in the sun or smoked, fish can be kept without refrigeration. A speciality in Saint-Louis, *cheb-ou-jen* is dried mollusc, *yète*, which has a strong, distinctive flavour that might not suit everyone's taste buds.

Since 90 percent of the population in this region are Muslim, pork is not widely consumed, nor available. Lamb, beef and goat are the most commonly used meats.

Both Dakar and The Gambia's Atlantic coast have a great selection of restaurants, where you can find pretty much everything, from Lebanese and Chinese to Indian and Ethiopian cuisine. For

COLONIAL HERITAGE

French influence in Senegal, though relatively unobtrusive in the cooking, has left the Senegalese with a taste for fresh French bread, dressed salads and hors-d'œuvre. British culinary practices have fortunately not affected Gambian cuisine, but have regrettably left their mark on some hotel kitchens, which have a tendency to serve unimaginative meat dishes in bland sauces, chips with everything, and unseasoned garnishes. Local dishes can be hard to find on their menus, though *benachin* and *cheb-ou-jen*, *domoda*, *mafé* and chicken *yassa* are sometimes offered.

the not so adventurous visitor, pizza and burger bars are also largely available. Better fast-food options, though, are the Afra places in The Gambia (*dibiteries* in Senegal). These are tiny grill houses, where you can watch your kilo of meat being prepared before your eyes. These places are particularly popular stopovers after a late night out.

For fresh vegetables, the choices can often be quite limited, particularly during the dry season. Aubergines, courgettes, carrots, cabbage, onions and tomatoes are the most commonly found veg; mint, coriander and parsley are popular herbs. Typical local vegetables include green leaves such as sorrel (*bissap*), dried baobab leaf (*lalo*) and okra (*gombo*), which is used in the gooey stew *soupakanja*.

Celebrations and thirst-quenchers

Festive dishes include *naan mboro*. Muslims eat this before mosque prayers on Korite (end of Ramadan), while Christians typically prepare it for Good Friday. *Lakh* with *sow* (sweetened soured milk) is typically served as the first dish at baptisms. At Tabaski, the Muslim Feast of the Lamb (commemorating Abraham's sacrifice of a lamb in place of his son), tradition demands the slaughtering of a lamb, which is then to be grilled and shared among family and friends.

When it comes to drinks, freshly squeezed juices can be bought all along the Gambian beach side. There's also an excellent range of local drinks, such as *bissap*, which is made from red sorrel flowers and drunk ice cold or eaten frozen as a home-made ice-lolly. Ginger juice (*gingembre* in French) is made from pounded fresh root ginger and is a perfect cure for a sore throat as well as a great energiser. *Ditakh* is made from a green fruit infused in water oozing vitamin C. A healthy day is best started with local herbal teas, reputed for their medicinal properties. The best-known one is *kinkeliba*.

In Senegal and The Gambia eating and drinking is a social event, with whole families gathering around a giant bowl for mealtimes. Preparation of food can take hours and is carefully done. The preparing and drinking of *attaya* especially is an event to partake in. In the afternoons you can find young boys and older men gathered outside the compound on the street corner chatting and socialising over a teapot. *Attaya* is a strong brew made from gunpowder green tea mixed with fresh mint, water and lots of sugar. The green tea, fresh mint and water are heated in a small metal teapot over charcoal. Skilled pouring from a great height from teapot to glass and back dissolves the sugar and forms a white froth on the surface through which the tea is drunk. There are three brewings – the first one is strong and bitter, the second sweeter and the third even sweeter, milder and more minty. If you accept the invitation to tea, you should stay for all three, so make sure you are not in a rush as the preparation takes a while.

In Casamance, the traditional drink is palm wine, a white, frothy and slightly sour liquid tapped from the oil palm. Drunk fresh it is as refreshing as juice, fermented it becomes a potent alcohol, and distilled as *cana* it turns into a lethal, high-percentage brew.

FAR LEFT: fish and rice is a popular dish. **LEFT:** serving *attaya* is a skill. **RIGHT:** *bissap* is a local Gambian drink.

Gambian specialities

Many drinks and dishes previously mentioned are also found in The Gambia – hardly surprising, since both countries share many cultural origins. But the presence of Yoruba and Sierra Leonean immigrants stretching back several generations has lent some distinctive flavours to The Gambia's cuisine.

Benachin, a Wolof dish (*bena* = one, *chin* or *kin* = pot, i.e. a one-pot meal) resembles *cheb-ou-jen* but is often served with meat instead of fish (Senegalese *cheb-ou-yapp*). The Mandinka dish *domoda* is The Gambia's national meal. It is made from vegetables and meat cooked in a thick groundnut sauce. This dish is similar to the

SWEET BAOBAB

The baobab tree is known to have many useful parts suitable for consumption. Its leaves are used in cooking and its stringy white fruit is used to make juice and porridge. The fruit is cracked open and emptied of its meat, which is cleaned from its many seeds and then pounded. Alternatively, the meat of the fruit is soaked in water and later poured through a sieve. Sugar is added to enhance the flavour.

widespread West African dish *mafé*. *Sisay yassa* is the same as chicken *yassa* (grilled chicken marinated in lime juice and onions).

Red palm oil goes into *plasas* (a corruption of Sierra Leonean "palaver sauce", itself coming from the Portuguese *palavra*), a stew made with smoked fish and greens that is particularly popular with the Aku people. Fish is fresh and plentiful and should be enjoyed. Care should be taken with oysters harvested from the creek mangroves, which have not had the advantage of sea-washing, as these can cause hepatitis.

In the market you can find snacks and finger foods such as *pastels* (small hot pastry fritters stuffed with spiced fish) and fish balls *(boulettes)*, fish cakes, *fataya* (meat-filled pasties of Lebanese origin) and, of course, roasted groundnuts, best bought hot and loose.

Traditionally, neither Gambians nor Senegalese eat prepared desserts, though especially in Senegal, the lasting influence of French cuisine means that restaurants generally offer sumptuous three-course meals. Delicious fresh fruit, such as pineapple, pawpaw (papaya), mangoes, watermelons, guavas, limes, bananas or soursop *(corrosol* in French) make fruit salad a fabulous dessert option. Yoghurts, *chakri* and a variety of tarts are also widely available.

CRAZY FOR NUTS

Mafé (or *Mafe*, *Maffé*, *Maffe*, or *Maafe*), a traditional dish of the Wolof people of Senegal and The Gambia, is one of the many variations on the African groundnut stew. It is a stew with meat simmered in a sauce thickened with ground peanuts and has a wonderful sweet-salty flavour. It can be made with lamb, mutton, chicken, fish (fresh or dried) or just vegetables. The basic *Mafé* recipe calls for meat, onions, oil, tomato paste, peanuts, a vegetable or two, chilli peppers, salt, black pepper and water.

Eating etiquette

Cooking and eating in both Senegal and The Gambia are based on the tradition of hospitality. If finances allow, meals are copious, geared to feeding a large family. As tradition demands, there's always enough for the unexpected guest. Food is served on a large flat tray, rice underneath and vegetables, meat and fish arranged over the top, with careful attention to final presentation. A mat on the floor serves as a "table", the family sitting around the dish, eating with either their hands or spoons. If you decide to use your hand, make sure it's the right one, as the left hand is the one you're supposed to wash yourself with. The eating technique looks simple but is hard to execute. A little rice is rolled up in the fingers, squeezed into a ball and popped into the mouth. Succulent pieces of fish, meat or vegetables are broken off by the hostess and tossed in front of the visitor because stretching is not good manners. A bowl of water is provided before and after the meal for hand washing.

ative variety of ways. *Niambe Niebbe*, for example, is a cassava dish served with cooked black-eye beans and the side serving of a hot sauce made with pepper, tomato and onion. If you are invited to a family home, you're unlikely to be served those dishes though, as they are considered a poor man's diet. Sadly for the vegetarian, the hostess will most probably have gone to lengths to find you an excellent chunk of meat or fresh fish. The best place to look for freshly prepared *niambe niebbe* is on street corners, where women sell them in mornings and evenings. You will get a slice of bread, senfour or the more filling *tapalapa* and fill it up with the *niebbe* and sauce.

Vegetarian food

Being a vegetarian in The Gambia or Senegal can be hard work. Most restaurants don't have a great deal of options for the vegetarian, much less the vegan visitor. As in many African countries, Gambian and Senegalese dishes mostly include meat or fish of some kind, and most locals will simply be bemused by the idea of someone voluntarily refusing to eat meat. Still, there are a few traditional vegetarian dishes.

If you know what you are looking for you can get well fed on black beans prepared in an imagin-

In the early morning hours you will find the breakfast winner *accara*, sold in big metal bowls outside the local shops. These are fried balls from peeled and pounded beans, which are eaten with pepper sauce and usually wrapped in bread.

For the dish *oleleh*, black-eye beans are ground to a powder and made into a bean cake. Wrapped in banana leaf, its beautiful presentation is enough to give you an appetite. It is sometimes made with dried fish, so enquire before buying.

If the struggling vegetarian really can't find enough valid options in restaurants, it might be a good idea to take a stroll to one of Senegal's or The Gambia's bustling markets, stock up on vegetables, fruits, cashews and peanuts and prepare big bowls of delicious fresh salad.   ❏

LEFT: colourful peppers on sale at a Gambian market. **ABOVE LEFT:** dried fish is used in many recipes. **ABOVE RIGHT:** you'll be spoilt for choice with exotic fruits.

FESTIVALS

Celebrations and festivals
are popular elements in both
Senegalese and Gambian culture

As elsewhere in the world, festivals involve the preparation of sumptuous food and the purchase of stylish new garments. Several weeks before the event, women will choose beautifully coloured materials at the local market and take them to the neighbouring tailor to be sewn into elegant *boubous* (wide, flowing robes). Creatively wrapped matching headscarves or a new hairstyle in the latest fashion is a must.

Muslim celebrations are the most important events for the majority of both Gambian and Senegalese people. Their dates change every year, as they depend on the lunar calendar. The main Muslim holidays are Tabaski, when most families slaughter a lamb in commemoration of Abraham's sacrifice, and Korite, the end of the fasting month Ramadan.

Christian holidays are of course observed by the small Christian population (e.g. the Aku who have come to settle in The Gambia from Sierra Leone), though the festive spirit of Christmas has spread to non-Christian communities as well. Around Christmas time you can witness the masked Kankurang roaming the streets of The Gambia to the sound of the sabar drum, the rattle of the natural maracas *kesseng kesseng*, whistle blows and much cheering. The Kankurang wears a costume made from leaves and other natural products, carries a machete and is accompanied by his troupe, which mock-terrifies the people it passes. If you ever get stopped by the Kankurang on the street, don't forget to give a small donation for the performance.

TOP: the Roots Festival takes its name from Alex Hayley's famous book *Roots*, in which he traces his origins back to the Gambian village of Juffureh *(see page 89)*. Excursions to Juffureh and the adjacent James Island are central to the festival. Especially for guests from the Diaspora, they are occasions to pay respects to distant ancestors at the slave fort at James Island.

MAIN PICTURE: Senegalese percussionist Doudou Ndiaye Rose with his group plays on Gorée Island for the opening of the Dakar-Gorée Jazz Festival.

ABOVE: festival participants parade through the rural town Podor during Baaba Maal's annual Blues du Fleuve Festival.

LEFT: traditional Gambian dancer.

RIGHT: koba player in Dakar.

SENEGAL FESTIVAL HIGHLIGHTS

One of the most enduring and most renowned events is the Saint-Louis Jazz Festival, held every May in bars and outdoor stages. It has featured some of the greatest names in jazz, as well as famous African performers such as Ali Farka Touré.

May is also the month of the Dak'Art Biennale, one of Africa's biggest visual arts events. Every two years, it lures art-lovers from across the world to see some of the best in contemporary African art. Particularly exciting are the over 100 "Off" exhibitions – informally organised fringe events – that spread the Biennale spirit across the entire city.

Banlieue Rythme is an urban festival that grew from the initiative of youngsters living in some of Dakar's roughest suburbs into a citywide music festival (June). Also in Dakar, Kay Fecc is an ambitious dance festival with a real Africa-wide outlook (December or June).

THE GAMBIA FESTIVAL HIGHLIGHTS

The Gambia's most famous party is the International Roots Festival, held every two years in the first week of June. Started in the late 1990s, it is held to commemorate the transatlantic slave trade, but also aims to encourage people in the Black Diaspora to come home, promoting a positive view on Gambian culture and creating a sense of unity among African people worldwide. It also promotes business and investment collaborations between the Diaspora and Africa.

Apart from the excursions, Roots offers a full programme of cultural events and concerts. Bakau Stadium is the centre for gigs of traditional and contemporary Gambian and Senegalese artists. Throughout the country, seminars, discussions and workshops on current affairs in The Gambia, Africa and the Black Diaspora draw in scholarly-minded guests, while partygoers fill the many nightclubs along The Gambia's coastline.

ABOVE: the Saint-Louis Jazz Festival.

RIGHT: beware of the Kankurang!

ABOVE: Muslims at prayer during Korite festival on Gorée Island, Senegal. Gorée also celebrates the Day of the Open Doors, granting rare glimpses into the beautiful courtyards of the Portuguese-style Gorée houses.

ARTS AND CRAFTS

Situated in the culturally rich region of West Africa, The Gambia and Senegal are great destinations for lovers of music, dance, painting and other arts

Senegal and The Gambia may not offer that clichéd backdrop of elephants or rhinos; instead, they lure the adventurous visitor with breathtaking arts scenes. In Dakar or Bakau, no night passes without live music, no week without a major arts event. The cities themselves seem to dress in artistic guises, with minibuses, walls and shopfronts all providing spaces for self-expression. Deepest tradition and cutting-edge city culture live here peacefully and harmoniously, and continue to inspire one another. Senegal's thriving capital Dakar in particular is home to vibrant music, film, fashion, theatre and visual arts scenes.

The Gambia is often teasingly called "Little Jamaica", as it has a reggae scene that seems several sizes too big for such a tiny nation. Right next to the pulsating urban scenes that infuse Dakar and The Gambia's Atlantic coast with their inimitable energy, you can also experience the still very vibrant roots of contemporary styles.

Amadou Hampate Ba, one of Africa's great philosophers once said that, in Africa, "When an old man dies, it is as if a whole library has burnt down."

Griot traditions, music and dance

In Africa, history has largely been kept alive orally, and in the Sahel region to which both Senegal and The Gambia belong, the crucial task of passing memories, facts, feats and legends from one generation to the next has been left to the professional occupational group of the *griots*. Traditionally, a "noble" (*geer* in Wolof) family, meaning one standing at the top of the strict hierarchical social order, would have one or more *griots* (*gewel*) responsible for preserving the story of their lineage and recounting it in the form of praise during various family celebrations. *Griots* are part of a "caste group", and their status, and with it attributes of character and behaviour, are determined by birth, whether a person exercises the *griot* profession or not. Their social status is lower than that of a noble person, yet they are empowered with the licence to praise or taunt, to enshrine your name in history or ruin it for ever, and thus still command much respect from higher-ranking members of society.

LEFT: record shop in Serekunda, The Gambia, where reggae is extremely popular.
RIGHT: local crafts markets abound.

Today, the *griot* tradition is very much alive. Most pop styles are grounded in it, and many of the countries' greatest stars are of *griot* background (e.g. Youssou N'Dour on his maternal side, Thione Seck, Jaliba Kouyaté or Coumba Gawlo). If you eavesdrop at weddings or baptisms, you'll often be able to hear a *griot* reciting the magnificent history of those present, perhaps to the accompaniment of *kora* or *xalam* (lute). A feast for ears and eyes are also the uber-glamorous women's events *mamaya*, frequently held at Dakar's Théâtre Sorano, where rows of established ladies in shimmering gowns and impressive make-up "spray" their favourite *gawlos* with banknotes and gifts.

The very same theatre is also the spot Senegal's national ensemble calls its home. Inspired by the neighbouring country Guinea, this group of traditional musicians was formed after independence with the clear task to preserve and enliven Senegal's deepest musical traditions. Though the ensemble still rehearses religiously, it rarely performs. But many of Senegal's great artists have passed through this "school" (e.g. Assane Mboup, singer with Orchestra Baobab).

Orchestra Baobab is today the most famous representative of Senegal's lively salsa scene, which dates back to the independence era of the 1960s and '70s. Back then, Senegalese "orchestras" –

YOUSSOU N'DOUR

Youssou N'Dour is one of the most celebrated African musicians in history. His mix of traditional Senegalese *mbalax* with eclectic influences ranging from Cuban samba to hip hop, jazz, and soul has won him an international fan base of millions. In the West, Youssou has collaborated with musicians Peter Gabriel, Neneh Cherry (with whom he duetted on the top single "7 seconds"), Paul Simon, Sting and Bruce Springsteen. He has also created a youth foundation to help children in need.

large bands featuring mainly guitars, drums, vocalists, horn sections and congas – experimented with a novel mix of the hugely popular Cuban styles and elements of Senegalese traditional music. In their creations, they were also strongly influenced by the cutting-edge music drifting in from The Gambia, a revolutionary mixture of funk, the sounds of Gambia's many traditions and a touch of Latin beats pioneered by the unforgettable Super Eagles (later re-formed as Ifang Bondi).

Those who grew up with the beats of that era still swear by it today, and so you can see contented couples swaying to the Sene-salsa inflections of Pape Fall, Medoune Diallo and, of course, Orchestra Baobab in hot Dakar nightclubs.

In terms of popularity, however, Senegal's great orchestras have long been superseded by *mbalax*, that inimitable rhythm forged in the steaming *quartiers* of Dakar. *Mbalax* was shaped in the early '80s by the artist who is still today the unrivalled leader of the pack – Youssou N'Dour. He

Mbalax dancing is as popular as ever, and you'll find it not only in nightclubs and social gatherings but in religious and cultural gatherings as well: weddings, birthdays and naming ceremonies for instance.

hard for styles from other ethnic groups, regions or backgrounds to get heard. Yet it's difficult to argue with a music that has kept two countries dancing to the same beat for close to 30 years, and has brought forth some of the world's greatest African stars, such as Youssou N'Dour, Baaba Maal and Omar Pene.

For those who like it quieter, Senegal in particular also has a vibrant folk and jazz scene, featuring young artists such as Yoro or Daby Balde on the stages of small restaurants, bars or live clubs.

Lovers of all things urban will find Senegal and The Gambia hard to leave. Senegal in particular has a strong hip hop culture, led by internationally

married popular styles with the feverish percussion the Wolof people knew and loved from *sabar* street and beach parties, and created almost overnight the seductive sound Senegal defines itself by *(see also panel opposite)*. Like the Wolof language, *mbalax*, with its complex rhythm and sensual dance moves, has over the years grown into a true national expression. More than that – even quarrelling neighbours Senegal and The Gambia are united in their love for that beat. Some people fret that the prevalence of *mbalax* makes it

LEFT: the *balafon* is a type of xylophone used in the *mbalax* musical tradition. **ABOVE:** *dundum* drums are just one type of West African drums. **RIGHT:** Podor-born musician Baaba Maal.

renowned artists such as Didier Awadi, Xuman and Daara J. Over the years, Dakar's youths have come up with ever new ideas of marrying Senegalese roots, the harsh twang of Wolof and the latest in hip hop beats.

The Gambia's hip hop movement has brought forth respected talents such as Smokey or Galaxy High, but the tiny nation is really the land of reggae. Rebellion the Recaller is perhaps the best-known name in Gambian reggae abroad, but there are plenty of young artists working towards their big breakthrough. Concerts by Njie B and Singateh are guaranteed entertainment, though the best place to experience reggae in The Gambia are regular street or beach bashes, with the One Tribe Sound System leading the way.

Modern writing

Few are the nations that have been led by writers. Senegal is certainly one of them. Its first president, Léopold Sédar Senghor, was a fine poet, and his love for the word has left its mark on the nation. He was also one of the main thinkers behind the philosophical idea of *Négritude* or blackness, which he had developed in Paris in the 1940s with West Indian writers Aimé Césaire and Léon Damas *(see also page 50)*. At the same time, Cheikh Anta Diop was researching his theory of the anteriority of African civilisation in world history, provoking emotive debates in intellectual circles.

Letter and Aminata Sow Fall are among the leading women writers. More recently the debut work *Le Ventre de l'Atlantique* (The Belly of the Atlantic) has sold hundreds of thousands of copies and instantly propelled the young emigrant author Fatou Diome to unexpected fame. Most Senegalese works are first published in French, and only very few have been translated into English.

Painting

All along the tourist zones of Senegal and The Gambia, you will be offered garish colour and sand paintings for cheap rates. But make no mistake. Away from the world of tourist trash, these

As president, Léopold Senghor encouraged artists to craft a distinctive visual vocabulary through which to share and celebrate a newfound sense of and belief in Africanness.

countries are home to serious arts traditions. Every two years, you can admire the works of some of the best artists at the Dak'Art Biennale, which features works from across the continent, but retains a strong local focus on home-grown talent.

The foundations for modern Senegalese art were laid in 1962, when the centre for research into black fine arts of the former Art College encouraged a modern African style called the École de Dakar. Its best-known representatives are Dioutta Seck, Maodo Niang and Amadou Ba. The pictorial conception of the École de Dakar is deeply rooted in the concept of *Négritude* and "back-to-roots" philosophy that swept Africa and the black Diaspora during the late 1960s. Pape Ibra Tall and Pierre Lods represented this movement.

Though Senegal's once flourishing publishing industry has largely disappeared, the country continues to bring forth many talented authors. Cheikh Hamidou Kane is one of the best-known male writers, his philosophical work *An Ambiguous Adventure* a profound debate of a society faced with colonisation. The works of female writers seem to make a particular impact in Senegal. Mariama Bâ, author of the stunningly beautiful *So Long a*

Today, trends are a lot more varied, and artists such as Ndary Lô, Soly Cissé, Douts Ndoye, Amadou Kan-Si and Cheikhou Ba surprise constantly with their new, imaginative interpretations of African realities.

A typically Senegalese tradition is the technique of reverse-glass painting, known as *sous-verre*. The style was initially affiliated with the Islamic world as a way of iconographic transmission and so was used to portray and diffuse religious contents and themes. As a result, it was temporarily banned under French colonisation. Nowadays, *sous-verre* painters such as Babacar Lô and Gora Mbengue adapt the style to contemporary con-

Thiaroye, *Xala* and his final work, *Moolaade*, released only months before his death in June 2007. He was often referred to as the "Father of African film". Today, there's a new generation of film-makers, encouraged by relatively cheap equipment and greater opportunities for international exchange. Moussa Sene Absa, director of the controversial and sexy movie *Carmen Geï*, leads the field, and young talents such as Angèle Diabang are taking documentary film to a whole new level. Strangely for a country with such a strong cinematic output, Senegal has no properly functioning movie theatre. African films are frequently shown at the Centre Culturel Français though.

tent and styles, while street sellers peddle "pop-versions" of the art in the form of caricaturist paintings, ubiquitous Bob Marley portraits and hilarious street scenes.

Film-making

Senegal has brought forth an impressive list of famous film-makers, including people like Djibril Diop Mambety, Paulin Vieyra and, of course, Ousmane Sembène. The last put West African cinema on the world map with works such as *Camp de*

Fashion

For the discerning fashion-lover, Dakar is fertile ground. Inspired by the worldwide success of African haute-couture queen Oumou Sy, a number of young designers have decided to make clothes their business. Colle Ardho Sow and Angélique Dhiedhiou find ever new, ever more glamorous uses for the humble woven cloth, while young artists such as Cheikha (Sigil) and Ndiaga Diaw (Fitt) capture the feel of urban Dakar in their stylish designs. Oumou Sy is also the founder of the annual Dakar Carnival and International Fashion Week in Dakar.

In The Gambia, the cute batik company Salam Batik leads the way with its modern take on classic tie-dye. ❏

THE GAMBIA

For such a small country, The Gambia has a lot to offer, whether it be long stretches of sandy beaches, exciting birdwatching opportunities or an interior rich in tradition

Among the most idiosyncratic legacies of the colonial carve-up of Africa, The Gambia protrudes finger-like into francophone Senegal (with which it shares all its terrestrial borders) along the course of the Gambia River. Its serpentine borders follow the river inland for a full 300km (180 miles), yet it is nowhere more than 50km (30 miles) wide, making it the smallest country on the African mainland.

Small it may be, but The Gambia has plenty to offer tourists. The resort-studded Atlantic coastline has emerged as perhaps the most popular African beach destination with English-speaking visitors, thanks to its accessibility from Europe, a long record of political stability, a blissful dry-season climate that coincides with the northern winter, and a justified reputation for offering value for money. And while beach holidays dominate, The Gambia is also renowned in ornithological circles as providing a superb (and unusually affordable) introduction to Africa's rich birdlife, with around 600 species recorded in an area the size of Yorkshire, and plenty of knowledgeable local guides to help first-time visitors track them down.

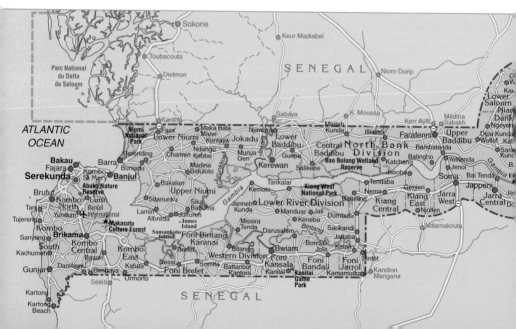

While sun-seekers flock to the coastal resorts, more adventurous travellers succumb to the more down-to-earth allure of the Gambian interior. Here, a quintessentially African landscape of dry savannah is bisected by the life-sustaining waters of the Gambia River, whose mangrove- and forest-lined banks are studded with traditional fishing villages. Although the tropical riverside ambience of upcountry Gambia arguably amounts to more than the sum of its individual attractions, there are highlights aplenty, ranging from the mysterious megaliths of Wassu and brooding colonial ruins of Janjanbureh to the chimps and hippos of the River Gambia National Park and stunning array of colourful birds to be encountered just about anywhere.

Coverage of The Gambia in this book spreads across three chapters. **Banjul and the North Bank** introduces the sleepy capital city, Banjul, which is located at the southern mouth of the Gambia River, as well as a

selection of north-bank historic sites whose association with the sombre days of the transatlantic slave trade led to their inscription on the Unesco World Heritage List as "Saint James Island and Related Sites" in 2003. Next, **Serekunda and the Atlantic Coast** focuses on the fabulous string of popular beach resorts running southward from Banjul and the densely populated area immediately inland of this. Finally, the **Gambia River Route** follows the winding course of the great river inland all the way to where it crosses from Senegal at the country's easternmost extremity. ❑

PRECEDING PAGES: the bustling fish market at Tanji; sunset on beautiful Kombo Beach. **FAR LEFT:** proud to be Gambian. **LEFT:** relaxing in style at Ngala Lodge. **ABOVE:** fighting hippos.

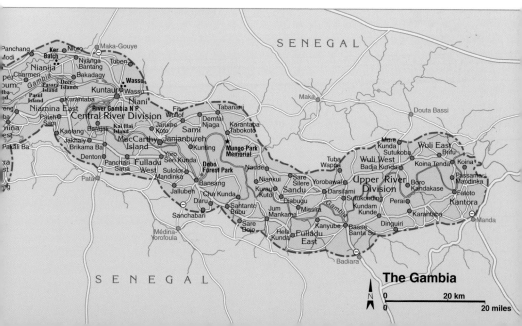

The Gambia

N

0   20 km

0   20 miles

BANJUL AND THE NORTH BANK

In comparison with the likes of Dakar, Banjul is
strikingly low-rise and sedate in character,
coming across less like a capital city than a small
and slightly time-worn provincial town

The most unassuming of African capitals, **Banjul** stands at the mouth of the Gambia River on St Mary's Island, a confined and low-lying patch of terra firma dislocated from the Gambian mainland by a maze of mangrove-lined creeks. Such is its isolation that the only road link to the rest of the country is Denton Bridge, built to replace an older namesake in 1986, the 21st anniversary of Gambian independence.

The foundation of Bathurst

Banjul was founded as a direct result of Britain's abolition of the slave trade in 1807. Until then, the main British outpost on The Gambia had been James Island, 25km (15 miles) downstream of the river mouth, but Sir Charles MacCarthy, Governor-in-Chief of British West Africa, believed that the only way to enforce abolition and curb illicit trade was to blockade slaving ships at the river's entrance. In 1816, Captain Alexander Grant bought St Mary's Island, then known locally as *Banjulo*, to establish a military stronghold at the river mouth, and the settlement that took root there was named in honour of the Earl of Bathurst, then the British Colonial Secretary.

In many respects, Bathurst was an unfortunately sited settlement. In the early days, the swampy mangroves that surrounded the island led to constant infestations of mosquitoes and malaria, while the minimal elevation ensured that flooding was a regular problem in the wet season until the construction of the dyke that now forms Kankujereh Road. Nevertheless, by 1821 the fledgling capital could boast a large military barracks, an officers' mess, a hospital and a courthouse, while a battery of six cannons guarded the river mouth from what is now the grounds of State House. The young settlement also attracted many traders from more established outposts such as Gorée and James Island, and by 1826 its population stood at 1,800. Bathurst was the obvious choice of capital when The Gambia was formally declared a British colony with its own administrative and judicial systems in 1843.

Main attractions

BANJUL:
ARCH 22
JULY 22 SQUARE
NATIONAL MUSEUM OF GAMBIA
ALBERT MARKET
NORTH BANK:
FORT BULLEN
ALBREDA
JUFFUREH
FORT JAMES
NIUMI NATIONAL PARK

LEFT: selling cashew nuts under Arch 22.
BELOW: "Welcome to Banjul" sign.

WHERE

Exploring Banjul, it helps
to know that the official
road name changes that
were implemented in the
1990s have not been
widely adopted by locals
(including taxi drivers) –
as a result most roads
effectively have two
interchangeable names.

Banjul

Renamed Banjul in 1973, the capital city
remains the seat of government and the
judiciary, and it still houses the country's
largest concentration of colonial-era
buildings. Over recent decades, however,
the physical limits imposed by its watery
surrounds have prompted a gradual economic drift out of Banjul to the mainland.
In terms of commerce, the main benefi-
ciary has been Serekunda, which has more
of the heaving bustle one associates with
an African city, and whose population
now exceeds that of Banjul by a factor of
10, but the Atlantic seafronts of Bakau,
Fajara, Kotu and Kololi have also experienced population surges. Meanwhile,
sleepy Banjul is quite possibly the only
African capital whose population is in
decline, from a high of 45,000 in the early
1980s to an estimated 35,000 today.

A sleepy town

Few would regard Banjul as a world city,
but it's an agreeable town all the same,
with an orderly and easily navigable layout, a relaxed but lively atmosphere and
a smattering of intriguing attractions,
headed by the very informative National
Museum and the somewhat more chaotic
Albert Market.

Given its proximity to the popular
resorts that line the nearby Atlantic coastline, Banjul seems oddly unaffected by

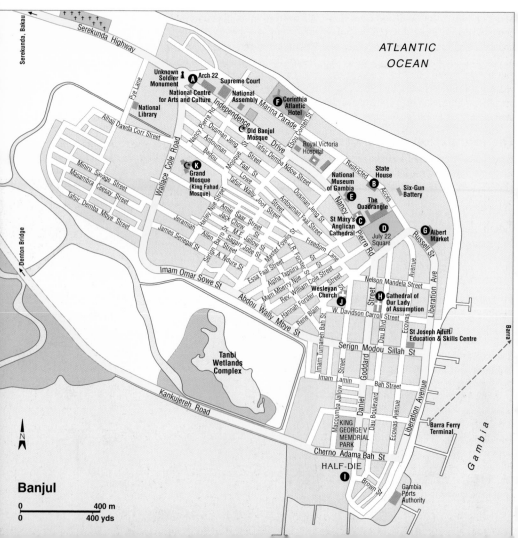

Banjul

0   400 m

0   400 yds

Recommended Restaurants and Bars on page 91

tourism, but this only adds to its charms, which emerge easily from the dust and disrepair. Some roads are in need of work, but the slower pace of locomotion this enforces gives one time to notice courtyards, arches, lattices, verandas, flowering trees, stand pipes and cooking pots and local clothing styles and headdresses, especially in the backstreets.

In this pedestrian-friendly city, people are always on the move. They crowd about their business, trading, hoping to sell or to make a bargain, visiting. The ethnic mix is a microcosm of the country, with Aku, Fula, Diola, Mandinka, Sarakholé, Serer and Wolof all represented, some immediately recognisable by attributes such as clothing or facial scarification, others less obviously so. The city is also home to many foreigners, most conspicuously a large population of blue-robed Mauritanians, but also Lebanese, Senegalese, Guineans, Malians and a wide variety of European expatriates, the last usually distinguishable from tourists by their clothing, colouring and deportment.

Several tour companies based along the Atlantic coastline southwest of Banjul offer introductory tours of the city, often

in conjunction with a trip across the Barra Ferry to the north bank. Banjul is compact and safe enough to be explored independently, though it would be advisable to leave inessential valuables in your hotel room, especially if you are visiting Albert Market, where pickpocketing is a minor but real cause for concern.

The easiest way to reach Banjul from the Atlantic hotel strip is to charter a tourist taxi, though this can be expensive as the driver will usually wait until you are ready to return. Alternatively, shared bush-taxis can be picked up in Bakau or Serekunda, and they cost next to nothing.

Children heading for school in their colourful batik uniforms.

BELOW: carrying his load to the market.

The National Museum of Gambia holds informative – if dusty – displays on the country's history.

BELOW: the white façade of St Mary's Anglican Cathedral.

Exploring the city

Banjul can be divided into three district quarters, each with its own distinct character. The oldest and most architecturally interesting part of town is the spacious and leafy administrative sector that runs northwest from July 22 Square along Independence Drive and Marina Parade. To the southeast from July 22 Square, the main commercial centre consists of a grid of roads between Albert Market and the Barra Ferry terminus. The main residential area lies to the southeast of Independence Drive and July 22 Square.

Around Independence Drive

The capital's most striking architectural landmark, **Arch 22** Ⓐ is practically impossible to miss, towering as it does above the northeast end of Independence Drive at the junction with the road from Serekunda and Bakau. A neoclassical triumphal arch supported by eight columns, it was designed by the Senegalese architect Pierre Goudiaby and unveiled on 22 July 1996 to commemorate the second anniversary of Jammeh's coup d'état. At 35 metres (112ft) high, Arch 22 is reputedly the tallest structure in The Gambia,

and even if bombastic military monuments aren't your thing, it is as good a place as any to start a walking tour of Banjul, if only for the splendid view over town from the airy café at the top. A bronze statue of a Jammeh-looking Unknown Soldier carrying a baby – a symbol of liberation from the oppressive former regime – stands in the circle below the arch.

Running parallel to each other, Independence Drive and Marina Parade are lined with administrative buildings dating from the colonial era. These include the **Supreme Court**, the **National Assembly**, the **Royal Victoria Hospital** (built in the 1840s) and various government offices. Unfortunately, the majestic **State House** Ⓑ is off limits to tourists, despite housing the Six-Gun Battery that was raised by Captain Grant to prevent slave ships entering the Gambia River (now a Unesco World Heritage Site).

The tiny but appealing **St Mary's Anglican Cathedral** Ⓒ at the southeast end of Independence Drive is a more demure colonial relic. Immediately alongside this, **July 22 Square** Ⓓ – formerly Independence Square and before that MacCarthy Square – is the one large open space in the city centre, and the site of a War Memorial and commemorative fountain constructed for the coronation of King George VI in 1937.

Also found on Independence Drive, the thoroughly worthwhile **National Museum of Gambia** Ⓔ (tel: 422 6244; www.ncac.gm; Mon–Thur 8am–6pm, Fri 8am–12.30pm, Sat 8am–3pm; charge) is located in an airy wooden-floored house that used to serve as the (whites only) Bathurst Club. A varied selection of well-annotated displays covers subjects as diverse as traditional Gambian societies, the early colonial history of Bathurst (complete with several fascinating old monochrome photos), the Senegambia Stone Circle sites of Wassu and Ker Batch, Iron Age societies in the Senegal River region, and the spread of Islam and the marabout tradition. The displays are divided into history and ethnography sections. The main hall and lower floor cover indigenous industries and technol-

Recommended Restaurants and Bars on page 91

ogy, music and dance. On the upper floor are the history and archaeology sections. Set aside at least one hour to take a proper look around, after which you might want to browse in the adjacent gift shop or grab a soft drink in the leafy garden, alongside the city's last functional well.

The four-star **Corinthia Atlantic Hotel** **F** located on Marina Parade is an attractive place to pop into for a light lunch or refreshing drink. Its forerunner, the original Atlantic Hotel, was the very first hotel in The Gambia, and it boasts a prime location in large leafy grounds running all the way down to the beach. It also has a notable bird garden, established in 1990, where no less than 150 different species have been recorded, including woodland kingfisher, red-cheeked cordon-bleu, shikra and red-billed hornbill.

After an exhausting sightseeing session around town, the amazing sea views and pleasant breeze at the pool bar are very welcome. On a clear day, you can see right across the river mouth to Barra on the north bank. One advantage this hotel has over the resorts dotted along the Atlantic coastline is a superior location for water sports.

Albert Market

The vibrant focus of market life in Banjul spreads eastward from July 22 Square along **Russell Street** to the famous, colourful and inexhaustible **Albert Market** **G**. Razed by a fire in 1988, this market has been going strong since the middle of the 19th century and it would take more than total combustion to end that run. Shortly after the devastating fire, a new façade was constructed by a team of Chinese contractors, promising a lasting elegance that is subverted by the makeshift lanes of local and imported produce inside. You will be spoilt for choice with all the shimmering fabrics, prints, beads, shells, kola nuts, hair extensions, skin creams, tea, vegetables and fruit that can be purchased here. A corner of the market is entirely devoted to local arts and crafts, and even if you don't want to buy anything, it is interesting just to watch the pointers and woodcarvers at work.

Goats roam freely in the streets of Banjul.

BELOW: batik fabrics on sale at Albert Market.

Gambians have a passion for football – including for European teams.

Liberation Avenue

The Lebanese cloth stalls running south from Albert Market along **Liberation Avenue** (Wellington Street) are full of bolts and rolls and odds and ends of gloriously varied lengths of cloth which ride marvellously on dark skins but need great discrimination to suit paler ones. As visitors quickly notice, the Gambians place enormous store on being well-dressed, and a woman's wardrobe is considered a major household expense. Excellent-quality cloth for men's lightweight suits, summer shirts and shorts can also be bought inexpensively. Local tailors wait to run up clothes for a third of European prices with great competence. Note that bargaining is essential. The Gambian cloth and clothes sellers concentrate on tie-dyed dresses and shirts, hand-painted T-shirts and "bush hats", which are seldom worn except by Europeans.

An important landmark in the commercial centre running towards the Barra Ferry terminus is the Catholic **Cathedral of Our Lady of Assumption** ⓗ (mass: Mon–Fri 6.45am, Sun 7am and 9.30am), on the corner of Daniel Goddard and Wilfred Davidson Carroll Street. More opulent-looking than its Anglican counterpart, this unusual building dates back to 1911 and has a banco-like adobe exterior supported by heavy buttresses.

Many other colonial structures are scattered around this part of town, several of them rather undistinguished former warehouses. One such building on Ecowas Avenue now houses the **St Joseph Adult Education and Skills Centre** (tel: 422 8836; Mon–Thur 9am–2pm, Fri 9am–noon), whose female students produce a selection of good-quality handcrafted clothes and other items.

Old Town

Further south, past the reliably chaotic **Barra Ferry** jetty, is one of the oldest neighbourhoods in Banjul, originally known as Mocam Town but now called **Half-Die** ⓘ in memory of the cholera outbreak that killed half its inhabitants in 1869. Here you'll find some of the last few surviving wooden and bamboo-

Recommended Restaurants and Bars on page 91

weave houses built in the so-called Creole style. Often on pillars raised above the ground, these buildings have steep corrugated roofs set above wooden upper floors, and are typically adorned with wrought-iron balconies, shutters and dormer windows.

Older still is the residential quarter running southwest from Freedom Lane to Abdou Wally Mbye Street. Here, at the junction of Macoumba Jallow and René Blain streets, the **Wesleyan Church** ❶ constructed in 1834 is the oldest surviving place of worship in Banjul. One block up, at 36 Hannah Forster Street, is one of the finest remaining examples of wooden Creole architecture, dating to the mid-19th century.

Further west, on Wallace Cole Road, you'll spot the sleek twin minarets of the **Grand Mosque** ❶, which was funded by King Fahad (it is also called **King Fahad Mosque**). For all its splendour, it is rather uncompromisingly modernistic in appearance, but is one of the few mosques in The Gambia large enough to accommodate a special section for female worshippers, who in most smaller mosques are confined to the veranda.

The restaurant scene

One victim of the recent economic drift from Banjul to the mainland has been its formerly thriving restaurant scene. Aside from the evergreen Corinthia Atlantic Hotel, the only established sit-down eatery is **Michel's Seafood Restaurant**, a tavern-like set-up on Independence Drive below Arch 22 that does a good line in sandwiches and *shwarmas* as well as all manner of fresh seafood. For a pleasant alfresco lunch, **Billy's International Cuisine**, set in the green park below Arch 22, is a new venture with a varied menu, while **Ali Baba's**, a door or two down from Michel's, is the best of several cheap *shwarma* houses serving greasy hamburgers and Lebanese pitta sandwiches stuffed with spicy mixtures of meat and salad. Cheaper still, but a long way from meeting Western hygiene standards, are the *tangana* or chop bars and casual eating tables dotted around the vicinity of Albert Market.

The Barra Ferry

Few tourists stay in Banjul these days, and day visitors from the coastal resorts less frequently venture into the capital for

The top of the Grand Mosque minaret.

BELOW: schoolgirls playing French skipping in the streets.

Magical Mudflats

The expanse of mudflats and mangroves designated as the Tanbi Wetland Complex on the southern outskirts of Banjul, readily accessible along Kankujereh Road (formerly Bund Road), is popular with birdwatchers and can be magical whether you visit at high or low tide. Old hulks, wrecks, little ships and plants sprouting through the islets of abandoned vessels emerge out of the shining water or glistening dark mud. Listed as a Ramsar Wetland and an Important Bird Area, Tanbi has a checklist of more than 200 bird species, with gulls and terns being particularly well represented. It is also a good place to see waders such as black-winged stilt and black-tailed godwit, and a variety of colourful kingfishers. Manatee and Nile crocodile are occasionally observed.

Markets are at the core of village life.

its own sake than as a point of embarkation for a "**Roots Tour**" to the various slave-related sites on the facing north bank. Remarkably, there is no bridge across the Gambia River anywhere in the country, and the only crossing point downstream of Farafenni-Soma is the **Barra Ferry ❷**, a motor ferry service that connects Banjul to the north-bank settlement of Barra.

The ferry crosses in either direction once every hour from 7am to 7pm, leaving Banjul from the crowded wharf at the southern end of Liberation Avenue. Vehicles, traders, passengers and animals all crowd onto the ferry, which brings the government a considerable income in fares. The crossing typically takes at least 45 minutes, sometimes longer depending on tides, and the fare for foot passengers is nominal.

Leaving the dockside, the ferry provides an excellent view over the water to Banjul and the beach leading down to the Corinthia Atlantic Hotel. However, this first sight of the Gambia River is not particularly exciting, as one can hardly distinguish its silt-filled waters from the sea – indeed, from the air the muddy flow of the river can be seen arcing far out into the Atlantic Ocean, creating vast sandbars that regularly shift position in the estuary. Port facilities in Banjul are very limited, and most large vessels anchor off the port and exchange cargoes by means of lighters and small boats, but you may see a few ocean-going steamers loading with peanuts or delivering containers of consumer goods and machinery.

Barra

The pier at **Barra** looks like any nondescript landing stage, but it's an important terminus for traffic between Banjul and sites upriver or in Senegal (the border at Fass is only 20km/12 miles further north). The town of Barra, which has grown around the ferry, supports a population of around 5,000, and it boasts a bustling market, a large lorry and bus park, and – should you get stuck there – a couple of indifferent local hotels and eateries. A giant groundnut factory with a covered conveyor and huge storage depots stands west of the pier.

Standing sentinel on the wave-lashed headland of Barra Point, a few hundred metres past the groundnut factory, **Fort**

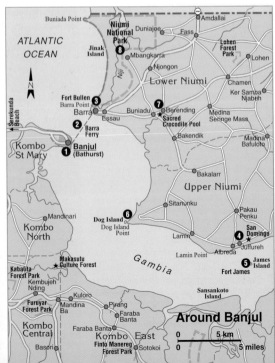

Around Banjul

Recommended Restaurants and Bars on page 91

Bullen ❸ (Mon–Sat 8am–7pm; charge) was the only fort ever built along the West African coast with the express purpose of helping to eradicate the slave trade. A rectangular laterite structure with a 1,200 sq metre (12,900 sq ft) floor area and a circular bastion in each corner, the fort was built in the late 1820s as a counterpart to the south bank's Six-Gun Battery, which didn't have sufficient range to protect ships from slipping along the north bank of the 13km (8-mile) wide river mouth. Fort Bullen was re-employed during World War II as an Allied point of observation and defence against potential naval attacks, and one of the four cannons in front of the northwest bastion dates to this time. Following major restoration, it is now part of the network of national museums.

Albreda and Juffureh

The most interesting of the north bank's historical sites, clustered some 30km (18 miles) upriver of Barra along a fantastically bumpy dirt road, are the old Portuguese, British and French slave-trading posts at the twin villages of **Albreda** and **Juffureh ❹**, which lie directly opposite James Island. Juffureh in particular has received world exposure through Alex Haley's book *Roots (see page 89)*, which purported to trace the author's ancestry from the tiny village, through the days of the slave trade, to modern America. An otherwise unremarkable Mandingo village, Juffureh has become a popular pilgrimage site, especially for Afro-American visitors to The Gambia, with the main focus of attention being the compound of the Kinte family claimed as kin by Haley. The locals play up to the tourist trade, posing for pictures and showing off their woodcarving skills at the craft market.

Juffureh is also the site of the **National Museum of the North Bank** (Mon–Sat 10am–5pm, Fri until 1pm; charge), housed in the Maurel Frères Building, which was built by the British in the 1840s and later used as a warehouse by the Lebanese trader after whom it is named. The small museum documents the slave trade out of West Africa in harrowing detail, and also has displays about the harsh treatment of slaves after they arrived in America, and a room full of paraphernalia relating to Alex Haley and the *Roots* phenomenon.

The Gambian Port Authority's building near the Barra Ferry.

BELOW:
anti-slavery statue facing the Gambia River in Juffureh.

The Freedom Flag-pole that once stood near the CFAO Building has long since disappeared, but guides will point out where it used to be. Legend has it that any captive who reached the flagpole without being felled by bullets would be granted his freedom.

So close to Juffureh that it is difficult to say where one begins and the other ends, Albreda, rented to French traders by the King of Niumi in 1681, was possibly the most important slaving post on the Gambia River prior to abolition in 1807. Little now remains from those harsh days except perhaps the rather time-worn double-storey building once occupied by the Compagnie Française d'Afrique Occidentale (CFAO), which overlooks the small wharf. In reality, it is questionable whether this **CFAO Building** was ever used by slave traders, since it was most likely constructed a decade or so after the slave trade along the Gambia River was curtailed by the twin fortifications at Bathurst and Barra. The ground floor, which used to serve as a shop and warehouse, is entered through an open arcade and veranda, while the first floor consisted of residential quarters for the company's agents. Close by is the substantial ruin of a Portuguese chapel that reputedly dates to the late 15th century, making it possibly the oldest such structure in West Africa.

Clearly signposted to the right about 1km (½ mile) east of Albreda, the trading post of **San Domingo**, founded in the late 15th century, was the first Portuguese settlement in the area. Back then, it was most likely inhabited by traders of mixed African and Portuguese descent, who acted as hosts and middlemen to visiting European ships. In its prime, San Domingo consisted of several large buildings set in large gardens with a freshwater well, but all that remains today is the ruin of a double-storey house set alongside a massive baobab tree. Whether this is the building "of two storeys with courses of mortar running through the laterite rock, plaster tinted pink, a yellow brick arch over one window as well as four rectangular windows beneath a wooden lintel" described by one contemporary visitor is unknown.

Fort James

The most important relic of the slave trade in this part of The Gambia is **Fort James ❺**, which once dominated **James Island**, a small rocky outcrop lapped by the salty waters of the Gambia River about 2km (1 mile) from Albreda. James Island's career as a trade outpost started in 1651, when it was settled by Latvians.

BELOW: the ruins of Fort James.

Recommended Restaurants and Bars on page 91

It would be seized 10 years later by English traders, who built a large fort there, and changed hands again several times after that, falling at various times to the French and the Dutch – even at one point a band of Welsh pirates – and its location ensured clear passage downriver for whichever power controlled it at the time. It was completely destroyed at least three times – twice by the French and once when the gunpowder stocks accidently went off. Following the British abolition of the slave trade in 1807, naval ships based at James Island intercepted more than 100 French and Portuguese slave vessels off the Gambian coast.

Today, all that is left of the once impressive fort are a few cannons, and some thick stone and brick walls held together by the roots of baobab trees and inhabited by lizards, rats and snakes. Part of the dungeon in which up to 140 slaves were impounded also survives. The beaches are littered by tiny beads, said to belong to female slaves who lost them in their struggles against the slave traders. The island itself is also fast eroding. Despite its ruinous state, it is a poignant site, and can easily be visited from Albreda by boat.

James Island is also a stopover on the Banjul–Juffureh boat trip.

Dog Island

Situated off the north bank halfway between Albreda and Barra, **Dog Island** ❻ also has a historical background. Its name dates to the 15th century, when passing Portuguese sailors mistook the barking of baboons for dogs. A British fort was built there in 1661, but it was abandoned five years later and few traces of it remain. In 1816, Captain Grant leased the island from a local king and quarried the stone for use in the early construction of Banjul.

An improbable local legend has it that it was off Dog Island or James Island that the boundaries of The Gambia were first established. As no settled frontier divided British Gambia from French Senegal, it was agreed that the extent of land each side of the Gambia River which would define the country would be decided by the firing range of a gunboat lying in the mainstream of the river. At low tide, it's possible to walk across from the facing mainland, but the island is rather barren, with little to show for its history.

WHERE

Inscribed as a Unesco World Heritage Site in 2003, Saint James and Related Sites comprises seven structures connected to the European presence on the Gambia River prior to formal colonisation. These sites are considered of special significance for their relation to the evolution and abolition of the transatlantic slave trade. One site is on the south bank, the Six-Gun Battery (1821), in what are now the grounds of Banjul's State House. The six north-bank sites are Fort Bullen, James Island, the San Domingo ruins, the Portuguese chapel, the CFAO Building and the Maurel Frères Building.

Alex Haley and "Roots"

One slave taken from the compound at Juffureh to an American plantation was Kunte Kinte. Captured from his village as a small boy, the youth could recall his kidnapping vividly – being taken from the compound to the longboat, being hauled on board, his last glimpse of light and breath of fresh air as he was bundled into the hold, and the weeks below deck in stifling conditions with little or no food and water.

The boy never forgot his heritage in Africa. He retained the thoughts, sounds, smells and traditions of family life back in The Gambia, and passed on every detail to his sons, their sons and their sons in turn, until in the 1970s a respected American writer called Alex Haley traced his ancestry back to Kunta Kinte in his book *Roots*.

Reaping critical praise, *Roots* earned Haley the Pulitzer Prize. The book sold 1,500,000 copies in its first 18 months, and the TV series was watched by millions in America alone. In addition, the book became a seminal "black studies" text, and Haley was invited to speak at campuses all over the US. The work

inspired many black Americans to make trips to The Gambia, Senegal and Guinea in search of their African heritage.

Then, in 1993, a year after Haley's death, the 200-year saga that purported to be a true story was exposed as invention. The evidence against Haley was conclusive, drawn from his own private papers and interviews with scholars and associates. There was no way the Kunte Kinte celebrated at Juffureh could have been Toby, Haley's hero. Records showed that Toby had been in America five years before the ship on which he was supposed to have travelled docked in America, and had been dead eight years before he was supposed to have fathered a daughter.

In spite of the exposé, the "Roots Tour" to Juffureh, Albreda and James Island remains one of the most popular excursions for tourists to The Gambia. Its emphasis is on the slave trade in general, but it includes a visit to the Kinte compound at Juffureh, helping to perpetuate the Haley myth.

Doves are not the most exotic bird species around but they are nonetheless frequently observed.

Berending

About 5km (3 miles) from Barra, at the junction of the main surfaced road along the north bank and the side road to Albreda, is the village of **Berending ❼**. It is the site of a sacred crocodile pool that attracts pilgrims from all over The Gambia and bordering parts of Senegal. According to local tradition, leaving an offering of kola nuts at this pool can cure anything from infertility to impotence, reverse bad fortune or protect against evil spirits. It consists of a series of small pools running along a shallow watercourse, most of which are dried up or shallowly filled with damp mud. The crocodiles here can be quite elusive and most are very small. Note that it is also a great site for birds, with turacos and robin-chats calling from the lush foliage, and jacanas, crakes and kingfishers active around the reedy shore.

Niumi National Park

The biggest natural attraction on the north bank is **Niumi National Park ❽** (daily 7am–6pm; charge), whose 50 sq km (20 sq miles) incorporate most of the Gambian coastline north of Barra, including a big portion of **Jinack Island**, an estuary-bound landmass that effectively forms a southern extension of the Siné-Saloum Delta in Senegal. Established in 1986, the park includes 11km (7 miles) of unspoilt coastline and several wide sandy beaches, from where dolphins are regularly sighted between November and February. It is also a popular spot with birdwatchers, often hosting large flocks of gulls, terns and migrant waders, as well as a varied selection of scrubland species. Somewhat incongruously, much of Jinack is densely cultivated with *Cannabis sativa* – marijuana.

Niumi is difficult to explore independently, but day tours are offered by most local tour operators, either crossing by motorboat from Banjul or taking a 4x4 from Barra followed by a short canoe ride across the Niji River. Alternatively, **Madiyana Safari Lodge** and **Dahala Lodge** both offer simple thatched hutted accommodation, good food and limited but clean facilities – the perfect unsophisticated desert-island escape for those who want to laze in a hammock, swim in the sea and go beachcombing along a swathe of white sand.   ❏

RESTAURANTS AND BARS

Restaurants

Prices for a main course
per person:
$ = under US$8
(D160)
$$ = US$8–15
(D160–300)
$$$ = over US$15
(D300)

All the restaurants
and bars featured in
this listing are located
in Banjul.

Ali Baba's Snack Bar
Nelson Mandela Street
Tel: 422 4055
$
As light on the pocket
as it tends to be heavy
on the calories, this long-
serving Lebanese eatery
located near the harbour
serves kebabs, *shwarmas*
(sliced grilled meat and
salad in pitta bread),
falafel sandwiches and
other Middle Eastern
staples to take away or
eat in. A reliable budget
bet, but it closes early
(5pm), so not really
an option for dinner.

Billy's International Cuisine and Bar
Cnr Independence Drive &
Marina Parade
$$
Set in park-like lawns
below Arch 22, Billy's
has the greenest setting
in the city centre, and
can be a very pleasant
place to enjoy an al-
fresco sundowner in view
of Banjul's best-known
landmark. The food is
standard Gambian fare –
grilled seafood and meat
dishes with chips or rice
– but it is well prepared,
even if service can be on
the slow side. Open from
lunchtime until late.

Corinthia Atlantic Hotel
Marina Parade
Tel: 422 8601
$$$
The formal indoor restaur-
ant at Banjul's leading
hotel closed in 2008, but
the pool terrace remains
a great spot for lunch or
dinner with the Atlantic
waves providing a lulling
aural backdrop. The set
menu tends to be a touch
predictable and indiffer-
ent value for money, but
the à la carte menu is
about as imaginative as
it gets in central Banjul,
and sensibly priced too.

Michel's Seafood Restaurant
29 Independence Drive
Tel: 422 3108
$$
Situated only a few
metres from Arch 22,
this unpretentious eatery
is reminiscent of a Euro-
pean tavern with its dark
wood-panelled walls.
Michel's is undoubtedly
the best place for an
indoor meal, snack or
drink in central Banjul,
serving a good selection
of mid-priced grilled
seafood and meat dishes
as well as cheap sand-
wiches and *shwarmas*.
Service is unusually
quick and efficient. There
is also a breakfast menu.
Open 8am–10.30pm.

Palm Beach Hotel
Serekunda–Banjul Highway
Tel: 420 1620
$$–$$$
Located only 3km
(2 miles) west of the city
centre, this stalwart of
the Gambia accommo-
dation scene offers a
superb beachfront set-
ting and is just five min-
utes out of town using
public transport. It's a
most agreeable spot for
a pre- or post-dinner
drink, and the à la carte
menu is usually strong
when it comes to sea-
food dishes. The buffet
option, on the other
hand, is best avoided.

ABOVE: Michel's Seafood Restaurant is the place
for an excellent indoor meal in Banjul.
RIGHT: chicken *kassa* being served up at the Atlantic
Hotel outdoor restaurant.

SEREKUNDA AND THE ATLANTIC COAST

Stretching for 50km (30 miles) south of Cape Point,
The Gambia's so-called "Smiling Coast" is known
as much for the warmth and hospitality of its
people as for the arcing white-sand beaches
that frame the peacock-blue sea

This short stretch of beautiful coastline forms the hub of The Gambia's hospitality industry: almost all of the 200,000-plus tourists that visit the country annually are bound for one of the myriad beach resorts, and a large proportion of these visitors barely stray more than a few hundred metres from the sandy coast, except when they are transferred to and from the airport.

The waters here are warmed to comfortable tepidity by the warm Guinea Current, while the shore, one of the most westerly in Africa, is cooled by northeast trade winds, making for an idyllic holiday climate, especially during the European winter, which roughly coincides with the dry season in The Gambia.

Orientation

The beaches begin immediately west of Banjul, with the first one stretching for almost 8km (5 miles) before it curves southwards at Cape Point, the southwestern tip of the Gambia River Mouth. South of Cape Point, the coastline can be divided into two broad sectors. The northernmost 10km (6 miles), effectively a coastal extension of the Greater Banjul area, runs from Bakau to Kololi, and is heavily populated and quite dense with tourist developments, including dozens of hotels, resorts and restaurants. The longer and wilder stretch of coast south of Kololi, dotted with small fishing harbours such as Tanji, Sanyang and Gunjur, is far less developed for tourism, though its scattering of rustic beach

retreats will hold great appeal to those looking for a relatively off-the-beaten-track getaway.

Less than 15km (9 miles) inland of the Atlantic coastline you'll find Serekunda and Brikama, the two largest towns in The Gambia. The 25km (15-mile) asphalt road that runs south from Serekunda to Brikama is flanked by two important tourist landmarks. The small but popular Abuko Nature Reserve, 8km (5 miles) southeast of Serekunda, is the country's most popular wildlife sanctuary, and an easy opportunity for a day trip from any

Main attractions
BAKAU
FAJARA
KOTU BEACH
KOLOLI
SEREKUNDA
ABUKO NATURE RESERVE
BRIKAMA
MAKASUTU CULTURE FOREST
TANJI
GUNJUR
KARTONG

LEFT: the rocky
point at Fajara.
BELOW: stand at
Brikama market.

*Woman carrying
her heavy load in
Kachikally.*

of the coastal resorts. Yundum, approximately 8km (5 miles) closer to Brikama, is the site of Banjul International Airport, which handles all international flights to and from The Gambia (though rather confusingly it is actually 20km/12 miles south of Banjul as the crow flies, and even further by road). Also in the vicinity of Brikama, the Makasutu Cultural Forest and Lamin Lodge are perennially popular retreats set alongside the implacable maze of mangroves and bolongs that line the southern banks of the Gambia River.

The area covered in this chapter spreads across several administrative districts whose name start with the word Kombo (eg Kombo St Mary, Kombo Central, Kombo South), for which reason Gambians frequently refer to it simply as "The Kombos".

Bakau

Sprawling southeast from Cape Point, the aptly named town of **Bakau ❶** – literally, "Big Place" – is the third-largest settlement in The Gambia, with a population of around 75,000, and the most populous anywhere along the country's Atlantic coastline.

Boasting both a dramatic and historic clifftop setting, Bakau is an important tourist hub, serviced by a wide selection of hotels and restaurants, but it is also very much a working town. The lively fruit and vegetable market set alongside Atlantic Boulevard, the main thoroughfare through town, stocks the widest range of fresh produce you'll see anywhere in The Gambia. Below this, the fishing beach and market – with its long metal jetty looking in imminent danger of collapsing – bustles with an array of colourful pirogues and mercantile activity throughout the day.

Legend has it that Bakau was founded in the early 17th century around the sacred crocodile pool at Kachikally. It was first mentioned by name by the Portuguese explorer Lemos Coelho, who landed there in 1669 and used it as a base for exploring

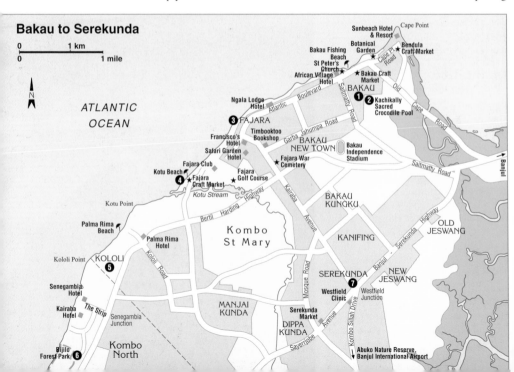

Recommended Restaurants and Bars on pages 108–9

the Gambia River over the next three years. Coelho later wrote that the "the port is very attractive", and that if he "were to return upriver today, he would live nowhere else", and also noted that a slaving post operated by European traders existed alongside the town. In 1882, Bakau became the site of one of the first schools in The Gambia, founded by the Quaker missionary Hannah Kilhan, and the small town was integrated into the British colony of The Gambia in 1888.

Much of Bakau's Old Town was destroyed by flooding in 1906, but several old colonial buildings still stand, including the tiny **St Peter's Church** overlooking the fishing bay and several grand residences, among them those of both the UK and US High Commissioners. Situated alongside the British High Commissioner's residence, at the junction of Atlantic Boulevard and Cape Point Road, the **Bakau Botanical Garden** (daily 8.30am–6pm; free) provides a peaceful retreat from the suburban bustle. Founded in 1924, the garden is small enough to explore thoroughly in 15–20 minutes, and it holds much of interest to hard-core botanists and birdwatchers. A

more contemporary and sporadically boisterous landmark, the **Bakau Independence Stadium** is the country's premier arena for football matches. Built with Chinese assistance in 1983, this massive stadium lies about 1.5km (1 mile) inland of Atlantic Boulevard, and has a capacity of 20,000.

Bakau's most popular and intriguing attraction, often visited as a day trip from elsewhere along the coast, the ancient **Kachikally Crocodile Pool ❷** (daily 7am–7pm; charge) is in the heart of the eponymous residential quarter. Poorly signposted, the pool is most easily reached by walking for about 1km (½ mile) along the sandy (and, thanks to the open sewer pipe that follows it, pungently ammonic) road that runs inland at 45 degrees from the T-junction of Cape Point Road and Atlantic Boulevard. This small, weed-clogged pool is actually much deeper than it looks, and it contains around 70 crocodiles, several of which are reliably to be found sunbathing on the concrete banks. Be very careful here, as crocodiles that seem docile enough on terra firma might well attack somebody who fell into their watery home.

The entrance to Kachikally includes access to the Kachikally Museum, which has some displays on the local Diola culture and traditional musical instruments, as well as the history of Bakau, and Gambian involvement in World War II.

LEFT: frangipani blooms in Bakau Botanical Garden. **BELOW:** beware of the crocodiles at the Kachikally sacred pool.

The water at Kachikally is considered to be curative, and barren women come to douse themselves in the little brick enclosure next to it – any child born after such ritual bathing is invariably named Kachikally. As well as barren women, the pool draws others in need of its fortifying powers, including wrestlers and politicians. The leafy grounds host a surprisingly varied birdlife, with the likes of black-headed paradise flycatcher and blue-breasted kingfisher likely to be seen flitting through the foliage.

Around Bakau

Plenty of hotels are dotted around Bakau. In terms of comfort and facilities, the five-star **Sunbeach Hotel and Resort,** overlooking Cape Point, is the uncontested leader of the pack, and well worth popping into for a drink and the great beachfront views even if you stay elsewhere. The more modest **African Village Hotel** is one of the longest-serving and popular mid-range package hotels along the Atlantic coastline, boasting a great clifftop position overlooking a small private beach, while the **Bakau Guesthouse**, perched above the fishing bay

Colourful fishing pirogue drawn up on Kotu Beach.

BELOW: the bar at Ngala Lodge.

and market, is the outstanding budget deal in this popular resort area.

When it comes to eating out, you could spend a week in the area without repeating venues, and there are also plenty of supermarkets for self-caterers. You'll find several cybercafés and banks offering foreign exchange facilities on Atlantic Boulevard, while the **Bakau Craft Market** at the junction of Cape Point Road is packed with stalls selling a varied range of woodcarvings, batik clothes and tablecloths, jewellery and other locally crafted items.

Fajara to Kololi

South of Bakau, at the junction of Atlantic Boulevard and Kairaba Avenue, the beach curves to the rocky point of **Fajara ❸**, which is also the name of a pleasantly leafy residential area favoured by foreign diplomats. Several decent hotels are clustered in this suburb, notably the upmarket **Ngala Lodge**, mid-priced **Safari Garden Hotel** and budget-friendly **Francisco's Hotel**.

Running southeast from Atlantic Boulevard, **Kairaba Avenue** is the most direct thoroughfare between the Atlantic beach-

front and central Serekunda, 3km (2 miles) inland. The seaward end of the road is flanked by restaurants, beauty salons, banks, supermarkets and other shops, including **Timbooktoo**, which is far and away the best source of local interest books (and other English-language reading matter) anywhere in Senegal or The Gambia. On the north side of Kairaba Road, the racism that underpinned the colonial experience is manifest in the **Fajara War Cemetery**, where some 200 graves of World War II casualties are segregated into several different clusters, some exclusively for soldiers of indigenous Gambian origin, others reserved for combatants of European descent.

At its southern end, Atlantic Boulevard terminates in a cul-de-sac at the **Fajara Golf and Country Club** (tel: 449 5456; daily; temporary membership and golf club rental available). Despite its recent facelift, the Club retains a certain time-warped charm, with an atmosphere somewhere between an old colonial clubhouse and an English village hall. The entrance hall is lined with glass cases of sports trophies and photographs of RAF crews, and the livelier bar dominated by a large-screen TV that draws big crowds for major international sporting events. Aside from the bar, temporary members also have access to the highly rated 18-hole golf course, swimming pool, tennis and squash courts, snooker table, and a reasonably priced restaurant serving decent pub grub.

Atlantic Boulevard may be a dead end for motorised vehicles, but pedestrians can continue along a narrow footpath flanking the golf course to fabulous **Kotu Beach ❹**, a long stretch of clean white sand that stretches for another 3km (2 miles) south to Kololi. On the way, as the path descends to the north end of the beach, you will pass the large **Fajara craft market**, which is one of the best places to buy souvenirs, with reasonable prices and a wide range of goods.

Kotu is the most populated beach in The Gambia, fringed by numerous low-rise luxury hotels and villas, but the sands are far from overcrowded. Holidaymakers are joined by traders touting woodcarvings and handsomely dressed women selling fruit and hair-plaiting services. The Gambia's top athletes generally prefer to train on the clean-washed beaches than the dirt track of Banjul's main stadium, and are

EAT

Fajara features a few good eateries, including the country's top Indian restaurant in the form of **The Clay Oven**, and the beer garden-like **Mama's Restaurant**, which often attracts a heaving crowd of tourists for its steady flow of cheap draught beer and varied selection of local and international dishes.

BELOW: playing football on Kotu Beach.

Green monkeys at the Bijilo Forest Park have grown used to the tourists.

BELOW: writing in the sand.

frequently to be seen running through the paces on Kotu Beach. All the big hotels have commandeered small patches of beach for their guests (though the beach as a whole is public) and employ security guards to chase away touts. The hotels also monitor swimming conditions, which are quite hazardous when the sea is rough – therefore on no account should you go swimming when the red flag is flying.

Immediately south of Kotu Beach, **Kotu Stream** can be reduced to a trickle in the dry season and forms a torrent in the rains, but it is popular with bird-watchers throughout the year for the wealth of aquatic and woodland species that can be seen along the walking trails that flank it. Two other notable bird-watching sites lie at Kotu: the surfaced **Cycle Path** that leads to the beach from near the Badala Park Hotel is good for grassland species, including yellow-throated longclaw, while the **Kotu Sewerage Ponds** opposite the same hotel

often host waterfowl and waders. A short distance past the mouth of Kotu stream, halfway towards Kololi, **Palma Rima Beach** – named after a popular package hotel that lies 500 metres/yards inland – is quieter than Kotu Beach but no less attractive, and is serviced by a good selection of beach bars and eateries.

More often referred to locally as "Senegambia" (after the eponymous hotel), **Kololi ❺** is the pulsating hub of The Gambia's beach tourism industry. Its best-known landmarks are the plush five-star **Kairaba Hotel**, with its wonderful Somerset Maugham-style cocktail bar, and the **Senegambia Hotel**, set in large beachfront grounds rustling with birdlife and monkey activity.

The short stretch of tar that connects these hotels to the main coastal highway, often referred to as "The Strip', is the one part of the Gambian coast that arguably resembles its more crowded Mediterranean counterparts. The two sides of The Strip are lined with perhaps a dozen restaurants apiece, battling it out for the tourist dollar by advertising cheap draught beer and happy-hour specials, and whose collective culinary variety can only be

described as globetrotting. Needless to say, this is an excellent place to do anything from curio shopping or internet surfing to arranging a day excursion or rental car, though the predominance of touts can be rather off-putting to the uninitiated.

The numerous hotels and tour operators in Kololi offer a varied selection of day and overnight trips. Most famous among these are the "**Roots Tours**" to James Island, Juffureh and the other slave-related sites of the north bank *(see pages 87–9)*, but other popular goals for **day trips** include Abuko Nature Reserve, Makasutu Culture Forest and relatively remote south coast villages such as Tanji and Kartong. Overnight trips inland to see the chimpanzees of Badi Mayo or birds of Tendaba are also extremely popular and worthwhile. Competition between companies is fierce, and tour representatives and hotel staff often warn against booking through smaller companies because they are anxious to get their commission by selling you a tour with their operator. Do not be put off – companies with a proper office will be pleased to show you their tour licence issued by the Tourist Authority.

Alternatively, if you prefer to discover The Gambia independently, you could cut a deal with a local taxi driver, or even use public transport, though the latter option can be uncomfortable and time-consuming. It is advisable, however, to refuse offers of tours made on the beach, where youths are out to make a fast buck and where you may find yourself travelling in an uninsured vehicle.

For those seeking a green interlude a little closer to their hotel, a short dirt track leads south from Kololi's Strip to the underrated **Bijilo Forest Park ❻** (daily 7am–6pm; charge; guides available), which protects some 50 hectares (125 acres) of coastal forest, a habitat that is increasingly rare in The Gambia. A 5km (3-mile) network of figure-of-eight trails leads through the park's cover of dense coastal scrub studded with lush borassus palms. The park's main attraction for most visitors is several troops of free-ranging but very habituated monkeys, with the widespread green monkey being supplemented by a population of around 50 of the rarer red colobus. Bijilo also supports one-third of all the butterfly species recorded in the whole of The Gambia, and a remarkably varied birdlife, with typical forest species being supplemented by a host of seabirds and flocks of waders.

Serekunda

The urban centrepiece of Greater Banjul, situated 3km (2 miles) inland of Fajara, **Serekunda ❼** is now the largest town in The Gambia, with a population estimated at 350,000, and the focal point of the national road-transport network. A relatively insubstantial village at the time of independence, this burgeoning town owes its rapid expansion to a steady influx of rural Gambians and migrants from neighbouring countries into Greater Banjul, and the restricted area of the island-bound capital 10km (6 miles) to its east. Serekunda's most important crossroads and transport hub, known as "**Westfield**" after the eponymous clinic, is the junction of the Banjul Highway, Kairaba Avenue and the South Bank Road towards Yundum and Brikama. The town sprawls outwards from West-

An African red-billed hornbill in Bijilo Park, which hosts a variety of birds.

BELOW: goats on the loose in a residential street of Cape Point.

Pots, pans and sieves for sale at Brikama market.

BELOW: market vendor waiting for customers.

field Junction in all directions, forming an amorphous low-rise sprawl that merges almost imperceptibly into the coastal suburbs of Bakau and Fajara and inland towns of Abuko and Lamin.

Lively bordering on chaotic, Serekunda – centred upon a labyrinthine **covered market** that sometimes threatens to engulf the entire town – is a far more representative slice of West African urban life than sleepy old Banjul, and its myriad bars and eateries are a little more louche. Located at the junction of Sayerrjobe Avenue and Mosque Road, **Serekunda Market**, with its clutter of several hundred stalls, differs from the craft markets at the coastal resorts not only in its vast size and claustrophobic mood, but also insofar as the proffered wares cater primarily to locals rather than tourists. That aside, Serekunda is decidedly lacking in landmarks, and best experienced by roaming the streets whimsically until you've had enough and decide to hail down one of its ubiquitous taxis.

A popular goal for day trips out of Greater Banjul, **Abuko Nature Reserve** ❽ (daily 8am–6pm; charge; guided tours available) lies on the right-hand side of the main Brikama road about 8km (5 miles) south of Serekunda. It's a 20–30-minute drive from most of the beach resorts, and is easily reached on public transport. Protected as a water catchment area in 1916 and gazetted as a nature reserve in 1968, Abuko is one of the smallest sanctuaries anywhere in Africa, extending over a mere 1 sq km (⅓ sq mile), but its forests, seasonal steams and perennial pools harbour a rich biodiversity, epitomised by its checklist of 270 bird species. Common mammals include green monkey, red colobus, bushbuck and Maxwell's duiker, all of which make regular appearances at the waterhole overlooked by the hide some 200 metres/yards past the entrance gate. A quiet vigil at this pool is also likely to yield sightings of Nile crocodile and monitor lizards, and a host of water-associated birds including black-headed night heron, squacco heron, African jacana and African darter.

Past this pool, the winding path through the cool forests offers the best opportunity in The Gambia to see a number of forest-dwelling birds, particularly in the early morning and late afternoon. Among the more conspicuous or interesting species to be seen here are the raucous African pied hornbill, stunningly colourful violet turaco, boldly marked double-toothed barbet, vociferous common wattle-eye and flighty black-headed paradise flycatcher. After approximately 1km (½ mile), this path emerges at the so-called **animal orphanage**, a rather depressing zoo-like set-up whose cages house a few disgruntled-looking patas monkeys and restless spotted hyenas. The orphanage once provided sanctuary to The Gambia's only lions, and was used to rehabilitate chimpanzees born in captivity prior to their release in the River Gambia National Park, but this is no longer the case.

About 1.5km (1 mile) past Abuko is the village of Lamin, where **Lamin Lodge** ❾, a charming, higgledy-piggledy restaurant-bar built on stilts, is the springboard for the "Birds and Breakfast" excursion featured in many tour programmes. One of the most enchanting experiences that The Gambia offers, this early-morning explo-

Maps on pages 94 & 102

Recommended Restaurants and Bars on pages 108–9

ration of the mangrove-lined creeks by dugout canoe, in the company of an ornithologist, is followed by a sumptuous breakfast at the lodge.

Yundum, 5km (3 miles) south of Lamin, is of little interest except as the site of **Banjul International Airport**, which started life as an Allied airfield during World War II. This is The Gambia's only international airport, and it consisted of little more than a few quaint barn-like sheds until as recently as 1997, when a new modern airport designed by the Senegalese architect Pierre Goudiaby was formally opened.

Brikama

About 10km (6 miles) south of Yundum, the main south-bank road passes through **Brikama ⑩**, which now ranks as the country's second-largest town, with a population of around 85,000. Brikama has a historic heritage: it was reputedly founded by Mandinka migrants from Mali in the 13th century and was twice destroyed by Muslim raids (in 1854 and 1874), but in both cases it soon recovered.

Brikama is a noted centre for woodcarvers, who produce their best workmanship in the shape of masks or gazelle groups, which, after jovial bargaining, can be purchased at very reasonable prices at the lively **Brikama Craft Market**. The majority of woodcarvings found for sale in the markets on the coast are actually made here. The town has also produced a high proportion of The Gambia's best-known Kora musicians, including the late Alhaji Bei Konte, his son Dembo Konte, and Tata Dindin. Surprisingly, the live music scene is rather tepid compared to Serekunda and the coast, though occasional concerts are staged at the Jokor Nightclub, about 200 metres/yards from the main road from Banjul.

The Makasutu Culture Forest

The most remote goal for regular day trips from the coastal resorts, situated about 5km (3 miles) east of Brikama, is the **Makasutu Culture Forest ⑪** (www.makasutu.com; full-day tours run from 8am–4pm; charge), which has become The Gambia's most prominent ecotourism project since it opened in 1999. A private reserve managed in collaboration with the surrounding communities, Makasutu protects about 10 sq km (4 sq

Potter at work in his shop in the Makasutu Culture Forest.

BELOW: homeware shop in Serekunda.

Mandina River Lodge offers four solar-powered floating lodges reached by elevated walkways or by dugout canoe.

miles) of riparian forest, savannah, mangroves and wetlands bordering the Mandina Bolong, a tributary of the Gambia River. It supports a varied range of fauna. The most prominent large mammal of the forest is the Guinea baboon, represented by many very habituated troops, but various antelope and small carnivores are also present. Conspicuous reptiles include agama and monitor lizards, and the birdlife is similar to the nearby Abuko Nature Reserve, though with fewer forest specialists.

Highly worthwhile and enjoyable, **day tours** to Makasutu start in an open clearing below a giant baobab alongside a tall termite hill. Guided bush walks are usually undertaken in the early morning, when wildlife is most active, and dugout trips into the mangroves offer a good

chance of encountering rarities such as white-backed night heron and African finfoot. These wildlife excursions are offset by several activities that place the spotlight on local Gambian cultures, ranging from a visit to a local marabout (Islamic holy man) to watching a palm tapper at work. The buffet lunch also places emphasis on Gambian food.

Exclusive accommodation is available at the beautifully designed **Mandina Lodge**, which consists of four stilted units along the river, and another four set further back in the lush fringing woodland, and is widely regarded to rank among the top five lodges and hotels of any sort in The Gambia.

The south coast

In comparison with the built-up Atlantic frontage between Bakau and Kololi, the southern coast of The Gambia is thinly populated, with just a handful of small towns and villages running along its 40km (25-mile) length, most notably Ghanatown, Brufut, Tanji, Tujereng, Sanyang, Gunjur and Kartong. Tourist facilities south of Kololi are also relatively few and far between, and the dozen or so lodges that do exist tend to be more rustic and integrated into the surrounds than their resort-like northern counterparts. The road that follows the coast south from Kololi to the Senegalese border was once notoriously rough going, but it is now surfaced in its entirety and well serviced by public transport.

Particularly as you head further south, the beaches here are among the finest in the Senegambian region. Great scallops of silver sand extend along the coast as far as the eye can see, hemmed in on the landward side by tall dunes, lagoons, mangroves, village compounds and small waterways, and largely unaffected by the sand erosion that has affected the north coast. Picturesque additions to the scene are occasional fishing boats being hauled over the sands, big-horned white zebu cattle slowly making their way down to the water's edge to lick the salt from the rocks, and mixed flocks of gulls, terns and other marine birds that thrive both

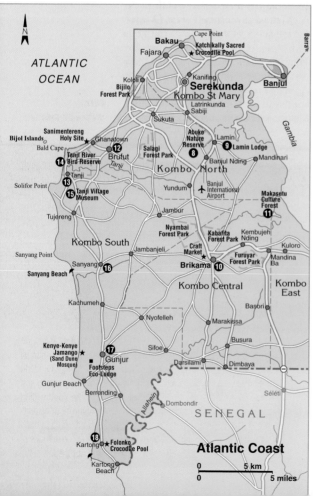

Atlantic Coast

Recommended Restaurants and Bars on pages 108–9

around the fishing villages and along more remote stretches of beach.

The first settlement, about 8km (5 miles) south of Kololi, on the great sandy curve that arcs between Bijilo and **Bald Cape**, are the twin villages of **Ghana-town** and **Brufut ⑫**. The former is a small rustic village populated – as the name suggests – almost exclusively by Ghanaian fishermen, who catch and smoke fish for export to their home country. Brufut, by contrast, is a larger and swankier centre, one whose stock has risen considerably following the recent opening of the five-star **Sheraton Gambia Resort**.

One of the most important animist shrines in Gambia, **Sanimentereng** lies close to Brufut Beach, and consists of an adobe prayer house, an ancient baobab tree, a sacred pool and an altar on which locals and pilgrims place gifts to the spirits. The ultra-exclusive **Sanimentereng AU Village** housed the many African heads of state who attended the 7th African Union summit held in Banjul in July 2006. The villas have since been sold to individuals as part of an upmarket gated-villa complex. Also on the outskirts

of town, **Brufut Woods** (daily; charge) is recognised as perhaps the best place in The Gambia to see the enormous Verreaux's eagle-owl, and it hosts a good variety of other woodland birds.

Agama lizards are the most common in Africa. They can be found in many sizes and colours.

Tanji

The only major south-coast village that actually runs right along the beach, **Tanji ⑬**, situated immediately south of the eponymous river mouth, is the busiest fishing centre along the Gambian coast. The sandy beach, strewn with fish offal, is a little too chaotic and dirty to make for comfortable swimming, but the dramatic fishing-associated activity at the beach, market and fish-smoking centre ensures that Tanji is included on many

LEFT: chillies for sale.

Fishing Beaches

Village life along the coast is entirely dominated by the sea, and every community has access to a strip of beach and keeps its own set of pirogues. These fishing beaches host one of the most colourful and animated scenes in The Gambia. The women of the villages wade out to the pirogues to help the fishermen unload their catch – their labours are rewarded in fish, which they either trade or keep for the evening meal. The painted pirogues drawn

up on the white sand, the catch itself – in its last natural tints – and the brilliant colours of the women's dresses and buckets are stunningly attractive. Flying fish, yellowtail, snapper, catfish, rock hind, mullet and sea bream all come tumbling out of the boats' gunwales, jumping and sparkling in the late sunlight. It's also worth visiting the boatbuilding yards, with pirogues at various stages in their construction, and the pungent and swelteringly hot smoke-houses behind the beach, where much of the fish is smoked or salted before being packed off to the markets of Banjul and Serekunda or to landlocked neighbouring countries.

A black kite looking for preys.

BELOW: smoking fish in Tanji.

day tours out of the more northerly resort hotels. Another popular tourist activity is the camelback trips along the beach offered by **Pepe Camel Safaris** (tel: 446 1083; daily 8am–6pm).

Gazetted in 1993, the **Tanji River Bird Reserve** (tel: 437 5888; email: wildlife@gamtel.gm; daily 7am–6pm; charge) protects 6 sq km (2½ sq miles) of marine wetland and savannah habitats bordering the Tanji River, as well as the only offshore islands in The Gambia. One of the country's most popular and rewarding birdwatching venues, the reserve supports over 300 bird species, including 34 types of raptor, alongside large mammals such as spotted hyena, bushbuck, green monkey and red colobus.

Situated about 1.5km (1 mile) offshore, the **Bijol Islands** form the country's most important roosting site for terns and gulls, with concentrations of 20,000 birds present on occasion. Green turtles nest on the islands' beaches, and Mediterranean monk seals and whales are observed from time to time. Visitors are free to walk where they please in the mainland part of the reserve, but the islands can be visited by boat only by special arrangement, and landings are thankfully forbidden during the peak breeding season.

Clearly signposted on the left-hand side of the main coastal road some 2km (1 mile) south of Tanji, the **Tanji Village Museum** (tel: 437 10 07; www.tanje. dds.nl; daily 9am–5pm; charge) was established in the 1990s by Abdoulie Boyo, former curator of the National Museum in Banjul, to educate tourists on traditional Gambian customs and lifestyles. The centrepiece is a life-size replica of a traditional Mandinka compound showing various types of huts and their uses, and the museum also hosts traditional craftsmen such as a blacksmith, weaver and *kora* player. Alive with birds and butterflies, a short nature trail in the grounds is of interest to botanists for its selection of labelled indigenous trees, and it also gives some background to traditional herbal medicines. An on-site restaurant can provide meals to tour groups with a couple of days' notice, and rustic accommodation is available, though its "back to nature" appeal is undermined somewhat by the rumble of traffic along the main road.

Sanyang

Straddling the surfaced coastal road about 15km (9 miles) south of Tanji, the small town of **Sanyang** ⓰ is quite a busy transport hub, lying as it does on the junction with the main road between the south coast and Brikama. Situated approximately 4km (2½ miles) east of the eponymous beach, Sanyang lies deeper inland than any other urban centre along the south coast, and as such it sees relatively few tourists. Having said that, **Sanyang Beach**, about an hour's walk from town along a sandy road, is one of the loveliest spots along the Gambian coast, serviced by a handful of rustic lodges and beach bars, and the fishing village is busy enough to be interesting without being so large that it ruins the beach from the perspective of swimming or sunbathing.

Gunjur

The largest town along the south coast, with a population of 13,500, **Gunjur** ⓱ has an aura of modernisation that denies it the charm of more traditional fishing villages elsewhere on the coast. Gunjur has been an important religious centre ever since it was visited by the Tidjiane marabout Cheikh Oumar Tall in the 1830s *(see page 46)*. The region's most famous religious shrine is Kenye-Kenye Jamango (literally "Sand Dune Mosque"), which was reputedly founded by Omar Tall and still attracts devout Tidjiane followers from all around the region. The makeshift mosque lies on the dunes overlooking Gunjur beach about 3km (2 miles) west of the town centre, and the surrounding buildings and gardens are also held sacred by local Muslims.

Whatever the town might lack in terms of tourist attractions, the nearby **Gunjur Beach** possesses it in spades. Situated about 25 minutes' walk from the main road, this idyllic long arc of sand, teased by gentle breakers and hemmed in by tall vegetated dunes, is the stuff of desert-island fantasies, and you can walk along it for miles without seeing another person. Inland of the dunes that line Gunjur Beach, an extinct waterway or lagoon supports a long row of palm-shaded smallholdings, where local farmers grow tomatoes and other vegetables using water from shallow wells that tap the subterranean flow.

Schoolchildren from the Kobisala Nursery School in Sanyang.

BELOW: woman and child washing a fish bucket on Tanji Beach.

The annual Kartong Festival (www. kartongfestival.org), organised in conjunction with the world music magazine Songlines, *usually features an exciting programme of local and international musicians and other performance artists. The inaugural festival took place in November 2005 and the fourth edition was held over Easter 2008.*

The leafy savannah that divides Gunjur Beach from the main road is the site of two excellent owner-managed upmarket lodges. The nine-chalet **Footsteps Eco-Lodge**, entirely rebuilt following a fire in 2006, is probably the most ecologically sound lodge anywhere in The Gambia. Among other things, it draws entirely on the sun's rays to electrify all the rooms and power the pumps that feed subterranean water into the freshwater swimming pool. Nearby **Gecko Lodge**, which opened in 2008, offers accommodation as well as excellent yoga courses in airy Afro-Mediterranean chalets scattered around lovely large leafy grounds.

Kartong

The most southerly town in The Gambia, situated approximately 2km (1 mile) from the border with the Casamance, **Kartong** ⑱ (also known as Kartung) was reputedly founded in the 16th century and today hosts a population of around 3,000. The oldest part of town is also the site of its best-known landmark, the sacred **Folonko Crocodile Pool** (daily), which is associated with the marabout Cheikh Oumar Tall, and is far less tourist-oriented

than its counterpart at Kachikally. The pool still forms an important Islamic pilgrimage site, especially for Gambian wrestlers, who believe a ritual bath there will ensure victory in combat, and for barren women who believe the sacred water cures infertility. Several large crocodiles are resident, and there's also plenty of avian activity around the pool. Crocodiles can also be seen at the **Gambia Reptile Farm** (daily; charge), which is located on the northern outskirts of Kartong, along with venomous and non-venomous snakes, turtles and chameleons and other lizards.

Despite its remoteness from any established package tourism circuit, Kartong is the closest thing to a beachfront town along the coast south of Tanji, and a cluster of low-key tourist facilities runs along the narrow band of vegetated dunes that divides the main road immediately north of town from an indisputably gorgeous beach. A well-known landmark here is the **Lemonfish Art Gallery** (tel: 772 8621; www.lemonfish.gm; Tue–Sun 9am–6pm), which opened in 2005 and displays the work of around two dozen contemporary Gambian and other West African artists. Situated 200 metres/yards

BELOW: eco-lodge near Kartong.
RIGHT: in bloom.

from the main road, the gallery lies in a large balconied house, and light meals and drinks are served at the in-house Riverside Café. There is also a shop where you can buy artworks and jewellery.

The pick of the accommodation options running immediately north from Kartong is **Boboi Beach Lodge**, which combines an isolated location in lush tropical garden and incredible palm-shaded beachfront setting with affordable rates and chilled-out staff, making it one of the best budget deals in The Gambia.

About 2km (1 mile) south of the town, **Kartong Beach** is a less attractive proposition for swimming than the beach north of town, if only because it is an active fishing beach and this tends to be strewn with fish offal and other forms of waste. It's an interesting spot, however, situated alongside the attractive mangrove-lined Hallalhin (or Allahein) River, which forms the border with the Casamance. For locals, the river constitutes an important source of catfish, oysters and other seafood, while tourists who take a local dugout onto the calm waters will be rewarded with some interesting birdwatching. Although this remote corner

Fisherman mending his nets on the calm Hallalhin River.

of The Gambia can easily be visited as a day trip from elsewhere on the coast, it's also possible to stay overnight at a Dutch-run eco-lodge called **Stala Adventures**, which runs a unique array of cultural and birdwatching excursions in collaboration with the local community.

Make sure you visit the offices of KART (Kartong Association for Responsible Tourism; tel: 449 5887; www.safari garden.com) – where you will learn all about its great work in the area; they also organise pirogue trips and birdwatching and walking tours. ❑

BELOW:
Kartong Beach.

RESTAURANTS AND BARS

Restaurants

Prices for a main course per person:

$ = under US$8 (D160)
$$ = US$8–15 (D160–300)
$$$ = over US$15 (D300)

Bakau

Chapman's Bar and Restaurant
Atlantic Boulevard
Tel: 449 5252
$$–$$$
This popular and spacious courtyard restaurant has a pleasant outdoor ambience and a varied menu of tasty grilled seafood and meat dishes. An exceptionally well-stocked bar includes beer on tap, and vegetarians are well catered for, too. Open Tue–Thur 3pm–late.

Fang-Fang Bar and Restaurant
Atlantic Boulevard
Tel: 449 7476
$$
What this Chinese eatery lacks in character is compensated for by the extensive menu, which has plenty of choice for vegetarians and carnivores alike, as well as the very reasonable prices. Indoor and outdoor seating available. Open 4pm–midnight daily.

Net Café Bistro
Atlantic Boulevard diagonally opposite Africa Village Hotel
$
The fastest internet connection in Bakau is on offer inside, while the pavement terrace serves very palatable and affordable burgers, *shwarmas*, sandwiches and other snacks from breakfast time until after dark.

Smiling Coast Brasserie
Atlantic Boulevard
Tel: 449 4653
$$
One of the more wallet-friendly eateries in Bakau, this outdoor restaurant serves a good selection of grilled seafood, chicken and meat dishes. Music-lovers should aim to be here on Mon, Wed, Fri or Sat evening, when there's usually live African or reggae music.

Fajara

Butcher's Shop
130 Kairaba Avenue
Tel: 449 5069
$$$
A Fajara institution for more than 15 years, this excellent restaurant has a menu dominated by meat dishes – beef, lamb, pork, chicken – as well as a fair selection of seafood meals. Portions are large. There's a great wine list and a leafy wooden deck. Open daily 8am–11pm.

The Clay Oven
Off Atlantic Boulevard near the junction with Kairaba Avenue
Tel: 449 6600
$$–$$$
The country's top Indian restaurant prides itself on efficient service and a dither-inducing menu of top-quality meat, prawn and vegetarian dishes.

With indoor seating only, it's an especially good option in unsettled weather, but can feel stuffy at other times. The all-you-can-eat buffet on Tuesdays is worth starving all day for. Open lunch and dinner daily.

Mama's Restaurant
Cnr Kairaba Avenue & Atlantic Boulevard
Tel: 447 7640
A la carte **$–$$**;
seafood buffet **$$$**
Cheap draught beer, a welcoming outdoor atmosphere and a varied selection of reasonably priced and generously proportioned African and European dishes ensure that Mama's is usually the busiest eatery in Fajara. The seafood buffet, though pricier than other dishes, is unbeatable value. Open Tue–Sun 9am–late.

Ngala Lodge
64 Atlantic Boulevard
Tel: 449 4045
$$$
Open to non-residents, the restaurant at this exclusive lodge is one of the finest in The Gambia, with an imaginative menu of both seafood and meat dishes prepared by a Belgian chef, and a good selection of daily specials. The clifftop setting overlooking the Atlantic is also extremely appealing. Open for breakfast, lunch and dinner daily.

LEFT: simple, fresh food at the Mandina Lodge.
RIGHT: setting the tables at Avocado, the Coconut Residence Hotel restaurant.

Yok Salon
Garba Jahumpa Road,
500 metres/yards east of the
junction with Kairaba Avenue
Tel: 449 5131
$$$
Tucked away in the leafy
Japanese-style garden
behind the African Living
Art Centre, the Yok is
renowned for its imagin-
ative pan-Asian fusion
cuisine and tantalising
menu of fruity cocktails.

Kotu Beach
Paradise Beach Bar and Restaurant
$–$$
Aside from hotel
restaurants, Kotu is
rather short on options
for eating out, the one
major exception being
this long-serving beach-
front restaurant, which
is a little seedy but offers
a shady retreat from the
sun, as well as a varied
menu of no-frills African
and European meat, fish
and vegetarian standbys.
Reliable rather than
exciting, it's open daily
9am–10pm, and very
reasonably priced.

Palma Rima
Luigi's Restaurant
Luigi's Complex,
Palma Rima Road
Tel: 446 0280
$$
Set about 100 metres/
yards back from the
beach, this Italian eatery
serves a varied selection
of pizza, pasta and other
dishes, as well as some
of the best desserts in
The Gambia. Open
noon–late daily.

Shiraz Lebanese and Seafood Restaurant
Opposite Palma Rima Hotel
Tel: 446 0434
$$–$$$
Probably the best
Lebanese restaurant in
the greater Banjul area,
the Shiraz is a particu-

larly good option for
groups due to its
extensive meze menu.
Sheesha pipes and
a good selection of
Lebanese wines
enhance the Middle
Eastern atmosphere.
Open 6–10pm daily.

Teranga Beach Club
Tel: 706 7864
$
This budget-friendly bar
and restaurant is the
only beachfront option
at Palma Rima. It serves
a variety of standard
meat or fish with
chips-style fare, and
there's usually live
Gambian music every
Sunday night.

Kololi
Al Basha Lebanese
The Strip, Senegambia
Tel: 446 3300
$$$
Among the less populist
of the countless eateries
lining the strip, this
excellent Lebanese
restaurant serves a good
à la carte selection, but
the meze special – seven
different dishes to be
shared between two – is
a real treat for the taste
buds. Open Mon–Sat
6pm–midnight.

Avocado Restaurant
Coconut Residence,
Bertil Harding Road
Tel: 446 3377
$$$
The elegant poolside
restaurant in Kololi's
top hotel is well worth
the short taxi ride
required to get there.
A tantalising fusion menu
combines elements of
European, Thai, Japan-
ese and Tex-Mex cuisine,
and the wine list is
second to none. Seafood-
and meat-lovers are well
catered for, but vegetar-
ians are poorly served
by the limited selection.

Jojo's Bistro and Grill House
Bijilo Road
Tel: 446 5151
$$** (lunch); **$$$ (dinner)
The funky orange-and-
yellow decor ensures
that this airy bistro with
both indoor and outdoor
seating stands out from
the pack. It serves a
limited selection of tasty
light lunches, including
salads and filled
baguettes, and a more
substantial evening
menu dominated by
seafood and steaks.

Kora Bar and Diner
Bijilo Road
Tel: 446 2727
$$$
This smart and trendy
restaurant, set in quiet
leafy gardens less than
five minutes' walk from
the hubbub of The Strip,
offers both indoor and outdoor seating and is known
for its relaxed atmos-
phere, classy service and
nifty cocktails. Specialities
include fajitas, seafood

platters and steak, and
you're advised to leave
room for dessert. Open
Mon–Sat 6pm–late.

Paradiso Restaurant
The Strip, Senegambia
Tel: 446 2177
$–$$
Inexpensive but good-
quality grills, pizzas and
pastas attract a steady
stream of budget-
conscious package
holidaymakers to this
pleasant Italian eatery,
which has indoor and
outdoor seating. There's
cheap draught beer too.
Open daily 8am–late.

Tao Asian Cuisine
Bijilo Road
Tel: 446 1191
$$** (à la carte); **$$$ (buffet)
The best Asian restaurant
in the Senegambia area
of Kololi, this place serves
a bewildering variety of
Thai, Chinese and other
Asian dishes, as well as a
sumptuous all-you-can-eat
buffet on Thursday nights.
Open daily 7–10pm.

Mangrove:
The Friendless Tree

Extending for 130km (80 miles) up the Gambia River, the mangrove is a tropical evergreen which clings to salty tidal mudflats spurned by other life

John Steinbeck wrote: "No one likes the mangrove." He was right: the ungainly tree with its roots buried deep in stinking mud, its gaunt branches and leathery leaves, has few sympathisers among the human population, but is attended by a veritable zoo, aquarium and aviary of wildlife. However, not only do the mangrove swamps provide shelter for a wide range of creatures, but man also feeds, either directly or indirectly, off the curious tree.

Large tracts of The Gambia's coastline and inland waterways are lined with mangroves, and the area may be growing because of the tree's ability to "create" land, though this is tempered by its use as firewood and timber. Small lagoons and creeks along the coast, often in places where the sea breaks over the coastal sandbar, are typical habitats of the dense vegetation and stilt-like root systems of the mangrove.

Some 20 mangrove families comprising more than 50 species are recognised worldwide. Most common in West Africa is the red mangrove, of which three species are present *(Rhizophora mangle, R. harrisonii* and *R. racemosa)*, but these are often found alongside the white mangrove *Laguncularia racemosa* and black mangrove *Avicennia germinans*. All these trees are salt-loving, ranking among the few plants which can cope with water of a high salinity. The mangrove may grow to 24 metres (80ft) in height and prefers regions with high rainfall. The trees grow in clumps between the low- and high-water marks and produce a particularly large quantity of vegetation and dead matter which decays into a very nutritious mire.

The roots, characteristically angled out of the mud, breathe in their oxygen requirement and almost leapfrog across the new banks of litter formed as the trees mature. The red mangrove sheds more than 1.2 tons of leaves per hectare (3 tons per acre) per year. In this way the mangrove adds to the coastal land and its special seed design and germination habits ensure that the "colony" grows.

Producing more than 300 seeds per year, the mangrove is a quick coloniser. The quill-like seeds germinate from the large, yellow, fleshy blooms while still on the tree. Between 15–30cm (6–12 inches) long, the germinating seed falls into the water surrounding the mother tree and inverts gradually because of its buoyancy. The sprouts touch land and the tiny plant takes hold and roots.

Should the seed be caught in a current, it will drift, alive, for up to a year until it is washed against suitable soil or further mudflats. Roots and debris along the coast break the force of the ocean waves and the sea grass, which grows in profusion beneath the stilt-lined waters, collects more vege-

ABOVE: fisherman on his canoe near the Makasutu Culture Forest. **TOP RIGHT:** African darter hawks from overhanging mangrove branches. **RIGHT:** the mangrove is thick and impenetrable.

table matter increasing the banks on which the mangrove are embedded.

Mangroves are also an important habitat for wildlife, with waterbirds being especially well represented, from the cormorants and kingfishers that hawk from overhanging branches to the herons and finfoots that shelter below them. The rare and elusive white-crested tiger heron is unique to mangrove habitats, while the enormous West African manatee is dependent on them for food.

From the seaward side man takes his canoes into the backwaters and creeks of the mangrove's mysterious domain. One knows neither when one is on new dry land nor a mile out in the Atlantic; the forest of semi-floating, knee-deep trunks and thick, green canopy all looks the same. Here, fishermen take an astounding variety of marine produce from shrimps and lobster to sea bass, electric eel, catfish and yellowtail snapper. Snook, tarpon and other game fish can be hooked in the mangrove margins. To the landward, man harvests oysters and mussels, crabs and other crustaceans.

The mangrove wood also makes excellent firewood for charcoal and it can be fashioned into carved implements and used as building material. However, indiscriminate felling has, in some areas of the West African coast, dangerously depleted the mangrove and as a result upset the

ecological balance. This is not yet the case in Senegal, nor in The Gambia.

Indirectly, the mangrove helps the human population by creating a "buffer zone" between the relentlessly buffeting waves of the Atlantic Ocean and the vulnerable, sandy-rocked shoreline. The plant also acts as a filter as it breaks down a good deal of waste which otherwise would pollute the shoreline. Finally, as the tree-line marches into the sea creating more land area, the rich soil behind it is eagerly tilled by local farmers. Unlovable maybe, but very useful. ❑

Game Viewing

It would be misleading to compare Senegal or The Gambia to East Africa when it comes to safari opportunities, but the region does have much to offer wildlife enthusiasts

The region's most important conservation area for mammal biodiversity is the Parc National de Niokolo-Koba, which sprawls across a vast tract of savannah in southeastern Senegal. Though somewhat remote from the coastal tourist circuits, this Unesco World Heritage Site is the last place in the region where elephant, lion and African wild dog still roam free.

A more realistic goal for a quick safari fix is the Réserve de Bandia, which protects a fabulous tract of baobab-studded savannah some 15 minutes' drive from the resorts of Senegal's Petite Côte, inhabited by forest buffalo, roan antelope, warthog and various monkeys.

Similar in conception, the Siné-Saloum's Réserve de Fathala protects giraffe, white rhino and roan antelope relocated from Bandia, and is the only place where visitors stand a realistic chance of spotting the spectacular Derby eland, the world's largest antelope. Fathala is easily visited as a cross-border day trip from The Gambia.

An encouraging recent development has been the reintroduction of Dama gazelle and scimitar-horned oryx – both hunted out in Senegal – to the accessible Réserve de Guembeul and more remote Réserve de Faune de Ferlo-Nord in northern Senegal.

The Gambia's protected areas are on the small side but can be very rewarding. Abuko Nature Reserve near Serekunda, though best-known for its birds, is a good place to see bushbuck and Maxwell's duiker. Bijilo Forest Reserve, bordering the coastal resorts of Kololi, is great for monkeys, while upcountry sanctuaries include the dry savannah of Kiang West National Park and moister River Gambia National Park.

Above: hippo mother and calf bathing in the Parc National de Niokolo-Koba in Senegal.

Below: forest buffalo are identified by their red-brown colour and short backward-sweeping horns

Right: a small herd of giraffe in Senegal's Réserve de Bandia were introduced from South Africa, along with a pair of white rhinoceros.

Recommended Restaurants and Bars on page 137

men are generally out working the fields (as opposed to the vegetable gardens, which are worked by women), extending or repairing their compounds or simply sheltering from the sun's heat. On Fridays, lines of men can be seen in their best robes walking to the nearest mosque.

Getting around

The easiest and most efficient way to see something of the Gambia River Route is on a guided tour from the coast. The most popular option here is a one- or two-night excursion to a specific lodge, such as Tendaba Camp or Badi Mayo, but longer tours can also be arranged. A more adventurous option would be to hire a self-drive vehicle, ideally a 4x4, or to use the extensive network of crowded bush-taxis that connects all major centres. There are only four places countrywide where motor vehicles can cross between the south and north bank: these are the large but slow ferries connecting Banjul to Barra at the river mouth and Farafenni to Soma on the Trans-Gambia Highway about 110km (70 miles) upriver, and the smaller and quicker ferries further east at Janjanbureh and Basse Santa Su.

Historically, the south-bank road was always regarded as a smoother option than its north-bank counterpart. This is no longer true, however, as the south-bank road has deteriorated badly in recent

Groundnuts for sale.

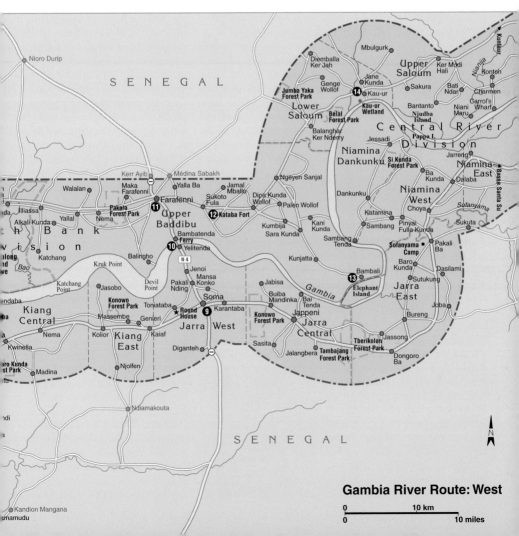

Gambia River Route: West

0   10 km

0   10 miles

years, while the north-bank road from Barra to Kerewan and Farafenni to Janjanbureh is now freshly surfaced. From Janjanbureh, the south-bank road is definitely the better option as far as Basse Santa Su. Further east, both roads are in relatively poor shape. These things do tend to change, so seek current advice.

The Western Division

East of Brikama, the south-bank road skirts marshes and mangrove swamps that extend inland from the river for almost a mile. This administrative area, known as the Western Division, ends at the large tributary of the Gambia called Bintang Bolong. About 35km (20 miles) out of Brikama, at Bessi, a sandy 7km (4-mile) track leads north to the bank of **Brefet Bolong**, a narrow channel separated from the main body of the Gambia River by marshy Sansankoto Island. It was here that the trading post of Brefet was established by the British Royal Adventurers in 1664, three years after they took control of James Island (5km/3 miles across the water). This beautiful site was later occupied intermittently by the French and other British, but all that

At Bintang Gereejal, one can see the ruined walls which outline the site of a tiny church and early Portuguese trading post (both long deserted).

remains today are a few overgrown and ruinous walls set below the sprawling kapok and baobab trees.

Some 15km (9 miles) past Bessi, a clearly signposted road runs north to the tiny village of **Bintang ❶**, which lies on the south bank of the Bintang Bolong about 10km (6 miles) south of its confluence with the Gambia River. The main tourist centre here is the attractively rustic **Bintang Bolong Lodge**, which consists of six stilted rooms above the mangrove-lined creek and another six rooms set further back on dry land. This is a favourite spot for boat excursions and fishing trips. Monkeys, crocodiles and, more occasionally, dolphins are among the larger creatures that might be seen in the vicinity, and the birdlife is excellent. Boat trips further afield to James Island and the north-bank villages of Juffureh and Albreda can also be arranged. A village of around 700 people, Bintang is also a good place to see traditional Kankurang dancers, whose Mandinka protagonists perform in a costume made of branches and leaves, wear body dye, and don a red face mask topped with demonic horns.

East of Bintang, the south-bank road runs roughly parallel to Bintang Bolong for approximately 40km (25 miles). At about the halfway mark, it passes through **Bwiam ❷,** a small but fast-growing village flanked by the southern bank of the bolong. Bwiam was once an important slave-trading post, and the foundations of a few old residences or warehouses are discernible near the recently rehabilitated wharf. A more contemporary landmark, the **Sulayman Junkung Hospital**, built at the initiative of President Jammeh in 2003, is now one of the country's top four medical facilities. Near the hospital, the **Saint Joseph Family Farm Centre** (tel: 448 9050; daily) is a welcoming community project that educates local women about sustainable agricultural practices.

Bwiam's best-known curiosity is an inverted three-legged *kalero* (metal pot) that sits half buried below a stand of giant kapok trees, a kilometre or so north of the main road. This centuries-old artefact is held sacred by locals, who claim

The Gambia River

The fourth-longest waterway in West Africa, the 1,100km (600-mile) Gambia River rises in the region's most important watershed, the moist and mountainous Fouta Djalon region of Guinea. It flows into the southeast of Senegal near Kédougou, bisecting the Parc National de Niokolo-Koba, where it is joined by several tributaries before it crosses into The Gambia some 300km (180 miles) east of its mouth as the crow flies. Just before it enters The Gambia, the river is funnelled through the Barrakunda Falls, a 7-metre (20ft) wide channel hemmed in by smoothed laterite walls. Below these rapids, the Gambia River is tidal and flat, registering a total altitude drop of less than 20 metres (60ft) west of Basse Santa Su. It becomes increasingly wide as it approaches the Atlantic, and is saline as far inland as Kuntaur, about 180km (110 miles) from the estuary. The river is technically navigable almost as far as the Senegalese border, but no formal passenger boats take advantage of this feature. The estuary, one of the widest in Africa, spans 20km (12 miles) and is crossed by a regular ferry service linking Barra on the north bank to the capital, Banjul.

Recommended Restaurants and Bars on page 137

hat it cannot be moved except of its own accord. However, legend has it that the pot would, during times of war, swivel around to indicate the direction of a forthcoming attack – a slice of folklore that might contain a kernel of truth if, as seems likely, the tripodal device is not actually an inverted cooking pot but a rotating artillery stand.

About 5km (3 miles) past Bwiam, a prominently signposted tar road runs south to **Kanilai** ❸, whose main claim to fame is as the birthplace of President Jammeh in 1965. Set snugly against the Senegalese border, this once obscure village is seldom depicted on pre-millennial maps of The Gambia, but it has risen to prominence under the leadership of its most famous son, who was raised and educated there, and returns regularly to his custom-made presidential palace. The introduction of street lights, asphalt roads and electricity has spurred a tenfold increase in Kanilai's population since the mid-1990s. The small town also now bills itself as the "Home of Festivals", hosting the **Kanilai International Cultural Festival** over two weeks in June on odd-numbered years, and the mock initiation ceremony peculiar to the **International Roots Festival** on even years.

Less successful has been an attempt to lure a steady stream of conventional tourism to town. Closer in spirit to a European safari park than a real game reserve, **Kanilai Game Park** (daily 7–10am and 5–7pm; charge; guide mandatory) is stocked with an arbitrary menagerie selection of rhinos, zebras, wildebeest and other South African imports that don't occur naturally in West Africa. By contrast, the government-owned **Sindola Safari Lodge**, a 40-room hotel built to service the adjacent game park and host presidential functions, is a worthy up-country counterpart to its coastal sister, the five-star Kairaba Hotel. Indeed, measured in terms of comfort and facilities – fancy restaurant, swimming pool, air-con etc – Sindola is easily the best hotel in the Gambian interior, even if Kanilai itself lacks any convincing attractions other than pure curiosity value.

Past the turn-off to Kanilai, the south-bank road veers northward at **Kalaji** ❹, crossing Bintang Bolong at its narrowest point as it exits Western Division. Kalaji is occasionally used as a terminal

At the end of the International Roots Festival (pictured), boats from Albreda or Juffureh moor at Kanilai laden with visitors eager to see the mock initiation ceremony.

BELOW: the Kankurang is the exorcist of evil spirits.

Carved wooden mask at Tendaba Camp.

BELOW:
the rondavels
at Tendaba Camp.

for pleasure craft from Banjul, and you might want to stop at the roadside to buy some of the delicious locally made peanut crunch. A few kilometres north of Bintang Bolong, the main road passes through **Sankandi**, where two British commissioners were killed in a clash with locals in 1900. From here, a rough track – suitable for 4x4s only – runs west for about 25km (16 miles) to Keneba, site of a Medical Research Council field station. North of this, **Tankular** is a tiny river port set close to a former Portuguese trading post, and its people treasure an old Portuguese ship bell that was recovered from the remains of the ruined trading post and dates back to 1711.

Pool with a view

By far the most popular of The Gambia's upriver lodges, **Tendaba Camp ❺** has a riverfront setting along a 5km (3-mile) dirt track signposted at the junction village of Kwinella, about 25km (16 miles) north of Kalaji on the main south-bank road. The facilities are those of a basic safari lodge, and include an electricity generator but no landline telephone. The accommodation is in African-style rondavels (round huts) with pointed, thatched roofs and en suite showers and toilets. There is a swimming pool and an open-sided riverfront restaurant serving decent meals and chilled drinks (it's advisable to drink bottled drinking water as the only water on tap is the slightly salty river water). Overnight stays are not expensive, and the camp embodies the sense of isolation associated with being deep in the African bush.

Established by a Swedish captain in 1972, Tendaba originally functioned as a hunting and fishing camp. Today, it is Gambian-owned and managed, and its main clientele consists of birdwatchers and tourists seeking a taste of upriver rusticity. Pirogue trips lead through the labyrinthine **Kisi Bolong** and **Tunku Creek**, which are lined with tall mangroves and home to hermit crabs, mudskippers and a daunting variety of birds, including the alluring African finfoot and white-backed night heron. For birdwatchers, the rice fields and woodland behind Tendaba Camp also merit exploration; regularly recorded species include ring-necked parakeet, Senegal parrot, Abyssinian roller, grey woodpecker, beautiful sunbird and black-headed bush-shrike.

You could charter a boat from Tendaba to **Bao Bolong Wetland Reserve** ⑥ (daily; free), The Gambia's largest officially protected area, extending over 220 sq km (85 sq miles) of marsh, woodland and mangroves on the north bank opposite Tendaba Camp. The reserve is named after the Bao Bolong, a tributary of the Gambia that rises in Senegal, where it only flows seasonally. The Gambian part of the bolong, though perennial, is dominated by fresh water that flows into the Gambia River during the rains, but this is replaced by a backwash of saline water from the main river when the inflow subsides during the dry season. One result of this unusual seasonal variation is that the mangroves lining the creeks of Bao Bolong are far larger than average, with a canopy up to 12 metres (40ft) tall.

A designated Ramsar Wetland Site, Bao Bolong supports a varied selection of mammals, including Cape clawless otter, West African manatee, marsh mongoose, red river hog and the rare sitatunga antelope. Dolphins sometimes swim this far upstream in the dry season, when water salinity is highest, while hippos occasionally stray here from the river's upper reaches during the rains. Massive Nile crocodiles are almost certain to be seen sunning on the mudbanks, and the scarcer dwarf crocodile is also present. The reserve is an important site for migrant waterbirds, with concentrations of more than 20,000 present between September and January, while a rich selection of resident species includes such rarities as white-crested tiger heron, Allen's gallinule, martial eagle and Pel's fishing owl.

Kiang West National Park

A popular goal for 4x4 day excursions out of Tendaba Camp is **Kiang West National Park** ⑦ (tel: 726 4982; daily 7am–6pm; charge), whose eastern boundary lies only 5km (3 miles) away as the crow flies. This 115-sq km (45-sq mile) tract of dry Guinean savannah, interspersed with a few tree-lined bolongs on the southern bank of the Gambia River at Tendaba Camp, is the most important sanctuary in The Gambia for terrestrial wildlife, and well worth a half-day visit. True, when it comes to spotting large mammals, Kiang West tends to be more miss than hit, but the birdlife is reliably excellent, with more than 300 species

The colourful Senegal parrot makes migrations within West Africa, according to the availability of the fruit, seeds and blossoms that make up its diet.

LEFT: the tranquil Gambia River.
BELOW: local smile.

Kiang West National Park's official emblem, the bateleur.

BELOW: river fisherman.

recorded, including many raptors and other large birds now scarce elsewhere in the country.

Kiang West provides sanctuary to all of The Gambia's naturally occurring primate species, including red colobus and patas monkey, and these might be seen anywhere in the park. Carnivores are well represented, and while you're unlikely to see anything larger than a mongoose, you might well come across the trademark chalky white spoor of spotted hyena, and the truly optimistic could hope for a fleeting glimpse of a secretive leopard, sightings of which are reported every few years, most recently in 2006.

As for birds, Kiang West's heftier residents include Abyssinian ground hornbill, martial eagle, long-crested eagle, helmeted guineafowl and white-backed vulture. The bateleur, a spectacular black, white and red eagle that's been adopted as the park's official emblem, is often seen flying overhead in its distinctive rocking manner. And even if you don't see much wildlife, there is a stirring sense of space associated with driving through the country's largest – and arguably last – tract of untrammelled African savannah.

The two road approaches to Kiang West both require 4x4s. Coming directly from the direction of Banjul on the main south-bank road, the closest option is a clearly signposted 1.5km (1-mile) track that runs west from **Dumbutu** to the park headquarters. However, the headquarters are frequently untended (unless a few baboons count), and the track on to the river is unclear, so it's probably advisable to bypass this junction unless you intend to take advantage of the inexpensive but rudimentary accommodation that's on offer (in which case, phone ahead).

The more useful approach to Kiang West is clearly signposted on the left-hand side of the feeder road to Tendaba Camp about 1km (½ mile) north of Kwinella. After 5km (3 miles), it leads to **Batelling** ⑧, where a quartet of rusting cannons under the tree opposite the mosque form the only enduring relic of European fortifications erected during the 18th century. For self-drive visitors, Batelling, 3km (2 miles) south of the unmanned park entrance gate, is where entrance fees must be paid, and it's also the best place to pick up a local guide to help find your way around the unsignposted roads, and to spot and identify wildlife.

Three main sites of interest lie close to Batelling. The first, reachable along a 500-metre/yard track that branches to the right immediately past the concrete bunker referred to as the entrance gate, is a large seasonal pan encircled by palms and overlooked by a low laterite cliff where you can park your car. This can be good for wildlife when the pan holds water, attracting baboon, warthog and various small antelope. The pan is sometimes visited by the handsome roan antelope, which is the country's largest surviving indigenous terrestrial ungulate, crossing into the area from the Casamance towards the end of the rainy season.

Returning to the entrance gate, the main track continues north to **Toubab Kollon** ("White Man's Well"), the site of a long-gone Portuguese trade outpost set on a flat stretch of river bank 2km (1 mile) further north. There's a picnic site here, or at least the crumbling remains

Recommended Restaurants and Bars on page 137

of one, and the view across the river is very pretty, though its unlikely to yield much in the way of wild mammals. More promising is a marshy, mangrove-lined stream that attracts plenty of wading birds. A rough sandy track follows this stream west for about 1km (½ mile) before connecting with the main track to **Kolonding Viewpoint**, set on a 20-metre (65ft) high slab of laterite that overlooks a series of shallow pools along the river bank. Sit here quietly in the late afternoon, and you're almost certain to see wildlife action below, most likely a few bickering baboons.

The Trans-Gambian Highway

Effectively forming the divide between the western and central river route, the Trans-Gambia Highway is the main thoroughfare for vehicles crossing between northern Senegal and the Casamance. Measuring all of 25km (16 miles), this Gambian interlude along the RN4 between Kaolack and Ziguinchor is punctuated by two of the interior's most substantial towns, Soma and Farafenni, as well as the crossing of the Gambia River – less than a kilometre wide here –

on the flat-bottomed, diesel-powered Yelitenda–Bambatenda Ferry.

Situated at the crossroads of the main south-bank road and the Trans-Gambia Highway, **Soma ⑨** is a dusty and amorphous junction town of around 12,000 people. It has good facilities, including a bank with foreign exchange, a couple of small lodges and eateries, a few filling stations and a bustling central market.

A worthwhile excursion in this area, situated just close to the crossroads at **Toniataba**, is the site of a great house built by an important local marabout (holy leader). This round structure has a circumference of 60 metres (200ft), and the marabout is believed to be buried beneath its floor. Nearby, a few old colonial buildings still stand at **Mansa Konko** (Mandinka for "King's Hill"), the former administrative capital.

Approximately 3km (2 miles) north of Soma towards Farafenni, there's not much to **Pakali Nding** aside from the Pakali Nding Trans-Gambia Highway Lodge, but this rustic lodge is easily the nicest option for overnight accommodation on transit between southern and northern Senegal.

Excursions to the Bao Bolong Wetland Reserve depart from the pier at Tendaba.

BELOW: pirogues poised for action.

TIP

Banks are scarce in
the area, so if you are
running low on cash
head to the Trust Bank
in Farafenni, the only
bank for miles.

BELOW: The
Waterhouse, which
is the main lodge
at the Chimpanzee
Rehabilitation Trust
in the River Gambia
National Park.

The **Yelitenda–Bambatenda Ferry ⑩**,
which ferries vehicles and passengers
between Yelitenda, on the south bank of
the Gambia River, and its north-bank
counterpart Bambatenda, runs every 30
minutes or so between 7am and 6.30pm,
though long queues often result in significantly longer waits. Coming from Soma,
vehicles must buy tickets at a roadside
weighbridge about 2km (1 mile) south of
Yelitenda, while vehicles coming from
the north will find the ticket office a few
hundred metres before Bambatenda.

Close to the ferry crossing, at the aptly
named Devil's Point, lies the hulk of the
MV *Lady Chilel Jawara* (named after
the then first lady of The Gambia), which
served as one of the world's last floating
post office-cum-ferries. A victim of the
unpredictable currents and sandbars that
claimed so many of the steamers that
once plied the river almost to the Senegalese border, MV *Lady Chilel Jawara*
sank after being grounded on a sandbar
in December 1984, less than nine months
after it had been launched, and claiming
the lives of four passengers.

Straddling the Trans-Gambia Highway
only 2km (1 mile) south of the Sene-

galese border, **Farafenni ⑪** is the main
route focus along the north bank – indeed,
with a population topping the 30,000
mark, it is upcountry Gambia's most populous urban centre, and the fifth-largest
town nationwide. It has good facilities,
including one of the country's largest and
newest hospitals, officially opened in
2003, and a scattering of banks, markets,
filling stations, small hotels and local
restaurants. Farafenni's strategic location
attracts a significant number of semi-
transient Senegalese, Guinean and even
Mauritanian traders, creating a certain
cosmopolitan buzz that's most evident on
Sundays, when the weekly *lumo* (market)
is held on the northern outskirts of town.
On other days of the week, there's really
very little to see in Farafenni itself, and
it's easy enough to move on.

Farafenni to Janjanbureh

Travelling east from the Trans-Gambia
Highway, there are three good reasons
for taking the north-bank road between
Farafenni and Janjanbureh in favour of
its south-bank counterpart. The first is
that this once horrendous 115km (70-
mile) road was resurfaced in 2006 and

Recommended Restaurants and Bars on page 137

now ranks as the smoothest drive anywhere in The Gambia. The second is that it offers access to the finest of the country's 100-odd megalithic sites, including Wassu and Ker Batch, which were inscribed as Unesco World Heritage Sites in 2006. Finally, the port of Kuntaur is the closest springboard for the pristine forested waterway protected within the River Gambia National Park and the renowned Chimp Rehabilitation Trust centred on Badi Mayo.

The first point of historical interest heading east towards Janjanbureh is **Kataba Fort** ⓬, which lies a short distance south of the main north-bank road about 8km (5 miles) from Farafenni. Now reduced to little more than overgrown foundations, the small fort was built with British assistance in the early 1840s by the king of Kataba (a Wolof kingdom that covered most of present-day Gambia north of the river) as defence against the rival Kemintang leader.

A longer side trip from the main road leads south for 20km (12 miles) along a bumpy dirt road via Sara Kunda to the remote village of **Bambali** ⓭, which lies on the forested stretch of river bank facing

Elephant Island. This is the largest island along the Gambia River, but it's a long time since any elephants were seen in the vicinity (the last individual recorded anywhere in The Gambia was shot in the 1920s). Still, this is the furthest point upriver where hippos are resident, and it's easy enough to arrange a boat at Bambali to seek them out. As you punt around the island, you might also disturb the occasional crocodile or flock of heron in the dense undergrowth, and are likely to see the resident green monkeys. To get an idea of the full extent of the birdlife hereabouts, ask the boatman to take you to the south-bank rice fields.

About 40km (25 miles) from Farafenni, **Kau-ur** ⓮ (also spelt Kaur) is one of two points where the north-bank road comes close to skirting the Gambia River. A few hundred metres before town, the roadside **Kau-ur Wetland** is a near-perennial swamp that often hosts an interesting bird selection, including Egyptian plover, painted snipe, purple gallinule, knobbilled duck, and thousand-strong flocks of collared pratincole. At **Nioro**, 25km (16 miles) past Kau-ur, a partially collapsed stone circle comprised of eight

You won't only see wild birds.

LEFT: girls looking for crabs in the river.
BELOW: the best time to see hippos is at low tide.

The Egyptian plover is also called the crocodile bird. According to a well-known myth by Herodotus, the crocodiles lie on the shore and the plovers fly into their open mouths to feed on bits of decaying meat lodged between the teeth. The crocs do not eat the plovers, as they are providing them with greatly needed dentistry.

megaliths lies in an open field 500 metres/yds north of the north-bank road. Just past this, the permanent **Panchang Swamp**, an extension of Nianija Bolong, hosts a rich birdlife, notably Egyptian plover, African jacana, Allen's gallinule and a resident population of African pygmy goose, which is most likely to be seen on open water covered with lilies and other floating vegetation.

Another 2km (1 mile) past Nioro, **Nyanga Bantang** is a busy little village at the signposted junction for the rough but easily followed 7km (4-mile) dirt road leading to **Ker Batch National Monument ⓭** (daily 8am–6pm; charge). Erected in the 1st millennium AD, the nine full circles at Ker Batch each comprise between 10 and 24 megaliths, making a total of 161 stones, the tallest of which are around 2.5 metres (8ft) high and 1 metre (3ft) in diameter. Ker Batch is the site of The Gambia's only lyre-stone, a Y-shaped megalith whose sym-

bolic purpose remains a matter for conjecture, though local legend holds that it marks the burial site of close relatives who died simultaneously. This unique stone was broken in the early 20th century, and the concrete repair work undertaken by the 1965 Anglo-Gambian Stone Circle Expedition could have been more subtle. A small but worthwhile site museum provides useful background to Ker Batch and the other Senegambian Stone Circles, as well as displays relating to more contemporary local cultures.

Ker Batch is but one of the 54 megalithic sites (containing a total of 115 stone circles) that flank the **Nianija Bolong** as it winds for 30km (18 miles) between the Senegalese border and confluence with the Gambia River. It is one of the largest of these sites, and widely regarded to be the most important on account of its lyre-stone, but archaeological enthusiasts travelling with a 4x4 could spend days exploring the area further. The most prodigious site is **Niani Maru**, which consists of 176 megaliths arranged into eight circles, and other sites with multiple circles include Ker Abdu Njay, Wilingara, Buntung and Ngedel.

Recommended Restaurants and Bars on page 137

The best-known and most frequently visited of the Senegambian Stone Circle sites, **Wassu** ⑯ (daily 8am–6pm; charge) is clearly signposted a few hundred metres east of the main north-bank road about 25km (16 miles) past Nyanga Bantang and a similar distance from Janjanbureh. Like Ker Batch, Wassu is a National Monument and World Heritage Site, and its tally of 200 individual megaliths arranged into 11 circles is the greatest concentration countrywide. The site is completely fenced off, and a site museum dedicated to megalithic stones in the Senegambia and elsewhere is housed in a small rondavel (round hut). About 200 metres/yards east of the site, the quarry where the stones were carved contains several megaliths that broke in transit or before they had been completed.

Only 2km (1 mile) south of Wassu, **Kuntaur** ⑰ is the last inland port accessible to ocean-going cargo boats, and a row of waterfront warehouses testifies to its former heyday as the main export centre for the local groundnut industry. Kuntaur is still a relatively significant town, with a population of around 7,500, but cargo boats are a rare sight these days. By contrast, following the completion of the surfaced road from Farafenni, tourism to Kuntaur – not only the closest town to Wassu, but also the best base for boat trips to the River Gambia National Park – appears to be on an upward spiral. The once dire accommodation situation in Kuntaur was rectified in 2007 with the opening of the **Kairoh Gardens Guesthouse**, which offers decent en suite accommodation in a riverfront setting, as well as boat trips into the nearby park.

Situated approximately halfway between the eastern boundary of the River Gambia National Park and Janjanbureh, the large island of **Kai Hai** ⑱ is said to be haunted by a dragon-like man-eating creature – possibly a folk memory of an outsized Nile crocodile that once preyed on local villagers? Visiting this island by canoe is an eerie experience. Overgrown foliage casts a permanent shadow over the few paths through its forest. However, approaching Kai Hai from the west reveals a part of the jungle that has been cleared, and there is evidence that at one time rice was grown on the haunted island. The nearest village on the north bank, also called **Kai Hai**, lies about 2km (1 mile)

Legend has it that there is a curse on those disturbing the Stone Circle sites. A Captain Doke, an expedition leader called Ozanne and the archaeologist Parker all died mysteriously shortly after excavating some of the sites. However, the team led by F.A. Evans, director of the Anglo-Gambian stone circles expedition in 1964–5, escaped the curse – though very little has been done to unearth the origins of these sites since.

LEFT: man playing the balafon in Wassu. **BELOW:** snapshot of river life.

The Senegambian Stone Circles

This Unesco World Heritage Site, consisting of over 1,000 different sites with a total of almost 29,000 laterite stelae, is shrouded with mystery

Between 240 and 480km (150–300 miles) up the Gambia River, running north along the banks of tributary Bao Bolong as it crosses into Senegal, and further north still into the Siné-Saloum Delta, a collection of ancient monuments stands as one of Africa's greatest anthropological and archaeological riddles.

Erected more than 1,000 years ago, these laterite megaliths are all that remains of what must have been a highly sophisticated culture more or less contemporaneous with the ancient empire of Ghana, or even predating it. In AD 1067, the Arab chronicler El-Bakri wrote of a royal city called Cantor, which must have stood near the site of the stone circles. The peoples who live in the region nowadays hold the stones to be the work of an earlier civilisation, but have little more to say about their constructors.

Many skeletons have been uncovered below some circles, as well as tools, pottery and various ornaments, suggesting that these ancient monuments were originally erected as elaborate gravestones, though it is difficult to explain why the human remains found at some sites predate their circular headstones by a matter of centuries. The circles are remarkably reminiscent of other megalithic tumuli such as those in Brittany in France, which are generally held to be disposed in such a way as to indicate a connection with the sun, and therefore sun-worship. No similar memorials exist elsewhere in West Africa, though interestingly the southern highlands of Ethiopia, at the opposite end of the Sahel, are dotted with megalithic grave markers of a similar size and vintage, though these are not generally arranged in circles.

Thought to have originally been covered by laterite earth mounds, the standing stones sometimes include oddities such as the strange "lyre" or "V" stone at Ker Batch. Archaeologists think the megaliths were made and erected over 1,000 years ago and have now weathered down to a smooth, knobbly rust-red surface, like solid iron ore. Most stones have flat or concave tops, but others are adorned with button-like protrusions. Most sites contain just one or two stone circles, while the most extensive contains more than 50 circles of varying circumference. Occasionally, circles are arranged concentrically – that is, one circle is contained entirely within another.

The Senegambian Stone Circles are one of the most under-publicised wonders of West Africa, and they warrant greater exposure, which might be forthcoming following their inscription as a Unesco World Heritage Site in 2006. The Unesco site consists of two Senegalese and two Gambian clusters. The most accessible is Wassu, which lies alongside the main north bank between Farafenni and Janjanbureh as it bypasses Kuntaur, but nearby Ker Batch is of special interest for its lyre-shaped stone. In Senegal, Siné Ngayène has the densest concentration of stone circles anywhere in the region, and Wanar has the most lyre-shaped stelae. Both sites can be reached by following the Bao Bolong east from Nioro du Rip. ❑

LEFT AND ABOVE: the stone circles at Wassu.

from the river bank and is the site of five megalithic circles. More esoterically, the birthplace of Sir D.K. Jawara, the first president of independent Gambia, a short drive west of Kai Hai at the village of **Barajali**, is listed as a Historical Monument. At **Sapu**, on the south bank, is a small landing stage from where one can take a short track to the Janjanbureh road.

River Gambia National Park

Established in 1978, the 6-sq km (2½-sq mile) **River Gambia National Park** ⓐ (daily; charge) protects a quintet of uninhabited islands downriver of Kuntaur. Scenically, it is an astonishingly evocative and beautiful stretch of river frontage, with banks swathed in the sort of steaming tropical rainforest you'd more likely associate with the Congo Basin than the Sahel. The ecological systems range from lush jungle rainforest to reeds, savannah and mangrove swamps. The wildlife here is truly exceptional. Mammals include red colobus monkey and Guinea baboon, both of which are common in the riverine woodland, while hippopotamus and crocodile are resident in the river, and the manatee is seen from time to time.

The national park is best-known for the chimpanzees that have been released onto three of the islands (including so-called Baboon Island) by the Chimp Rehabilitation Trust (CRT), an organisation that has its roots in Stella Brewer Marsden's work with orphaned chimps at Abuko Nature Reserve in 1969. Some 20 chimps, mostly animals that had been mistreated in captivity, have been released onto the islands since 1979, and many more have been born there. Today, the CRT is the longest-running and arguably most successful venture of its sort, supporting a total population of 80 chimpanzees split between four communities on three islands.

Tourists are forbidden from setting foot on these islands, but boat trips along the shore can be arranged with operators or boatmen in Kuntaur or Janjanbureh. These boats cannot enter the western channel that divides Baboon Island from the river bank (preserved exclusively for the use of the CRT), but they still offer a good chance of seeing chimps, especially in the mid- or late afternoon. In addition, you are almost certain to see hippos, crocs and a variety of monkeys and birds

The name "colobus" is derived from the Greek word for "mutilated", because, unlike other monkeys, colobus monkeys do not have thumbs.

BELOW: baby chimpanzee holding on to its mother at the River Gambia National Park.

TIP

If you see a hippo, make sure you keep a safe distance. Remember: they are responsible for more deaths in Africa than any other animal. Hippos don't kill to eat (they are vegetarians, after all), but to protect their territory.

BELOW: getting the ferry to Janjanbureh.

– most conspicuously the handsome palmnut vulture and African fish eagle, the secretive African finfoot, flotillas of pelican, and a host of hornbills, barbets, shrikes, turacos, parrots and other woodland species – and the lush riverine setting really is fantastic.

Formerly closed to tourists, the CRT opened an exclusive bush camp called **Badi Mayo ⑳** ("River Monkeys") on the western river bank in 2006. Consisting of just four stilted furnished tents set on a tall laterite cliff overlooking the river, this camp is on a par with some of the best upmarket bush camps in East Africa, and it looks set to become *the* premier goal for short (ideally 2–3-night) upriver excursions from the coast. The highlight of any visit here is likely to be the boat trips, which are timed to coincide with chimp-feeding times, so that close-up sightings – and photographic opportunities – are guaranteed. A network of short guided walks out of camp offer great birdwatching opportunities.

Badi Mayo is set not in the national park but within the community-owned Nyassang Forest Park directly opposite. The community-orientated dimension to the project is revealed when you take a donkey cart to the village of Sembel Kunda, whose school and clinic are both funded by the CRT. Sembel Kunda is also home to the Gambia Horse and Donkey Trust, which helps educate locals to treat their working equines properly, thus improving farming productivity and the welfare of the animals.

Stella Brewer Marsden, the founder of all these projects, was awarded an OBE for her work for animal welfare in 2006. She died in January 2008 aged 56 and is buried at Badi Mayo. Her husband and sons will continue her work to ensure the long-term welfare of her chimpanzees.

Janjanbureh (Georgetown)

The oldest town in this part of Gambia, and the most popular with tourists, the sleepy port of **Janjanbureh ㉑** stands on an eponymous island in the middle of the Gambia River. Both the town and the island have been officially called Janjanbureh since 1995, but locals still tend to stick to the colonial names of **Georgetown** and **MacCarthy Island**. Coming from Banjul, the drive takes at least five hours whether you follow the north- or south-bank road (the former is a quicker and smoother drive, but the Barra Ferry invariably delays things by an hour or so). The island is linked to the north- and south-bank roads by vehicle ferries that usually cross every 15–20 minutes in either direction, and are seldom full.

Situated beyond the reach of ocean-going boats, Janjanbureh Island – then known as Lemaine Island – might periodically have served as a European trading post prior to the 19th century, but there is little evidence to support local claims it played a significant role in the slave trade. On the contrary, the town we know today dates to 1823, when Captain Alexander Grant, acting on behalf of the British crown some 16 years after it had abolished the slave trade, leased the island from the king of Kataba to create a settlement for freed slaves. The island was named after Sir Charles MacCarthy, the incumbent British governor to West Africa and a dedicated enforcer of aboli-

Recommended Restaurants and Bars on page 137

tion, and the fort and town established by Captain Grant were named after King George IV. The island-bound town was the most important administrative centre upriver of Banjul throughout the colonial era, as well as being the second-largest town anywhere in The Gambia. Even more than Banjul, however, Janjanbureh has suffered a sharp post-independence economic decline, and the latest population estimate of 7,500 places it outside the country's 15 largest towns.

Janjanbureh today is a genuine backwater, lethargic in mood, run-down in appearance and with a level of economic inactivity that creates a weekend atmosphere whatever day you actually visit. The town centre, a tight grid of dusty roads lined with colonial-era relics, is so compact it can easily be explored without a guide, but several willing youths will offer their services, and it may be wise to follow the path of least resistance. Several 19th-century architectural landmarks can be seen along Owen Street, among them an intact Creole-style wooden house that was originally built by the Jones family, one of the 200 liberated slaves brought to MacCarthy

Island in 1832, and a Methodist church constructed in the early 1830s under the Reverend William Fox. Other noteworthy buildings include the former Divisional Commissioner's residence, located on the western edge of town, and the nearby Armitage High School. This is the country's only boarding school, established in 1923 for the progeny of district chiefs, and many of its alumni achieved prominent government positions in the post-independence era.

The "slave house" in Janjanbureh was probably created after the abolition of slavery in the British colonies in 1807.

In recent years, overenthusiastic – or plain cynical – local guides have manufactured a set of tourist attractions that greatly exaggerate Janjanbureh's tenuous link with the slave trade. The impressive waterfront ruin of Fort George, built under Captain Grant to enforce abolition two decades after it had been enshrined under British law, is now touted as a former slave market, while a subterranean storeroom of a ruinous former warehouse has been converted retrospectively into

LEFT: the African fish eagle.
BELOW: admiring the birdlife.

EAT

There are a few eating options outside the camps *(see restaurants on page 137)*, as well as basic eateries clustered along the wharf area *(badala)*, close to the ferry terminal.

BELOW: nesting bird. **RIGHT:** local vegetation.

a slave dungeon, lit by flickering candles to enhance its sinister mood. Then there's the Freedom Tree, planted in front of the police station to replace the "original" in 2002, and subject of a legend similar to the one associated with the Freedom Flag at Albreda *(see page 88)*. Needless to say, the local guides are adept at taking financial advantage of any guilt induced in naive tourists by this parade of horrors.

There is no shortage of accommodation in Janjanbureh, though the two most alluring options both lie well outside the town centre. The more upmarket of these is **Bird Safari Camp**, which offers accommodation in standing tents and smart en suite bungalows on the eastern tip of Janjanbureh Island about 3km (2 miles) out of town. The camp has large gardens distinguished by a bustle of birdlife and the only swimming pool on the island, making it a great goal for a day walk even if you opt to stay close to town. Alternatively, **Janjang-Bureh Camp** is idyllically located in a patch of riverside forest rattling with green monkeys and birds in the village of Lamin Koto on the mainland directly opposite the island. It offers candlelit accommo-

dation in en suite circular mud-brick and whitewashed rondavels (round huts) overlooking the river. Just five minutes from Janjanbureh by pirogue, this camp also makes a great goal for a day trip, with a good chance of spotting monkeys in the gardens while you lunch, and the option of wandering about 1.5km (1 mile) back along the Kuntaur Road to see the Lamin Koto Stone Circle, the closest megalithic site to Janjanbureh.

Janjanbureh is a useful base from which to visit several attractions further afield, including the megalithic sites of Wassu and Ker Batch, or the River Gambia National Park, which is best reached by boat. Another site of local historical interest is the **Musa Molloh Mausoleum**, which lies at Keserah Kunda about 2km (1 mile) from the village of **Boraba** near the junction of the main south-bank road and the turn-off to Janjanbureh. Reputedly born a slave, Musa Molloh was an important leader of Fulani resistance in the late 19th century, when his influence extended over most of The Gambia as well as parts of southern Senegal and Guinea, and he played a largely successful diplomat double game with the

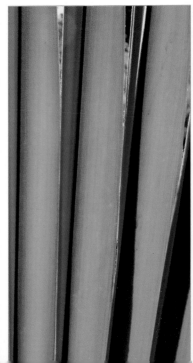

Recommended Restaurants and Bars on page 137

French and British. He died at **Kesereh Kunda** in 1931.

Boraba and Kesereh Kunda are also two of the four villages that have set aside a combined 2 sq km (¾ sq mile) of forest and palm-lined riverfront and Guinean savannah to form the new **Kunkilling and Tankandam Community Forest Park** ㉒ (tel: 990 8599; daily; charge; guides available), on the south bank 5km (3 miles) east of Janjanbureh. Serviced by five short eco-trails, this excellent community-based venture is home to all five primate species that occur naturally in The Gambia, including the lovely red colobus monkey, while other mammals seen with varying degrees of frequency include warthog, banded mongoose, bushbuck, Gambian sun squirrel, hippopotamus and West African manatee. The birdlife is outstanding. For dedicated twitchers, it is the only known Gambian locality for the rare Adamawa turtle dove, while less esoteric highlights include white-backed vulture, Pel's fishing owl, Baudouin's snake-eagle, African finfoot, shining-blue kingfisher and black-faced firefinch. Unlike in most government reserves, visitors are encouraged to walk at dusk and dawn, when wildlife is most active.

Eastern Gambia

East of Janjanbureh, the south-bank road continues towards Basse Santa Su through wild, relatively undulating country covered with tangled scrub and dry bush. A potential stop en route, **Bansang** ㉓ is a market town of 8,500 people that lies about 10km (6 miles) east of Janjanbureh, and has largely superseded it as regional economic hub. Remarkably, Bansang is the first point east of Banjul where the south-bank road more or less skirts the Gambia River, though you need to leave the main road for decent river views. Home to the largest hospital upriver of Farafenni, Bansang's compact town centre seems decidedly energetic after a couple of days in Janjanbureh, and there are a couple of adequate local hotels for those who want to enjoy the riverside location or to explore further.

A popular stop on ornithological tours, **Bansang Quarry** on the outskirts of town is famed for its breeding colony of red-throated bee-eater. Recently fenced by the Gambia Birding Group, the quarry is pock-marked with breeding holes used by at least 100 pairs of this spectacularly colourful bird, which is resident but most active during the rains. The birds often leave the roost to forage further afield during the day, so the best time to visit is towards sunset. Scattered pools often attract a varied selection of finches and other seed-eaters.

Established in 2005, the **Dobo Forest Park and Community Forest** ㉔ (tel: 567 6200; daily; charge) protects 1 sq km (⅓ sq mile) of forest and thicket adjacent to the oddly named village of Bush Town. It lies on the north bank directly opposite Bansang, to which it is connected by a regular passenger ferry. Best visited in the early morning or late afternoon, Dobo has a short walking trail, and English-speaking guides are available. Small though it is, the forest protects an impressive variety of mammals, ranging from bushbuck and warthog to red colobus monkey and Guinea baboon, and

The region is famous for its pottery, which has a distinctive red hue that echoes the colours of the surrounding laterite hills, and ranges from tiny clay pots, decorated with incisions or paint, to giant earthenware water containers.

BELOW: fishermen out on their pirogue.

hippos are sometimes seen in the river. More prolific still is the birdlife, which includes all 10 kingfisher species recorded in The Gambia, a variety of hornbills, flycatchers and parrots, and the rather scarce little green bee-eater and four-banded sandgrouse.

The north-bank road is longer than its south-bank counterpart, and inferior in condition, but the journey is more exciting and offers access to two notable historical sites. At **Karantaba Tenda**, 30km (18 miles) by road from Janjanbureh, the **Mungo Park Memorial** ㉕ is an obelisk marking the spot where its Scots namesake disembarked in 1804 on his fateful second expedition to locate the source of

the Niger. Another 30km (18 miles) past Karantaba Tenda, the road returns towards the Gambia River and the twin villages of **Kurau Kuto** and **Diabugu** ㉖ which host a concentration of 26 megalithic stone circles spread across four different sites. Finally, at **Yorobawal**, a side road connects by ferry to Basse Santa Su on the south bank.

In purely architectural terms, **Basse Santa Su** ㉗, more often referred to as plain "Basse", might easily be characterised as Janjanbureh revisited – yet another decaying colonial port whose riverfront is dotted with a few time-worn Victorian buildings. Basse, however, is refreshingly untainted by the aura of eco-

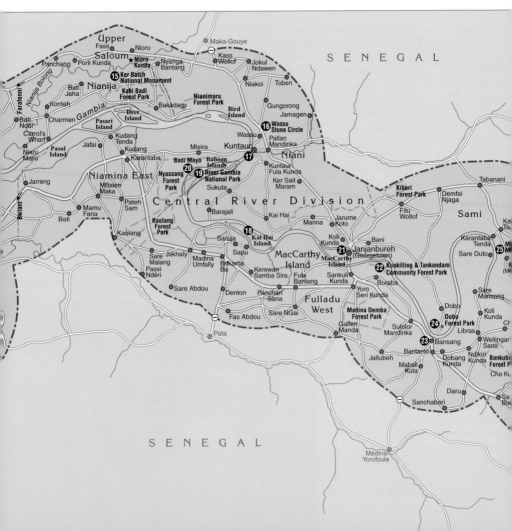

Recommended Restaurants and Bars on page 137

nomic stagnation that haunts Janjanbureh – on the contrary, the whole town comes across as one gigantic and rather chaotic market, its narrow streets spilling over with shops and stalls that sell all manner of imported and locally produced goods. Basse has strong trade links across the border with Senegal, and further afield into Guinea and Mauritania, and this combination of mixed cultural traditions and modern marketplace bustle make it the most emphatically African of all Gambian towns. Basse is a main depot for the local peanut and cotton trade, and its economic resurgence is reflected in a population surge from around 5,000 in 1983 to 18,000 in 2008.

Basse saw quite a bit of tourist development in the 1990s, but the deteriorating state of upcountry roads since the millennium has seen a reversal in this trend, as fewer tourists are prepared to drive all the way from the coast. The premier tourist facility is **Fulladu Camp**, which lies on the northern river bank facing the town centre, and has a similar feel to Tendaba or Janjang-Bureh camps, with clean bungalows and a large open-sided restaurant overlooking the river. In the town centre, the **Jem Hotel** is

The malachite kingfisher is one of the 10 recorded species of kingfishers in The Gambia.

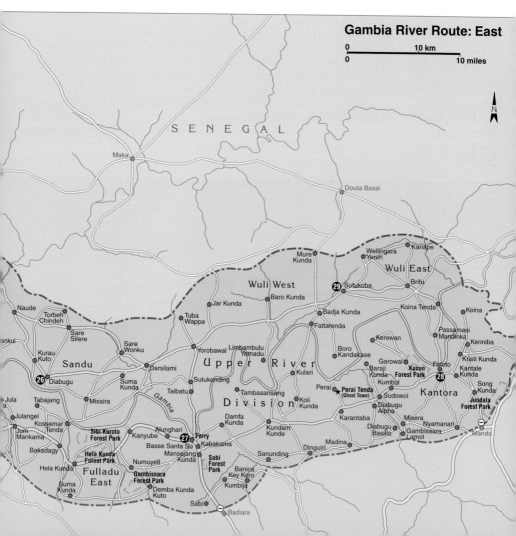

Gambia River Route: East

Monitor lizards are generally large reptiles with long necks, powerful tails and claws, and well-developed limbs. Almost all of them are carnivorous.

BELOW: children in Damfa Kunda, a village set between Basse and Sukutoba.

the best of an indifferent selection, while **Traditions** – formerly a restaurant set in one of the 19th-century trading houses on the riverfront – was in the process of reinventing itself as a hotel in 2008. Facilities include several banks, filling stations, supermarkets and one erratically functioning cyber café.

Basse is renowned among birdwatchers as the most reliable place to see the localised Egyptian plover, which are more or less resident along the muddy riverfront between Traditions and the main ferry jetty. Sightings are most frequent in the early morning between June and February. The best way to see more of the wildlife around Basse is to negotiate an afternoon boat ride with one of the pirogue owners who ferry passengers across the river. Green monkeys are numerous in the riverine forest, as are gigantic monitor lizards, while birders are in for a real treat, as the area supports several species that appear to be less common further west, including the beautiful blue-bellied roller

and the red-fronted and northern carmine bee-eaters that breed in the mudbanks.

The largest town east of Basse Santa Su is **Fatoto** ㉘, about 35km (20 miles) away on the rough and dusty south-bank road. A diversion off this road is the ghost town of Perai Tenda, where abandoned shops and colonial trading posts testify to the prosperity of early riverside trading ports. The much longer and even dustier north-bank road to Fatoto passes through **Sutukoba** ㉙ about 40km (25 miles) out of Basse. This is the ancient site of a large settlement and trading town which thrived in the early 15th century. It lies on the edge of the Djolof Empire's territory, and its old name means Great Sutuko. Excavations are under way in this historic area, north of which are the two hamlets of Gunjur Kuta and Gunjur Koto – one old and one comparatively new – located on the border with Senegal and noted for the traces found there of early civilisation. Twenty-four km (15 miles) further on, the road rejoins the Gambia River opposite Fatoto. The town has a groundnut collection factory and a ferry. To reach the Senegalese border, you would need to cover the last 10 miles (16km) of the river by canoe. ❑

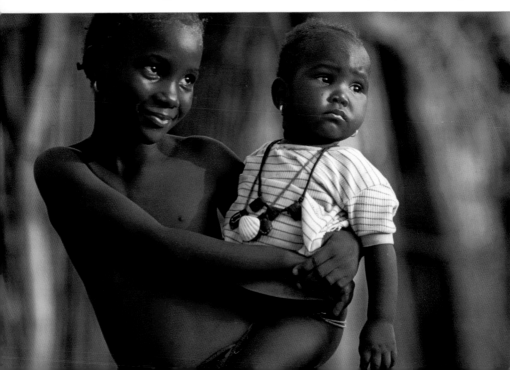

RESTAURANTS AND BARS

Restaurants

Prices for a main course per person:

$ = under US$8 (D160)
$$ = US$8–15 (D160–300)
$$$ = over US$15 (D300)

There aren't really any stand-alone tourist-oriented restaurants in this area. If you stay overnight, it is best to eat at your hotel, which will almost certainly rustle up a decent meal of chicken/fish and chips/rice with a few hours' notice. Alternatively, most towns have a scattering of local eateries serving very cheap Gambian dishes and stalls

selling filled baguettes and/or omelettes.

Farafenni
Eddie's Hotel and Restaurant
200 metres/yds west of the main circle. Tel: 573 5225 **$**
Assuming you have plenty of time on your hands, this is the best eatery on the Gambian portion of the Trans-Gambian Highway, which isn't saying much. If time is at a premium, head for one of the stalls around the market.

Tendaba
Tendaba Camp
Tel: 554 1024 **$$**
The setting is superior to the food, but the open-sided restaurant at The Gambia's most popular

upriver camp does serve adequate à la carte meals and a nightly buffet.

Janjanbureh
Bendula Bar
Owen Street **$**
Set behind the market, this cheap 'n' cheerful bar serves draught beer – a rarity upriver – and a few snacks and light meals (made to order, so expect at least one hour's wait).

Janjang-Bureh Lodge
North Bank. Tel: 567 6182 **$$**
The evening buffets at this peaceful riverfront retreat are well prepared, generously proportioned and include a good range of dishes. Lunch is à la carte, and well worth crossing the river for.

Basse Santa Su
Aminita's Café
Fatoto Road **$**
Close to the F&B Bar, this is probably the best local eatery in Basse, serving tasty Gambian and Sierra Leonese staples. The breakfast omelettes are good too, and the obliging woman owner can usually prepare Western-style dinners with a bit of notice.

Traditions
Basse Wharf. Tel: 566 8760 **$$**
A few years ago this was the best eatery in Basse, but now the emphasis is on developing it as a guesthouse. All the same, with a couple of hours' notice, the obliging management will prepare a tasty chicken or fish dish.

BELOW: preparing a fish stew in a traditional cooking pot.

SENEGAL

Senegal is a scenic and cultural mix of stunning coastlines, lush mangrove-lined creeks and grand colonial architecture

Senegal is 20 times larger than The Gambia, and boasts a great deal more scenic and cultural variety – though beaches, predictably, do form the *raison d'être* of the national tourist industry. We explore Senegal over nine chapters, starting at **Dakar and the Cap Vert**. Dakar ranks among the most vibrant and compelling of African capitals, and its lively markets and nightlife provide a wonderful introduction to contemporary Senegalese culture. Facing the capital, but totally different in mood, **Île de Gorée** is a sleepy former colonial outpost whose shape has changed little since the 19th century.

Heading north, all the way to the Mauritanian border, the former capital of **Saint-Louis**, set on a small island in the Senegal River Mouth, comes across as the perfect hybrid between Dakar and Gorée. Steeped in history and studded with grand colonial architectural relics, Saint-Louis also has a lively restaurant scene and nightlife that place it squarely in the 21st century. By contrast, the **Senegal River Route** explores an area steeped in traditional culture, ranging from the curvaceous adobe architecture of Matam and Île à Morfil to the harsh swathes of semi-desert inhabited by colourfully robed Tukulor herders around Bakel.

The country's main tourist hub is the **Petite Côte**, the string of beach resorts that runs along the short sandy stretch of coastline southward from Dakar to Joal via Saly Portugal and Mbour. Further south, the labyrinthine **Siné-Saloum Delta**, a wilderness of mangrove-lined creeks at the mouth of the Siné and Saloum rivers, is particularly popular with game fishermen and birdwatchers.

The **Central Interior** has a haunting quality to its vast baobab-studded plains, and the holy city of Touba and ancient stone circles near Kaolack are worthwhile goals for adventurous travellers. Even more untamed in spirit, **Southeast Senegal** is dominated by Niokolo-Koba, the country's largest national park, and it's also an important centre of traditional animist cultures. Finally, the lush **Casamance** – all but isolated from the rest of the country by The Gambia – is practically a destination in its own right, with its rich Diola culture, lovely traditional villages, and some of the finest beaches anywhere in West Africa. ❏

PRECEDING PAGES: the pelicans in the Parc National des Oiseaux du Djoudj.
LEFT AND ABOVE: welcome to Senegal.

Senegal

0   50 km
0   50 miles

ATLANTIC
OCEAN

Rosso
Senegal
Thillé
Boubakar
Podor
Guédé
Ga
Sa
Nd

Parc National
des Oiseaux
du Djoudj N 2
Rosso-
Sénégal
Dagana
Ndiayène

Richard
Toll
Keur Mor Ibra
(Souiléne)

Ross-
Bethio
Lac de
Guiers
Diaglé
S a i n t - L o

N'Gnith
Niassant
Mbidi

Ndiol
Yamané
Male

Saint-Louis
Bowdé
Doudal
Wéndou
Tiengôli

Parc National de la
Langue de Barbarie
M'Pal
Tessékré
Forage
La

N'diébène
Rao
K. Momar
Sarr

Léona
N 2
Négue
NdiayèH ne

Sag
Louga
Dik Do
Poram

Toundé Malèye
Koki
Mouye
Yang
Yang
Duro
Séno

Lompoul
Guéoul
Mouk
Mouk
Doundodji

Diokoul
Kébémèr
Tiamène
Ndiagne
Boulal
Dara
N 3
Linguère
Belka

Fas Boye
Sagata
Touba Mérina
Sagata
L o u g a
Barkédji
Diou

Ndandé
Sam Yabal
Tiargni
Lindé
Samali

M'Boro
N 2
Mékhé
Darou
Marnane
Darou-
Mousti
Touba
Bélef
Afé
S E N

Noto Gouye Diama
Baba-Garage
Véling

Kayar
Tivaouane
Gawane
Ndindi
Sival
Tiél
Kh

Pikine
Maljke
Thies
Kbombole
Ndoula
Mbaké
Touba
Sadip
Gassane
Ranch
de Doli
Patakour

Dakar
Rufisque
T h i è s
Diourbel
Kaël
Taif
Kolobane
Mbo

Bambey
Touba
Mboul
Mbar

Fissel
Diourbel
Mbabane
Loumbol

Popenguine
Somone
Ngayokhém
Gossas
Ndiène
Lagane
Bondié
Ndioum
Guènt
Ribe
Escal

Saly-Portugal
N 2
F a t i c k
Somb
Gagnik
Mbos
Guènt
Pate
E

Mbour
Fatick
Gandiaye
Guinguinea

Pointe-Sarène
Nguéniène
Bifkelane
Kaffrine

Mbodiène
Diofior
Kaolack
N 1

Joal-Fadiouth
Foundiougne
Passi
Mbelbouk
Niahène
Kdurnp

Palmarin
N 5
K a o l a c k
Diokoul
Kour

Djifer
Sakone
Ndofane
N'Ganda
Ndia
Ba

Toubacouta
Wak
N'Gouna
Nioro
du Rip
Kaymor
Kau-ur

Parc National
du Delta
du Saloum
Prokhane
Sotokoi
Kuidang
Kuntuar
River
Gambia N.P.
Janjanbareh

Karang
Nimn
National
Park
Nia Kunda
Farafenni
Bansa

Bakau
Fajara
Kerewan
Salikene

Serekunda
Banjul
Kiang West
National Park
Kwinella
Soma

Tujering
N 4

Tiptinto
Gambia
Tankon
Dialaba
Diéri
Soulabali

Gunjur
Brikama
Sibanor
Bwiam
Bessi

Kartung
K o l d a
Sa
Bo

Diouloulou
Bounkiling
Kandiadiou

Kabiline
Diaroumé
Saré
Bidji
Diana
Malari
Kolda
Ca

Kafountine
Badiana
Baila
Sindian
N 4
Soungnougnou

Z i g u i n c h o r
Marasassoum
Diendé
Diareng
Karantaba
Sandinier
N 6
SaréYoba
Dièga

Balingor
Bignona
Sédhiou
Saré
Ndiaye

Tionk Essil
N 4
N 6
Tanaf

Diakène
Mlomp
Ziguinchor
Goudomp
Samine
Escale
Barro
Farim
Conte

Diembéring
Siganar
São
Dominigos
GUINE

Cap Skirring
Parc National de la
Basse-Casamance
Cacheu
Bissora
Olossato
Mansaba
BISSA

Kabrousse
Varela
Cacheu
Bachille
Gebac

DAKAR AND THE CAP VERT

Dakar ranks among the most vibrant and compelling of African capitals, and its lively markets and nightlife provide a wonderful introduction to contemporary Senegalese culture

Main attractions
PLACE DE L'INDÉPENDANCE
CATHÉDRALE DU SOUVENIR AFRICAIN
MUSÉE THÉODORE MONOD D'ART AFRICAIN
GRANDE MOSQUÉE
PARC NATIONAL DES ÎLES DE LA MADELEINE
LAC ROSE

Dakar is not merely the capital city of Senegal. This vibrant and cosmopolitan city of 2.5 million people is also the country's commercial and economic hub, the site of its most important seaport and airport, and its very social and cultural pulse, a meeting point not only of African and European cultures, but also of the great many different ethnic groups and religious sects that inhabit the vast Senegalese interior. Little wonder, then, that Dakar has been dubbed the Paris of Africa, a label that rightly reflects its elevated status within Senegal and throughout West Africa, yet could mislead first-time visitors into expecting something a little less uncompromisingly African than the actuality. For Dakar, despite its long links with France and rich colonial architectural heritage, has an energy that is emphatically and unmistakably African, providing an exciting, occasionally daunting but always fascinating introduction to Senegal, or indeed the whole of West Africa.

Dakar ❶ lies at the southern end of the Cap Vert, a wedge-shaped peninsula of volcanic origin that terminates at Pointe des Almadies, the most westerly landfall in Africa. As early as 1444, the Portuguese navigator Dinis Dias landed at Pointe des Almadies and christened it Cabo Verde ("Green Cape") on his pioneering voyage south of the Senegal River. At this time, the peninsula was scattered with several small Lébou fishing villages, several of which are still in existence today. Over the next four centuries, the focus of European activities in this part of Senegal was not Cap Vert itself but Gorée Island, which lies in the sheltered bay offshore of present-day Dakar. Indeed, the mainland saw little in the way of permanent European settlement prior to 1840, when a few warehouses were constructed by French traders at Rufisque.

The name Dakar is a French bastardisation of Ndakarou, the Wolof name of the mainland village that originally stood on the same site. Founded in the early 17th century, Ndakarou prospered as a

LEFT: guarding the Palais Présidentiel.
BELOW: taking a dip in the lagoon.

Dakar

0   500 m
0   500 yds

esult of its proximity to Gorée, whose traders it supplied with food, drinking water and other fresh produce. As a result, Ndakarou practically selected itself as the site of the capital of the Lébou Republic, a polity formed in 1795 when the people of Cap Vert revolted against Cayor rule under the breakaway leadership of the Islamic Diop family. It was also the most obvious location when a French military outpost was established on Cap Vert by Governor Faidherbe in 1857. Under Faidherbe, Lébou was effectively annexed to France, but the colonisers didn't interfere much in its domestic politics, and the Serigne (king) of Ndakarou is officially recognised as its traditional leader to this day.

Renamed Dakar, the nascent city was soon earmarked as a centre of development by the colonial authorities. By 1885, its deep harbour was serviced by a large jetty and other port facilities, and had also become the southern terminus for the telegraph and railway lines to Saint-Louis. Dakar was incorporated into the French commune of Gorée in 1872, but was recognised as a full commune in its own right 15 years later, and it replaced

Saint-Louis as the capital of French West Africa in 1902. The city's importance as the main regional transport and economic hub was further consolidated in 1923, with the completion of the railway

Waving the flag for Senegal.

line connecting it to Bamako (Mali). Its status came full circle in 1929, when the increasingly sidelined commune of Gorée was disbanded and became part of Dakar.

As the colonisers built up Dakar, so the city came to represent French power and influence over the whole of West Africa. As a result, the city centre still possesses an impressive collection of colonial edifices, though unlike Saint-Louis or even Gorée, this French architectural legacy persists as a small enclave within a sprawling modern city. At the start of the 20th century, the population of Dakar was fewer than 20,000, but the post-World War II boom had increased that figure to 300,000 by 1960. Today, as with most other African capitals, Dakar suffers from serious overcrowding as more and

BELOW:
a colourful way
to travel in Dakar.

Fresh fruit in abundance from the many markets dotted around the city centre.

BELOW:
descaling fish
at Marché Kermel.

more rural dwellers migrate towards the city in search of elusive employment. Recent estimates place the population of Dakar at slightly more than one million, while the greater Dakar metropolitan area, inclusive of Pikine, supports at least 2.5 million people.

Central Dakar

The obvious place to begin a tour of Dakar is the large oblong **Place de l'Indépendance** Ⓐ, which has been the central point of the city ever since it was a village 150 years ago. Most of the banks and airline offices are located in or near this square. Contrasting with modern multi-storey blocks such as the Hôtel de l'Indépendance on the western edge of the square and the Sofitel Teranga in the southeast corner are traditional French structures such as the marble War Memorial, the Chamber of Commerce and the Foreign Ministry (in colonial times the law courts).

To the east of the Place de l'Indépendance, the leaf-shaded **Avenue Albert-Sarraut** leads down towards the sea at the Pointe de Dakar. The end of the avenue is marked by the tall ochre-and-brown bank building designed by the celebrated architect Goudiaby. Beside it, set back from the avenue, is the large modern **Novotel** which enjoys panoramic views over the sea to the island of Gorée. In the late afternoon the Avenue Sarraut buzzes with life as housewives do their shopping at the supermarkets or at the circular **Marché Kermel** Ⓑ a block to the north. The cool dark bar of the **Hôtel de la Croix du Sud** or the leafy courtyard of the Korean **Restaurant Le Séoul** a little further along are good places to stop for refreshments.

Running west from Place de l'Indépendance, **Avenue Pompidou** Ⓒ (formerly Avenue Ponty and still widely referred to by this name) runs up to the crossroad by the big neo-Sudanese-style **Marché Sandaga** Ⓓ *(see page 152)*. Formerly the heart of the French colonial shopping and business district, Avenue Pompidou is rather run-down nowadays, but it remains a hive of downmarket commercial activity, lined with small dimly lit shops and populated by an occasionally overwhelming cast of beggars, hustlers, pickpockets and street vendors selling everything from cola nuts to digital watches. Avenue Pompidou is no longer the nightlife hub it used to be, with much of the action having

Recommended Restaurants and Bars on pages 160–1

ing relocated to suburbs such as Point E and Les Almadies, but a lining of restaurants, coffee shops, bars, jazz clubs and cinemas survive as seedy ghosts of its halcyon days. If you want to explore this part of town, be warned that Avenue Pompidou and Marché Sandaga together form the main pickpocketing and bag-snatching hotspot in central Dakar, so carry nothing more than the cash you need.

Around Avenue Pompidou, mainly to the south, is a grid pattern of side streets containing many pleasant stuccoed colonial buildings with balconies or interior courtyards, and bougainvillea and other climbing plants draped over the walls. In the early evening, many Dakarois take a stroll along Avenue Pompidou to window-shop, regularly stopping to chat with acquaintances or to have a drink in one of the French-style café-bars with terraces opening onto the pavement. The biggest crossroads on this road is with **Avenue du Président Lamine-Gueye**, which leads southward from Sandaga Market to the **Place de Soweto**, and is similarly popular for an evening stroll. On this street one may also find kneeling worshippers spilling over from the small mosque on the corner of **Rue El Hadj Assane Ndaye**.

West of the Sandaga Market junction, Avenue Pompidou becomes **Avenue André-Peytavin**, and passes a large compound containing two-storey colonial buildings with wide shaded balconies running all the way round the four sides of the first floor. These are now occupied by various government departments. The avenue ends at the cliff edge overlooking the wide bay of the **Anse des Madeleines**. Turning right, one enters the long, sweeping **Route de la Corniche Ouest**, which leads out of the city centre to the northwestern suburbs past Soumbédioune. Turning left, one enters the **Boulevard de la République** which runs back into the city centre, not quite parallel with Avenue Pompidou, emerging towards the east of the peninsula on **Avenue Léopold-Sédar-Senghor** about 500 metres/yards south of Place de l'Indépendance. The Boulevard contains the **Théâtre National Daniel Sorano** ⓔ,

Street sign for Avenue Léopold-Sédar-Senghor, Senegal's first ever president.

LEFT: Place de Soweto. **BELOW:** local kora musician.

A Presidential Guard relaxes off-duty.

BELOW: the Cathédrale du Souvenir Africain.

Senegal's major centre for the performing arts, where ballet, music and drama are presented throughout the year.

Further east along Boulevard de la République is the Roman Catholic **Cathédrale du Souvenir Africain** . An imposing edifice holding 2,000 worshippers, the cathedral has within its precincts a large garden and an elementary school. It was built in 1929 in a mixture of styles, with two towers reminiscent of minarets, a great pseudo-Byzantine dome and a massive monumental façade. Continuing east, one comes upon the great wrought-iron gates of the **Palais Présidentiel** at the T-junction formed with Avenue Léopold-Sédar-Senghor at the end of the boulevard. The gates are guarded by the red-uniformed Gardes Présidentiels, who do not object to being photographed. The palace itself is a majestic white mansion, green-tiled and built in 1907, set in a lovely garden with the ocean as a backdrop.

South of the Plateau

Having walked the above circuit of the **Plateau** – the central and oldest part of Dakar – you will have noted that the simple grid pattern is easy to get to grip with. Almost opposite the Presidential Palace is a massive 10-storey block housing a considerable number of government functions. This edifice, known universally as *le building*, commands wonderful view of the peninsula and the surrounding sea from its roof terrace, and it is possible to obtain permission to go up to take advantage of this fact. Proceeding south from the Presidential Palace along Avenue Léopold-Sédar-Senghor you first pass the main hospital and, following west as the road becomes the **Avenue Nelson-Mandela** (formerly Avenue Courbet), you enter the Place de Soweto (formerly Place Tascher).

Overlooking this large circular place is the modern building of the Assemblée Nationale and beside it the neo-Sudanese style **Musée Théodore Monod d'Art Africain** (tel: 33 825 9890; daily 8am–12.30pm and 2–6.30pm; charge). Founded in 1938 and known as the musée de l'IFAN until 2007, this is a "must" for anybody with an interest in traditional African arts and cultures, housing a limited but superb collection of ethnographic displays focusing on the Bassari and

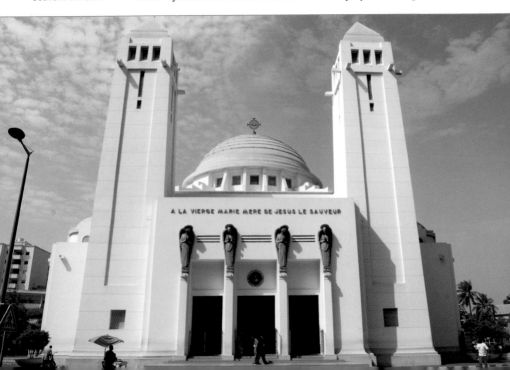

her tribes of the southeast, as well the ogon of neighbouring Mali. It also has ood collections of masks and musical struments from all around West Africa, d is used as a venue for the fascinating ak'Art Biennale exhibition, which displays art by contemporary international d African artists.

Facing the museum is the Avenue Pasur, which passes the **Hôpital Le Dan- c**, the **Institut Pasteur** and the **British mbassy** as it heads south towards the o of **Cap Manuel** ❶ with its powerful ghthouse (which may be visited for nother splendid view). Returning north owards the Place de l'Indépendance by e seafront route, you travel along the inding **Route de la Corniche Est**. Be arned that this road has something of a eputation for muggings by day or by ight, and it is wiser not to walk it alone.

Passing **Pointe Bernard** ❶ and the ttle bay of **Anse Bernard** with its good each, you continue along the rocky ceanfront, looking across at tranquil orée Island *(see pages 163–7)*, to the ituristic low concrete buildings of the **estaurant Lagon I** and associated **ôtel Lagon II**.

North of Place de l'Indépendance

Shaded by its tall trees, **Allées Robert- Delmas** leads north from the Place de l'Indépendance, passing the 1914 colonial **Hôtel de Ville** and the **Poste Principale**, to the port on the **Boulevard de la Libération**. To the left is the magnificent colonial railway station with its vaulted brick façade ornamented by coloured tiles and its great canopied interior. To the right, the boulevard goes past the docks to the end of **Pointe de Dakar**, with its half-finished sea wall protruding into the Atlantic. The road to the port passes the ferry jetty for Gorée Island.

The port of Dakar is the largest and best-equipped between Morocco in the north and the Côte d'Ivoire in the south. It was the first major port in West Africa and an automatic stopover for ships on the way south from Europe, and today it hosts extensive oil, groundnut and fish depots and several great cranes. About 1km (½ mile) northwest along **Avenue de l'Arsenal**, which runs parallel to the railway lines, **Gare Routière Pompiers** is the closest bush-taxi station to the city centre, despatching a steady stream of

Contemporary sculpture on view at the Dak'Art Biennale.

BELOW: a container ship leaving the port of Dakar.

Markets of Dakar

The numerous markets that stud the city centre and suburbs showcase West African culture at its most lively and flamboyant

The city's markets are easy and safe enough to visit independently, though first-time visitors to Africa prefer the company of a local guide, and the presence of pickpockets and other petty thieves makes it advisable to carry as little as possible into any market – ideally just enough cash to see you through the day, tucked away discreetly in a tight pocket rather than an easily snatched bag.

A good starting point is the **Marché Sandaga**, at the crossroads at the west end of Avenue Pompidou. This is the city's largest and busiest market, a warren of shoe shops, cloth-sellers and tailors, fishwives cutting up great silver-scaled *thiofs* and butchers hacking at slabs of fly-covered meat, stalls selling music CDs (many pirated or bootlegged) and vendors selling illicit DVDs. Craft-lovers will enjoy leather work, ready-made or made to measure, pottery, rush and basketwork and *bou-bous* or the cloth lengths to make them (known as *pagnes*).

Also very central, **Marché Kermel** off Avenue Sarraut is housed in a beautiful circular building rebuilt in 1997 to mimic the 19th-century original, which was razed in a fire. Less overtly African in feel than Sandaga, this market is heavily frequented by expatriate Europeans. Its speciality is flowers – a gloriously colourful profusion, offered by women whose dress and demeanour are often scarcely less colourful. It is also reasonably good for craft objects, though prices tend to be slightly higher than elsewhere.

Two more specialised markets in the city centre are worth a look: the **Marché Touareg** in front of the Hôtel de l'Indépendance is an excellent place to buy colourful Malian jewellery, while the **Marché Malien** on Avenue Faidherbe sells traditional items used by lovelorn Senegalese women to lure their desired one.

Further out of town, in the Médina near the Grande Mosquée, the **Marché Tilène** is on Avenue Blaise-Diagne, opposite the Medissa School complex. The least Westernised of Dakar's markets, Tilène mainly sells fresh produce and manufactured household items, but it also has a fascinating traditional medicine section, where charms, *gris-gris* and magic love potions are the main stock in trade, though browsing among the stalls you may also find monkey paws, ground antelope horns, wings of owls and much more besides. About 2km (1 mile) further, on Avenue C.A. Bamba, the **Marché des HLM** is the best place to buy traditional and imported fabrics, which can be tailored to conform to the latest Senegalese fashions.

West of the Médina, reached from the Plateau via the Corniche Ouest, with its joggers (and occasionally muggers), the village of **Soumbédioune** is the site of the busiest fishing beach within the confines of suburban Dakar. Every evening the beach fills at five o'clock with the returning boats, and the housewives come to buy the day's catch for their evening meal. Between the beach and the Muslim cemetery is the **Village Artisanal** (craft market). This complex of up to 100 stands, created in 1961, is where many of Dakar's finest craftsmen – carvers, leatherworkers, weavers and tailors – work and sell their wares. ❏

LEFT: fruit-seller inside Marché Kermel.
ABOVE: the distinctive entrance to Marché Kermel.

vehicles to suburban Dakar and places further afield. The Gare Routière is usually a seething mass of travellers, drivers, vehicles in various states of dilapidation, and a thousand vendors with trays of drinks, oranges, cigarettes and virtually everything else a traveller might require on their journey.

Further out still is the big portside industrial zone and an adjacent district of HLMs, the French-system mass low-rent housing units. Immediately northwest of the Plateau district, on the **Avenue Malik-Sy**, is the **Grande Mosquée**  of Dakar. Built in 1964 with financial assistance from the late King Hassan of Morocco, the building is inspired by the Mohammed V mosque in Rabat and in the Maghreb style. It is possible to climb its tall minaret every day except Friday, when the mosque is open only to Muslims for prayer.

In the lee of the Grande Mosquée, to its northwest, lies the "African quarter", as it once was, of the **Médina**. This tightly packed district of low plaster houses set in a square grid of streets was built in the 1920s to house the survivors of the plague epidemic of 1914–15. By day a bustle of vendors and craftsmen in little workshops, the Médina at night buzzes with Dakarois walking the darkened streets to meet, talk and visit the little blue- or red-lit *dibiterie* cafés or rudimentary bar/discos. Two blocks from the Grande Mosquée is the great concrete **Stade Iba-Mar-Diop**, where various sports take place. This used to be the place to watch traditional wrestling over the weekend, but these days it is mostly used to hold football matches.

The closest substantial tract of greenery to the city centre, about 5km (3 miles) further north off the Route de Rufisque, is the **Parc Zoologique et Forestier de Hann** ❷ (tel: 33 832 3875; daily; charge), which extends over some 60 hectares (150 acres) of woodland and reclaimed marsh between the suburb of **Hann** and the **Pointe de Bel-Air**, the most easterly point on the Cap Vert Peninsula. Founded in 1903, the park consists of two parts, of which the 8-hectare (20-acre) zoological garden, with its caged lions, leopards,

tigers and other indigenous and exotic mammals, is the better-publicised but more superficial. By contrast, the arboretum, with 300 plant species and an even larger area given over to forest and other natural vegetation, is a lovely place for a gentle weekend stroll, particularly for those with an interest in birds.

Cap Vert: the southwest shore

The Route de la Corniche Ouest leads westward from the city centre to the suburb of Soumbédioune, renowned for its beachfront fishing market, and the office for the **Parc National des Îles de la Madeleine** ❸ (tel: 33 821 8182; daily 8am–6pm; charge). Here, pirogue trips can be arranged to cross the short stretch of sea to Senegal's smallest national park, which contains two offshore volcanic outcrops and their resident breeding colonies of marine birds. A small bay on the sea-facing side of the larger Île de Sarpan provides a safe landing point and has a small secluded beach. Sarpan is also known as Île des Serpents (Snake Island), and, while snakes are present, this moniker probably results from a mis-

Freshly baked baguettes for sale.

BELOW:
the richly decorated exterior of the Grande Mosquée.

A detail from a contemporary mural.

hearing of Sarpan, the name of a French soldier who was detained there after being convicted of a misdemeanour. From the bay, a footpath leads uphill to a viewpoint overlooking the small craggy Îles de la Madeleine, their guano-streaked cliffs a squawking mass of great cormorants. One can follow the footpath around the full circumference of Île de Sarpan, with its unusual cover of stunted and misshapen "dwarf" baobab trees. Many different birds can be seen circling above the cliffs, ranging from the glorious red-billed tropic bird, notable for its outrageously long-tail streamers, to pairs of osprey hawking above the ocean. Diving trips to the islands can be arranged through the Océanium Dakar (tel: 33 822 2441; www.oceanium.org).

About 4km (2½ miles) northwest of the city centre along Av Cheikh-Anta-Diop, the prosaically named suburb of Point-E is the site of the **Université Cheikh Anta Diop** (UCAD) ❹. The largest and most prestigious institute of higher education in Francophone Africa, UCAD has its roots in a medical school that was founded by the French colonists in 1918. This was extended to be a public university attached to the University of Paris in 1957, and was known as the University of Dakar until 1987, when it was renamed in honour of an eminent Senegalese professor whose research into the antecedents and early social and political structures of African peoples were of profound influence. Today, it is attended by some 60,000 students. Over recent years, Point-E and the area around the university have emerged as something of a hotspot for nightlife, with a range of clubs and bars that eclipse their counterparts around Avenue Pompidou if not in quantity then certainly in quality. Among the livelier nightspots here, **Just 4 You** hosts quality live Senegalese music almost every night, the **Alizé Club** is the place to dance to boisterous local *mbalax* music, while **Pen'Art** tends to be more jazz-orientated.

Further out of town than the university, the **Mermoz** district is named after the famous French aviator who flew the Atlantic from Senegal in the 1920s. Nearby **Ouakam** ❺, one of the oldest Lébou villages on the peninsula, is the site of a busy fishing beach complete with colourful pirogues, as well as the

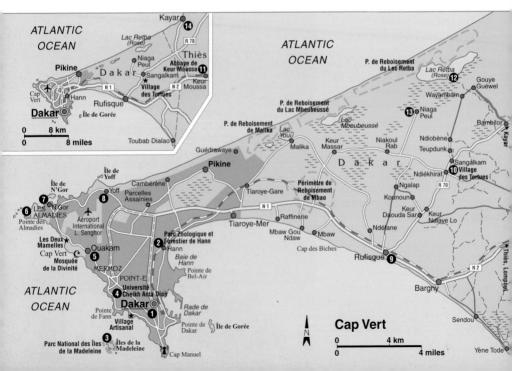

magnificently futuristic **Mosquée de la Divinité**, whose green-capped twin minarets rise impressively between the cliffs and the ocean. The cliffs that hem in Ouakam's beach and mosque are the southern slopes of **Les Deux Mamelles** ("The Two Teats"), a craggy pair of volcanic cones that rise to an altitude of 105 metres (350ft) to form the highest point on the Cap Vert peninsula, if not anywhere along the Senegalese coast. The twin cones offer great views over the rest of Dakar, and the taller and more northerly peak is the site of the most powerful lighthouse on the Atlantic coast of Africa, the **Phare des Mamelles** (daily; free), an attractive whitewashed colonial building constructed in 1864 and extended in 1911.

West of Ouakam, the coastal road skirts the southern end of the runway of Senghor International Airport before emerging at the relatively trendy and well-to-do suburb of **Les Almadies**. The suburb terminates at **Pointe des Almadies ❻**, the most westerly tip of the African continent, protected by a series of jagged outcrops that have caused a great number of ships to come

to grief as they attempted to circumnavigate the point. The origin of the name "Almadies" is somewhat obscure: it may refer to the bark canoes used by the local Lébou fishermen at the time of the first European landfall, but could also derive from the Portuguese *Alma Dia* (Day of the Soul).

The 1km (½-mile) long western shore of Pointe des Almadies now falls within the grounds of two chain resort hotels. The **Club Med Pointe des Almadies** contains two restaurants, a large swimming pool, a nightclub and the usual beach and sports facilities, and the southern tip of its beach is *the* most westerly point on Cap Vert, for those collecting geographic landmarks. North of this, the plush **Le Méridien President Hotel** extends across almost 20 hectares (50 acres) of lush green grounds, which incorporate a nine-hole golf course that runs down to the beach on two sides. As with Point-E, this part of Cap Vert is well endowed with restaurants and nightclubs.

Pointe des Almadies, the most westerly tip of the African continent.

BELOW: the Mosquée de la Divinité boasts a great sea view.

Cap Vert: the north shore

A short distance east of Pointe des Almadies is the traditional Lébou fishing village of **N'Gor** ❼, with its maze of houses, small mosque and nearby naval station. The fine sandy beach here, protected by the eponymous island, is reputedly one of the safest on the Cap Vert peninsula for swimming. Several small hotels line the beach, and for many tourists this is a far more attractive option than staying in Dakar itself. Even more relaxed are the landward beaches on **Île de N'Gor**, which lies about 500 metres/yards offshore, and can easily be reached from the mainland beach by pirogue.

Continuing east along the coast from N'Gor, **Yoff** ❽ is one of the oldest Lébou fishing villages on the Cap Vert peninsula, reputedly founded in the early 15th century. Home to the **Centre de Conférences de Dakar**, with its bold modern triangular buildings, Yoff is also the site of the **Aéroport International Léopold Senghor**, the main port of entry for fly-in tourists to Senegal. Today, it would be a stretch to call this bustling settlement of around 50,000 people a village, but it does retain a strong sense of community,

thanks in large part to its almost exclusively Lébou population, most of whom belong to the Layène brotherhood founded by the marabout Seydina Limamou Laye in 1884.

The **Mausolée Layène**, where Said Limamou Laye was interred after his death in 1909, has subsequently been expanded to become the large and attractive domed Grande Mosquée that dominates Yoff beachfront. It attracts pilgrims from all around the country, and is especially busy on Friday afternoons, when the Layène followers that comprise the entire population of Yoff come to pray there in their distinctive white robes. Yoff's rubbish-strewn beach is also the site of a busy fishing market, centred about 1km (½ mile) west of the mosque. The beach has long been associated with the traditional *ndeup* ceremony, a Lébou animist ritual that appeases bad spirits and, though fascinating to witness, is very unpredictable when it comes to timing.

A few kilometres further east, **Cambérène** is another traditional Lébou village with strong Layène presence. An important Layène mosque was established here in 1914 by Seydina Issa Rohou Laye.

Pirogues of Senegal

On the formerly French parts of the West African coast, canoes are referred to as pirogues. The smaller boats usually consist of a long, narrow, double-prowed dugout carved in one piece from the buoyant wood of the baobab tree, and are used to ply rivers and creeks. The larger pirogues, drawn up on the beaches as one travels along the coastal road north of Dakar, are carved-built. Almost every beach and bay from Cap Skirring to Saint-Louis sports fleets of these colourfully decorated boats lining the high-water mark.

The boats are the product of generations of craftsmanship and design. Constructed from an easily carved red wood similar to teak, the main frame consists of planks warped to a flat centre board which defines the pirogue's narrow, high-sided profile. In length, the traditional pirogue can vary from 2 to 20 metres (65ft), and its width generally accommodates side-by-side paddlers with a central well for net and catch.

At each end of the craft a curious prow gives the pirogue its knife-like shape, and the entire construction is fashioned by a team working with hand adzes and finished by bringing it up to a smooth surface ready for paintwork.

To watch the laborious work of the boat-builders on the Senegal coast is like watching the progress of a hand-built car. Working under an awning of woven palm thatch, the foreman directs the precise measurements and guides each adze stroke until the form is perfect. Often broken glass is used to prepare the surface for its final coat of paint. Blues, black, patriotic greens, yellows and reds are applied in layers to a stylised pattern, along with exquisitely painted crescents, stars, diamonds, hearts and flowers, and the names of saints, either Christian or Muslim, are inscribed in Roman or Arabic script, often with intricate scrollwork – and finally the proud beak of the bowsprit is often adorned with a Senegalese flag.

he eldest son of Seydina Limamou Laye nd his successor as caliph, after an epidemic swept through the original Layène community at Yoff. The beachfront mosque constructed here is clearly modelled on its counterpart at Yoff, and the nearby mausoleum of Seydina Issa Rohou Laye attracts numbers of pilgrims on important Islamic holy days.

Further east along the north coast of the peninsula, a number of new suburbs and districts have sprung up to cater for the overspill from the burgeoning city, and most support a more diverse ethnic mix than traditional Lébou villages such as Yoff and Cambérène. **Patte d'Oie** (Goose's Foot), **Parcelles Assainies** and **Guédiawaye** are sprawling areas of mostly new housing catering mainly to working-class migrants from elsewhere in Senegal. However, the most telling example of the rapid demographic changes around Dakar is **Pikine**, which lies to the east of Dakar, on what would have been thinly populated Lébou frontier territory in the 19th century, when a boundary wall of sand and clay was built to repel invaders. Founded in 1952 to house former Dakarois residents who

were relocated to make way for new developments, Pikine mushroomed from out of the sand in the late 1960s and now supports a population estimated at around 1 million – as many as Dakar itself.

East of Dakar

The first major town along the RN1/RN2 east of Dakar is **Rufisque** ❾, which lies on the south coast of Cap Vert about 20km (12 miles) from the capital as the crow flies. The site of a Wolof village since the 16th century, Rufisque – a bastardisation of the Portuguese *Rufisco* – also predates Dakar as a colonial port and settlement. Settled by French merchants from Saint-Louis and Gorée in 1840, the town was annexed to the French colony of Senegal in 1859, when a fort was built and work began on laying out the commercial and administrative waterfront, which has changed little in shape since the 1860s. Throughout the 19th century, Rufisque was an important centre for peanut-processing, and it was one of the initial four *communes* (along with Gorée, Dakar and Saint-Louis) represented in the French National Assembly in 1887. Today, though largely overshadowed by

The beachfront mosque at Yoff.

BELOW:
Yoff is a Layène pilgrimage site.

TIP

The best time to visit the Abbaye de Keur Moussa is on Sunday morning, in time to catch the 10am mass, which is sung to the accompaniment of traditional Senegalese instruments such as the *kora* – a unique and very powerful musical experience. The monks also sell a 17-track CD entitled "Sacred Chant & African Rhythms from Senegal".

BELOW:
a baby African spurred tortoise.

nearby Dakar, it remains the seventh-largest city in Senegal, with a population of around 160,000, and all roads to the interior pass through it.

Sangalkam, 10km (6 miles) northeast of Rufisque, is the site of the **Village des Tortues** ⑩ (tel: 776 589 984; daily 9am–5pm; charge), an internationally sponsored "tortoise village" where chelonians rescued from captivity or other threatening situations are bred for eventual restocking back into their natural habitats. Several species of turtle, terrapin and tortoise might be on display in the pens here, but the star of the show is the gigantic African spurred tortoise, which is the largest species associated with any of the world's continental landmasses. Situated in the Réserve botanique de Noflaye, the village also showcases a variety of medicinal and other indigenous Senegalese plants, and a small shop sells local crafts.

A short northerly diversion from the RN2 towards Thiès, approximately 25km (16 miles) past Rufisque, leads to the **Abbaye de Keur Moussa** ⑪ (literally "House of Moses"), a monastery founded in 1961 by the Solesmes Congregation, a Benedictine order dedicated to reproduction of the traditional Latin liturgy and Gregorian chants.

To the north of the Cap Vert peninsula a **string of large lakes**, Youi, Malika, Mbeubeussé and Retba, is divided from the coast by an extensive area of forest. The roads running north from Sangalkam and Keur Moussa both lead to the last and most interesting of these, **Lac Retba** or **Lac Rose** ⑫, the pink-hued apparition that inspired the English composer Sir Michael Tippett's final orchestral work *The Rose Lake*, scored over 1991–3. Lac Rose is also of some historical curiosity, as the site used by the famous aviator Jean Mermoz (who created the first airmail service to South America in 1930) to land his seaplanes before Yoff Airport was established outside Dakar, while its most recent claim to fame is as the finish of the Paris–Dakar Rally.

Extending over 3 sq km (about 1¼ sq miles) and nowhere more than 3 metres (10ft) deep, Lac Rose indirectly owes its unusual pink colour to salty minerals that were deposited over several millennia. Although the lake lies less than 1km (½ mile) from the Atlantic, it has a salinity level 10 times higher, allowing swimmers to be buoyed through the foul-tasting water in a manner reminiscent of the Dead Sea, though less extremely so. This inhospitable salinity level also prompts one particular type of microscopic aquatic bacteria to produce a red protective pigment, the direct cause of the lake's pink hue. The degree of pinkness varies greatly, but in full flush, a phenomenon that's most likely in the early morning or late afternoon towards the end of the dry season, Lac Rose contrasts strikingly with the surrounding landscape of tall white dunes.

About 1.5km (1 mile) east of the main car park, the fascinating Peul village of **Niaga Peul** ⑬ can be reached by a sandy road fringing the lake. Amounting to little more than a row of rudimentary huts housing a total population of around 500, Niaga Peul is nevertheless a thriving salt-extraction centre, still worked by the traditional method of trawling the

Recommended Restaurants and Bars on pages 160–1

lake floor in a simple pirogue. Hundreds of piles of coarse salt, each marked with the initials of their owner, line this stretch of the lake shore, to be sold to traders from the capital. Tourists are welcome to look around the village, and the boatmen are always eager to supplement their meagre income by paddling visitors around the lake for a negotiable fee.

Although the lake is primarily of scenic interest, bird enthusiasts are drawn to the small flocks of flamingos that sometime gather in the shallows, and the many wading birds that haunt the sandy shore. It is easily visited as a day tour from Dakar or the resorts of the Petite Côte, though you ideally need to join an organised tour or hire a taxi, as public transport is rather erratic. Few visitors spend the night at Lac Rose, but there are several decent camps on offer, most clustered close to the car park where the road from Dakar and Rufisque reaches the lake, and staying overnight does tend to allow you to escape the attentions of the hustlers and vendors who latch onto day visitors. Active visitors may choose to take a buggy ride or horseback excursion through the dunes, run by various operators based at the lake, and more sedate 4x4 trips are also on offer.

About 10km (6 miles) northeast of Lac Rose as the crow flies, or 60km (37 miles) from Dakar by road, **Kayar** ⑭ is a medium-sized port of around 18,000 inhabitants situated at the juncture of Cap Vert and the thinly inhabited Grande Côte that runs northeast towards Saint-Louis. The Atlantic coastline here consists of long, straight, sandy beaches and drifting dunes topped with hummocks of sea-grass. From the fishing beach at Kayar, hundreds of colourful pirogues plunge through the breakers to follow the shoals of migrating fish such as sea bass, tunny, hake, swordfish, barracuda and shark. Huge drying frames and long fish-smoking huts are crammed onto the shore. There's not much choice of accommodation at Kayar, but the **Auberge de l'Océan Bleu** has simple rooms and – as might be expected – a good seafood menu. ❏

Man in Rufisque.

BELOW: piles of salt line the shore at Niaga Peul.

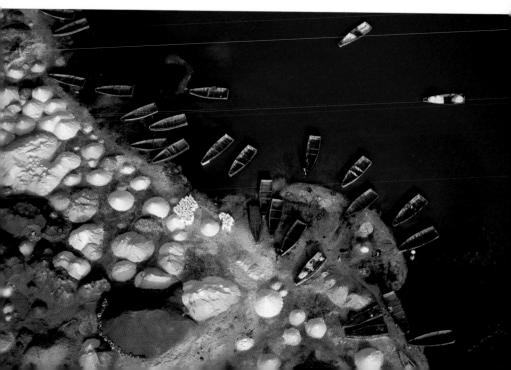

RESTAURANTS AND BARS

Restaurants

Prices for a main course per person:
$ = under US$8 (CFA 3,200)
$$ = US$8–15 (CFA 3,200–6,000)
$$$ = over US$15 (CFA 6,000)

Dakar

Chez Loutcha
101 Rue Moussé-Diop
Tel: 33 821 0302
$
It's run-down, smells strongly of cleaning products and noisy. And still, Chez Loutcha maintains an odd popularity among Dakarois working folks and curious tourists. During lunch hours it's almost impossible to get a seat here – proof enough of its enduring status. The Senegalese *plat du jour* is always a very generous portion of a well-prepared local meal.

Le Dragon
35 Rue Jules-Ferry
Tel: 33 821 6676
$$
Dakar has the best variety of Asian food for many miles, and the popular Le Dragon restaurant is no exception, serving delicious Vietnamese dishes. Closed Sunday.

La Fourchette
4 Rue Parent
Tel: 33 821 8887
$$$
Decked out in shiny tiles and comfy sofas, this chic place has successfully defended its well-earned place as classiest restaurant in town for several years now. The menu is an assembly of carefully chosen global flavours. Dishes come at a price – but every bite is worth it. Be sure to book in advance. Closed Sunday.

La Galette
16 Avenue Pompidou
Tel: 33 823 6363
$$
The long queues at the patisserie downstairs are a foolproof indicator that this is one of Dakar's best place for delicious cakes, fine tarts and croissants. Don't stop there – upstairs, you'll discover a brilliant restaurant that specialises in refined European cuisine and stands out for its great coffee and excellent service. Best for dinner.

Jardin Thaïlandais
10 Blvd du Sud
Tel: 33 825 5833
$$$
This has got to be the best Thai food you'll taste in Senegal. The dishes are a bit on the pricey side, but you won't regret it. Closed Sunday.

Keur Ndeye
68 Rue Vincens
Tel: 33 821 4973
$
Senegalese food should always be served in generous portions, and this is what this place does best. At lunchtime, a *plat du jour*, usually tasty

yassa chicken or chebbu-jen, arrives within minutes – don't even bother ordering anything else. There's usually a *kora* player to sweeten the slightly stark atmosphere.

Lagon
Route de la Petite Corniche
Tel: 33 821 5322
$$$
The ship-deck decor and waiters' uniforms are cringingly tasteless, and prices are steep. Still, this fish and seafood restaurant overlooking the ocean has remained one of Dakar's top addresses for years. Dishes are prepared with know-how and maybe even love. A brilliant dinner place to savour the flavours of the sea.

Le Layal
40 Rue St-Michel
Tel: 33 842 7313
$$
This intimate Lebanese café is one of Dakar's best-kept secrets. Service is great, the atmosphere friendly and the generous portions of *couscous royal* and other Lebanese and North African specialities among the best you'll find in the capital. Closed Mondays.

La Palmeraie
20 Avenue Pompidou
Tel: 33 821 1594
$
Centrally located and handy for a quick snack to eat in the centre of town. Sandwiches, cakes, coffee and fruit juices are on the menu.

Restaurant Farid
51 Rue Vincens
Tel: 33 821 6127
$$

Located in the Hôtel Farid near Place de l'Indépendance, this popular Lebanese and Senegalese restaurant has a first-class menu. Sample Senegal's national dish, *thiéboudienne*, rice in a thick sauce with a combination of fish and vegetables.

Le Séoul
75 Rue Amadou-Assane Ndoye
Tel: 33 822 9000
$$
Set in an attractive leafy courtyard, Le Séoul serves an array of delicately seasoned Korean dishes. Open for lunch and dinner.

Point-E
Les Ambassades
4 Bvd de l'Est
Tel: 33 825 5587
$$
Every taxi driver in Dakar knows this place. It's not pretty, nor is the food outstanding. But for a quick pizza or no-frills burger, this fast-food place and patisserie leads the way. It's always open, and usually full. You can also have home delivery from this better-than-fast-food-but-not-quite-a-dinner joint.

Ethiopian Restaurant Lalibela
Rue A
Tel: 77 510 1569
$
Now you may not have come to Senegal to savour Ethiopian cuisine, but this cheap and brilliant little place should make you reconsider. The Ethiopian owners have turned this into a speck of real Addis, and are gradually succeeding

in weaning the Senegalese regulars off the rice and on to Ethiopian bread. It gets full at dinnertime, so try booking in advance.

Mermoz
Shéhérazade
Behind Immeuble Rose
Tel: 33 860 1383
$$
Tucked away behind an impressive block of flats, this lovely garden restaurant has become one of the top addresses for North African and French cuisine. The intimate atmosphere is best soaked up during one of the place's frequent live concerts, often by some of Senegal's biggest stars.

Pointe des Almadies
Le Récif
Tel: 33 820 1160
$$
It simply has to be part of your perfect Dakar trip – a dinner at Africa's

westernmost point. There are plenty of restaurants on this small oval overlooking the ocean, and most of them are good. This airy eatery is one of the places to come to enjoy lobster. You get to pick your own from the tank in the back of the restaurant. Perfect for a Sunday lunchtime chill.

N'Gor
La Cabane des Pêcheurs
N'Gor Beach
Tel: 33 820 7675
$$$
The fish and seafood at this beach-view restaurant is so fresh you feel it may have been caught especially for you. Few places make a simple grilled fish taste that great. It's the perfect place for lunch after a morning on the beach – and one of the safest kitchens in town for lobster and oyster acts of bravery.

LEFT: Keur Ndeye restaurant.
RIGHT: assembling a delicious *thiéboudienne*.

*All tourists visiting
Gorée must pay
a tourist tax of
CFA500. Payment
can be made at the
tourist information
booth near the
ferry terminal.*

BELOW:
Gorée's beach is
used for swimming
and fishing.

million West Africans shipped across the Atlantic to a life of bondage in the Americas. However, many historians believe that Gorée's link with the slave trade has been overstated: the small island, with its limited natural resources and dense population of settlers and traders, would have been an unsuitable site for a major slave depot. So, while it's probable that a small number of slaves were exported from Gorée on boats trading primarily in less nefarious items, it's highly unlikely that the slave ships that transported 500-plus slaves in one transatlantic voyage ever collected their cargo there.

None of that changes the fact that slaving would have played a huge part in Gorée's economic prosperity during the 18th century. The European trading companies based there stocked their warehouses high with guns, gunpowder, cloth, salt and other imported manufactured goods, and sent parties across to the mainland to trade these items with powerful Wolof leaders for gold, hides, gum, ivory, other local produce – and, undoubtedly, slaves.

A highly influential social component of 18th-century Gorée were its *signares*

(a corruption of the Portuguese *senhora*), women of mixed European and African descent who acquired great wealth and power via liaisons with the island's European merchants, administrators and military men. The richest *signares*, such as Anne Pépin, Victoria Alberis and Cathy Louette, had large houses and substantial entourages of slaves and servants – who reputedly paraded behind their employers displaying their jewellery.

Life after Abolition

Following Abolition in the early 19th century, the British (and later French) naval forces engaged in the suppression of the slave trade were based on Gorée. As a free port, the island also attracted considerable commercial activity, and the population peaked at 5,000 in 1832. The subsequent overspill to Cap Vert led to the foundation of Dakar in 1857, and commerce followed. After the establishment of groundnut cultivation on the mainland, and the construction of the railway to Saint-Louis, Gorée was left to the religious and educational communities, and its population gradually declined, totalling just 600 in 1931.

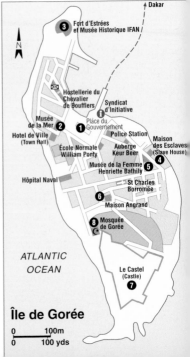

Dakar

Fort d'Estrées
et Musée Historique IFAN ①

N

Hostellerie du
Chevalier
de Boufflers / Syndicat
d'Initiative
Musée ② Place du
de la Mer Gouvernement ①
Hotel de Ville Police Station
(Town Hall) Maison
École Normale Auberge des Esclaves
William Ponty Keur Beer (Slave House) ④
Musée de la Femme ⑤
Hôpital Naval Henriette Bathily
St Charles
Borroméé
⑥
Maison Angrand

Mosquée ⑧
de Gorée

**ATLANTIC
OCEAN**
Le Castel
(Castle)
⑦

Île de Gorée

0   100m
0   100 yds

An important historical figure associated with Gorée is Jean-Stanislas de Boufflers, who was appointed Governor of Senegal in 1785. A poet, aesthete and member of the Académie Française, de Boufflers was an outspoken critic of the darker excesses of the slave trade, while as a conoisseur of feminine beauty, he found ample scope to indulge himself among the *signares* of Gorée. The island's most celebrated son, however, is Blaise Diagne, who became the first African representative in the French parliament (from 1914 until his death in 1934), and the Chairman of the first Pan-African Congress in Paris (1919).

Gorée today

Gorée's history is given concrete form in its architecture, most of which dates from the 19th century or earlier. Thanks to Unesco, the Senegalese government and several other agencies, the more important structures have been renovated since Gorée was listed as a World Heritage Site, but many of the dwellings that surround these landmarks are crumbling, while others have been turned into holiday homes or guesthouses.

The arrival of the launch from Dakar is usually accompanied by what passes for a flurry of activity on the sleepy island. Arriving tourists might be approached by guides, who will offer to show them around the island for a negotiable fee, but it's safer to arrange a guide through the waterfront tourist office of the **Syndicat d'Initiative**. A knowledgeable local guide will provide a great deal of background to the island's history and architecture, but it is also fine to walk around the small island unescorted, and there's little danger of getting lost.

Laundry drying in the hot wind; in the background, the tall buildings of Dakar.

Place du Gouvernement

The obvious starting point for a walking tour, **Place du Gouvernement** ❶ faces the ferry jetty and hosts an informal marketplace and cluster of craft shops and curio stalls. Several historic buildings surround the square. The **police station**, the island's oldest stone building, is depicted as a store on a 17th-century map, and shares its foundation with the

BELOW: the terracotta walls of the Musée Historique.

THE PETITE CÔTE

A string of dazzling white-sand beaches,
luxurious hotels and a laid-back atmosphere make
the Petite Côte Senegal's most popular and enticing
destination for sun-worshippers; but it has more to
offer, like water sports and nature reserves

The sun-drenched heart of Senegal's tourist industry is the stretch of Atlantic frontage that runs for 75km (45 miles) as the crow flies southward from Dakar to Joal-Fadiouth via La Somone, Saly, Mbour and various smaller resorts. Strung with one scenic beach after another, pampered by an idyllic tropical climate and serviced by countless modern hotels, the so-called **Petite Côte** has far more to offer tourists than the rougher waters of the relatively undeveloped Grande Côte to the north of Dakar. Its shimmering white beaches are cooled by constant trade winds, shaded by towering cocoa palms and lofty kapok trees, and serviced by a range of restaurants, cafés and patisseries that wouldn't look out of place in France itself.

As such, the Petite Côte is perfect for holidaymakers with little hankering for the more adventurous side of Senegal, and its innumerable resorts attract an annual pilgrimage of tens of thousands of sun-seekers during the European winter – many of whom see nothing more of Senegal than the resort where they stay and the view from the vehicle that transports them there.

But if the attractions of the beach do pall after a while, visitors in search of more active pursuits can easily explore further afield, whether they join a short safari into the brooding African savannah protected in the Réserve de Bandia, take a boat trip into deep-blue coastal waters that teem with a bewildering variety of fish, explore the shell-scattered

alleys of Fadiouth Island, or take a stroll through the bird reserves bordering La Somone and Popenguine.

Most of the Petite Côte's inhabitants are Serer or Lébou, and the area is predominantly Catholic, with Portuguese and French influences still evident in many churches, missions and schools. As might be expected, the main population centres lie along the seashore, and the main industry is fishing, as testified to by the hundreds of pirogues that line the wide sandy beaches. Nowhere are these colourful boats so densely concentrated

Main attractions
POPENGUINE
RÉSERVE DE BANDIA
LA SOMONE
SALY
MBOUR
NIANING
JOAL
ÎLE DE FADIOUTH

LEFT: fishermen on Mbour Beach. **BELOW:** a friendly welcome awaits visitors.

The giraffes flown in from South Africa to Bandia thrive in their new environment.

BELOW: the indigenous brown buffalo, Bandia.

the alleged apparition. The best day to visit is Sunday, when a mass is held at 9.30am and a rosary takes place at the sacred grotto at 4.30pm. On other days of the week, the church is open for evening mass at 6.30pm.

About 1.5km (1 mile) south of the village centre, the **Réserve Naturelle de Popenguine** (tel: 33 956 4951; www.popenguine.org; daily; charge) was created at the initiative of the Popenguine Women's Group for the Protection of Nature (known by its French acronym RFPPN) in 1988 and received formal recognition by the Senegalese government 10 years later. Extending over approximately 10 sq km (4 sq miles), the reserve protects the wonderful unspoilt beach running south of town, a belt of baobab woodland behind the beach, and the spectacular laterite cliffs that tower 75 metres (240ft) above them both.

One of the main reasons behind the reserve's creation is that it forms an important overwinter site for the blue rock-thrush and several more common Palaearctic migrants, but the bird checklist is now close to the 200 mark, with marine terns and gulls likely to be seen alongside woodland species such as Senegal parrot, yellow-crowned gonolek and long-tailed glossy starling. The varied fauna also includes bushbuck, common duiker, spotted hyena, golden jackal, porcupine, green monkey, rock python and monitor lizard. Guides are available from the RFPPN office on the road between the town and the reserve.

Call of the bush

As the crow flies, Popenguine lies only 8km (5 miles) north of La Somone, the next major holiday resort along the Petite Côte, but the wide estuary that separates the two small towns means that driving between them entails a circuitous 30km (18-mile) trip along the RN1 via **Sindia** and **Nguékokh**. Clearly signposted on the east side of the RN1 between Sindia and Nguékokh, the private **Réserve de Bandia** ❸ (tel: 33 958 2024; www.reservedebandia.com; daily 7am–6pm; charge) was created in 1990 and first opened to the public in 1997, since when it has become one of the most popular and rewarding day trips from the nearby resorts, offering a bush atmosphere that recalls East Africa and contrasts strongly

Recommended Restaurants, Bars and Cafés on pages 184–5

with the rest of the Petite Côte. Following extensions in 2001 and 2006, Bandia now covers around 35 sq km (14 sq miles) of dry woodland dominated for the most part by tangled acacia scrub, although the southern part of the reserve protects a stunning area of open grassland studded with massive baobab trees. The seasonal Somone River flows through Bandia, feeding two permanent watering holes.

For casual visitors, the main attraction of Bandia is a selection of animals that have been introduced from outside the country. These include a pair of white rhinoceros, which are most often seen at one of the watering holes in the late afternoon, as well as giraffe, greater kudu, common eland and impala, all of which were flown in from South Africa. The presence of these creatures in Bandia is somewhat bizarre in pure ecological terms, since they belong to races or species that are totally exotic to West Africa, but most are doing well in their new environment – indeed, the four giraffes originally introduced in 2000 have reproduced to form an 18-strong herd, and common eland and impala are both very easily observed. Pending a fur-

ther increase in the reserve's area, plans to introduce lion and elephant are also in the pipeline.

One of the two white rhinos that were introduced to Bandia.

Species under threat

Rather more important in genuine conservation terms are the many animals that have been reintroduced to Bandia from the beleaguered Niokolo-Koba National Park, whose wildlife is under increasing threat as a result of decades of poaching. The most conspicuous of

BELOW: a herd of roan antelopes amongst the tall baobabs in Bandia.

The Village Artisanal in Saly is a good place to purchase traditional souvenirs.

BELOW: the exquisite Plage des Cocotiers in Saly.

useful facilities – though note that the nearest bank and ATM is about 10km (6 miles) away in Saly.

Wetland habitat

In 1999, the estuary of the Somone River was set aside as the centrepiece of the 7-sq km (2¾-sq mile) **Réserve Naturelle de La Somone** (daily; free), a community reserve whose creation, like that of the bordering Réserve Naturelle de Popenguine, was initiated by a local women's group. Plenty of pirogues at the estuary mouth below Club Baobab offer short excursions into the reserve, which supports vast flocks of birds, including greater flamingo, pink-backed pelican, Caspian tern, lesser crested tern and up to a dozen species of wader at any given time.

Rising near Thiès before it passes through the Réserve de Bandia, the river supports a belt of gallery forest and grassland, which can be explored further upriver. Serious birdwatchers should follow the side road that angles right about 200 metres/yards before the main road reaches Club Baobab and leads to a small beach offering great views over the bird-lined sand flats and mangroves. This

beach also appears to be the centre of I Somone's booming oyster and muss industry; the fresh produce can be boug on-site to make a great meal for tho staying in self-catering accommodatio

Senegal's Riviera

Linked to La Somone by a busy surfac road following the coast, **Saly ❺** – al sometimes spelt Sali – is often cited Senegal's answer to the French Rivier and for good reason. The clean, san beach here is arguably the most attra tive in the country, and certainly t most popular, lined with dozens of hote ranging from swish all-inclusive beac front package deals to cosier *auberg* along the back roads.

However, this Senegalese beach Mec differs from its Mediterranean counterpa in several crucial respects. For one, Sa possesses a distinctly exuberant Afric character, epitomised by the makeshi market stalls that jostle for space among the plusher eateries and salons that li the main tourist drag. It also has a deci edly low-rise architectural style, with fe hotels or other buildings standing mo than two storeys high. Best of all, t

Recommended Restaurants, Bars and Cafés on pages 184–5

olden sands of Saly's beaches are seldom anything close to crowded, even during the peak tourist season.

Saly can be divided into three distinct sectors: **Saly Portugal** (also known as Saly Portudal), **Saly Niakhniakhal** and **Saly Nord**. The established core of the tourist industry, **Saly Portugal** is centred on a large traffic roundabout at the end of a well-maintained and clearly signposted feeder road that branches west from the RN1 approximately 3km (2 miles) north of Mbour.

As reflected in its name, this once modest village was settled by some Portuguese mariners in the 17th century, when it served as one the first slave-trading posts in West Africa. The small town's present-day prosperity is based on an altogether more salubrious trade, namely tourism, and this is reflected in a good range of modern facilities ranging from hairdressing salons and internet cafés to banks with ATMs and well-stocked supermarkets.

There are dozens of hotels here. Several four-star establishments fringe the palm-lined beach, among them the **Hôtel Espadon**, **Palm Beach Hotel**, **Saly Hotel** and **Savana Saly**, all of which offer accommodation, food and facilities to top international standards. Saly Portugal is also densely packed with restaurants, cafés and bars, along the RN1 with most international cuisines well represented, and one could easily eat out at a different place every night for two weeks without straying much beyond a 500-metre/yard radius of the main traffic roundabout. And if you want to make a night of it, there are plenty of nightclubs and bars dotted around the village, too.

For curio-hunters, the **Village Artisanal Saly**, located about 20 metres/yards from the main roundabout, is packed with all manner of African craft products, from carvings and paintings to bracelets, beads and batiks, and the pressure to buy isn't overwhelming.

Almost immediately south of Saly Portugal, easily reached along a stone beachfront footpath or sandy back road, Saly Niakhniakhal's tongue-twisting

name seems to reflect its character, which comes across as uncompromisingly African in comparison with its touristy neighbour. But this is gradually being subverted by the growing demands of the tourist industry, and most of the waterfront is now dominated by tourist hotels, though these are matched one-for-one by more idiosyncratic accommodation establishments such as the fine Belgian-run **Auberge Khady** and the somewhat farm-like **Ferme de Saly**.

Away from the beach, **Saly Niakhniakhal** retains a sedately suburban residential feel, but its sandy roads support a good number of quality restaurants, most of which are significantly cheaper than their counterparts in Saly Portugal, along with a sprinkling of shops, supermarkets and internet cafés.

Saly Nord

If **Niakhniakhal** comes across as the most organic part of Saly, then the upstart **Saly Nord** (North) – which lies about 3km (2 miles) northwest of the main roundabout in Saly Portugal, along the surfaced coastal loop road to La Somone – is undoubtedly the most contrived. A

A proud Senegalese.

BELOW: peacock perched on a hotel balcony in Saly.

This baobab on Fadiouth Island is considered sacred.

BELOW: fishermen's carts line up the beach on Fadiouth.

What tourist development does exist in Mbour tends to be rather low-key, and suited more to backpackers and other independent travellers than to package tourists. The largest hotel by far is the moderately priced **Centre Touristique Coco Beach**, located near the Préfecture, which offers 90 rooms, most with air-conditioning. Although somewhat run-down in comparison with most Saly hotels, Coco Beach has a friendly atmosphere, a clean swimming pool, and it fringes a clean private beach, lined with swaying palms, only a couple of minutes' walk from the hubbub of the fish market.

Plenty of smaller hotels are dotted around town, but it is more usual for those seeking a conventional beach holiday to stay at one of the resorts at Saly or elsewhere along the Petite Côte and to visit Mbour market as a day trip. Organised tour groups can regularly be seen wandering through the lines of fishing craft on the beach at Mbour or photographing the wooden racks used for curing fish, and there are now several craft stalls in town.

Nianing

At a central junction in Mbour, the RN1 branches inland towards Fatick, Kaolack and Tambacounda, but a secondary surfaced road continues along the coast for 30km (18 miles), terminating at Joal-Fadiouth. Some 6 miles (10km) south of Mbour along this coastal road, the delightfully isolated beach resort of **Nianing** ⑦ is the location of the **Domaine de Nianing** (tel: 33 957 1120; www.domainede nianing.com; charge for day visitors), a 260-bungalow holiday village that sprawls in thickly wooded 150-hectare (370-acre) gardens stretching down to a fabulous beach. Founded in 1969, this unusually spacious resort contains a small private zoo with caged antelope and birds, and more than 150 bird species occur naturally in the baobab- and palm-studded gardens and a quartet of lakes, while semi-tame troops of patas and green monkeys are also common.

The joy of Fadiouth

Situated about 115km (70 miles) south of Dakar by road (though much closer as the crow flies), **Joal ❽** is the second-largest port on the Petite Côte, sharing a population of around 40,000 with the small island of **Fadiouth**, and it sprawls for several kilometres along the main tarmac road from Mbour before this terminates at the parking lot facing the islet. According to local tradition, Joal was settled by Serer immigrants in the 11th century and was soon thereafter regarded as the most important naval gateway to the medieval Siné Empire.

Then also known as Joola, the port attracted significant Portuguese settlement in the 16th century, and by 1635 the navigator Francisco Coelho noted that "the port of Joal is well recognised, with calm and stable waters, and a most agreeable and healthy climate". Joal-Fadiouth has a Christian tradition dating back to the Portuguese period, and it has several old churches, but it also served briefly as the residence of the 19th-century Islamic icon El Hadj Oumar Tall, and a mosque is dedicated to his memory. The wide main street that dominates

the town is overlooked by a few mid-19th-century colonial houses, most of which are in a poor state of repair. The poet and first president of Senegal Léopold Sédar Senghor was born in Joal in 1906, and his family home – called *Mbind Diogoye* ("House of the Lion") – is still open to visitors.

The setting of Joal, across the water from **Île de Fadiouth**, is picturesque, and there are also interesting sights in the surrounding countryside. Around Joal the great mounds of dry earth known as *tanns* are used as defences against the sea, bolstered by huge banks of sun-bleached shells some 8 metres (26ft) wide. Giving the scene a somewhat desolate look, hundreds of ancient gaunt baobabs are the only life to survive on the heaped shells and arid soil. These barren areas give the region a ghostly atmosphere which is even more pronounced around the fishermen's graveyards.

According to local tradition, the island-bound village of Fadiouth was founded in the 13th century by Massa Waly, a refugee leader from the distant Ghana Empire, and his locally born niece Fadiara Diakhanora. The village now has

Bust of Léopold Sédar Senghor in his family home in Joal.

BELOW: the pirogues and old wooden footbridge of Fadiouth Island.

RESTAURANTS, BARS AND CAFÉS

Restaurants

Prices for a main course per person:
$ = under US$8 (CFA3,200)
$$ = US$8–15 (CFA 3,200–6,000)
$$$ = over US$15 (CFA6,000)

Toubab Dialaw

La Mimosa
Tel: 33 894 7326 **$$**
With its shady veranda decorated with African art overlooking a lush garden, this friendly little hotel is a lovely spot for a leisurely meal. Pizzas and other Italian cuisine are the main speciality, but Senegalese and other European dishes are available. Make sure you taste one of their delicious fruit punches. Open 8am–10.30pm.

Popenguine

Keur de Sable
Tel: 33 957 7164
$$
Tasty French and Senegalese food is prepared at this attractively situated small hotel on the slopes of Popenguine. Popular with Dakarois weekenders, it has indoor seating and a cocktail bar, but most people prefer to enjoy the breezy vine-draped veranda. Open 8am–10pm.

Réserve de Bandia

La Bandia
Tel: 33 958 2025
$–$$
Situated immediately inside the entrance of Senegal's most popular wildlife sanctuary, this shady outdoor restaurant serves a good selection of grilled meat and fish dishes, as well as pastas, pizzas, light snacks and a full range of alcoholic and soft drinks. The food may not be the best on the Petite Côte, but it's more than adequate, and the birdlife and crocs at the adjacent pool are great fun. Open daily 8am–6pm.

La Somone

Café Creole
Ngaparou Crossroads
Tel: 33 958 5191
$–$$
This funky café at the four-way junction about 2km (1 mile) outside La Somone is one of the livelier eateries on the Petite Côte, serving an innovative selection of Caribbean and European dishes. Senegalese and reggae music are prominent on the play list, and there's live music every Thursday night. Open 7.30am–1am.

Saly Portugal

La Dolce Vita
Route de La Somone
Tel: 33 957 1478
$$
One of the more moderately priced eateries along the main strip through Saly, this offers the rather odd combination of Italian and Cantonese menus. Fortunately, both are good, and they are supplemented by the more usual Senegalese selection of seafood and brochettes. The large veranda is very pleasant, and there's indoor seating too. Open 9am–10.30pm.

L'Éventail

Route de La Somone
Tel: 33 975 2681
$
Set back from the main road in pretty green gardens, this small and cosy Vietnamese restaurant makes a great – and inexpensive – break from the standard Franco-Senegalese fare served up at most of the more moderately priced places along the main strip through Saly. Open noon–late.

Lenny's Bar and Restaurant

Route de La Somone, opposite the Village Artisanal
Tel: 77 714 0918
$$
Boasting a breezy first-floor location overlooking the main drag through Saly, this unpretentious French restaurant presents a lengthy menu that includes the usual seafood and meat dishes supplemented by a barbecue menu and the more unusual likes of rabbit and quail. Cheap beer and house wine make this an excellent spot for a leisurely drink and meal as you watch Saly life go by. Open 7pm–late.

La Riviéra

Place de Coursel
Tel: 33 957 0724
$$–$$$
With its large, inviting swimming pool and amazing selection of excellent seafood, meat and vegetarian dishes topped up with a lavishly stocked cocktail bar, this is justifiably one of the most popular eateries on the main strip through

Saly. Youngsters and the not-so-hungry are well catered for by the pizza, sandwich and burger menu. Steeply priced drinks notwithstanding, it's good value, and one place you can rely upon to be open 24/7.

Wine Lounge Bar

Place de Coursel
$$
Situated behind La Riviera, this newly opened bar has one of the best wine lists on the Petite Côte, and a limited menu of light meals and snacks. Stylish African decor and an upstairs cigar room with leather chairs and DVD/TV create a very pleasant ambience to accompany the wine.

Saly Niakhniakhal

Escale Adji

Tel: 77 277 8745
$
Situated where the asphalt terminates as the road enters Saly Niakhniakhal, this new restaurant has a really funky contemporary African feel, with terracotta floors, canvas roof, hardwood furniture and outdoor eating in a green garden. The bar is well stocked and the Senegalese menu is as good value as you'll find around Saly.

Le Frangalaise

Tel: 33 954 9022
$
Situated on the sandy main road through Saly Niakhniakhal, this airy and friendly restaurant has indoor and outdoor seating and an excellent selection of mostly seafood dishes at very

competitive prices. Open lunch and dinner.

Habana Café

Saly Beach
Tel: 33 957 1730
Snacks and plat du jour **$**; other dishes **$$**
Standing out from the crowd with its cheerful banana-yellow exterior, this laid-back beachfront café has a good selection of cocktails and other drinks, as well as a long, varied menu of delicious French and seafood dishes, including an inexpensive plat du jour. Excellent service. Open 9am–late.

Le Pontoon

Hôtel des Cocotiers
Tel: 33 957 1491 **$$**
One of the longest-serving eateries in the Saly area, this is notable as much as anything for its stilted beachfront location with waves breaking below the balcony, but it also serves very good seafood and other dishes

at wallet-friendly prices. Open 11am–11pm.

La Terrazzo

Saly Beach
Tel: 33 973 3317
$$
Home-made pasta and seafood are the specialities at this perennially popular seafront Italian restaurant, but the real draw is the breezy location right on the beach.

Joal-Fadiouth

Le Sénégaulois

Tel: 33 957 6241
$–$$
Thatch-shaded tables in compact green grounds overlooking the Fadiouth channel make this moderately priced bar-restaurant next to the bridge to the island the obvious place for a meal or drink in Joal. The standard Franco-Senegalese menu of seafood and meat grills/brochettes is supplemented by filled baguettes and other snacks.

LEFT: fresh and dried chillies are present in many Senegalese dishes. **RIGHT:** fish croquettes make excellent on-the-go-snacks.

MARINE AND AQUATIC BIRDS

For a country characterised by low rainfall, Senegal – and for that matter The Gambia – is unexpectedly well endowed when it comes to estuarine and freshwater wetlands and associated bird species. In essence, this is because the coastline extends inwards along a series of long, wide, westward-flowing rivers – most importantly, from north to south, the Senegal, Saloum, Gambia and Casamance – that together form a sprawling network of meandering streams and creeks (known locally as *bolongs*) before they eventually empty into the Atlantic Ocean.

Indeed, of Senegal's six national parks, four exist primarily to conserve riverine/estuarine habitats. These include the Parc de la Langue de Barbarie at the mouth of the Senegal River, the Parc du Delta du Saloum, and the Parc de la Basse-Casamance on the Guinean border. There's also the Parc National des Oiseaux du Djoudj, a Unesco World Heritage Site and one of the most important wetland habitats anywhere in the world. Situated on the Mauritanian border, this vast network of saline and freshwater habitats is the first watering point south of the Sahara, and as such it provides sustenance to an estimated 3 million Palaearctic migrants every winter – as well as supporting large resident populations of pelicans, flamingos, crowned cranes, terns, gulls and storks.

The estuarine reserves of Senegal and The Gambia contain several avian breeding colonies of global significance. Île aux Oiseaux in the Saloum Delta, for instance, supports up to 40,000 royal tern nests, making it the largest such breeding colony in the world. Langue de Barbarie often supports more than 10,000 nesting pairs of various terns and gulls in a good season.

ABOVE: the large flocks of great white pelican at Djoudj and pink-backed pelican near Mbour are among the most important colonies for these charismatic birds anywhere in West Africa.

ABOVE LEFT: white heron. **LEFT:** the large saddle-billed stork is easily spotted: apart from its distinctive beak, it has a wing span of up to 270cm (9ft).

AQUATIC RARITIES

Several of the 'ticks' most eagerly sought by visiting birdwatchers are waterbirds, and many can be seen quite easily when you know where to look. The gorgeous blue-grey Egyptian plover, also known as the crocodile bird for its reputed mutualistic feeding behaviour of cleaning crocodiles' teeth, is unlikely to be seen unless you visit Basse Santa Su, where it is practically resident at the harbour from June–Feb, or Niokolo-Koba, where it is often seen from the veranda of Hôtel Simenti.

Boat trips through the mangrove-lined *bolongs* around Makasutu or Lamin Lodge are good for several rarities such as the African finfoot, which looks like a red-billed cross between a duck and a cormorant, and tends to swim elusively at the water's edge below overhanging branches. The secretive white-backed and back-crowned night herons are also regularly seen in these mangrove habitats, but you'll need a bit more luck to spot the ultra-rare white-crested tiger heron, or the immense Pel's fishing owl.

Noteworthy matches between location and species include the pygmy goose and the pools covered in floating vegetation at Panchang on the north bank of the Gambia River, and the red-billed tropicbirds that haunt the Îles de la Madeleine off Dakar.

ABOVE AND LEFT: many of the more common water-associated birds can be observed near almost any river or wetland habitat – among them the hadeda ibis, cormorant, wattled plover, grey heron, great white egret, African spoonbill, and the peculiar little hamerkop, which builds the largest nest of any African bird.

ABOVE: the elegant great white egret.
LEFT: the African darter bird is also known as the snake bird: as it swims along, only its long neck and head are visible above the water.

*Young Nile crocodile.
All three African
crocodile species are
present in the delta.*

however, the main attraction of Siné-Saloum is the rich sense of place associated with boating silently through the mangrove-lined waterways, and the opportunity to interact with the local fishing communities that subsist on the delta's rich harvest.

A bird-lover's paradise

The most conspicuous component of the Siné-Saloum's fauna is the marine and terrestrial birdlife that attracts ornithologists from around the globe. Hundreds of mudflats, sandbars and vast areas of mangrove swamps provide an ideal habitat for waterbirds. Throughout the year, herons and storks wade between

The delta is also of considerable interest to wildlife enthusiasts, providing sanctuary to such endangered aquatic creatures as marine turtles, dolphins and manatees, along with a rich selection of birds. For many independent travellers,

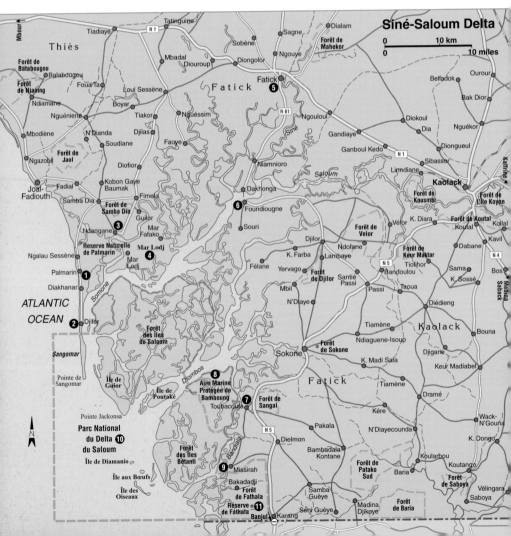

e gangling roots of mangroves, search-
g out frogs, fish and other aquatic
rey, while overhead a variety of water-
ssociated raptors – osprey, African fish
agle, palmnut vulture, long-crested eagle
nd grey kestrel – can be seen wheeling
ver the fish-stocked waters.

Back on terra firma, shrikes ("butcher
irds") impale their catches – from
rasshoppers to small rodents – on the
narp prongs of thorn bushes, while palm
lantations and patches of acacia wood-
nd provide perfect cover for an assort-
nent of more colourful species, among
nem blue-bellied roller, bearded barbet,
enegal parrot, violet turaco, blue-
heeked bee-eater, violet-backed starling
nd yellow-crowned bishop.

Bird numbers are boosted in the Euro-
ean winter, when concentrations of more
nan 100,000 individual marine birds are
egularly recorded. The delta is the world's
nost important breeding site for the royal
ern, with more than 30,000 nesting pairs
resent in season, and it's the busiest
verwintering for the great white egret
nywhere in West Africa. Other marine
pecies that congregate in numbers include
reater flamingo, western reef egret,
urasian spoonbill, pink-backed pelican,
ied avocet, grey plover, Kentish plover,
urlew sandpiper, Caspian tern, lesser
rested terns, Sandwich tern and slender-
illed gull. In short, this is one place where
good bird field guide, a pair of binocu-
ars and a camera are essential.

Relatively few large creatures inhabit
he Siné-Saloum, though all three African
rocodilian species are present, includ-
ng the massive Nile crocodile, as is the
npressive water monitor, a type of large
izard, and a variety of swimming snakes.
ourneying by boat through the maze of
vaterways, one can sometimes see a
chool of dolphins join the wake of the
raft or dive across the pirogue's bows,
nd there are also said to be several fam-
lies of hippopotami in the deltas, but
hese are seldom sighted.

More alluringly, the Siné-Saloum is
lso the most important Senegalese
efuge for the West African manatee, a
ylindrically shaped all-grey aquatic

mammal large that weighs up to 500kg
(1,100lb). Associated with tropical estuarine and riverine habitats along the
Atlantic coastline of Africa, the West
African manatee – which is also known
as the sea cow – is sometimes spotted in
the channels, where it feeds on mangrove
shoots and seaweed. The West African
manatee is one of four aquatic mammal
species placed in the order Sirenia, a
name that refers to this oddball creature
being the probable source of the mer-
maids and sirens of ancient legend.

A land of national parks

Away from the water, large mammals
still inhabit the terrestrial habitats of the
Parc National du Delta du Saloum.
The largest land animal found here naturally is the red river hog, a secretive
nocturnal species associated with dense
riparian vegetation. More common is
the diurnal warthog, which should be
treated with great respect, and the handsome bushbuck. The pythons here often
grow to considerable size; by contrast
the duiker antelopes that sometimes venture into the mangroves are no bigger
than a small dog. Guinea baboon, green

Children playing in the delta at sunset.

BELOW:
the delta abounds
with birdlife.

monkeys and patas monkeys are frequently encountered in all wooded habitats, and the sanctuary also supports a few troops of the elusive red colobus monkey. The best game-viewing in the delta can be had at the **Réserve de Fathala**, a fenced-off section of the national park where rhino, giraffe and various other large mammals have been introduced for the benefit of tourists.

There's plenty of small invertebrate life in the delta. The dark, pod-like appendages festooning the exposed roots of the mangroves are a variety of oyster, a delicacy in this region. Walkways constructed between settlements across shallows are usually built of mud surfaced and strengthened with the shells of oysters. On the black mudbanks, the thousands of small holes are the burrows of sand and fiddler crabs which will emerge in their hundreds if one keeps still. Mud skippers, with adapted front fins, walk across the banks from pool to pool and may even be seen climbing the mangrove roots. Unfortunately, however, the mangrove ecosystems of Siné-Saloum have been the subject of much ecological study, and it is feared that the coastal

defences of naturally formed sandbanks are gradually being eroded, both by the forces of nature and by man, whose hunger for firewood has resulted in the slow loss of the vegetation that binds the banks together.

Sangomar

With the waves of the Atlantic crashing on its western shore, and the mangrove-lined waters of the Saloum River flowing along its east, the **Sangomar peninsula** – the sliver of sandy land that tapers southward from Joal-Fadiouth to the remote Pointe de Sangomar – forms something of an intermediate zone between the contrasting ecotypes of the Petite Côte and Siné-Saloum Delta. Indeed, from a visitor's perspective, this long narrow band of shifting sand arguably offers the best of both worlds, boasting some superb swimming beaches, as well as good access into the mangrove-lined delta. There are no substantial towns on the peninsula, only a few sleepy fishing villages, and this innate feel of rusticity is complemented by the low-key nature of tourist development. But while Sangomar doesn't aim to attract the sort of package tourism associated with Saly Portugal and surrounds, the peninsula does host a couple of the Petite Côte's most exclusive up-market resorts, as well as a selection of basic camps attuned to the needs of independent travellers.

The well-maintained shell road to Sangomar branches east from the surfaced coastal road at Joal-Fadiouth, a few hundred metres before the tar terminates. The shell road runs inland for about 12km (7 miles) via Fadial to **Samba Dia** (also the junction for a rough sandy piste to Ndangane), where it veers back towards the coast in the southwesterly direction, reaching the north end of the peninsula at the small town of **Palmarin** ❶. Before reaching Palmarin, however, the road runs for several kilometres along a causeway flanked by a network of tidal flats and shallow pools protected in the **Réserve Naturelle de Palmarin**, a 105 sq km (40-sq mile) community reserve created in May 2001. There's plenty of

The Réserve Naturelle de Palmarin is of special significance as a breeding site for green and olive Ridley turtle, both IUCN (International Union for Conservation of Nature) listed as endangered, and it was also once used as a breeding site by the critically endangered leatherback turtle.

BELOW:
a pirogue builder
on a tea break.

birdlife to be seen along the way, ranging from flamingos and pelicans to large mixed flocks of gulls and terns, including the localised Audouin's gull. Spotted hyena and side-striped jackal, still present in small numbers, are often heard calling eerily after dark, and the latter is more occasionally seen in daylight.

Palmarin is not so much a town as a loose semi-urban agglomeration of half a dozen villages harbouring a combined population of around 5,000–6,000. The name Palmarin is probably European in origin, alluding to the many palms that line this stretch of coast, but dates back for centuries. The French sailor Geoffrey de Villeneuve, who visited the area in 1785, noted that "Palmarin, also called Grand Joal, is enclosed on one side by the river to which it gives its name, on one side by the sea, and on the other by marsh". According to the same writer, "Its inhabitants, emboldened by this position, once refused to pay taxes, and even massacred collectors, until the king of Siné discovered a land bridge to the island and crossed with his army, who surprised the people and captured them as slaves". Today, the villages are most notable for

their unusual construction – often on ancient banks of shells – and for the pointed-topped rice stores built on stilts away from the rising waters. Two superb upmarket resorts border Palmarin: first the **Lodge des Collines de Niassam**, whose 13 rooms are perched treehouse-like among the baobabs or stand on stilts above the lagoon, and the more conventional but winningly stylish **Royal Lodge**, with its wonderfully isolated location on a beach studded with mighty baobabs. One hut at the Royal Lodge even has its own private swimming pool.

Pointe de Sangomar

At one time, the Sangomar peninsula extended southwards for almost 40km (24 miles) south of Joal-Fadiouth to the **Pointe de Sangomar**, and it is still shown that way on many maps. However, the topography of the area was radically transformed in 1987, when a storm created a

The hut dwellings on Plage d'Or, on Île des Palétuviers. The resort is linked to the Hôtel Les Palétuviers, (see page 199).

BELOW:
pelicans take flight.

Boy from the delta region practising his judo skills.

BELOW: women gathering for the annual National Women's week.

breach in this natural barrage of sand and dunes, and the most southerly portion of the peninsula was transformed into a serpentine island measuring about 10km (6 miles) from north to south. The fish factory that once scarred the southern tip of the peninsula was abandoned shortly after this, and its activities were transferred to Mbour. Today, the most southerly point on the peninsula is Djifer.

A rustic fishing village of around 2,000 inhabitants, **Djifer ❷** (or Djifère) lies about 20 minutes' drive south of Palmarin along an erratic unsurfaced road. Dolphins and other marine creatures are often seen from the village, and the local pirogue sailors are noted for their exceptional skills, making it an excellent spot for informal trips deeper into the delta. Several small hotels are dotted around the Djifer area, with the perfectly located **Campement La Pointe de Sangomar** being a recommended base for exploration. From here, it is possible to visit the little fishing villages of **Dionevar** and **Niodior**, built on islets in the winding estuary waters that face the part of the Sangomar peninsula that has now become an island.

North of the Saloum

No bridge spans the Saloum downriver of Kaolack, which means that the northern and southern verges of Siné-Saloum are serviced by discreet road circuits, connected only by the vehicle ferry that links **Fatick** to **Foundiougne** a few times daily, assuming that it is in service. The closest surfaced road to the northern delta is the smooth RN1 between Mbour and Kaolack, from where two more erratic access roads run southwards to the banks of the Saloum. The more westerly of these roads branches south about 35km (20 miles) east of Mbour, between **Tiadiaye** and **Tatinguine**, and passes through **Diofior** before terminating at **Ndangane** after 40km (25 miles). Ndangane can also be accessed directly from Joal-Fadiouth following a short but rough road track through **Samba Dia**. Further east, at Fatick, an extremely corrugated 27km (17-mile) road runs south to **Dakhonga**, the ferry terminal for Foundiougne on the south bank.

For those without private transport, bush taxis cover the RN1 and both routes leading to Ndangane with fair regularity, but are rather scarce along the road from Fatick to Dakhonga.

Ndangane

Set on a wide *bolong* with good fishing grounds on both sides, the rapidly expanding village of **Ndangane ❸**, sometimes spelt N'Dangane, is the main tourist focus on the northern shores of the delta. The village, whose name derives from the Serer word for harbour, consists of two parts, connected by a kilometre-long dirt road along a causeway fringed by salty mudflats that teem with wading birds.

Most tourists end up at the smaller but more developed sector, which lies at the end of the surfaced road, leading down to a muddy beach packed densely with pirogues offering trips out into the delta. One of those bizarre enclaves of tourist bustle in which Senegal and The Gambia specialise, this part of Ndangane consists of maybe 300 metres/yards of road packed densely on either side with lodges, restaurants, bars and craft shops

Recommended Restaurants and Bars on page 203

and its incongruity is accentuated by its isolation from Ndangane proper, a fishing village of approximately 1,000 people that is seldom visited by tourists.

There's no shortage of accommodation options in the touristy part of Ndangane. At the top end of the range, you'll find the **Hôtel Le Pélican du Saloum** and **Hôtel Cordons Bleus**, both classy and long-serving establishments that offer comfortable rooms and excellent seafood, as well as a welcoming swimming pool. A large number of small and more affordable hotels are packed along the main strip, ranging from the well-run and homely **Gîte Rural Le Cormoran** to the more backpacker-oriented **Campement Le Barracuda**.

You're spoilt for choice when it comes to eating and curio shopping too, with the open-sided, thatch-roofed **Le Temarko Restaurant and Boutique** offering the opportunity to do both, in an unbeatable waterfront location. And having made a short tour of the village and its surrounds, don't miss out on a boat trip into the delta, following the river southwest along a sandy spit inhabited by large groups of waders and waterfowl.

Mar Lodge

Across the creek, about 20 minutes from Ndangane by pirogue, **Mar Lodj** is one of the largest islands in the delta, extending over about 150 sq km (60 sq miles), and it supports a population of 5,000 spread across four villages, of which the largest are Mar Fafako and Mar Lothie. Like much of the delta, Mar Lodj isn't noted for its altitudinal variation – the highest point isn't even 10 metres (30ft) above sea level – but its cover of moist woodland and savannah supports an exceptionally varied birdlife, as do the channels that enclose it. A row of likeable but little-used **campements** lines the island's shore, their aura of remote rusticity enhanced by the island's lack of electricity (they are powered by generators or solar panels, but it's a good idea to bring a torch).

A popular landmark on Mar Lodj is a heavily buttressed *fromager* (kapok) tree whose trunk has become intertwined with those of an African mahogany and a borassus palm – locals have claimed this particularity as symbolic of the peaceful coexistence of the island's Muslim, Christian and animist populations.

TIP

It's possible to arrange a pirogue to take you all the way upriver from Ndangane to Foundiougne, a two- to three-hour trip through wide waterways and narrow creeks that allows travellers without private transport to combine estuarine sightseeing with some fairly efficient avoidance of circuitous bush taxis!

LEFT: a boat trip is the best way to see the delta fauna.

Fishing

Senegal provides some excellent opportunities for game fishing, especially along the offshore fish migration route where the warm Guinea current meets the cold current of the Canaries, and in the labyrinthine creeks of the Siné-Saloum. Over 20 of the larger species fished in these waters are recognised by the Florida-based International Game Fish Association, and at least 30 other game fish are prevalent, among them swordfish, blue marlin, tunny, sea bass, wahoo, yellowfin, sailfish, barracuda, sawfish, blackfin and rays of all sorts – even the massive sunfish. A few shark species, including hammerhead, have been caught here too.

Fishing trips can be arranged through most hotels in the Petite Côte and Siné-Saloum Delta. They usually last from 8am to 4pm. Boats carry four to six passengers and provide meals and refreshments. Most are equipped with VHF radio, outriggers, downriggers, electronic depth sounders and even fish finders. With all this sophisticated equipment on board, it is somewhat humbling, several miles out into the Atlantic Ocean, to meet up with a fishing pirogue that has no technology more advanced than 20 strong oarsmen.

The pool area at the Hôtel Les Palétuviers.

BELOW: The Plage d'Or, also run by Les Palétuviers, on Ginak Island.

road. The town has a busy market and a few old colonial buildings – the Courthouse, Lutheran Church and Préfecture are all worth a look – but otherwise it is of interest solely as the junction for **Dakhonga**, from where a vehicle ferry leaves five times daily for **Foundiougne** on the south bank of the Saloum River.

The **Dakhonga–Foundiougne Ferry** is the only place upriver of Kaolack where vehicles can cross between the southern and northern delta. The crossing is inexpensive and it only takes a few minutes, but with just five daily departures in either direction, it is worth planning around these times.

Crossing times from Foundiougne to Dakhonga are 7.30am, 9.30am, 11.30am, 3pm and 7pm, while they run at 8.30am, 10.30am, 12.30pm, 3.30pm and 6.30pm in the opposite direction daily, except on Wednesday when the 3pm and 3.30pm runs are scrapped. This timetable has changed little in decades, and departures are generally as punctual as could be expected, but the boat is subject to increasingly frequent breakdowns, in which case there will be no ferry and you're in for a long trip via Kaolack.

Back on the RN1, **Fatick** ❺ is the principal town of the northern delta and capital of the eponymous administrative region, supporting a population estimated at around 25,000. Facilities include a post office, cybercafés and shops to prepare for your trip further into the region. The town is set alongside the wide salty mudflats that flank the Siné River, and one of its major economic activities is salt production, which is still undertaken manually, as can be seen from the main

Recommended Restaurants and Bars on page 203

outh of the Saloum

he administrative centre of **Foun-iougne ❻**, recognised as a municipality nce 1917, boasts a few interesting colo-al buildings but has a relatively modest opulation of around 6,000 people. Con-ected to the north bank by a motor ferry, is minor port and major important fish-g centre is also an increasingly popular ase for independent travellers and shermen, who are catered to by a var-ed selection of bars and restaurants, hile accommodation options range om the smart **Hôtel Foundiougne** to a ariety of camps, including the friendly verfront **Les Bolongs** and **Le Baobab ur Mer**. In the vicinity of town are umerous creeks, reed beds and water-ays that warrant exploration by irogue. Most camps will offer boat ours, at similar prices.

From Foundiougne, a passable 33km 20-mile) surfaced road arcs through Djilor to the junction town of **Passi**, vhich straddles the surfaced (but in arts densely potholed) RN5 to Banjul Gambia) about 30km (18 miles) south-vest of Kaolack. A further 18km (11 niles) southwest, **Sokone** is the largest town on the RN7, supporting a population of 12,500. It's a useful place to stop for lunch or fuel en route from Kaolack to Banjul, but there is little reason to linger beyond that.

Toubacouta

A more popular stop along the RN7 is **Toubacouta ❼**, a sprawling small town that runs north of the main road to the south bank of the Bandiala River. Set among tall mangroves on a thickly wooded stretch of the shore, Toubacouta is easily one of the most beautiful spots of the delta. It is also home to some of the finest hotels in the Siné-Saloum region, notably the excellent **Hôtel Keur Saloum** and **Les Palétuviers**, both of which offer accommodation in comfortable air-conditioned bungalows, and have a swim-ming pool, world-class restaurant and bar. A legend among the game-fishing community, the Hôtel Keur Saloum has been organising angling expeditions into the delta and open ocean for decades, and its clients hold many records (includ-ing the world record for red snapper), but similar excursions can be arranged through several other operators.

Les Palétuviers' excursion buses are sparkling clean.

LEFT: mask typical of the region.
BELOW: making a run for it.

Fun and games.

Toubacouta is also well placed for wildlife enthusiasts, as it offers regular excursions to the Île des Oiseaux, which is a seasonal home to 40,000 nesting terns, and is better-placed for game drives into the national park and Réserve de Fathala than any other lodge. As the closest access point to the delta from Banjul (The Gambia) and the furthest from Dakar, Toubacouta attracts more English- and Dutch-speaking tourists than most other parts of Senegal.

The island on the opposite side of the Bandiala River to Toubacouta is the site of the **Aire Marine Protégée de Bamboung** (Bamboung Protected Marine Area), a community conservation project monitored by 14 villages on the Bamboung Bolong, a creek that arcs northward through the mangroves for about 10km (6 miles) before its confluence with the Diombos River. The core purpose of the project is to curb the illegal fishing that threatens the sustainability of the local marine harvest elsewhere in the delta, and the high level of community involvement – local villagers act as rangers, regularly patrolling the *bolong* in motorised pirogues – has ensured its

BELOW: hut accomodation.
RIGHT: seeing the world upside-down.

success. The volume of fish in the *bolon* is reckoned to be at its highest level decades, and recent years have witnesse the welcome return of several specie that had become scarce as a result overfishing, as well as an increase resident populations of piscivorous bir such as herons, egrets and kingfisher

An eco-lodge called **Keur Bamboun** (www.oceanium.org) has been establishe alongside the *bolong*, to help genera funds for the project. It offers accomm dation in a dozen organically constructe huts that use solar electricity and well rain water, as well as guided walks an pirogue rides in the mangroves, whic harbour a rich birdlife as well as sma populations of warthog, spotted hyen and green monkey. Visits must be arrange at the main office in central Toubacout from where transfers to the island – v pirogue and donkey-cart – take less the half an hour.

Some 12km (7 miles) from Touba couta along a good dirt road, the bus fishing village of **Missirah** has pretty location on the bank of the Band ala, and could be a pleasant place for day trip were it not for the incessar

Recommended Restaurants and Bars on page 203

demands for money made of visitors. Its best-known landmark is an enormous buttressed *fromager* (kapok) tree that stands a short distance back from the river, approximately 100 metres/yards left of the main road as you enter the village, and is reputed to be more than 1,000 years old – probably not true, but the tree is very impressive all the same.

There's no accommodation in Missirah, but the modestly priced, peaceful and very comfortable **Gîte de Bandiala**, situated immediately outside the boundary of Parc National du Delta du Saloum, only 3km (2 miles) from the village, is one of the best bases in for wildlife-lovers anywhere in the delta region. Reminiscent of a South African bush lodge, this small camp is set in thick woodland, rattling with birds and lizards, where a small waterhole overlooked by an elevated hide attracts a steady stream of green and patas monkeys, as well as warthogs and other animals. Bandiala is a wonderfully restful spot, full of character, though inconvenient to travellers without their own transport as it lies 30 minutes' walk from any bush taxi route and a similar distance from the water.

Parc National du Delta du Saloum

The main entrance to the **Parc National du Delta du Saloum** ❿ (tel: 33 832 2309; daily 7am–6pm; charge) is in Missirah, at the office of the ecoguards. The guards will then take you to the park headquarters, 6km (4 miles) away. Extending over 750 sq km (290 sq miles), this is the second-largest national park in Senegal, protecting much of the marine side of the delta, along with an extensive tract of dry savannah woodland running towards the Gambian border. The sea parts of the park allow mainly for birdwatching. The forest section protects a range of large mammals, most abundantly warthogs, hyenas, phacochers and monkeys, but poaching and sanctioned hunting have both taken their toll, so that formerly common antelope such as bushbuck and red-flanked duiker are now rather scarce in most areas.

The national park is host to many species of monkeys, including green, red colobus and patas.

BELOW:
French lesson at a Toubacouta school.

The stunning Abyssinian roller can be spotted at the Réserve de Fathala.

BELOW: roan antelopes take their name from the "roan" colour (a reddish brown).

However, interest in the park is likely to be stoked by the formal opening of the IUCN-sponsored **Circuit Écotouristique de Bakadadji** in 2008. Based out of the village of Bakadadji, which is located 4km (3 miles) from Missirah, this development consists of a land circuit that can be explored either on foot or by mountain bike, as well as an aquatic circuit undertaken by motorised pirogue, and personable guides are available in the village.

Among the sites included on the circuit are a baobab forest that was once inhabited by a legendary marabout, Île des Hyènes (Hyenas Island, where you are sure to see hyena dens, if not the actual animals), Île des Oiseaux (inhabited by pelicans, egrets and cormorants among plenty of other species) and various other baobab-studded shell islands and densely vegetated *bolong*s.

Réserve de Fathala

Open to the public since 2003, some 20 sq km (8 sq miles) of thick tree savannah within the national park has been fenced off as the **Réserve de Fathala** ⑪ (tel: 33 637 9455; daily 7am–7pm; charge). Clearly modelled on the Réserve de Bandia *(see page 172)*, Fathala has been stocked with indigenous wildlife from both Bandia and Niokolo-Koba parks, including roan antelope, kob, buffalo and Defassa waterbuck, as well as a pair of white rhino and trio of giraffes of Southern African stock, and it also hosts good numbers of naturally occurring mammals such as green monkey, patas monkey, Guinea baboon, bushbuck, red-flanked duiker, warthog, forest buffalo and side-striped jackal.

For serious wildlife enthusiasts, the big draw here is a herd of 17 western giant eland, which has been introduced from Niokolo-Koba and might well represent around 10 percent of the wild global population of this endangered subspecies of the world's largest antelope. Most of these species are likely to be seen in the course of a two–three hour guided game drive, as is an excellent variety of woodland birds, ranging from the dashing Abyssinian roller to the handsome palmnut vulture.

The Forest of Fathala is sadly being threatened by excessive livestock grazing from the surrounding villages, intensive illegal logging, fruit and bark gathering and poaching.

The entrance gate to Fathala lies on the right-hand side of the RN5 approximately 20km (12 miles) past Toubacouta not far before the small town of Karang on the Gambian border. Self-drive visitors must have a 4x4 and can arrange guides on the spot, but open-sided safari vehicles with drivers are also on offer to visitors. Whether or not you drive yourself at Fathala, the overall package inclusive of entrance fees works out at around double the cost of a similar safari in Bandia, and it seems rather exorbitant when compared to similarly small reserves elsewhere in Africa – so don't visit on a tight budget!

RESTAURANTS AND BARS

Restaurants

Prices for a main course per person:
$ = under US$8 (CFA3,200)
$$ = US$8–15 (CFA 3,200–6,000)
$$$ = over US$15 (CFA6,000)

Ndangane

Le Pic Bœuf
Main road
Tel: 77 574 7385 **$**
Set about 100 metres/yds back from the beach opposite the junction to Joal-Fadiouth, this inexpensive eatery with shell-strewn floor and thatched roof has a well-stocked bar, an espresso machine and a varied menu that includes seafood, meat and pasta dishes. Open 9am–10pm.

Le Temarko
Ndangane Pier
Tel: 77 594 9413 **$$**
Boasting the prime position in Ndangane, this open-sided waterfront restaurant has an ambience to match its location, with an African decor topped by a tall thatch roof. Lively Senegalese music and a warm welcome complement the decor, and the seafood-dominated menu is good value. Open 10am–11pm.

Foundiougne

Hôtel-Campement
Le Baobab sur Mer
Route de la Corniche
Tel: 33 948 1262 **$–$$**
Situated on a peninsula above the Saloum River, the thatched restaurant at this popular small hotel serves good Senegalese and French fare, and the well-stocked bar is usually lively in the evenings. Open lunch and dinner.

Toubacouta

Brasserie de Toubacouta
Tel: 33 652 9605 **$–$$**
Set in the heart of Toubacouta, 200 metres/yds from the waterfront, this is the most popular bar-restaurant in town, thanks to its bright decor, thatched umbrella-style seating, clean open-sided kitchen and a satellite TV that gets hauled out for major international sports events. It serves up moderately priced seafood and meat dishes. Open noon–3pm and 6pm–late.

Campement du Centre
$
This local-style campement in the heart of Toubacouta is brightly painted, with a shady thatch roof, and the beers and meals here are as cheap as it gets in this part of Senegal. The menu is dominated by seafood and meat grills/brochettes.

Les Palétuviers
Tel: 33 948 7776 **$$$**
Situated in lovely grounds centred on a large swimming pool, this smart hotel welcomes non-resident diners to its legendary seafood dinner buffets, and it also serves a varied selection of à la carte dishes at lunch.

BELOW: tables set for dinner in the lovely baobab- and kapok-shaded grounds of Les Palétuviers.

Recommended Restaurants, Bars and Cafés on pages 214–15

SAINT-LOUIS

Explore this atmospheric seaport, whose spectacular Grande Mosquée sits amid elegant French colonial architecture; a little further afield are wildlife reserves teeming with birds

he capital of Senegal's most northerly region, **Saint-Louis ❶** is the country's sixth-largest city, with a population of around 170,000, and its third-largest seaport (having been superseded by Mbour in population terms back in 2003). Situated on N'Dar Island a few kilometres upstream of the Senegal River Mouth, Saint-Louis lies less than 10km (6 miles) south of the Mauritanian border, and it is connected to Dakar by a well-maintained 260km (160-mile) highway.

France's first settlement

Cold statistics, however, do scant justice to the historical significance and rich ambience of this most distinctive and enjoyable of Senegalese cities, which was founded by French traders in 1659, and baptised Saint-Louis-du-Fort in honour of King Louis XIII. Not only is Saint-Louis the oldest French settlement in Senegal, but it also served as the main centre of their West African operations for two centuries prior to 1902 (when Dakar was made capital of the Afrique Occidentale Française; *see page 48*), and it remained the administrative capital of Senegal and Mauritania until 1958.

Prior to the establishment of Saint-Louis, the island was reputedly uninhabited, though the Portuguese explorer Lançarote set anchor nearby in 1445, and Thomas Lambert, a former governor of the Compagnie de Normandie, landed here in 1638. It was Louis Caullier who started constructing the first permanent buildings 21 years later. With its fine harbour and easily defended position at the mouth of the Senegal River, Saint-Louis flourished as an important centre for trade with Europe and the Sahara. It also became one of the most important centres of the slave trade. By the late 18th century, the population had grown to 10,000. As on Gorée, a distinct wealthy and privileged elite was formed by the ladies of mixed African and European descent known as *signares*. In 1816 and again in 1824, René Caillié, the first European to visit the legendary city of

Main attractions
PONT FAIDHERBE
MUSÉE DE L'AÉROPOSTALE
JEAN-MERMOZ
PLACE FAIDHERBE
HÔTEL DE LA POSTE
PARC NATIONAL DE LA
LANGUE DE BARBARIE
RÉSERVE DE GUEMBEUL

LEFT: Pont Faidherbe is a feat of engineering.
BELOW: the streets of Saint-Louis.

A Saint-Louis street boulangerie.

Timbuktu (in Mali), used Saint-Louis as the starting point for his explorations of the West African interior.

Two governors had considerable influence on the development of Saint-Louis. Baron Roger, governor from 1822 until 1827, was responsible for the building of the Maurel et Prom trading house, one of the most important buildings of its time in Senegal, and for the erection of a cathedral on the site of an earlier wooden church. When Louis Faidherbe became governor in 1854, he embarked on extensive improvements. In 1880 the town hall was built and, three years later, Saint-Louis was linked to Dakar by rail. Faidherbe also supervised the construction of the **Pont Moustapha-Malick-Ga** (originally called Pont Servatius), whi still forms the only link between N'D Island and the mainland suburbs of **Gu N'Dar** and **N'Dar Tout** on **Langue Barbarie** (Barbary Tongue), the lon narrow spit of sand that separates t calm waters of the Senegal River fro the more turbulent Atlantic Ocean.

Whether coming from Dakar or els where in the country, the sole point access to central Saint-Louis is the Gu tave Eiffel-designed **Pont Faidherbe** the impressive metallic structure whi has linked N'Dar to the eastern mainla since 1899. Before reaching the bridg you first pass through the sprawlin mainland suburb of **Sor**, which is larg and more populous than the old tov centre, and has a more modern Afric feel. Sor holds little that is of specif interest to travellers, though it is the si of the city's main *gare routière* (bus ar taxi station) as well as the railway statio which dates back to 1908 but is no long used by regular passenger services.

Colonial elegance

Steeped in colonial history, Saint-Lou has some of the finest examples French architecture in Africa, includi several structures that date from the 18 century, when the city was at its mo prosperous. Many of these older buil ings are double-storey residences co structed around a cool central courtyar with wooden balconies on the first flo and painted with a flaking coat of past orange, yellow or red. On first contac the somewhat Mediterranean appearan of the city centre might seem at od with the predominantly Afro-Islam population, but one soon recognises ho these disparate elements have integrate to generate a unique and absorbing sen of place. This singularity of atmosphe – reminiscent of Gorée but on a far grand scale – has been greatly enhanced sinc by Saint-Louis's inscription as a Unesc World Heritage Site in 2000. Mar buildings that were very run-down even in ruins before the turn of the m lennium have since been restored to the

Saint-Louis

ormer glory and freshly painted, creating a strong aura of urban rejuvenation.

The compact city centre, built to a grid pattern which covers N'Dar Island in its entirety, is easily covered on foot. It is perfectly possible to do this unescorted, but there is also much to be said for employing the services of a registered local guide, which can be arranged at the helpful **Syndicat d'Initiative** (tourist office; tel: 33 961 2455; daily 9am–1pm and 3.30–6.30pm) around the corner from the post office opposite the Pont Faidherbe. Even if you prefer to explore under your own steam, the tourist office is a useful source of current travel advice.

Next door, the **Musée de l'Aéropostale Jean-Mermoz**  (tel: 33 961 455; daily 9am–1pm and 3.30–6.30pm; harge) which opened in 2005, documents the history of the early 20th-century airmail service between Europe and aint-Louis, and the dashing pilots who manned the flights.

a Savane

ituated behind the Syndicat d'Initiative, the most obvious starting point for a walking tour of the city is the central **Place Faidherbe** (known locally as "La Savane"), which lies in the oldest part of Saint-Louis, site of a 17th-century fort and cemetery, both of which were later built over. Alive with birdsong, Place Faidherbe is an oasis of shady greenery in the otherwise built-up city centre, watched over by a statue of the French colonial governor after whom it is named, which is in turn shaded over by a rather odd artificial palm tree in a shade of pink blancmange.

The square is surrounded by houses from the Louis-Philippe (1930–48) period, most of which are intact. The **Hôtel de l'Administration** (Governor's Palace) partially obscured from view by a stand of tall leafy trees, is an imperious example of early 19th-century architecture.

Opposite, the large Catholic **Cathédrale** , founded in 1828, is reputedly the oldest extant church in Senegal, though its dimensions seem somewhat

The total length of the Pont Faidherbe is 507.35 metres (1,664½ft) and the width is 10.5 metres (34½ft). The total weight of the deck is 1,500 tonnes.

BELOW:
the impressive staircase inside the Maison des Sœurs.

The excellent Saint-Louis Jazz Festival attracts musicians and fans from all over the world.

excessive today as the city's population is predominantly Islamic.

Six blocks south of the cathedral, facing the hospital on Rue Chassagnol, the former **Maison des Sœurs** (House of Sisters), originally housing an orphanage and now used as government offices, also dates from the early 19th century and is notable for its unique circular internal stairwell.

At the southeastern tip of the island, behind a row of five intricately carved palm stumps, the **Musée du Centre de Recherche et de Documentation** (Research and Documentation Museum; daily 9am–noon and 3–6pm; photography forbidden; charge) hosts some interesting displays relating to the history of Saint-Louis. Displays about the adobe mosques on Île à Morfil and the French forts built along the Senegal River in the 19th century make an excellent primer for travellers planning to journey further upriver.

Ancient and modern

The part of N'Dar to the north of Place Faidherbe, much of which was laid out in the 1870s, contains fewer individual historical landmarks, although many of the older buildings have attractive features such as iron fretwork balconies, wooden shutters, and elegant arcades and colonnades. At one time, no building on the island was allowed to be higher than the **Grande Mosquée** , a spectacular structure set in the grounds of an ancient fortified mansion between **Quai Roume** (on the northeastern riverfront) and **Avenue Jean-Mermoz**. Another attractive **mosque** is to be found a few hundred metres west of this on the Boulevard du Général-Giraud.

For all its historic qualities, Saint Louis also possesses a definite contemporary and cosmopolitan buzz, certainly when compared to most towns in the interior. **Rue Blaise-Diagne** and **Rue Abdoulaye-Sack**, the main drags running north from Place Faidherbe, are lined with street cafés, patisseries, French and Moroccan restaurants – eating out is a highlight of hanging around in Saint Louis. You will also find trendy boutiques, internet cafés and the inevitable proliferation of curio stalls and craft emporiums. Like its American namesake, the town has long been associate

ith live music. There's no shortage of osy bars and livelier clubs where you n stay out until the small hours – try larco's for background classic jazz om the 1930s–60s, the Iguana Café ith its relaxing sofas and contemporary &B and African music, or the water-ont Flamingo Bar for a breezy alfresco ·ink backed by the lapping of water gainst stone. Serious jazz enthusiasts ill need little persuasion to try to fit eir itinerary around the annual **Saint-ouis International Jazz Festival**, hich takes place in May and attracts :lebrated musicians from all over Africa id the rest of the world.

andmark hotels

ne of the city's best-known landmarks, uilt in the mid-19th century, the **Hôtel e la Poste ⊙** on the waterfront opposite ont Faidherbe is a red-tiled three-orey building with painted frontage, olourful awnings, a cosy veranda and a rge swimming pool. From the river, the otel and its neighbouring mansions in arious shades of pastel present a pic-resque vista reflected in the water. The otel interior is worth lingering over, as

it manages – perhaps a little self-consciously – to embody all the qualities one associates with an overblown but romantic colonial outpost, with a bar furnished in mock leopard skin and animal heads mounted on the pink walls.

The Hôtel de la Poste, while typical of the colonial architecture of Saint-Louis, is not as luxurious as the newer **Hôtel Pointe Sud** and **Hôtel Sindone**, both of which are modern multi-storey constructions with air-conditioned rooms, situated on the southern part of the island close to the museum. When it comes to value for money, however, the pick of Saint-Louis's hostelries has to be the **Hôtel de la Résidence**, a long-serving family hotel that resembles the Hôtel de la Poste in some respects, but is smaller and more homely, and it retains a strong period feel refreshingly free of stuffed animal heads.

Over to Guet N'Dar

Outside of the town centre, another interesting walk from Place Faidherbe leads across Pont Moustapha-Malick-Gaye to **Guet N'Dar** on the Langue de Barbarie. Continue straight ahead after crossing the bridge, past the whitewashed **Monu-**

Fans of modern African music are urged to pop into the Teranga Music Shop, which has a great selection of CDs by Senegalese, Malian and other African artists, as well as a wall entirely covered in old Afripop LPs that will have vinyl buffs salivating.

The Year's Finale

Most spectacular of all the festivals in Senegal are the Saint-Louis Fanals. Likened by some observers to the carnivals of Latin America, the Fanals take place between 21 December and 1 January. They date back from colonial times when the predominant religion of Saint-Louis was Roman Catholicism. Christmas Eve mass was an important social occasion during which the Saint-Louis *signares* (ladies of mixed African and European descent) competed with each other to display the most sumptuous gowns and the richest jewellery.

Every year the gowns became more extravagant. The rich half-castes, often mistresses of the elite merchant class, employed pages to support their trains and carry lighted lanterns in their path. While the ladies attended the service, the lantern-carriers held their own competition outside the church to see whose paper lantern was most artistically

constructed. Coloured paper, cloth and tinsel were fashioned into fabulous shapes lit from inside by candles.

Today the Fanals are real works of art sponsored by local businessmen and paraded through the streets of Saint-Louis in a whirl of excitement and a carnival air. Paper and cardboard, silver foil, gilt, tinsel and coloured cloth are used in order to create spectacular designs. Ships, aeroplanes, buildings and monuments, masks – even replicas of mosques – are displayed in a great procession. A prize and the honour of best exhibit are awarded to the company responsible for the most attractive lantern. Visitors flock to Saint-Louis to witness this great spectacle, which is as vibrant as many of the carnivals of the Caribbean or Brazil. If you're not around at the right time of year, an example of a Fanal is exhibited in the Musée du Centre de Recherche et de Documentation *(see opposite)*.

Market stalls along Avenue Dodds.

BELOW: the tranquil waters of the Parc National de la Langue de Barbarie.

waters of the Atlantic as they land or out to sea.

Turning south from the market alo **Avenue Dodds**, running down the ce tre of Guet N'Dar, one comes to a ve different part of Saint-Louis. The wh walls and red-tiled roofs give way t more randomly constructed sector, onl few metres from the elegant 18th-cent quarter and its tree-lined avenues. H the Wolof fishermen have set up th village. Amidst their huts and pirogu nets are mended, fish are dried on rac or cured in smoke-houses, and there i constant bustle of people. The river s of the narrow spit is carpeted with patchwork of vegetable gardens.

Pressing on through the village, ab 1km (½ mile) south of the market is t strange and impressive **Cimetière d Pêcheurs** (fishermen's cemetery), who rough tombs covered with fishing n lend a weird and uncanny air to the vi of sea, sand and low huts.

About 2km (1 mile) further south, t attractive dunes and beaches have recent years spawned a clutch of low-k but comfortable resorts, including t **Hôtel Mermoz**, **Hôtel Cap Saint-Lo**

ment aux Morts (War Memorial) to the main marketplace, where Wolof tribesmen wearing loose embroidered shirts guide their fabulously decked-out wives around the maze of booths, and Peul women commandeer odd corners to set out their dried fish or red and green chillies. The beach in front of the market is particularly worth visiting in the late afternoon, when dozens of colourful pirogues can be seen riding the choppy

nd **Hôtel l'Oasis**, catering to tourists hose interest lies primarily in beaches ther than cities.

At the southernmost point of the spit is e **Hydrobase**, once the headquarters of e famous French airman Jean Mer-oz's airmail service. The buildings here ave now fallen into disrepair, and an ura of decay clings to the whole area. evertheless, the huge sand dunes run-ing along the shore still attract plenty f picnic and bathing parties. As the ydrobase and the beach are quite a dis-ance from the centre, you may decide ou want to hire a taxi or horse-drawn arriage for the journey.

Outside Saint-Louis

One of the more popular excursions from aint-Louis, described more fully in the **enegal River Region** chapter, is the orld-famous Parc National des Oiseaux u Djoudj *(see pages 218–20)*, which is 0km (36 miles) from Saint-Louis by oad and hosts some of the greatest aterbird concentrations in West Africa, s well as other wildlife.

Another recommended excursion for ird enthusiasts, only 18km (12 miles) om Saint-Louis, the **Parc National de Langue de Barbarie** ❷ (daily 7am– pm; charge) is named after the spit of and separating the Senegal River from e Atlantic Ocean. Somewhat confus-gly, however, the national park protects ot only the very southern end of Langue e Barbarie, but also a long stretch of the ain coast. For this reason, the entrance ate, in the mainland village of **Mouit** pposite Langue de Barbarie, is reached y driving back towards Dakar for 5km 3 miles), then taking a right fork south nd driving another 15km (9 miles). lthough most visitors come to this park n a day trip, comfortable rooms, camp-g space and good home cooking are all vailable at the Swiss-owned **Campe-ent Zebrabar** in Mouit, 500 metres/ ards from the park entrance.

The rangers at Mouit will arrange otorised pirogue trips into the park ith reliable boatmen at a fixed price. In ddition to visiting the **Senegal River**

Mouth, where common dolphins are occasionally seen, the boat trip goes past **Île des Oiseaux**, which supports resident colonies of white pelican, grey-headed gull, great cormorant and various terns, egrets and herons. During the European winter, this sandy stretch of coast also attracts a wide variety of migratory waterfowl and waders. The marine fauna includes four species of turtle, which have adopted the lonely coastline as a nesting ground, underlining the park's international importance.

Alongside the main road to the Parc National de la Langue de Barbarie and only 12km (7 miles) south of Saint-Louis, lies the 700-hectare (1,730-acre) **Réserve de Guembeul** ❸ (daily 8am–6pm; charge). Originally set aside in 1983 as a bird sanctuary, it now hosts a unique breeding project for four species of Sahe-lian antelope that have been hunted to extinction in Senegal. These are the scimitar-horned oryx (IUCN-listed as Extinct in the Wild), Dama gazelle (Crit-ically Endangered), addax (Critically Endangered) and Dorcas gazelle (Vul-nerable). Small herds of Dama gazelle and scimitar-horned oryx were intro-

KIDS

The Campement Zebrabar is a perfect place to stay if you're travelling with small children – they'll love the mini playground the friendly owners have built especially for them.

BELOW: a ghost crab in the Parc National de la Langue de Barbarie.

Royal terns in the Parc National de la Langue de Barbarie.

duced to Guembeul in 1994 and 1999 respectively, initially into small holding pens, but they have bred so successfully that they now roam freely throughout the reserve. Some of their offspring have been relocated to the Réserve de Ferlo-Nord, and are currently in holding pens there, for eventual release into the wild. The success of this project has led to the relocation of six addax from captivity in Canada to a holding pen in Guembeul in 2006, followed by 20 Dorcas gazelle from Spain in 2007, with the hope that they too can be released into the wild and eventually form a sustainable population.

Guided tours of Guembeul can be undertaken by motorised vehicle (ideally 4x4), donkey-cart or on foot. You'␣ unlikely to miss the addax and Dorca␣ gazelle in their pens, and the chances ␣ tracking down the free-roaming popula␣ tions of 45 scimitar-horned oryx and 3␣ Dama gazelle are pretty good too, thoug␣ the latter can be quite skittish. In add␣ tion to antelope, the terrestrial patas mo␣ key is quite often seen in the reserve, ␣ are warthogs. The classic Sahelian acac␣ savannah of Guembeul hosts a varie␣ selection of woodland birds throughou␣ the year, boosted by large flocks ␣ aquatic species in the rainy season, whe␣ the seasonal floodplains fill with wate␣

Lac de Guiers

Some 50km (30 miles) inland of Sain␣ Louis, the remote **Lac de Guiers** is th␣ largest lake in Senegal, extending ov␣ 180 sq km (70 sq miles) when full. Low␣ lying and shallow, it has a somewhat se␣ pentine outline, stretching for 35km (2␣ miles) from north to south along th␣ Ferlo River Valley, but nowhere mor␣ than 7km (4 miles) wide. The lake ␣ linked to the Senegal River by a can␣ that flows past the town of Richard To␣ and supplies water to its sugar refinerie␣

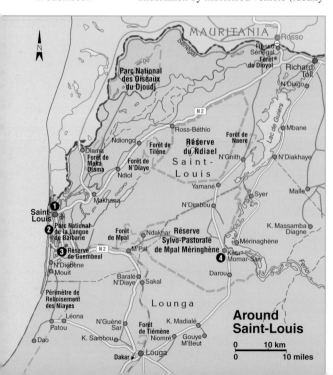

as well as to several small towns and villages dotted around its shores. It also provides 30 percent of Dakar's drinking water via a subterranean system of pipes running southwest from its shores for 250km (150 miles). The lake isn't formally protected, but it is recognised as an Important Bird Area for the wealth of aquatic birds – in particular African and European spoonbill, glossy ibis, lesser flamingo and a variety of colonial nesting herons and egrets – that frequent the open shallows and reed-lined shore.

Market town

The most important town to be found on the lakeshore is **Keur Momar-Sarr** ❹, many of whose 8,000 residents work at the nearby water-treatment plant and pumping station for Dakar. On Saturdays, the town makes way for the most important market in the region, attracting a colourful mix of Fulani herders and Wolof fishermen from miles around, as well as a fair number of day trippers from Saint-Louis. Situated on the lake's southwestern shore, Keur Momar-Sarr can eaily be reached from Saint-Louis along a good 120km (72-mile) surfaced road via Louga, but those with a 4x4 can almost halve the distance by following a sandy track that branches east from the main road at **M'Pal**.

Culturally, the Saturday market at Keur Momar-Sarr is the highlight of the rough road circuit that encircles Lac de Guiers, but the road also passes through several small Fulani and Wolof villages that see few tourists. For birdwatchers, the shore around Keur Momar-Sarr is so densely vegetated that it practically blocks access to the lakeshore, but it is possible to continue north from here to Richard Toll via **N'Gnith** along a rather rough track.

A better option, though one that still requires a 4x4, is to cross the southern end of the lake from Keur Momar-Sarr to the west-bank settlement of Mérinaghène, set in a pastoral region known for its rice production. From here, you can travel north along the western shore to Richard Toll via **Syer**, **Mbane** and **N'Diago**. Around the area of Mbane many small lakes stretch out along the Ferlo River, surrounded by numerous tiny fishing villages, while Syer is know for its fishing co-operative. ❏

The gigantic Sulcata tortoise, a vulnerable Sahelian endemic and the world's largest mainland tortoise (weighing up to 50kg/ 110lbs), breeds in sand holes in a fenced enclosure near the reserve headquarters.

BELOW:
the Saturday market at Keur Momar-Sarr.

RESTAURANTS, BARS AND CAFÉS

Restaurants

Prices for a main course per person:
$ = under US$8 (CFA3,200)
$$ = US$8–15 (CFA 3,200–6,000)
$$$ = over US$15 (CFA6,000)

Aux Délices du Fleuve
Cnr Rue Guilabert and Quai Roume
Tel: 33 961 4251
$
This legendary coffee shop and patisserie is *the* place to head to for a mid-morning or afternoon shot of caffeine and sucrose, and it also serves a limited selection of light meals. Open daily 7.30am–1pm and 3–6pm.

Bar Marco Jazz
Quai Roume
$
Situated opposite the Flamingo Restaurant, this self-consciously dingy bar brilliantly evokes the golden musical era of Saint-Louis's American namesake, with its deep-blue velvet sofas, monochrome photos of old jazz artists adorning the black walls, and an excellent sound system blasting music remastered from scratchy old 78s. No food served. Open 6pm–late.

La Case Crevettes
Rue Abdoulaye-Seck
$
One of the best cheapies in the town centre, this serves a variety of inex-pensive and simple seafood dishes.

L'Embuscade
Rue Blanchot
Tel: 33 961 7741
$
This cosy central bar is known for its reasonably priced beers, well-stocked spirits bar and contemporary selection of music, mostly American and Senegalese R&B and hip hop. Tapas and other light snacks are on the limited food menu.

Flamingo Restaurant
Quai Roume
Tel: 33 961 1118
$$
On a secluded riverfront location around the corner from the sister Hôtel de la Poste, this spacious indoor and outdoor restaurant is a nice spot to enjoy a breezy evening drink overlooking the iconic Pont Faidherbe, and the varied and moderately priced menu – pizzas, pasta, seafood, meat grills, etc – is a good reason to stay on for dinner.

Hôtel de la Résidence
159 Rue Blaise-Diagne
Tel: 33 961 1260
Main courses $$;
set menu $$$
The small and intimately decorated restaurant at this evergreen family-managed hotel serves a small but interesting selection of traditional French and fusion dishes, dominated by seafood

BELOW: L'Embuscade is a popular beer and tapas place.

but including more unusual items such as duck and liver. The service is commendable and prices are very competitive for a place of its quality and reputation. Open for lunch and dinner.

Hôtel Sindone
Quai Henri-Jay
Tel: 33 961 4244
$$$
The moment you step onto the palm-shaded floating deck of the Sindone's restaurant, you realise how few of Saint-Louis's eateries offer a view of the river. The fact that it's an exception is reason enough to eat here, but the seafood is also among the finest on the island. Open for lunch and dinner.

Iguana Café
Cnr Rue Bisson and Rue Abdoulaye-Seck
$

Eclectically decorated and very comfortable with its sofa-style seating, this cigar bar serves one of the widest selections of drinks in town, and there's usually some good African music blasting away in the background. Drinking, smoking and lively conversation are the main lines here, but it does serve snacks and sandwiches too. Open 9am–late.

Palais Saint-Louis
Cnr Rue Blanchot and Ababacar-Sy
Tel: 33 961 1772
$
Combining traditional colonial architecture with bright contemporary African decor, the bar and patisseries of this hotel are great places to chill out in Saint-Louis, whether it's for a morning coffee and croissant or a bleary nightcap.

Occasional live music. Open 7.30am–1.30am.

La Pirogue
Rue Marie-Parsins
Tel: 33 376 8104
$$
The intimate mood of this tiny restaurant – only six tables – is enhanced by the earthy decor, punchy selection of West African and sixties soul music, and warm Senegalese management. The Franco-Senegalese menu is dominated by seafood, but meat dishes are also available. Dinner only.

La Saigonnaise
33 Place de Liège
Tel: 33 961 6481
$$
Endorsed by a roll call of foreign ambassadors, this popular restaurant on the northern tip of the island offers great views over the water from the stylish terracotta balcony

and the glass-sided indoor area. French menu, with seafood being the main speciality. Good wine list. Open daily 11am–11pm.

Restaurant de Fez
Ave Ababacar-Sy
$
This homely and good-value restaurant – again, just six tables – is owned by a welcoming Moroccan lady and serves cuisine typical of that country, including chicken with couscous or stewed lamb tajine. Contrary to expectations, alcohol is served.

Restaurant Galaxie
265 Ave Abdoulaye-Seck
Tel: 33 961 2466
$
Budget travellers should seek out this popular local eatery, which serves filling and inexpensive seafood and other Franco-Senegalese fare. Open 8am–11pm.

BELOW: La Saigonnaise offers tasty food and a spectacular view looking to Mauritania.

Recommended Restaurants and Bars on page 231

THE SENEGAL RIVER REGION

Starting at Saint-Louis, the Senegal River Route
follows West Africa's second-largest waterway for
hundreds of kilometres. It is dotted with crumbling
relics of the early colonial era and characterised
by traditional cultures and architecture

More than 1,000 miles (1,600km) in length, the Senegal River is still less than half the length of the Niger, which is West Africa's longest river. Rising in the Fouta Djalon mountains in Guinea, the river creates a large curve embracing both The Gambia and Senegal itself, of which it forms the northern boundary. Its wide arc flows around great plains of near-desert, such as the Fouta and the Ferlo.

Along the river

Senegal is named after West Africa's second-longest river, which rises in the Guinean highlands and runs along the country's eastern and northern border before emptying into the Atlantic Ocean near Saint-Louis. Meandering through a vast swathe of arid and unproductive land, the river's Senegalese banks support numerous small villages and half a dozen more substantial towns, namely Richard Toll, Dagana, Podor, Matam, Bakel and Kidira.

The dominant people along the river are the Tukulor, a branch of the Fula whose colourful dress code provides a striking contrast to the sepia-tinged scenery of the dusty plains, and whose attractive style of *banco* (adobe) architecture is reminiscent of neighbouring Mali. Islam has been a powerful force here since the 10th century, and most towns and villages are dominated by at least one large mosque, but social codes are relatively liberal, particularly when it comes to how women dress and behave in public.

With the exception of the popular Parc National du Djoudj near Saint-Louis, few tourists explore this remote corner of Senegal, and facilities tend to be relatively basic, though the package-tour industry has expanded upriver as far as Podor following the resumption of services by the legendary cruise ship *Bou el Mogdad* in 2005 *(see page 229)*. Further upstream, the Senegal River is followed by the well-maintained RN2, which connects Saint-Louis and Kidira and forms an attractive option for adventurous travellers heading to Mali or the

Main attractions

PARC NATIONAL DES
  OISEAUX DU DJOUDJ
RICHARD TOLL
DAGANA
ÎLE À MORFIL
PODOR
MATAM
BAKEL
KIDIRA

LEFT: looking out to Mauritania, on the other side of the river. **BELOW:** music festival in Podor.

African darters in the Parc National des Oiseaux du Djoudj. Around 3 million birds pass through the park every year.

Niokolo-Koba region. With the RN2 now being surfaced it its entirety, the travel time between Saint-Louis and Tambacounda via Kidira is about the same as the more popular route via Dakar, but it's worth allowing at least four days to make the most of sightseeing opportunities.

The Djoudj Basin

Immediately inland of Saint-Louis, the vast low-lying area bounded by a crook in the Senegal River to the northwest and the Rosso-Sénégal road to the southeast is known as the Djoudj Basin. This is the

site of Senegal's third-smallest and most northerly national park, namely the **Parc National des Oiseaux du Djoudj**  (tel: 33 968 8708; daily 7am–7pm; charge), whose entrance gate lies about 60km (40 miles) from Saint-Louis, a short distance downstream of the reservoir created by the Barrage de Maka-Diama. Extending over some 16,000 hectares (40,000 acres), the park was created in 1971 and designated a Unesco World Heritage Site 10 years later, in recognition of its status as one of the world's 10 most important waterfowl sanctuaries.

Although it's worth seeing at any time of the year, Djoudj comes into its own during the European winter, when up to 3 million migrant birds pass through during any given year. Djoudj's significance derives from its location at the south of the Sahara: it is the first body of water encountered by Palaearctic birds when they migrate to sub-Saharan Africa. While many of these birds will eventually fly further south, a great many settle in for the whole winter, when the marshes becomes a seething mass of waterfowl and waders. Although populations vary from one year to the next,

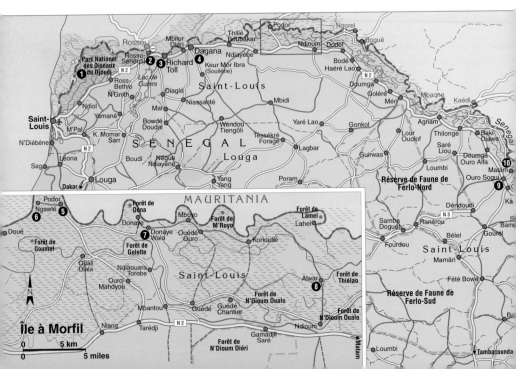

Recommended Restaurants and Bars on page 231

migrant species often seen in large numbers include northern shoveller, northern pintail, garganey, ferruginous duck, European spoonbill, pied avocet, purple swamphen, sand martin, ruff and a variety of nondescript warblers.

Djoudj also forms an important winter breeding ground for the great white pelican. Up to 15,000 of these strikingly comical birds congregate on one island to form a heaving, squawking breeding colony. This is a particularly spectacular sight from January to March, when the males are in full breeding plumage and the black-downed young are still nest-bound. Pelicans are, however, abundant in the area throughout the year. In addition, many thousands of brilliant-pink greater and lesser flamingos feed seasonally in the algae-rich shallows, and an extraordinary variety of herons, storks, gulls, terns and other large waterbirds are likely to be observed.

Many people visit Djoudj as a day trip from Saint-Louis, a 90-minute drive in either direction. More dedicated birdwatchers generally prefer to spend longer there, using the **Hôtel du Djoudj** as a base. This well-equipped hotel is located on a wooded river bank alongside the park headquarters, and its large swimming pool is a welcome sight in this hot climate. A couple of cheaper camps can also be found close to the park entrance, which is serviced by one or two unreliable bush taxis daily, but is far more easily reached on an organised tour or private vehicle from Saint-Louis.

The waterways of Djoudj are best explored by motorised pirogue. This can be arranged through the national park office at the entrance gate or the adjacent Hôtel du Djoudj. The pirogue jetty is located 7km (4 miles) from the entrance gate, which can be a problem for those who travelled to Djoudj by bush taxi. The normal goal for pirogue trips is the pelican colony, which is reached along a creek lined with ducks, waders, egrets and other waterbirds, including a small breeding colony of the normally elusive black-crowned night heron. Crocodile and monitor lizard are often observed from the boat.

A network of dusty roads runs through the terrestrial part of the park, which is ideally explored in a sturdy 4x4. There is some wildlife around, most visibly the

An unusual product from the Senegal River region is gum Arabic, which is harvested from Acacia nilotica trees for use in the textile and pharmaceutical industries.

BELOW: More than 350 species have been recorded in the national park.

Senegal River Region

ubiquitous families of warthog that trot along the plains, tails held aloft, but black-backed jackal, patas monkey and small antelope might also be observed. Terrestrial birds worth looking out for include the crested lark, black scrub robin and spectacular Arabian bustard. An excellent goal for self-drive expeditions is the Grand Lac (also sometimes known as Lac Tigue), a vast shallow seasonal pan fringed by several photographic hides, though these often overlook little but an expanse of flat dust during the dry season.

Choking Djoudj

Despite the abundance of birdlife, the ecology of the Djoudj wetlands has been adversely affected by the construction of the Barrage de Maka-Diama a short distance downriver. Water salinity levels have dropped since the dam was built, creating ideal conditions for the propagation of freshwater weeds that threaten to choke what was formerly open water. By contrast, terrestrial salinity levels are thought to have increased because the area is no longer washed over by annual floods. In 2000, Djoudj was placed on

Unesco's shortlist of World Heritage Sites in Danger, as a result of the threat posed to its indigenous aquatic vegetation by a south American invasive called *Salvinia molesta*. Fortunately, however, this infestation has been brought under control, leading to the park's removal from the danger list in 2006.

Rosso and Richard Toll

The first Senegalese town of any significance upriver of Saint-Louis, **Rosso-Sénégal ❷** is situated exactly 100km (60 miles) from the regional capital along a well-surfaced road, a trip that takes up to three hours by bush taxi and half as long in a private vehicle. Rosso-Sénégal is of interest mainly as the site of the most popular border crossing into Mauritania, and is far smaller than its north-bank counterpart **Rosso,** to which it is connected by a regular ferry service. Supporting a population of around 50,000, Mauritanian Rosso is the third-largest town in that thinly populated country, mainly due to its significance as the only river port along the solitary land link between the Mauritanian capital of Nouakchott and the likes of Saint-

Recommended Restaurants and Bars on page 231

Louis and Dakar. From Rosso it is 200km (120 miles) to Nouakchott. If you need to stay overnight in Rosso-Sénégal, your best – indeed only – option is the modest **Auberge du Walo**.

Roughly 12km (7 miles) east of Rosso as the crow flies, **Richard Toll** ❸ is a rather amorphous settlement of around 70,000 people that sprawls along the south bank of the Senegal River for several kilometres either side of its confluence with a major tributary called the Ferlo. Its architectural high point and main tourist attraction is the **Château du Baron Roger** (free), a palatial two-storey riverfront residence that looks every bit as incongruous in this part of Africa as an adobe hut planted in the Bois de Boulogne in Paris. The château was constructed for the eccentric Baron Jacques-François Roger during his tenure as Governor of Senegal in 1822–7. It later served as a residence to Governor Louis Faidherbe, and has also been used as a school and monastery. Often referred to as the "Folie" (Lunacy) du Baron Roger, the building subsequently fell into disuse, but it remains structurally solid almost two centuries after it was constructed, and its monumental façade, carved columns, grandiose stairway and numerous terracotta statues are highly impressive. Unsurprisingly, the château has been the subject of several rescue plans, in particular for conversion into a hotel, but no such scheme has thus far come to fruition.

The naming of Richard Toll

The name Richard Toll originally referred to the ornamental garden that surrounds the Château du Baron Roger. A keen amateur horticulturist, Baron Roger instructed the colony's gardener-in-chief, Jean-Claude-Michel Richard, to establish a botanical garden and nursery on the river bank close to the village then known as Ndiao in 1822. The baron built his château in the heart of this lavish garden, where a wealth of plants imported from France and its colonies were cultivated alongside groves of date and coconut palms and indigenous trees. Richard left Senegal in 1825 to become the director of the famous botanical garden at Saint-Denis in Réunion, but the name Richard Toll – "Richard's Garden" in the local Wolof language – stuck.

The ornamental gardens around the château have been neglected, and their appearance is now more jungle-like.

BELOW: the "Folie" du Baron Roger.

Aside from the overgrown and untended château grounds, there's nothing very garden-like about Richard Toll today, though it does lie at the core of a 6,000-hectare (14,000-acre) irrigation scheme developed by France over 1949–57. This expanded agricultural land, evident in the patchwork of rice fields in the surrounding countryside, looks like little squares of bright green carpet when the rice is young. Rice is grown throughout the year but the main harvest, when the grain is picked by hand, takes place in November. The main sugar-growing area is to the east of the town, and the farmers produce more than 12,000 tonnes of sugar a year.

If you want to overnight in Richard Toll, or just enjoy a relaxed lunch, the **Gîte d'Étape** is a well-maintained place with air-conditioned rooms, a fine restaurant, a nightclub, a swimming pool and a fantastic river-bank location. It is owned by Baaba Maal, the famous musician who comes from Podor. A few other hotels are scattered around town, but most are rather basic and indifferently located. Other facilities include a few restaurants and banks, and there's plenty of transport to Saint-Louis and Podor.

Dagana

Bypassed by the main surfaced road running eastward to Podor, the "frontier" settlement of **Dagana** ❹ lies on th south bank of the Senegal River som 25km (15 miles) upstream of Richard Tol. Reputedly founded in the 13th century, th town marks the traditional divisio between Wolof and Tukulor territory which lie to the west and east respectively and is most probably named after it founder. Dagana lies at the heart of a majo rice- and tomato-growing region, and i industrial centrepiece is the large SOCA tomato concentrate canning factory, visibl on the right as you enter town. The pecu liar mushy orange mounds sold by th bucket-load alongside the roadside ar the pulped by-product of this industry

A bustling town of around 20,000 resi dents, Dagana is well worth a 3km (2 mile) diversion from the main road. Th main point of interest is the well sign posted Quai Historique, which runs alon a tall riverfront embankment for a fev hundred metres, and is lined with severa attractive 19th-century warehouses an residences. At its southwest extrem stands Fort Faidherbe, a rather plai

Recommended Restaurants and Bars on page 231

ouble-storey building constructed by its amesake in 1835, and is earmarked for estoration before 2010. Also on the waterfront, the private Galerie d'Art et 'Exposition (tel: 77 641 4518; free) is worth a quick look, while the alley running one block behind the embankment s the site of a busy market selling fish, ruit and other fresh produce.

'odor and Ile à Morfil

Around 50km (30 miles) upstream of Dagana, the Senegal River emerges from meandering network of small streams nd channels (known locally as *marigots*) hat enclose numerous marshes and low-ying islands. The most significant of hese is the 100km (60-mile) long **Île à Morfil** (or Morphyl), which extends over ome 1,250 sq km (480 sq miles), making t the largest island on the West African nainland. Morfil is also a fascinating epository of traditional adobe architecure, dotted with small towns and villages vhose *banco* houses and West Sudanese-tyle mosques have more in common vith Mali than the rest of Senegal.

At the northernmost tip of Morfil (and f Senegal itself), some 20km (12 miles) rom Tarédji junction on the RN2, the leepy port of **Podor ❺** is one of the ountry's oldest and most interesting owns. Boasting a population of 12,000, 'odor has long been ignored by Sene-al's beach-oriented tourist industry, and remains very low-key in terms of tourist evelopment. Since 2005, however, its tock has risen somewhat following the evival of the cruise ship *Bou el Mogdad see page 229)* and the more recent con-ersion of the waterfront La Maison uillaume Foy to a guesthouse redolent vith period character.

vory and gold

he name Morfil probably derives from he Portuguese *marfim* (ivory) and ties n with a legend that the island was once n "elephant graveyard". There may be ome truth in this, as the marshland along his stretch of the Senegal River would rovide suitable grazing to old elephants vith failing dentition. A more likely

explanation, however, links to Morfil's significance as a trade outpost under the Tekrour Empire, when it could well have supplied trans-Saharan trade caravans with tusks shipped along the river from more remote hunting grounds further afield. Morfil remained an important trade centre for gold and other commodities when Europeans first documented its existence in the late 17th century – indeed, Podor's name derives from the French *pot d'or* (golden jar).

Immediately north of the town centre, the **Fort de Podor** is the most impressive historic building in town and the site of the **Musée Régional de Podor** (tel: 77 351 4201; Mon–Fri 9am–5pm, Sat–Sun by appointment; charge). It stands on the same site as an older fort built in 1744 by Pierre-David Bartholomew and occupied by the English from 1758–83. A new fort was built under the French Governor Faidherbe in 1853–4 and used by the colonial administration until independence, when it was taken over by the Senegalese army and later the local police force, prior to being abandoned in 1997. In poor condition at the time, the stone ramparts and three double-storey

Dagana is the industrial hub for tomato concentrate, a staple in Senegalese recipes.

BELOW: the Fort de Podor.

The Senegal River

The Senegal River meanders through an arid landscape dotted with relics from the French conquest of the interior

As the most northerly river along the Atlantic coastline of Africa, the Senegal was reached by several Mediterranean navigators in ancient times. It is almost certainly "the river Bambotus, full of crocodiles and hippopotami" mentioned in the writings of Pliny the Elder, and its mouth was visited by Hanno the Navigator c.450 BC, resulting in a low-key trade relationship with Carthage prior to its fall in 146 BC. The river also appears in certain medieval Arabic writings, and it was one of the first landmarks encountered during the Portuguese naval exploration of the Atlantic – the navigator Dinas Diaz entered its mouth in 1445, mistaking it for a western arm of the Nile. In the mid-19th century, the Senegal was the most important conduit of French colonial aspirations inland of Saint-Louis, and the traditional Tukulor architecture that characterises many ports such as Podor and Bakel is complemented by a miscellany of French forts, warehouses and other colonial relics.

The Senegal is 1,790km (1,110 miles) long and has a 480,000-sq km (187,500-sq mile) drainage basin. Its main sources are the Semefé and Bafing, which rise in the Fouta Djalon region of Guinea and join at Bafoulabé (Mali). Further downstream, the confluence of the Senegal and Falémé rivers, between Kidira and Bakel, forms the three-way border between Senegal, Mauritania and Mali. The river then flows in a wide arc along the northwestern boundary of Senegal, embracing the semi-desert plains of the Fouta and Ferlo regions, and forming a natural divide between the sparse woodland of the Sahelian belt and the Saharan sands of Mauritania.

The pasture on the river banks is generally too poor to support grazing, so the local economy is centred on subsistence fishing. Spears, rods, all types of net and even basketwork traps are employed, as are all manner of dugout canoes, from one-man skiffs to six- or eight-paddle craft. When the river bursts its banks every rainy season, it creates fertile fields that support seasonal crops of millet, rice, maize, sweet potatoes, sorghum, tobacco, onions and tomatoes.

The Senegal flows throughout the year, but is subject to great annual fluctuations in volume, determined by seasonal rainfall patterns in its upper basin. High-water season runs from July to October, with water levels peaking in September, after which the river gradually subsides to reach its lowest point from May through to July, when the shrinking waters reveal large mudbanks and sandbars. These obstacles to navigating craft make the river very treacherous, as they move during the heavy rainy season and their whereabouts cannot be accurately plotted.

Two big dams were built on the river in the 1980s. In Mali, the Manantali reservoir was created to regulate the river's erratic flow, though it also feeds a hydroelectric station. It has helped curb the risk of incidents such as the devastating floods of 1890, 1906 and 1950, or the drought that crippled the area in 1972–3, though the Rosso area was hit by heavy flooding in late 2005. By contrast, the main purpose of the Barrage de Maka-Diama, 25km (15 miles) upriver of Saint-Louis, was to prevent the saltwater intrusion that has at times infiltrated the river up to 200km (125 miles) inland of its mouth. The barrage also aimed to feed a proposed network of artificial irrigation channels and embankments through the lower Senegal River floodplain, expanding the extent of the region's rice paddies and cane fields, but this plan never progressed far beyond the drawing board. ❏

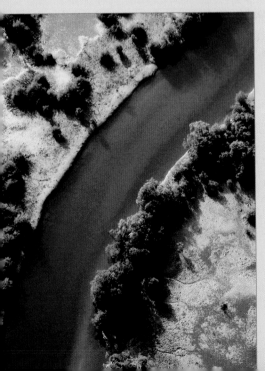

LEFT: the Senegal meanders its way through arid land.

buildings inside were renovated (at a cost of around 4 million Euros) with French cooperation over 2002–5, and they now house several interesting exhibits about the town and its surrounds.

The historic waterfront of Podor is lined with more than a dozen tall 19th-century residences and warehouses. The condition of these old buildings varies greatly, but several have undergone recent restoration, notably **La Maison Guillaume Foy** (tel: 33 965 1682; www.podor-rivegauche.com; free), originally constructed by its namesake in the 1850s and restored as a guesthouse in 2006. The house is well worth a look, even if you aren't staying there, for its graceful architecture, leafy courtyard, and collection of historical memorabilia.

Next door, the Presbyterian Church has restored another old warehouse as a school and library. A couple of doors down, a more decrepit colonial relic now houses an anonymous but well-stocked bar where you can sip a chilled beer as colourful pirogues cross the river to the Mauritanian shore, and local businessmen bicker over a game of *pétanque* on the sandy waterfront.

Morfil has supported centralised Iron Age societies since the 3rd century AD or earlier, and the ancient empires of Tekrour and Ghana both left their mark. Of particular interest to historians are a series of ancient burial mounds scattered in the vicinity of Podor. The most significant of these was discovered near Podor airport in 1958, when a local tractor driver inadvertently ploughed open a midden containing a veritable treasure trove of earthenware jars filled with copper and gold bracelets, leg rings and other artefacts. Most probably deposited

Podor's most famous modern export is the internationally acclaimed singer and guitarist Baaba Maal. Although his albums were recorded in Dakar or overseas, Baaba Maal visits to play occasional concerts.

BELOW:
the fort barracks.

Woman standing in front of her yellow banco house in a village on Morfil.

BELOW: festival revellers in Podor.

by the Serer people, who dominated the area before the 11th century, several other such mounds have since been excavated, and while none are open to the public, several artefacts unearthed in the area can be seen in the National Museum of The Gambia in Banjul *(see page 82)*.

Historic villages

The most accessible of the many historic villages that dot Morfil, **Ngawlé ❻** lies a mere 3km (2 miles) outside Podor along a poorly marked sand piste that runs inland of a much longer bend in the river. Arguably the prettiest village in Senegal, Ngawlé is most easily reached by donkey-cart, which can easily be arranged through the staff of La Maison Guillaume Foy. You could also walk, though it's quite easy to get lost, or hang about waiting for Air Ngawlé, a solitary bush taxi that ploughs backwards and forwards from Podor a few times daily. Ngawlé has a lush riverfront location, and its 1,000-odd inhabitants almost all live in traditional compounds of earthily curvaceous flat-roofed *banco* houses, made of smooth mud-bricks and often adorned with curved windows and painted orange or yellow.

Most of the other historic villages of Morfil are difficult to reach without private transport, ideally 4x4, though the area is serviced by a limited network of bush taxis emanating from Podor.

On the north bank of the island 11km (7 miles) from Podor, **Donaye Walo ❼** is a tiny village of traditional *banco* compounds, many of which now stand abandoned following flood damage in 1999. The centrepiece of Donaye Walo is its mosque, an attractively modest West Sudanese construction that was built in the 1870s and is still used by the 17 families that stayed on after the floods. Interesting Sudanese-style mosques of a similar vintage can also be seen at **Mboyo**, which also lies on the north bank about 10km (6 miles) further east, and at **Guédé**, on the south bank about 16km (10 miles) from Donaye Walo.

The most revered village on Morfil, **Alwar ❽** (also known as Halwar) was the birthplace of El Hadj Oumar Tall, founder of the short-lived but influential Tukulor Empire that extended over much of Senegal, Mali and Guinea in the mid-19th century and provided staunch resistance to French colonial expansion up

Recommended Restaurants and Bars on page 231

ne Senegal River. The *banco* house where Oumar Tall was born in 1797 is maintained as something of a shrine oday, and the village is also the site of ne oldest and most impressive of Senegal's 19th-century mud-brick mosques, a handsome building with carved doors, a tall rounded minaret, and six other urved protuberances on its otherwise lat roof. Home to around 1,000 people oday, Alwar lies about 45km (27 miles) rom Podor along a variable dirt road hrough Donaye Walo and Mboyo. In a imilar vein, the ornate mausoleum of Cheikh Ahmadou Madiyou, a contemporary of Oumar Tall, can be visited at Ouro-Mahdyou along the main feeder oad between Tarédji and Podor.

The Upper Senegal

Upon leaving Podor, the RN2 runs parallel to, but out of view of, the Senegal River for approximately 220km (132 miles) before arriving at the twin towns of **Ouro Sogui** and **Matam**, which espectively lie on the main highway and the southern river bank. Best undertaken n the relative cool of the early morning, t's an uneventful drive, both in terms of scenery and passing traffic, passing through a classic Sahelian landscape of flat, dry, sun-baked plains punctuated by an occasional stand of acacias or baobabs or a small Tukulor village – it seems barely credible that at any given point you're within a few kilometres of one of Africa's 10 largest rivers.

Ouro Sogui and Matam

Linked by a 10km (6-mile) causeway across a seasonal floodplain, Ouro Sogui and Matam have both been in existence since the 17th century, and a combined population of around 32,000 is divided almost evenly between the two towns, but otherwise they could scarcely be more different in character. Straddling the RN7, **Ouro Sogui** ❾, as might be expected, is the better-equipped of the two towns, serviced by a handful of decent hotels and restaurant, a few supermarkets, two banks with ATMs and a couple of fuel stations, but in all other respects it comes across as a typical junction town, bustling and functional, but somewhat devoid of character.

Matam ❿, by contrast, is a minor urban gem, with a lovely riverfront setting

EAT

In Ouro Sogui, the best place to eat is the Oasis du Fouta *(see page 231)*. Alternatively, you can try the cheap eateries and *dibiteries* (stalls selling grilled meat), such as Le Teddungal.

BELOW: atmospheric Matam.

Typical mud-brick house in Matam, with its circular and triangular openings for aeration.

and atmospheric Old Town, though the latter is easily overlooked if you don't know where to find it. The name Matam reputedly dates to the slave-trading era and derives from the Tukulor phrase *Matama* ("Pay in cash"). The story goes that Peul slave raiders regularly passed through the port, initially paying for the hospitality of the local Tukulor in the currency of their trade: captive slaves. However, having bartered away their slaves, the Peul then came back after nightfall and stole them back while the Tukulor slept, so the townsfolk started demanding cash for their services instead.

Coming from Ouro Sogui, the main road to Matam passes through a couple of blocks lined with small supermarkets and bars before terminating at a lively modern waterfront market. A right turn from here leads to the sedate old colonial part of town, where pleasant accom-

modation is available at the Hôtel Résidence des Fleuves, which reopened in 2006 following extensive renovations. This part of town was the site of one of many waterfront forts built by Governor Faidherbe in the 1850s, but the battlements of this colonial relic were carried away by a flood in the early 20th century and nothing much remains today. The same is true for the Résidence de Djourbivol, also built by Louis Faidherbe on the river bank downstream of Matam.

Of greater interest is the Old Town, which can be reached by taking the last left turn from the main road and then passing through the market for perhaps 100 metres/yards. Here, a maze of cart-width alleys is lined by traditional flat-roofed *banco* houses reminiscent of small-town Mali, though the mud-brick houses of Matam differ from their cross-border counterparts insofar as the outer walls are more generously aerated by circular and triangular openings. At least two dozen of these traditional adobe houses remain, often tucked away quietly behind tall compound walls, and some are said to be the best part of a century old. The only other building of note

Recommended Restaurants and Bars on page 231

Matam is a moderately attractive mud-bricked mosque topped by two tall minarets in the heart of the Old Town.

Returning via Ouro Sogui to the RN2, the southbound road once again follows a course parallel to the Senegal River. However, it maintains sufficient distance to ensure the road is out of the reach of seasonal flooding – and the river is well out of eyeshot from the road. The surfaced road runs for 90 miles (150km) from Ouro Sogui before it reaches the town of Bakel, a trip that takes up to three hours by bush taxi, and about two hours in a private vehicle.

It's a really hot drive, passing through sparsely vegetated countryside that appears dry even by Senegalese standards, but there are plenty of small, traditional Tukulor settlements along the way. It can be fascinating to stop at one of the *wadis* (dry riverbeds) crossed by the road between Ouro Sogui before it reaches the town of Bakel and watch the colourfully attired Tukulor villagers launder their clothes and water their livestock from temporary wells dug into the sandy base of the watercourse.

Bakel

Bakel ⑪ is a historic town situated approximately 30km (18 miles) north-west of the junction of the three-way border between Senegal, Mauritania and Mali. Originally, the town's inhabitants formed part of the powerful Ghana Empire, which once spread across a vast section of West Africa. Later, the invasions of Malinké tribes into the southern Casamance region originated in the area of Bakel. These migrations left the township rather depopulated until its reoccupation by a mixture of Sarakholé and Bambara peoples.

From 1690 the entire region came under the rule of the Boundou branch of Islam. University towns were set up throughout the area which were linked to the Kairouyine Mosque in Fez, Morocco and the Grand Mosque city of Tlemcen in Algeria. These included Bakel and towns in what is now western Mali. Despite the great military strength of the Islamic rulers, the French were able to take the town of Bakel in 1819 and establish an outpost under a treaty with the local chief.

The French forces began to organise a system of commercial traffic with barges on the river, building a fort overlooking the waterway in 1847. Louis Faidherbe, who became Governor of the French West African territories in 1854, visited the town three years later and supervised the construction of more substantial fortifications. Faidherbe's defences also included the installation of a gunboat just offshore with the aim of protecting shipping and warding off an attack by Omar Saidou. The great marabout of the Sarakholé ethnic group, Mamadou Lamin, laid siege to Bakel in 1885 but was shot outside the fort. Retreating to Kayes, in Mali, Lamin died of his wounds and the town returned to rule under the French for another five years.

Strategically located at the head of the Senegal River, not far from its confluence with the Falémé, Bakel represents the terminus for commercial river traffic. This historic town has a number of colonial houses worth a visit and several

Bakel is a most picturesque village thanks to its intact colonial architecture, a beautiful reminder of its time as a flourishing rubber and peanut centre.

Bou el Mogdad

Tourism to the often-overlooked Senegal River region was given a real boost in 2005 following the relaunch of the *Bou el Mogdad*, a legendary passenger and goods ship that serviced the stretch of river between Saint-Louis and Podor from 1950 until the start of the Barrage de Maka-Diama in 1982. The renovated cruise ship now undertakes an overnight run between Richard Toll and Podor once a week in either direction, part of a five-day tour that also takes in Saint-Louis, the Djoudj National Park and Dagana. Luxury accommodation comprising 28 cabins is complemented by excellent French cuisine and facilities – there's even a swimming pool on the lower deck – and can be booked through the Compagnie du Fleuve (tel: 33 961 5689; fax: 33 961 8320; www.compagnie dufleuve.com). The boat takes its name from an explorer who accompanied Faidherbe on his Mauritanian travels.

French explorer René Caillié (1799–1838) was the first European to return alive from the town of Timbuktu.

BELOW:
the fort in Bakel.

attractive mosques. The most impressive building in town is the fortress built by Louis Faidherbe, which stands on a tall bluff above the river. Regarded as Senegal's third-most important fortress, it now serves as the main office for the Préfecture of Bakel, and as such it is not formally open to the public, though visitors are generally allowed to wander around the courtyard within the sandstone outer fortifications.

In 1819, Bakel was the staging post for the French explorer René Caillié's first unsuccessful expedition in search of the legendary lost city of Timbuktu (in present-day Mali). Now a very run-down private residence, the house where Caillié reputedly stayed in Bakel can still be visited, and is readily visible from the fort, standing as it does on a wide pavilion at the pinnacle of the town's tallest hill. Whether or not it was ever really inhabited by Caillié (or was later used as a stopover point for the military commanders Dupont and Dusseault), the house is of limited architectural merit, and visitors are more likely to be impressed by the hilltop views over the town and river.

With a population estimated at 15,000, Bakel is far and away the most important trade focus for miles around, and the unexpectedly chaotic market makes an enjoyable goal for a couple of hours' exploration. Regular canoes connect Bakel to Gouray on the facing Mauritanian shore – indeed, you could probably wade across towards the end of the dry season – but the absence of a formal border post means it's illegal for foreigners to undertake this short trip.

Of the two hotels in Bakel, the new Hôtel Boundou is the standout, with friendly staff and a riverfront location, but those arriving by public transport should note that it is some distance from the *gare routière* (bush-taxi rank). Other facilities include several fuel stations and a bank, but there is no internet access, nor anywhere to change or draw money.

Kidira

The last stop on the Senegal River route, the border town of **Kidira** lies about 640km (400 miles) upstream from Saint-Louis and some 64km (40 miles) from Bakel. Once in legendary bad condition, the road between Bakel and Kidira is now surfaced in its entirety, and the drive takes less than one hour in a private vehicle, passing through the scenery that you could be forgiven for describing as mountainous if you've spent a while in Senegal. Built on the Dakar to Bamako railway, Kidira is of no real interest to tourists except as the site of the eastern-most railway station in Senegal, and the first stop for traders and visitors entering the country from Kayes, in Mali, or from further east.

Although Kidira is an important crossroads it offers no accommodation to travellers. For this reason, it is easier to travel straight through from Bakel to **Tambacounda**, a trip that shouldn't take longer than four hours in a private vehicle. Tambacounda is the administrative capital of the southeast and a springboard for trips to the Parc National de Niokolo-Koba; several hotels are scattered around the town, which is described in the relevant chapter (see page 258). ❑

RESTAURANTS AND BARS

Restaurants

Prices for a main course per person:
$ = under US$8 (CFA3,200)
$$ = US$8–15 (CFA 3,200–6,000)
$$$ = over US$15 (CFA6,000)

The ports along the river have few restaurants meeting Western standards. As in other parts of the region that see few tourists, the best place to eat will be your hotel, though stalls selling cheap food are usually found at the *gare routière* and central market.

Richard Toll
Le Gîte d'Étape
Signposted 50 metres/yards from the main road
Tel: 33 963 3240 **$–$$**
This is the most attractive place to eat in Richard Toll, set in lovely gardens overlooking the river. A good selection of French-style meat and fish dishes is supplemented by sandwiches and other snacks. Service can be on the slow side.

Podor
La Maison Guillaume Foy
Tel: 33 965 1682
$** (or **$$ for the full menu)
Best ordered a few hours ahead, the French-style food served here is the best in town, with the option of taking the full three-course dinner or just the main course.

Ouro Sogui
Hôtel Oasis du Fouta
Tel: 33 966 1294 **$**
A few metres north from the main roundabout, this popular hotel has a pleasant open-sided restaurant. The menu is unremarkable, with little in the way of fish or vegetarian fare, but the Franco-Senegalese meat and chicken dishes are well prepared, and there are crêpes for dessert. Open daily 7am–10pm.

Matam
CRTEF Canteen
$
Part of the eponymous college on the western outskirts of town, this place isn't easy to find, but anybody will point you in the right direction (just ask for "cretef"). As might be expected of a college canteen, there's no alcohol and not a great deal more ambience, but the simple fare – chicken and chips or stewed meat with couscous – is well prepared and good value. Open 8am–9pm.

Bakel
Hôtel Boundou
Tel: 33 983 5280 **$**
The best hotel in Bakel also prepares meals to order, usually requiring a couple of hours' notice. The courtyard has a good atmosphere, the food is simple but generously proportioned, and there's a well-stocked bar to sustain you while you wait.

BELOW: women selling potatoes in Dagana market.

Recommended Restaurants and Bars on page 255

THE CENTRAL INTERIOR

The open plains of the Senegalese interior
are hot, dry and unremittingly flat, and those
who undertake the trip will swiftly sense they
are passing through Senegal's spiritual heartland

ot, dry and unremittingly flat, the open plains of the Senegalese interior possess a strong sense of enic uniformity. Sun-baked sandy red ils support a sparse cover of contorted obabs, barbed acacias and tangled oundnuts, dotted by the occasional ango-shaded village, and overhung for uch of the year with a hazy Harmattan-induced sky of faded sepia.

You could travel for days here without seeing anything that might generally be described as a hill, let alone a ountain, and there's not much wildlife n show either, though the hump-backed ng-horned zebu cattle that trample the ains can be an awesome spectacle, d birdwatchers will find endless distraction in the regular fleeting flashes f avian colour that regularly brighten e roadside.

True, this parched setting does receive annual lease of fresh life during the l too brief rains, but for most of the ear – including the dry months that incide with the main tourist season – e dusty badlands of the Senegalese terior epitomise the creeping desertification that threatens the Sahel.

Wide open spaces

his is no place for agoraphobics, but r travellers in the right frame of mind, e wide empty roads through this dehydrated and featureless landscape can ke on an oddly mesmerising quality. unctuating the long tracts of asphalt rmac, a dozen-or-so medium-large

towns – most notably Thiès, Louga, Diourbel, Touba-Mbaké and Kaolack – form the obvious focal points for visitors to this area. The majority of these towns have a worthwhile market, a memorable mosque or two, possibly even a scattering of time-warped colonial buildings but, as with the surrounding plains, they tend to be short on prescribed "tourist" attractions.

As a result, any trip through the Senegalese interior soon takes on the mood of travel for its own sake, an experience centred more on the journey itself than

LEFT: the salt mounds in Kaolack.
BELOW: routing for Kaolack.

The marabout, a scholar of the Qur'an, presides at various ceremonies, makes amulets for good luck, and in some cases actively guides the life of the follower.

on any specific destination. And those who do undertake the trip will swiftly sense that they are passing through the country's spiritual heartland, a remote region that eschews the cosmopolitan aspirations of Dakar or Saint-Louis, preferring to look back across the Sahel and Sahara at Mali and Morocco and the other great Islamic nations of Africa. Indeed, any outsider who hopes to gain insight into the rich tradition of mystical marabouts and brotherhoods that informs the modern Senegalese consciousness will most likely find it in the central interior.

As for travel practicalities, roads running through the central interior are almost all surfaced and in good condition, and an excellent network of buses and bush taxis means that hopping between towns could scarcely be easier.

The majority of towns of any size have a handful of decent hotels (the one notable exception being lodging-free Touba) along with a few restaurants, internet cafés, supermarkets and banks, though it would probably be unwise to rely solely on ATMs for money in this particular part of the country.

Unambiguous travel highlights are few and far between, but would arguably include the monumental mosques at Touba and Rufisque, both of which are the subject of million-strong annual pilgrimages, while Thiès and Kaolack both have the kind of bustling urban ambience that could tempt those on a relaxed itinerary to settle in for a few days. Top of the list, however, are the mysterious megalithic stone circle sites that scatter the area between Kaolack and the Senegalese border, two of which – Sine Ngayène and Wanar – were inscribed as Unesco World Heritage Sites in 2006.

Wolof heartland

The Senegalese interior was the heartland of the Empire of Djolof (Wolof) which was founded by Ndiadiane N'Diaye c.1250 AD and in its heyday covered

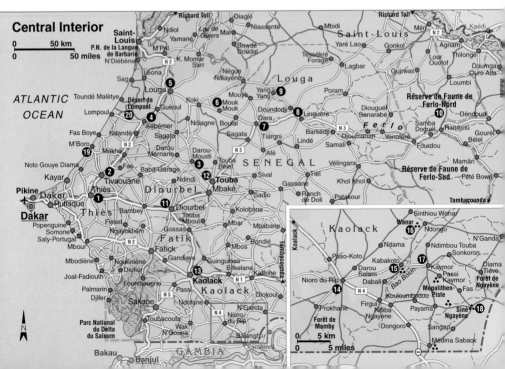

Recommended Restaurants and Bars on page 255

most of the region between the rivers Senegal and Gambia. For three centuries, this powerful empire, centred inland in the vicinity of present-day Linguère, presided over several coastal vassal states, whose leaders all paid tribute the Bourba (King) of Djolof.

However, the booming coastal trade with Europeans in the middle of the 16th century led to a sharp economic shift westwards and the dissolution of Djolof into its six component states. These were the southerly Serer states of Siné and Saloum, the central states of Baol and Cayor, and the northerly state of Walo, while Djolof itself remained landlocked in the northeast. All six states remained functional polities into the late 19th century, when their autonomy was crushed in the name of French imperialism. Nevertheless, their legacy looms large in the Senegalese landscape today.

Thiès

The gateway town to the interior, **Thiès** ❶ is typical of many market and trading centres in Senegal in that it grew around a route crossroads. Situated 100km (60 miles) west of Dakar, Thiès has been a key railhead since the line between Dakar and Saint-Louis opened in 1885, and its significance was further boosted when it became the junction for the Dakar-Niger line (to Bamako, Mali) built over 1906–23. And while rail transport has faded in significance over recent decades, Thiès still forms the pivotal crossroad between the RN2 northeast to Louga and Saint-Louis, and the RN3 east to Diourbel, Touba and Tambacounda.

Originally known as Dianxène, Thiès was established in the 17th century as a trade funnel through which the Cayor Empire supplied slaves, ivory and other goods to the French and Portuguese settlers on Gorée (at that time a more important settlement than Dakar).

In 1859, a French plan to construct a telegraph line between Dakar and Saint-Louis was opposed by the celebrated Cayor leader Lat Dior Ngoné Latyr Diop, and the area became a focal point of hostilities between the indigenous empire and its aspirant colonists. A French military outpost was established at Thiès in 1864, followed by a fortress in 1879, when Lat Dior signed a treaty with Governor Faidherbe agreeing to the

The name Thiès – pronounced "chess" – dates to the early days of French expansion into Cayor and is most likely a corruption of the French caisse, an allusion to the caches of ammunition that the colonists brought to quell Cayor resistance.

BELOW:
local crafts for sale.

Desert Driving

With careful planning, driving through Senegal's wide open desert areas can be a rewarding and enjoyable experience

More than a third of Senegal is desert and a good part of the rest of the terrain is laterite rock and sandstone through which tracks have been carved. At times these routes can be impassable: heavy rain creates gorges and pot-holes, and sometimes even landslides.

Not all of Senegal is so daunting to the motorist. In fact, the country has an excellent network of good, surfaced roadways between its major urban centres. Nearly 3,200km (2,000 miles) of asphalt roads link all the main towns and more than 10,000 laterite roads support the network.

However, it is in the outlying regions of open desert and the sandy central plateau that one is likely to run into some difficulties. This is not to discourage drivers from touring Senegal by car, merely to remind them that care and planning are necessary. When choosing a vehicle to hire, opt for the most rugged. Hot climate specifications – which usually comprise extra air filters, reinforced suspension and steering, and sump guards for the engine – are desirable. Four-wheel drive can be a huge asset when you get stuck or need to drive through banks of sand, and it also usually comes with good clearance for rocky or rutted roads.

The list of equipment needed for desert driving is a long one: an oil temperature gauge, towing cable, lock on the petrol cap, laminated windscreen and replacement kit, car compass, jump leads, a full set of tools, an extra spare wheel, corrugated metal track lengths for sand-driving, a powerful hand lamp for night-driving, foot pump, first-aid kit, a jack (particularly one with a wide base plate), puncture repair kit and tyre levers, replacement spark plugs, fan belt and extra filters.

Petrol, water and oil are life-savers in desert driving. Pinpoint the locations of all water and petrol stops on a good map and try to confirm this information by asking along the road (garages and petrol stations may have gone out of business or even have run out of stock). Make sure all petrol tanks, plus a reserve, are topped up at every available opportunity. Take plenty of oil, and make regular cooling-off stops. Water will be needed both for the radiator and for human consumption. In desert conditions the human body requires up to five litres (nine pints) of water a day, without any strenuous activity.

When driving in sand, the trick is to maintain sufficient speed to get through loose patches without becoming bogged down. If you do, however, either reduce the tyre pressure to increase traction or, better still, lay metal sand tracks in front of the wheels, having first dug the sand away from around them.

At night, sound your horn or flash your lights repeatedly when approaching an oncoming vehicle. For security reasons it is wise to take a local guide and travel in a convoy of at least two vehicles. In the event of a breakdown, stay with the vehicle, flag down passing help but be watchful over possessions when it is being rendered. ❏

LEFT: an encampment in the Lompoul Desert.

Recommended Restaurants and Bars on page 255

onstruction of the Dakar-Saint-Louis ailway through his territory. Soon after, at Dior reversed his decision and unched a series of attacks on the line hile it was under construction, leading several bloody clashes with Faiderbe's troops.

Lat Dior was killed by the French in e Battle of Dékhélé on 26 October 886, the year after the line opened. hortly afterwards Thiès, along with the st of Cayor, was annexed to the astal French colony of Dakar, Gorée d St Louis. The town was accorded unicipal status in 1904 and within ten ars it supported a population of 3,000. day, Thiès is the third-largest city in enegal, with a population estimated at ound 320,000.

Despite being located on a major ansport crossroads, Thiès receives few avellers, and public transport from akar to more distant destinations uses modern bypass that skirts the town mpletely. But while it hardly qualifies a must-see, Thiès is a pleasant enough opover, thanks partly to a climate and ood that fall midway between the eezy big city to its west and the more

parched and parochial interior, and partly to a layout that seems unusually spacious and cohesive compared to most other Senegalese settlements.

The obvious focal point is the enormous park-like traffic roundabout that stands in front of the modern Hôtel de Ville (town hall), which is overlooked by several low-rise office blocks and banks. **Avenue Léopold-Senghor**, named after the first Senegalese president who had previously served as Mayor of Thiès (1956–61), is the main thoroughfare, running north from the town hall towards the railway line. Shaded by tall trees, this avenue is lined with a good selection of tempting patisseries, restaurants and cafés, with a few banks (all with ATMs), internet cafés and other shops to be found in between.

North of the railway line, the funkily decorated **Palais des Arts** is a live music venue opened in 2007 by Waflash, the town's most famous pop group.

Waflash are an African band whose eclectic style and strong vocals have earned them renown far beyond the borders of Senegal. The band members started their musical careers in 1988 when the town's university was closed because of civil unrest.

Fortress museum

The fortress constructed by the French in 1879 is now the **Musée de la Région de Thiès** (daily 9am–6pm; charge). It

BELOW: the Musée de la Région de Thiès.

One of the colourful tapestries produced from the tapestry factory in Thiès.

can be reached from Avenue Léopold-Senghor by turning left into Avenue Lat-Dior, which runs parallel to the railway line, with the century-old railway station to the right and several colonial mansions and other buildings to the left. After approximately 500 metres/yards, Avenue Lat-Dior terminates at a T-junction with the fort standing prominently before you. Expect to wait a few minutes while somebody locates the man with the key, and be sure to clarify and pay the entrance fee upfront – unwary visitors to the fortress are frequently overcharged by a factor of ten.

Once inside, the highpoint of the museum is a sequence of paintings that depict Lat Dior's resistance to French occupation, but the museum has several other moderately diverting displays, covering everything from the history of the Dakar–Niger Railway to Neolithic stone tools sites in Thiès Region. Inside the fort is also a small library and café.

World-class tapestries

However, Thiès's best-known attraction is undoubtedly the **Manufactures Sénégalaises des Arts Décoratifs** (tel: 339 511 131; email: msadthies@yahoo.com; daily 8am–1.30pm and 3–6pm; free), a tapestry factory founded by President Senghor in 1966. The factory is located about 100 metres/yards from the fortress, and a few dozen tapestries are hung for display in a distinctive circular exhibition hall. The immense tapestries are based on paintings by such celebrated Senegalese artists as Amadou Seck, Souley Keita, Maodo Niang and Ousmane Faye, and samples now hang in such prestigious locations as Buckingham Palace and the Vatican. The weaving is done on manual looms and can take many weeks to complete. You can see all the stages of work from creating a design to dyeing the various wools. You will need to phone ahead if you want to take a look round the workshops.

Recommended Restaurants and Bars on page 255

Selling at around €750 per sq metre in 2008, these colourful tapestries are well beyond the means of most tourists, but if they stimulate a shopping itch, you can always alleviate it around the corner, where the Village Artisanal de Thiès is crowded with stalls selling all manner of more affordable local crafts.

North of Thiès

Skirted by the RN2 some 22km (13 miles) northeast of Thiès, **Tivaouane** ❷ is a town of some historic pedigree. It was an early capital of Cayor, which most likely served as the inland residence of King Zucholin, mentioned in the writings of the 15th-century explorer Luigi da Cada Mosto. Following the arrival of the Saint-Louis railway in 1885, Tivaouane prospered as a bustling centre of local trade, and by 1904 it was listed as Senegal's largest inland settlement – a title it has long since forsaken, though it remains a substantial place, with a population of around 40,000.

In 1902, the religious teacher El-Hajj Malick Sy selected Tivaouane as the base for his Tidjiane brotherhood (a sect with roots in 18th-century Algeria), in large part thanks to its location on the railway. Tivaouane is now considered to be the holiest Tidjiane city in West Africa, and the second-most important pilgrimage site in Senegal.

Tivaouane's limited range of tourist attractions includes three listed Historic Monuments: the double-storey 19th-century railway station, the mausoleum of El-Hadj Malick Sy, who died here in 1922, and the mosque built in honour of his son and successor Serigne Babacar Sy after his death in 1957.

The attractive Grande Mosquée whose three tall minarets dominate the town's skyline was built in the 1980s. It attracts up to one million pilgrims annually to celebrate Moulid (the birthday of the Prophet Mohammed), which falls on a different date every year according to the Islamic calendar, an event known locally as Gamou.

Aside from religion and groundnuts, the biggest industry in Tivaouane district is phosphate, sourced from two large open-cast phosphate mines at **Taiba** and **Pallo**, and later converted into fertiliser. For those interested, it is possible to arrange a guided tour of one or other of

BELOW: keeping an eye on the livestock in Louga.

the mines whose combined output is Senegal's most important source of export revenue. Make enquiries at your hotel as to how to go about this.

Some 26km (15 miles) north of Tivaouane, the RN2 passes through **Mekhé**, a railway town of around 15,000 residents with very little to offer tourists, though it does mark the start of a well-maintained 100-km (60-mile) surfaced road east leading to Touba. This road runs through acres of groundnut fields, baobab and palm groves as well as several small villages.

Great piles of groundnuts can be seen at the village collecting station of **Darou-Mousti ❸**, a typical Wolof village located on the crossroads with a surfaced road leading back to the RN2 at **Kébémer ❹**. It has a medium-sized railway station and a regular market, but Kébémer is best known perhaps as the home town of President Abdoulaye Wade, who was born there in 1926.

To the edge of the Sahara

Another 38km (23 miles) north of Kébémer, **Louga ❺** is the eponymous capital of a vast administrative region that stretches deep into the semi-desert fur ther east. It is Senegal's second-large city in area, but its 82,000 inhabitar place it tenth in terms of populatic Sprawling eastward from the RN Louga offers some useful facilities – se eral hotels, restaurants and banks – b the thick sand drifts along the surfac roads create a feeling of impermanenc as if the whole town might be swallow up by the encroaching desert were y to turn your back for too long. Econor ically, Louga is notable as a major dep for both the collection and processing groundnuts, generating 10 percent of t nation's total income from the crop, b it has little to offer tourists, and mc people heading north along the RN bypass it entirely.

East of Louga, a little-used but une pectedly good surfaced road runs f 87km (52 miles) through to **Dara**, on t junction of the RN3 between Diourb and Linguère. Among the most remc of Senegalese roads, the run east fro Louga passes through arid plains of re sand that support little vegetation ar even fewer people, though every so oft you'll pass a tiny village of thatch

Dara is best known for the racehorses bred by the Centre de Recherches Zootechniques (CRZ) founded in the colonial era.

BELOW:
musicians gather together in the Ferlo.

Recommended Restaurants and Bars on page 255

quare mud-brick houses whose Wolof inhabitants eke out a tough pastoral existence in a region plagued by rapid desertification and regular infestations of locusts and other pests.

At **Mouk-Mouk** ❻, about 50km (30 miles) past Louga, look out for the deep wells where herders from all over the surrounding area gather to water their cattle or to load up donkey carts with filled jerry cans.

The rather lightweight hooded vulture is often abundant in Senegalese villages and can be seen walking along on the ground, scavenging and clearing up refuse. The Louga-Dara road is one of the few places outside of game reserves where larger species of raptor – white-backed, Rüppell's griffin and even lappet-faced vulture – are regularly observed perching rather ominously in the bare baobab branches.

Desert market town

Set in the heart of the semi-desert, **Dara** ❼ is as sizzling and sandy as might be expected, and facilities aimed at outsiders are limited to the **Auberge-Restaurant Ker Guy**, a decent little place with a few air-conditioned rooms and a restaurant that rustles up some tasty local dishes at short notice. Dara is a surprisingly substantial town, with an estimated 30,000 inhabitants, and where traditional attire is still very much in evidence, with both men and women kitted out in brightly coloured smocks.

Several markets are held here, most famously the weekly livestock market which takes place in an open field about 1km (½ mile) out of town along the Linguère road – if you do visit Dara, make sure it's on a Sunday, so you can witness this lively event. Cattle, goats, sheep and even camels are all in evidence at the livestock market.

Linguère ❽, 42km (25 miles) further east along a stretch of the RN3, is a smaller administrative town set alongside a dry watercourse in the Ferlo River Valley. On the way, the road passes a few tall red dunes where herds of skinny white cattle march mournfully alongside the occasional group of camels. Incredibly parched, dry and dusty, Linguère has a distinct end-of-the-line feel, and it does indeed form the terminus not only of the surfaced road but also of a long defunct railway line from Dakar and Saint-Louis. Not very many travellers pass through and the only place to stay or have a sit-down meal in Linguère is the Hôtel Thiossane opposite the market.

The last Bourba

Considering that it's a former capital of Djolof, there's actually very little to see in Linguère itself, though adventurous travellers with a 4x4 could follow the riverbed northwest for about 30km (18 miles) to the intriguing village of **Yang-Yang** ❾. Today a mere village of around 300 people, Yang-Yang was the capital of Djolof prior to its annexation to Fouta Djalon in the 1870s and colonisation by France two decades later. It was also the

A hooded vulture gets ready to pounce.

BELOW:
collecting seed pods for animal feed.

The Ferlo village water supply; a well and tank.

BELOW: essentials for tea-making.

paying for the excavation of dozens rural wells. Prior to his death in 1952, also became an active figure in the cam paign for independence. The former re idence, mosque and fortifications of t Bourba of Djolof are preserved as H torical Monuments in Yang-Yang, alon with the ruins of a French military o post built during the Faidherbe era colonial rule.

The historical significance of Linguè is embedded in its name, which w also the title bestowed upon the "que mother" of Djolof – usually the moth or eldest sister of the king.

seat of the penultimate Bourba of Djolof, namely Alboury Biram Penda, who died in battle against the French in 1890, and the birthplace of his son and successor Alboury N'Diaye, who was recognised as the last Bourba by the colonial administration in 1896.

Far from being a colonial puppet, however, the overseas-educated Alboury N'Diaye was instrumental in the development of Djolof during the colonial area, pushing for the construction of a railway to Linguère in the 1920s, and

The Ferlo

Linguère isn't quite the dead end might seem. A rough 220km (130 mi road does run east from the town Ouro Sogui and Matam on the Seneg River, passing through the heart of t **Ferlo**, a semi-desert region desert th extends over 70,000 sq km (27,000 miles) of northeastern Senegal – on third of the country's total area.

Named after the tributary of the Sen gal River that flows through the Lac Guiers, this thinly populated region

Recommended Restaurants and Bars on page 255

sometimes referred to as the Ferlo River Valley, but this is rather misleading: the Ferlo is essentially a subterranean stream for most of its length, rising above ground only after heavy rain, and the surrounding terrain is flat even by Senegal's sparsely contoured standards. The Ferlo doesn't quite qualify as a true desert, receiving an annual rainfall of 250–350mm (10–13½ inches), but this falls almost exclusively over July to September, and it certainly feels like a desert the rest of the year.

As might be expected, the Ferlo is very thinly populated, though it does support a scattering of semi-nomadic Fallana pastoralists, whose settlements consist of tiny round mud-and-thatch huts, often built miles away from any visible water source – though many villages in fact lie close to the subterranean Ferlo and draw water from shallow wells in the river bed. Typical of these villages are **Barkedji**, **Dioumanan**, **Fonoféré**, and **Fourdou**, all of which lie within a few kilometres of the main road between Linguère and Matam.

As one travels progressively deeper into the region, the villages appear more and more poverty-stricken and the advancing sands of the Sahara gradually dominate the skyline. Little herds of gaunt, humped cattle with huge horns wander great distances in search of fodder when the river disappears underground during the dry season. The largest town along this long, almost empty road, with some 1,600 Fallana residents is **Ranérou**, which lies about 150km (90 miles) past Linguère.

Both the Réserve de Faune de Ferlo-Nord and Sud are best visited from December to June.

Ferlo's nature reserves

Just before Ranérou, the Linguère–Matam road forms the boundary between the twin reserves that extend across a vast swathe of the Ferlo region. Covering 4,870 sq km (1,900 sq miles) and 6,340 sq km (2,475 sq miles) respectively, the **Réserve de Faune de Ferlo-Nord ❿** and **Réserve de Faune de Ferlo-Sud** were set aside in 1972 and together form the largest protected area anywhere in the Sahel; portion of land in which no grazing is permitted.

Both reserves are listed as Important Bird Areas, and their combined checklist of 180 species includes the likes of Abyssinian ground hornbill, Arabian

BELOW: carved wooden crafts.

African sculpture.

BELOW: many stalls sell exquisite embroidery.

bustard and Savile's bustard, alongside a wide variety of raptors and possibly the last wild population of ostrich in Senegal. Smaller and more localised dry-country species include little grey woodpecker, black scrub-robin, cricket warbler, chestnut-bellied starling and Sudan golden sparrow.

The large mammals of the Ferlo have suffered heavily from hunting over the past century, but a reduced population of red-fronted gazelle just about survives, and smaller predators such as jackal still range freely throughout the two reserves. Ferlo North is the setting for a project to reintroduce two handsome Sahelian antelope species that once roamed the region in hundred-strong herds but now sadly teeter on the brink of extinction. These are the scimitar-horned oryx, which is IUCN-listed as "Extinct in the Wild" but quite well-represented in zoos, and the Dama gazelle, which is listed as Critically Endangered, with a total wild population estimated at just a few hundred animals.

Eight oryx and five gazelle from the Réserve de Guembeul were released into a 5 sq km (2 sq mile) fenced enclosure

alongside the Katane Ranger Post 2003 and both species have bred succes fully in this protected environment. On stocks are sufficiently high, a few ind viduals will be released to fend for ther selves – and if successful, these ra creatures will roam freely on Senegal soil for the first time in many decade

Diourbel Region

The second smallest of Senegal's administrative regions (after Dakar Diourbel closely approximates the exte of the former kingdom of **Baol**, one the autonomous states that emergo from the 16th-century collapse of great Djolof. The regional capital, also call Diourbel, lies close to the site where t last emperor of a united Djolof w killed in battle in 1549.

More importantly, Diourbel Regio is the spiritual focus of the Mouric Brotherhood, a progressive form Sufism that took shape in the early 20 century under the leadership of the my tic scholar Cheikh Ahmadou Bamba a his most prominent disciple, Cheik Ibrahim Fall. The town of Mbak where Ahmadou Bamba was born 1853, is situated in Diourbel Region, is the holy city of Touba, which I established in 1888.

Diourbel

The regional capital of **Diourbel** home to around 100,000 predominant Wolof residents, overlooks the Si River at the junction of the RN1 ar RN3, some 75km (45 miles) east Thiès. A compact city that took its pr sent shape in the colonial era, it w once an important stop on the Dakar Niger Railway, and its centre is sca tered with early 20th-century building including the Gare (railway station Préfecture and Bureau de Poste, a listed as Historic Monuments. Despi its size, Diourbel has a sleepy smal town atmosphere, though the place transformed during the annual pilgrin age to nearby Touba, when the popul tion doubles to accommodate transie pilgrims. The surrounding plains a

Recommended Restaurants and Bars on page 255

one of the country's richest sources of peanuts, and food production and processing form supplementary industries to groundnut collection.

The woodcarving booths lining the marketplace and the Village Artisanal are favourite attractions with visitors, as are the many stalls selling exquisite local embroidery. Leatherwork and gold and silver jewellery are also produced in the market, and paintings depicting the anti-colonial exploits of the national hero Lat Dior make decorative, if a little bulky, souvenirs.

Cheikh Ahmadou Bamba, whose image can be seen on posters and walls all over the country, was placed under house arrest in Diourbel in 1912 and remained there until his death in 1927. The immense compound he occupied during this period is still referred to as the **Maison du Grand Maître** (literally "House of the Great Master") and is inhabited by his descendents.

The Grand Mosque

Opposite the house stands the earliest Mouride **Grande Mosquée**, built under the supervision of Ahmadou Bamba

CHEIKH AHMADOU BAMBA
1853–1927

during his house arrest. A more classical construction than its famed counterpart at Touba, Diourbel Mosque is built in the Ottoman tradition, with a pinkish central dome and four corner minarets, and it makes for an impressive sight among the groves of deep green palm trees that surround it.

Non-Islamic visitors are welcome to enter the building except during prayer times, as long as they are appropriately dressed: women should cover their legs,

Posters of Cheikh Ahmadou Bamba are found all throughout Senegal.

BELOW:
the pink-hued Grande Mosquée in Diourbel.

head and shoulders and men should wear long trousers. The balcony around the main minaret affords a fine view of the town and its surroundings.

Founded in 1796 by a great grandfather of Cheikh Ahmadou Bamba, **Mbaké** was the second-largest town in Diourbel (after the eponymous regional capital) until the 1980s. Now, it is effectively little more than a satellite of Touba.

Capital of the Mouride

In the centre of the defunct kingdom of Baol, 30 miles (50km) north of Diourbel, **Touba**  is the country's fastest growing urban centre, with a population that has shot up from a few thousand in the early 1960s to more than half a million today, making it easily the second-largest city in Senegal. In theory, Touba lies some 8km (5 miles) north of Mbaké, the birthplace of its founder Ahmadou Bamba, but in practice the twin towns now form one vast urban sprawl that runs along the RN3 for kilometre after scruffy kilometre, with no clear divide as to where one begins and the other ends.

Touba is the *de facto* capital of the very powerful Mouride brotherhood,

practically functioning as a state within a state where the word of local religious leaders carries far greater weight than that of the secular central government. As such, it has emerged as a serious economic rival to Dakar, and its sprawling black market serves as the main national funnel for illicit imported and exportable goods, ranging from grey electronic equipment and automatic weapons to the fake Rolexes, Ray-bans and other branded items sold by Mouride emigrants in the cities of Europe and North America.

The modern ascent rise of Touba is almost entirely down to its association with Cheikh Ahmadou Bamba, who experienced a transcendent vision there in 1888 whilst sitting under a baobab tree, which he named after the Koranic "Tree of Paradise" (Tuba) that represents spiritual wholeness in the Sufi tradition. This isolated holy site remained just that until 1926, when a small mosque was constructed as a mausoleum for the ailing cheikh, who died a year later. After the death of its founder, however, the Mouride chose Touba as the site of their grandest mosque, which took practically

The Grand Magal attracts over two million followers, and with a sizeable crowd there are bound to be some risks, including criminal activity, so be aware.

BELOW: the impressive interior of the Mosquée de Touba.

Recommended Restaurants and Bars on page 255

40 years to build, and was inaugurated in 1964. Since that date it has undergone several relatively minor extensions and modifications.

Touba's mosque

Arguably more impressive than it is beautiful, the **Grande Mosquée de Touba** is the tallest such edifice in sub-Saharan Africa and third-highest in the world, and its five minarets that are visible from miles away as you approach from the flat plains to the north. The tallest minaret, known as Lamp Fall after Cheikh Ibrahim Fall, is one of the country's most celebrated religious icons, towering 87 metres (285ft) high and culminating in a white four-tiered structure reminiscent of a gigantic wedding cake. Its shorter companions are fashioned of pink marble and are topped with what looks like a quintet of garish purple Easter eggs.

As in Diourbel Mosque, non-Muslims are welcome to walk around inside the mosque, provided that they remove their shoes and are suitably attired – men should wear long trousers and shirts, and women should wear flowing garments that cover their knees, shoulders and hair.

The mosque's interior is truly immense and fabulously ornate, adorned with innumerable concrete pillars, arches, detailed plaster decorations and stained-glass windows. By contrast, the adjacent Mausoleum of Cheikh Ahmadou Bamba, distinguished by its domed green top, is a rather modest construction, as are the tombs of the five sons who serially succeeded him as caliph.

The Grand Magal

Touba Mosque is the focal point of an annual pilgrimage, the Grand Magal, which usually falls on the 10th day of the 11th month of the Islamic calendar to mark the end of Bamba's exile by the French colonial government in 1907. More than one million Mouride devotees from Senegal and elsewhere in West Africa descend on Touba and Mbaké for the Grand Magal, and both towns celebrate throughout the night.

In Touba the ceremonies are more reserved and religious in character, so most non-Islamic visitors tend to stay in Mbaké, making the short trip to Touba during the day. If you want to visit the town during pilgrimage, remember to

Pilgrims pray five times daily in Touba.

BELOW: families come to see the mausoleum of the saints of Mouridism in Touba.

Women wait in line to enter Touba mosque.

BELOW:
open for business
in Kaolack.

refrain from smoking or drinking (neither of which will be tolerated in Touba during Magal). Also, bear in mind that big crowds, even devoted ones, tend to attract criminals so be careful.

Touba, presumably for religious reasons, is possibly the largest town anywhere in Africa without a single hotel or any other formal accommodation option, and there's only one small *campement* in Mbaké. However, a large Mouride-managed campsite opens especially for the duration of the Grand Magal, and the people of Mbaké also open their houses to strangers during the

pilgrimage, so you will often find a be and food. A donation is always welcom and appreciated.

One measure of how recent the rise c the Mouride brotherhood has been is tha five of the six caliphs that followe founder Cheikh Ahmadou Bamba wer also his eldest surviving son at the tim of their succession. These were Mouha madou Moustapha Mbaké (from 1927 Mouhamadou Fallilou Mbaké (fror 1945), Abdul Ahad Mbaké (from 1968 Abdou Khadre Mbaké (from 1989) an Saliou Mbaké (from 1990), all of whor are now buried outside Touba Mosque When Saliou Mbaké died in 2007 at th grand age of 92, he was the last c Ahmadou Bamba's sons to go, but toda the dynasty remains secure with th appointment of a grandson, Mouhamado Lamine Bara as the seventh caliph on 3 December 2007.

Kaolack

Most if not all roads through the centra Senegalese interior converge on th bustling market town of **Kaolack** ⑬ which stands on the north bank of th Saloum about 115km (70 miles) uprive

Recommended Restaurants and Bars on page 255

of its mouth, and 190km (115 miles) southeast of Dakar. An important stop on the Dakar-Niger Railway and RN1 connecting Dakar to Tambacounda, Kaolack is also a useful springboard for travel onto The Gambia or Casamance, located at the junction of the Trans-Gambia Highway (RN4) southeast to Farafenni and Ziguinchor and the RN5 southwest to Banjul. The town is serviced by good public transport connections in all directions, with southbound vehicles departing from the Gare Routière Sud located near the market, and northbound ones using the Gare Routière Nord, which is found along the main Dakar road.

Kaolack lies approximately 8km (5 miles) downriver of Kahone, which was the capital of the Saloum Empire from the 16th to 19th centuries, and oral tradition states it was originally founded by two princesses from Baol. The last point along the river navigable by ocean-going vessels, it was selected as a French river-port in 1860, when the road grid of the present-day town centre was laid out. By the early 20th century, Kaolack was a peanut processing and maritime export

centre of note, and its fortunes were further boosted with the arrival of the railway line from Dakar in 1911. By 1936, it was the second-largest town in the whole country, with a population reaching the 40,000 mark.

In more recent years, improved road transport has reduced the deep port on the town's southern outskirts to a mere shadow of what it was in its colonial heyday. Aside from the groundnut industry, Kaolack is an important producer of salt, which is mined along the rather pungent stretch of riverbank opposite the port, accounting for what looks like an isolated, blindingly white sand dune towering to the west of the main road as you head southward out of the town.

Open-air market

Today, Kaolack is Senegal's fourth-largest town (population 185,000) and one of its most pleasant. Good facilities include several banks, internet cafés and supermarkets, as well as a choice of accommodation and eating out options that seems positively extravagant by comparison to the rest of the central

TIP

If you are in Kaolack on a Saturday night, head to the **VLC** (Village Loisir Club; Thur–Sun 9pm–3am), where you'll have to make your way through the crowd to hit the dancefloor.

BELOW: women collecting salt along the riverbank.

interior. There is also a reasonably well-equipped hospital located on Avenue Valdiodio-Ndiaye.

As for sightseeing, a scattering of old colonial buildings populate the town centre, but the main point of architectural interest is the covered marketplace, which is one of the largest in Africa, adorned with fine Sudanese-style arches and small arcades. In fact, the whole of the town centre can come across as one giant open-air market, which can be fun when you're in the mood for leisurely browsing and buying, but rather enervating when you are simply trying to head from A to B.

A refreshing break (if break you need) is to be had at the courtyard restaurant-bar operated by the **Alliance Franco-Sénégalaise** (Rue de France; tel: 339 411 0611; http://kaolack.af-senegal.org; daily 8am–late; free). Built and decorated in a striking blend of local and French influences adorned with mosaics, this is also the town's main library, and it hosts regular musical and other performances.

Kaolack has vied with Tivaouane as the most important centre of the Tidjiane Brotherhood since 1930, when El-Hajj Ibrahim (Baay) Niasse founded **Médina Baye** (literally "Town of Baye", about 3km (2 miles) north of the town centre as a base from which to spread the teachings of the Tidjiane brand of Sufism across West Africa and further abroad. Médina Baye remains something of a town apart, and its Grande Mosquée – oddly reminiscent of a colonial railway station – is one the most famous in Senegal, built in the Moroccan style with tall twin minarets flanking a large central green dome. Somewhat more unusual is the new mosque that stands prominently on the west side of the Dakar roads as you enter town – with its tall rocket-shaped minarets, you could be forgiven for thinking it represents phase one in an attempt to make sure the first African to reach the moon is Senegalese!

Towards The Gambia

Nioro du Rip ⑭ is the largest town along the RN4 (Trans-Gambia Highway) as it runs southeast for 110km (65 miles) between Kaolack and the Medina Saback/Farafenni border with The Gambia. The former capital of the small but influential Rip Empire, Nioro was

The new mosque in Médina Baye was commissioned by the late Senegalese millionaire Ndiouga Kébé, as part of his ambitious "future city" project which never really materialised.

BELOW: the rocket-shaped minarets of Médina Baye's new mosque.

Recommended Restaurants and Bars on page 255

founded *c.*1850 by the revolutionary marabout leader Maba Diakhao Bâ, with the dual goals of uniting the area north of the Gambian border under Islam and abolishing the traditional caste system associated with the Serer states of Siné and Saloum. Maba did succeed in deposing the traditional leadership of Saloum prior to his death in battle in 1867, but he is best remembered for his influence on such iconic Senegalese figures as Lat Dior and Cheikh Ahmadou Bamba, both of whom lived briefly in Nioro du Rip. Today, this unassuming settlement of 15,000 shows few outward signs of its former significance, though what remains of the Tata (Fortifications) built by Maba Diakhao Bâ is preserved as a Historic Monument.

There is no accommodation in Nioro du Rip, but air-conditioned en-suite rooms are available 14km (9 miles) east of town at **Campement Dabali** (tel: 337 913 610; www.campementdabaly.com), which lies on the north bank of the **Bao Bolon** alongside the village of Bolong (which is also known as Dabali). This can be reached by following the RN4 southeast of Nioro du Rip for 9km (5 miles) then taking the clearly signposted dirt road to the left at the tiny settlement of **Firgui** shortly before the main road crosses the river. Situated in a hunting concession leased from the regional administration in Nioro du Rip, Campement Dabali has traditionally catered predominantly to the hunting fraternity during the open season of January to April, with game birds being the main speciality, along with medium-sized mammals such as warthog. This is changing, however, and horseback safaris are also on offer, as well as birdwatching and cultural trips in the surrounding Peul-dominated countryside.

Megalithic stone circles

The main tourist attraction in this area is the world's largest concentration of **megalithic stone circles**, with more than 1000 such sites comprising almost 29,000 laterite stelae recorded in the area between the Gambia and Saloum rivers.

Surprisingly under-publicised and seldom visited by tourists, these mysterious prehistoric relics are likely to receive a profile boost following the inscription of two Senegalese and two Gambian clusters as the **Stone Circles of Senegambia** World Heritage Site by Unesco in 2006 *(also see page 128)*. The largest and most important of these megalithic sites flank the Bao Bolon to the east of Nioro du Rip. These include Senegal's two Unesco-inscribed sites, namely **Siné Ngayène**, which has the densest concentration of stone circles anywhere in the Senegambia region, and **Wanar**, which boasts the biggest concentration of lyre-shaped stelae.

With private transport, ideally 4x4, the two inscribed Senegalese sites (and several minor ones) can easily be explored over the course of a day trip from Kaolack (or en route between Kaolack and The Gambia) following a rough 50km (30 miles) road loop running east from the RN4 near Nioro du Rip. Alternatively, organised trips to the main sites are offered by Campement Dabali, while budget-minded independent travellers could easily get to **Siné Ngayène**, the

Time to slow down in Kaolack.

BELOW: overloaded.

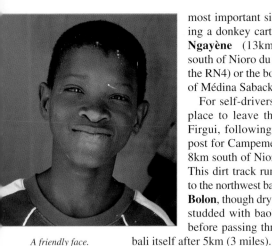

A friendly face.

most important site, by hiring a donkey cart in **Ndiba Ngayène** (13km/8 miles south of Nioro du Rip along the RN4) or the border town of Médina Saback.

For self-drivers, the best place to leave the RN4 is Firgui, following the signpost for Campement Dabali 8km south of Nioro du Rip. This dirt track runs parallel to the northwest bank of **Bao Bolon**, though dry scrubland studded with baobab trees, before passing through Dabali itself after 5km (3 miles).

After another 5km (3 miles), the first megalithic site, located immediately before at the village of **Kabakoto** ⓯, is easily visible on the right side of the road and consists of four circles, each comprising of around a dozen metallic red laterite stelae. Kabakoto itself is an atmospheric settlement of perhaps two dozen traditional mud-and-thatch compounds, housing more children than seems humanly possible, and a mosque listed as a Historic Monument.

Approximately 1.5km (1 mile) further, to the right, a long causeway crosses Bao Bolong, and you'll return to this later, but first follow the northwest bank of the bolong for another 5km (3 miles) to **Wanar Megalithic Site** ⓰, which lies in the open fields about 1.5km (1 mile) before the village of the same name, flanked by the villages of Siné Madame and Keur Ndaye about 1–2km (1 mile) to the west and east respectively. Wanar is made of of 396 megaliths arranged in 21 circles, including one concentric example, but it is best known for its tally of seven collapsed and nine standing lyre-shaped stones, three of which form a unique line in front of a larger circle. Wanar is currently unfenced and unmonitored, though the local community have long acted as informal caretakers, and there are plans to fence the site, restore several broken and collapsed stones, and erect some interpretative signboards.

Returning along the northwest bank of the river, cross the above mentioned causeway to the southeast bank and, approximately 1km (0.6 miles) further, before entering the substantial village of

Recommended Restaurants and Bars on page 255

aymor **17** look out for the remains of a tumulus consisting of 10 stones on the left side of track. As the road enters Kaymor, turn along a rough track through a massive stand of baobabs, passing a large mosque to the right and a wooden footbridge to the left. About 1km (0.6 miles) past this junction, at **Passi Kaymor**, you pass an amazing baobab forest where careful inspection will reveal several collapsed megaliths including at least two with knob-like "buttons" (which rather resemble battery terminals) and, reputedly, an elusive example of a lyre-stone.

Fork left at the mosque at Passi Kaymor, then continue for 6km (4 miles) along the rough track – looking out for a small solitary circle positioned under a tree to the left, then a cluster of several circles obscured in thicker undergrowth until you reach **Fas**, an attractive traditional Peul village of approximately 00 compounds.

About 3.5km (3 miles) past Fas, the Siné Ngayène **18** complex is housed in a conspicuous fenced 5 hectares enclosure on the outskirts of the village of the same name. The most extensive site of its type in the world, it consists of 1,102

cylindrical and polygonal carved stones describing 52 circles, including one concentric example referred to locally as the royal tomb. Siné Ngayène is also notable for the variety of carving styles and alignments on show, the presence of several "button" stones and circular engravings, and the overall good state of conservation. Excavations at this and other sites suggest it is essentially a vast funerary complex created by a prosperous and well organised society over several centuries in the 1st millennium AD. The quarry where the monoliths were excavated lies about 1km (0.6 miles) to the east, along the road to Tiékène, as does a large grinding stone used to carve their distinctive shapes.

Siné Ngayène is currently unmanned and no entrance fee is charged, but this is most likely to change following the planned construction of a visitors' centre, toilets and information boards. From Siné Ngayène, you can return to the RN4 at **Ndiba Ngayène**, a drive of around 15km (9 miles) passing through the villages of **Payama** (here stones from circles have been pulled up to support buildings) and **Koloumbodou** en route.

The finely worked individual stones at both Wanar and Siné Ngayène display precise and skillful working practices.

BELOW: the mighty baobab tree.

which supports around 12,000 inhabitants and is easily accessed by bush-taxi or private vehicle from Tivaouane, which lies 25km (15 miles) to the southeast along the RN2 between Dakar and Saint Louis. There is no accommodation in the town itself, but a couple of simple resorts can be found at the seaside M'Boro-sur-Mer 5km (3 miles) to the west.

Lompoul Desert

Even more scenically worthwhile is the 18-sq-km (7-sq-mile) **Désert de Lompoul ⓴**, which lies about 10km (6 miles) inland of Lompoul-sur-Mer along the road to Kébémer. The rippled peach coloured dunes here stand up to 50 metres (170ft) tall, and are almost entirely non-vegetated, creating a landscape reminiscent of the larger and better known Sahara or Namib.

An excellent base for exploring this area is the **Gîte de Lompoul**, which offers accommodation in Mauritanian style tents in the heart of the small section of desert and 3km (1.8 miles) from the sea (*see Travel Tips page 327*). Several agencies in Saint-Louis organise day trips to the desert.

Fishermen coming back ashore in Lompoul-sur-Mer.

The Grande Côte

The 150km (90 miles) coastline that separates the Cap Vert from Saint-Louis is arguably more beautiful than the Petite Côte, and it's certainly a lot less urbanised and touristy, boasting some wonderfully untrammelled dunescapes. Unfortunately, however, the combination of high breakers and treacherous currents makes the so-called Grande Côte ill suited to a typical beach holiday, assuming that swimming is high on your agenda, and very few tourists ever head this way.

BELOW: leading camels through the Désert de Lompoul.

The largest and most accessible town along the Grande Côte is **M'Boro ⓳**,

RESTAURANTS AND BARS

Restaurants

Prices for a main course per person:
$ = under US$8 (CFA3,200)
$$ = US$8–15 (CFA 3,200–6,000)
$$$ = over US$15 (CFA6,000)

With the exception of Thiès and Kaolack, the towns of the central interior are found wanting when it comes to quality restaurants. If you stay in any of these towns, your best bet for a sit-down meal will be your hotel. Otherwise, there are always plenty of stalls selling local staples, filled baguettes and the like around the *gare routière* and central market.

Dara

Auberge-Restaurant Ker Guy
Rue Linguère
Tel: 33 968 6310 **$**
This very acceptable local eatery, attached to the town's only hotel, serves filling plates of chicken or fish with rice at short notice, and may be able to rustle up something more elaborate with a bit of warning.

Kaolack

Café Waw
Rue Galliène
Tel: 33 941 1061 **$**
Attached to the Alliance Franco-Sénégalaise, this brightly decorated courtyard café is open for drinks and coffee all day, and serves an inexpensive *plat du jour* (usually chicken or fish) from around 7–10.30pm. Service is a little slow, but the funky ambience, sensible prices and fruit-bats that flap overhead after dusk are ample compensation. There is live music, too, upon occasion.

Le Brasero
Avenue Valdiodio-N'Diaye
Tel: 33 941 1608 **$–$$**
Run by an elderly French couple, this superb and centrally located courtyard restaurant serves delicious grills and seafood, as well as a selection of Senegalese dishes, adequate pizzas, and inexpensive beers and carafe wines. A large screen satellite TV ensures big crowds are present for major sporting events.

Chez Maty
Rue Cheikh Tidiane Cherif
Tel: 33 941 9000 **$**
Simple and cheap food is on offer at this bustling eaterie. Clean and presentable. Open 11am–2pm and 7pm–midnight. Closed Sunday.

Thiès

Croissant Magique
381 Avenue Lamine-Gueye
Tel: 33 951 1878 **$–$$**
This large centrally located patisserie/restaurant is a real winner on all levels, whether you're looking for a peppy espresso and freshly prepared croissant or sandwich on the shady street veranda, a full-blown French dinner in the airy indoor dining hall – or, for that matter, a yummy confectionary to take back to your hotel room. This is a popular place. Open daily 7.30am–late.

La Case à Teranga
232 Avenue Léopold-Senghor
Tel: 77 611 5125 **$$**
This unusually cosmopolitan restaurant combines conventional Franco-Senegalese dishes with an eclectic mix of Asian and Caribbean surprises. Although it's open for drinks and light snacks from 10am–midnight, main courses are available only in the evening. Live music is played at the weekend.

La Vieille Marmite
43 Rue Yacine-Boutou
Tel: 33 951 4440 **$**
A popular lunch stop with the Peace Corps, whose Senegalese headquarters is in Thiès, this busy little restaurant serves a good mix of affordable Senegalese and French staples to its loyal clientele of locals and resident foreigners. Open 9am–3pm.

Les Délices
300 Avenue Léopold-Senghor
Tel: 33 951 7516 **$**
The terrace here is a great spot for a central midday snack of coffee, and it also serves a reasonable selection of inexpensive Lebanese and French main dishes. Good for pastries and pizza too.

RIGHT: in rural areas, food is prepared in rustic pots.

Recommended Restaurants and Bars on page 269

SOUTHEASTERN SENEGAL

Visit Niokolo-Koba, the largest national park in West Africa, rich in wildlife and staggeringly beautiful, then tour hill villages where customs have remained unchanged for centuries

he far southeast of Senegal is distinctly different to the rest of the country. Bordered by Mali to the east and Guinea-Bissau to the south, this thinly populated region supports a cover of equatorial savannah dominated by fields of tall elephant grass and dense tangled woodland. It lies in the shadow of the Fouta Djalon mountains, whose rolling hills and peaks reach altitudes of up to 400 metres (1,300ft), and whose slopes are swathed in hardwood forests of teak and mahogany. Ribbons of lush riparian forest and swaying palms follow the upper reaches of the region's three largest rivers: the **Falémé**, which runs along the Malian border to its confluence with the larger Senegal River, and the **Gambia** and tributary **Niokolo-Koba River**, which are joined by a web of smaller tributaries, including the **Nieri Ko** and **Koulountou**. Further northeast, the terrain is flat and desert-like, supporting a sparse cover of hardier trees such as baobab, shea and acacia. In the mountain regions hard woods such as teak and mahogany are common.

The southeast is visited by relatively few tourists, certainly when compared to the bustling beaches of Cap Vert and the Petite Côte, but it has much to offer the adventurous traveller.

The main attraction is undoubtedly the **Parc National de Niokolo-Koba**, a vast tract of untamed wilderness flowed through by the wide Niokolo-Koba and Gambia rivers. The largest national park in West Africa, Niokolo-Koba is Sene-gal's most prominent safari destination, home to a varied selection of monkeys, smaller antelopes and birds, though considerable time, patience and luck are required to see more alluring and elusive species such as chimpanzee, lion, elephant and Derby's eland. Further southeast, the hilly Guinean border region near Kédougou offers great opportunities for rambling and hiking among the small hamlets of the Bédik, and for encounters with the traditionalist Bassari people, whose colourful initiation ceremonies take place annually between April and June.

Main attractions

TAMBACOUNDA
PARC NATIONAL DE
NIOKOLO-KOBA
MOUNT ASSIRIK
PAYS BASSARI
IWOL
ETHIOLO
CHUTES DE DINDÉFELO

LEFT: crossing the Niokolo-Koba River.
BELOW: a kob ewe with her young.

The best time for birdwatching in Niokolo-Koba is the European winter, especially the months from December to March, when as many as 3 million migratory birds visit the area from the northern hemisphere.

Tambacounda's attractions

The gateway to the southeast, **Tambacounda ❶** is also the largest town in the region, with a population estimated at 80,000. An important regional administrative centre and public transport hub, this strategically located town is accessible by road from several directions. The most common approach is the 300-mile (480km) bitumen RN1 from Dakar, but the stretch of road east of Kaolack is now in poor condition, and the journey takes at least six hours in a private vehicle, longer by bush taxi. Tambacounda can also be reached by road from the Gambian capital of Banjul, a trip that entails following the Gambia River east as far as Basse Santa Su, then veering south along a rough and sandy road through the Badiara border post to Vélingara, from where it is reached along an excellent 95km (57-mile) surfaced road running northeast. Other possible approaches are from Ziguinchor via Kolda and Vélingara, and from Saint-Louis via the Senegal River and Kidira.

Tambacounda owes its existence to its crossroads location on the colonial railway line connecting Dakar with Kidira

and the Malian capital of Bamako, and remains a pivotal stop on the train servic that links Dakar and Bamako onc weekly in either direction. The iron framed rail station, though poorly main tained, was placed on the Senegalese lis of Historical Monuments on its centenar in 2003, as were the colonial-era Hôte de Ville and Préfecture building. Thes somewhat esoteric landmarks aside, Tam bacounda boasts little in the way of for mal sightseeing. It has an engagingly aur of urban bustle, however, and it can b pleasant to wander around exploring th markets, tree-shaded avenues and smal craft shops, and noting the cultural diver sity of its Peul, Sarakholé, Tukulo Malinké, Bambara and Wolof inhabitants

Tambacounda has good facilities including a varied selection of hotels The pick is **Le Relais de Tamba**, whic lies in shady grounds on the RN1 o the outskirts of town, and offers 2 rooms with air-con, satellite TV, fre wireless internet, swimming pool an bistro restaurant. A popular option fo more budget-orientated travellers is the **Hôtel Niji**, which offers basic but clea rooms with en suite facilities and air

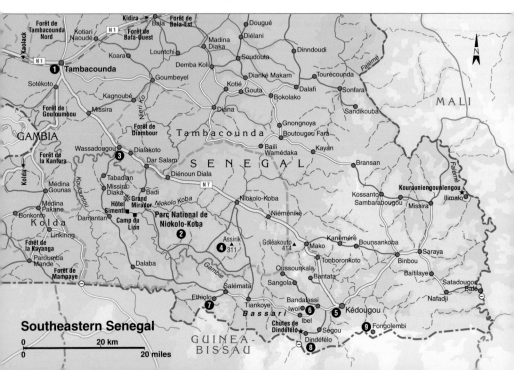

Southeastern Senegal

Recommended Restaurants and Bars on page 269

conditioning, and also has a swimming pool and good food. There are several internet cafés in Tambacounda, two banks with ATMs where you can draw money using international credit cards, and shops and supermarkets to stock up provisions for Niokolo-Koba.

Senegal's largest park

One of the few West African reserves that exists on a scale comparable to the great safari destinations of eastern and southern Africa, the **Parc National de Niokolo-Koba** ❷ extends over some 9,130 sq km (3,560 sq miles) of mixed woodland, savannah and riverine habitats. Geographically, much of the reserve is rather monotonous, though the flat plains are bisected by the perennial Gambia River and its various tributaries, and it does include one relatively significant outcrop in the form of the 311-metre (1,020ft) Mount Assirik in the southeast.

Named after a tributary of the Gambia River, Niokolo-Koba started life as a hunting reserve in the 1920s and was upgraded to national park status in 1954. It was inscribed as a Unesco World Heritage Site in 1981, on the basis of being "the most important site of its type in West Africa, and the best-managed… providing a spectacle of outstanding wildlife and a safe habitat for endangered species". Back then, Niokolo-Koba was renowned for the large herds of elephant, buffalo, hippo and smaller ungulates that congregated along the rivers, and the area was famed for the number and size of its lions, reputedly the largest in the whole of Africa.

Today, Niokolo-Koba remains the nearest part of Africa to Europe and the United States where a wide variety of large mammals can be seen in their natural state, but the wildlife isn't nearly so prolific as it was in the park's heyday. An alluring checklist of 70-plus mammal species includes four of the so-called Big Five, namely lion, leopard, elephant and buffalo, a quartet of other species on the IUCN endangered list (African wild dog, common chimpanzee, red colobus monkey and Derby's giant eland) and a host of other safari favourites, ranging from giraffe and hippo to warthog and Guinea baboon. However, the majority of these safari favourites are now so rare that casual visitors stand little chance of seeing them in the course of a few days' visit.

The giraffe, for instance, was long ago poached to extinction in Niokolo-Koba, while elephants are heading the same way, with the population of several hundred in the early 1980s survived by fewer than 10 individuals according to a survey undertaken by the African Parks Foundation in 2006. The same census suggests that several other large ungulate species are in serious trouble in Niokolo-Koba, with estimated 1990 populations of 24,000 kob antelope, 8,000 buffalo, 6,000 roan antelope and 5,000 hartebeest respectively down to 100, 500, 700 and 150 in 2006. Lions are under immediate threat of local extinction, with fewer than 30 individuals thought to survive, and leopard numbers have also dipped in recent years, though these secretive nocturnal predators are notoriously difficult to monitor. In June 2007, the World Heritage Site responded to the imminent crisis by placing Niokolo-

The area around Tambacounda is strongly associated with the Djembé drumming tradition, and it is said that the town's name describes the sound of the local drums.

BELOW: poaching has decreased the sightings of leopards.

Koba on the shortlist of World Heritage Sites in Danger, stating that it "is endangered by poaching and by plans to construct a dam on the Gambia River… [that] threatens to stop the flooding of the grassland essential to sustain wildlife."

Few African national parks display quite such a disparity between their potential as a safari destination and the on-the-ground reality, but Niokolo-Koba is emphatically still worth a visit, provided it is approached with realistic expectations.

Despite the high level of poaching, the thick woodland that characterises the main tourist circuit around the Hôtel Simenti still supports a fair amount of wildlife. Most common, perhaps, is the warthog, which is often seen trotting into the bush in small family groups, tails held comically erect, and the very lucky visitor might also catch a glimpse of the more secretive red river hog. The most conspicuous antelopes in this area are bushbuck, Defassa waterbuck, kob, and the tiny but elegantly marked red-flanked duiker. The handsome roan antelope, though more common in areas of open grassland, is also frequently observed. The buffalos of Niokolo-Koba are an unusually variable form, and a small herd might contain a combination of black, yellow and intermediate individuals – while not as common as they once were, they still inhabit the parklands between the rivers, and are occasionally viewed near riverbanks or clustered around waterholes.

Screaming and chattering in the riverbank vegetation and perching high in the ancient palm, mahogany and kapok trees, a wide variety of monkeys are found in Niokolo-Koba. In the Simenti area, green monkeys leap in squadrons from tree to tree, only to be chased off by troops of Guinea baboon, which is the most numerous large mammal in the park, with a population estimated at around 10,000. In grassland and other open habitats, the terrestrial patas monkey outnumbers the green monkey.

The most visible of Niokolo-Koba's predators is the dainty side-striped jackal, often glimpsed trotting through the woodland at dusk and dawn. Also likely to be encountered by tourists are mongooses, of which six species are found in the park. The nocturnal spotted hyena roams widely, but is rarely seen, while

smaller predators such as civet, genet and serval are difficult to spot in their favoured habitat of dense riparian woodland. It is thought that several packs of African wild dog still roam the plains of Niokolo-Koba, forming what is probably the last viable West African population of a predator that has become increasingly rare throughout its African range due to its vulnerability to diseases spread by domestic dogs. Other smaller mammals inhabiting the wooded riversides range from the striped ground squirrel to the crested or brush-tailed porcupine.

The rivers that run through the park once supported an estimated 3,000–4,000 hippopotami, and while no recent figures are available, several pods are resident in the Gambia River where it passes through the Simenti area. The Nile crocodile, which can grow to a length of 3.5 metres (10ft), is also common in the rivers, along with 60 different varieties of fish, amphibian and aquatic reptile. Two-metre (7ft) long monitor lizards are frequently seen basking along river banks together with small terrapins, the occasional water snake and colourful butterflies.

Avian jewels

Some of Africa's most prolific birdlife either passes through, or resides in, Niokolo-Koba. More than 330 species have been reported in the varied habitats of the park, feeding off a cross-section of vegetation that ranges from borassus palms to the giant baobab trees, as well as the prolific insect life. Grasslands attract all manner of busy weaver birds, such as the northern red bishop, white-billed buffalo weaver, spectacled weaver and the village weaver, whose tightly knit nests hang decoratively from thorn and silk cotton trees. Stork and heron nests are easily spotted along any of the waterways through the parklands, and spoonbill can be seen in great flocks on some of the more open expanses of water. The largest nests of all are the massive platforms built of twigs by the comical hamerkop.

Driving through the woodland around Simenti, one's eye is frequently caught

An African forest buffalo wallowing in the water.

BELOW:
wildlife-spotting along the river.

Grasslands attract many weaver birds such as the northern red bishop.

BELOW: the striking plumage of the West African crowned crane.

by colourful flashes of avian activity. The cobalt-blue Abyssinian and blue-breasted rollers are abundant, as is the cumbersomely designed long-tailed glossy starling, and the tiny red-billed fire-finch and red-cheeked cordon-bleu. A persistent grinding and churring duet in the waterside tangle might signal the presence of a pair of secretive yellow-crowned gonolek, with its brilliant red, black and yellow markings, while several species of dazzlingly coloured bee-eater – northern carmine, red-throated and little – might be seen hawking from the canopy of acacia trees.

The marshes and floodplains around Simenti support a variety of wetland species, ranging from the dainty African jacana to the outsized spur-winged goose. A variety of storks and herons nest along the waterways, and African spoonbill and black crowned crane congregate near open expanses of water. Also near water, one is likely to encounter the massive platforms built as nests by the small hamerkop, and a variety of kingfishers, ranging from the outsized giant kingfisher, which favours wooded river banks, to the jewel-like malachite kingfisher, which is most often seen perching low on waterside reeds.

Because of its vast size, Niokolo-Koba provides refuge to a number of large birds which are now extremely rare elsewhere in the country. Large raptors include the spectacular bateleur, long-crested and martial eagles, while pairs of African fish eagle emit their eerie, piercing duets from perches high above the water, alongside the similar-looking palmnut vulture. Another common raptor is the hooded vulture, which might sometimes be observed alongside the larger white-backed and lappet-faced vulture. The truly enormous Abyssinian ground hornbill is a regular crowd-pleaser, with its comical gait and long rather camp eyelashes.

Exploring Niokolo-Koba

The most straightforward way to visit the Parc National de Niokolo-Koba is on an organised safari. These can be booked through any major tour operator based in Dakar or the Petite Côte region, as well as through most operators in the Banjul and Serekunda region of The Gambia. Generally, drive-down tours from the coast will be four to five days in duration, while tours that fly as far as Tambacounda are a little shorter. A more affordable option is to get to Tambacounda on public transport and arrange your safari into Niokolo-Koba from there. The best place to organise 4x4 hire is at one of the hotels in Tambacounda, and the Hôtel Niji runs regular day and overnight trips into the park.

A cheaper option is to negotiate a deal with a taxi driver, bearing in mind that while the main road to Hôtel Simenti is passable in an ordinary car during the dry season, much of the rest of the park is accessible by 4x4 only. Finally, any bush taxi or other vehicle heading between Tambacounda and Kédougou will drop you at the Dar Salam entrance gate, where there is a small camp, or you can ask the rangers at the gate to radio the Hôtel Simenti to organise a transfer.

Entrance gates are open from 7am 6pm daily throughout the year, thoug

Recommended Restaurants and Bars on page 269

the official season runs from 15 December until 30 April only. A daily entrance fee is charged per person, and there is also a one-off vehicle fee and a daily fee per party for the mandatory guide. Game-viewing is best towards the end of the dry season (March to early June), when the vegetation has thinned out, offering good visibility, and the wildlife congregates in the vicinity of the river and other permanent water sources close to Simenti. Roads may be impassable during the rainy season, which usually runs from July to October, and wildlife is difficult to locate. Self-caterers will need to bring everything they need from Tambacounda, and should remember to stock up on bottled water, which is very expensive in the park.

Most game-viewing circuits start from locations along the surfaced N7, the road which transects the park between Tambacounda and Kédougou. The closest point of entry coming from Tambacounda is just after **Nieri Ko**, a tributary of the Gambia River, at the village of **Wassadougou** ❸. This village overlooks a ford across the Gambia River, and the road across the ford leads into

one of the main entrances to the Parc National de Niokolo-Koba and an area where roan antelope are common and wild dog are regularly observed. The **Campement Hôtel de Wassadou** (www. niokolo.com) located about 2km (1 mile) from the village along a signposted dirt road, offers comfortable air-conditioned rooms and French home cooking on a site overlooking a forested bend in the Gambia. Although this hotel doesn't lie within the park, the facing riverbank forms its northernmost boundary and is occasionally visited by groups of antelope and monkeys. From Wassadougou, a short boat trip takes visitors to a colony of carmine bee-eaters, and there is a good chance of spotting hippos, crocodiles and a variety of waterbirds along the way. The *campement*-hôtel also maintains a fleet of 4x4s, which are used to run individualised camping safaris into remote parts of the national park such as the Mount Assirik region.

The main point of entry is the Dar Salam entrance gate, which is located alongside the RN7 approximately 80km (50 miles) from Tambacounda and 15km (10 miles) past Wassadougou. Adjacent

The Gambia River is a hotspot for two eagerly sought water-associated birds, the secretive African finfoot and the very localised Egyptian plover, both of which might be seen from the verandas of the Hôtel Simenti.

BELOW: pitching a tent in Niokolo-Koba.

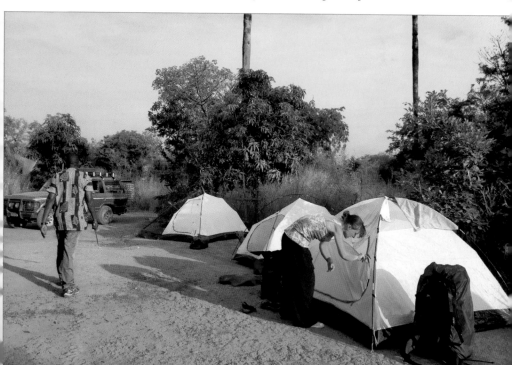

Mother and baby baboon take an early morning stroll.

BELOW:
a *campement* in Kédougou.

to the gate, the small **Campement Dar-Salam** comprises a few rather basic rooms, only likely to be used by travellers who get stuck at the gate, as well as a shaded restaurant serving cold drinks and simple meals. There is also a poorly maintained educational centre.

A rutted 30km (18-mile) dirt road, passable by saloon car during the dry season, leads from Dar Salam to the **Hôtel Simenti**, which is the most popular accommodation in the park. Simenti has a flawless location, overlooking a lushly vegetated stretch of the Gambia River where groups of hippos wallow in the depths, crocodiles bask on the shore, a steady stream of antelopes comes down to drink, and waterbirds such as Egyptian plover are regularly seen. Also within the hotel grounds, an excellent hide overlooks the Mare de Simenti (floodplain), which attracts large numbers of Guinea

baboon, green monkey, kob and waterbuck during the dry season, and also offers some superb birdwatching. Unfortunately, the hotel doesn't quite match its immaculate setting, though standard of accommodation, food and service have definitely improved in recent years, and the creaky air-conditioning and clean swimming pool are both very welcome in this hot climate.

A 10km (6-mile) road leads eastward from Hôtel Simenti to Bafoulabé, where the rustic **Camp du Lion** offers a more affordable but rather basic alternative to budget-conscious travellers at the confluence of the Niokolo-Koba and Gambia rivers. This camp also lies close to the Gambia River, but doesn't offer the grandstand views of the hotel. For independent travellers, both the Hôtel Simenti and Camp du Lion run organised game drives every morning and evening, following the excellent network of game-viewing tracks along the river, as well as visiting several small lakes. Game drives normally include a short guided walk on a rickety wooden suspension bridge across the Niokolo-Koba River near the confluence of tracks known as **La Patte**

Oie. Another spot worth making a
version for is the **Grand Mirador**
ewpoint over the river about 15km
miles) west of Simenti.

Most visitors restrict their exploration
Niokolo-Koba to the developed cir-
it around Simenti, but those with a pri-
te 4x4 could explore further afield.
eading east along on the RN7 from Dar
alam, the highway passes through
ienoun Diala, a further 10km (6 miles)
, from where another road leads around
s north boundary towards the east and
e road to Mali. Even on public trans-
rt, it is worth scanning the bush care-
lly on this stretch of the N7, as there
a good chance of seeing warthog, small
telope, and Abyssinian ground horn-
ll. Another 10km (6 miles) on from
ienoun Diala, a track leads into the
rest from the village of **Tali N'de
oulou**. Another 30km (18 miles) on,
ne comes to **Niokolo-Koba** village,
hich is bisected by the river for which
e national park is named, and the site of
large ranger station.

A few hundred metres after crossing
e Niokolo-Koba River, a rough dirt
ack to the right leads towards the allur-

ing and little-visited **Mount Assirik** ❹,
which lies roughly 20km (12km) south
of the RN7. This is the best place in the
park to see red colobus, chimpanzee,
elephant and giant eland. A primitive
campsite, the **Camp de l'Éland**, lies
about 10km (6 miles) south of the mountain at **Wouroli Ford**, where a great bank
has been constructed to contain the frequent floods of the Gambia River. Also
located on the banks of the Gambia,
between Simenti and Wouroli, the
"haltes" of **Gue Malapa** and **Badoye**
are free camping places.

Accessible only by 4x4, all three of the
above campsites are used occasionally by
organised tours, who will provide for all
their customers' needs on an overnight
safari. Independent travellers are urged
to check current road conditions and ask
advice of the park rangers before heading to this and other relatively remote
parts of the park. The campsites have no
food, water or electricity; they should
only be visited by independent travellers
who are prepared to carry everything they
need (it should be remembered that an
adult needs at least 5 litres/9 pints of
liquid a day in this climate).

*All visitors to
Niokolo-Koba
must have a vehicle
as walking is not
allowed except near
the campements
and hotels or when
accompanied by
a park ranger.*

LEFT:
scaling the mighty
baobab tree.

The fauna at Mount Assirik

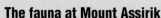

The forested gorges of Mount Assirik form a
distinct niche ecosystem within the more
open woodland typical of Niokolo-Koba, one
that supports isolated populations of two
forest-associated primate species, namely the
common chimpanzee – more closely related
to humans than to any other living creature –
and the smaller and more arboreal red
colobus monkey. The chimp community at
Assirik, estimated at around 100 individuals in
the 1980s, is now thought to number fewer

than 30. It is not used to human visits, but fleeting chimp sightings are quite
likely over a couple of days' visit to this remote area, which is accessible only
by 4x4, and ideally visited with a view to camping overnight.

Another animal to watch out for in the grassland around Mount Assirik is
Derby's giant eland *(pictured)*. This is the world's largest antelope, and it's
far more colourfully marked than the better-known common eland of eastern and southern Africa. An estimated 170 Derby's eland reside in Niokolo-
Koba, and they are of great significance to conservationists as the largest
and possibly only viable breeding population of the species' western race.

Feeding the chickens in the fascinating Bassari village of Ethiolo.

BELOW: Bassari village dwelling.

Bassari Country

At the far southwest of the N7 highway, 230km (140 miles) from Tambacounda and 150km (90 miles) from the Dar Salam entrance gate to Niokolo-Koba, **Kédougou ❺** is an important crossroads town located on the north bank of the Gambia River about 15km (9 miles) from the border with Guinea-Bissau. The town dates back several centuries to the gold trade of the Mali Empire, when it was founded by the Diakhanké people, a sub-group of the Mandingo, and its name translates as "Country of Men". It later expanded to service the iron mines at **Nafadji** in the Falémé district, and is now the largest town in the far southeast, with a population estimated at around 18,000. In striking contrast to the usual straw-roofed huts associated with rural Senegal, many houses in Kédougou are built with marble quarried in the nearby hills, and they bear the multiple hues of this stone.

The accommodation situation in Kédougou has improved greatly in recent years, especially since the road from Tambacounda was surfaced. There is now one proper upmarket hotel in the town, complete with swimming pool, as well as a smart camp and a few mor low-key lodgings catering mainly t backpackers. Other facilities include cyber café, fuel station and lively ma ket, but there is no bank or ATM. As fa as tourist attractions go, Kédougou cor tains little to delay the visitor, but th town was once used as a base by man early explorers into the headwater regior of the Gambia River, and it remains th obvious base from which the moder traveller can explore the remote village of the surrounding countryside.

The region around Kédougou is know as **Pays Bassari** (Bassari Country) afte the Bassari people, one of several strong traditional cultural groups that live in th area. Kédougou marks the end of the ta and the dirt roads that lead from the tow to outlying villages are variable in con dition – most can be traversed by an ord nary saloon car in the dry season, bu some may require a 4x4 during the rain While bush taxis run all day throug between Kédougou and Tambacound these services are generally restricted t local market days in other parts of th region. For this reason, most indepe dent travellers are forced to arrang

Recommended Restaurants and Bars on page 269

excursions by hiring taxis, a procedure which generally involves protracted haggling over the price.

The Bassari and other people of this area maintain a number of traditional ceremonies worthy of the attention of anthropologists and exciting to photographers. In addition, experts are studying the merits of the traditional remedies and medications evolved by the Bassari, who are now mainly employed in growing cotton, fishing, hunting and, of course, making souvenirs. A favourite local souvenir is the woven blankets and cloaks, most of which are imported from Guinea. Over the initiation season of April to June, visitors might have the opportunity to take photographs of these ceremonies, which mark the rites of passage of young Bassari men, but it is vital to ask permission before pulling out a camera on these sensitive occasions.

One of the most interesting and straightforward excursions in the area is to the small hilltop village of **Iwol** ❻, about 20km (12 miles) west of Kédougou near **Ibel** on the road to Salémata. From Ibel, a predominantly Fula village, a steep 30-minute walk uphill

takes one on to Iwol. On arrival at the village, which has a picturesque location in a rocky depression studded with immense baobab trees, visitors will be met by the official guide, who will ask them for a donation to the community before showing them around.

The most prominent baobab in the centre of Iwol village is held sacred, and may not be touched, while another baobab immediately outside the village is said to be the largest in the country, measuring about 23 metres (75ft) in diameter. The Bedik people of Iwol claim to have migrated to the area from Mali centuries ago and show some cultural affinities with that country's renowned Dogon. The women are particularly striking, with their elaborate braided hairstyles, colourful beaded necklaces, innumerable metal earrings and noses pierced with porcupine quills. Curio-hunters may want to buy one of the clay figurines, complete with porcupine quill through nose, that are sold by the children in the village. With a local guide, it is possible to explore the hills further, visiting other Bedik villages such as **Etchouar**, **Sangola** and **Landiéni**,

Taking part in a traditional ceremony.

BELOW:
daily life in Iwol.

Chimpanzees are easily observed in the village of Ethiolo.

BELOW: the Chutes de Dindéfelo, the tallest waterfall in Senegal.

all of which lie within a short distance of each other along tiny forest tracks.

Situated close to the Guinean border about 80km (50 miles) west of Kédougou, the village of **Ethiolo** ❼, reached from the main road at **Salémata**, is one of the most rewarding spots in Bassari Country. It has a stunning backdrop comprised of a circle of mountains, including the sacred peak of Patée, and is frequently claimed to be the largest traditional Bassari village in Senegal, with a population of around 700 divided between 65 households. Here there is a health centre and some small boutiques. For wildlife enthusiasts, Ethiolo is probably the best place in Senegal to see chimpanzees, thanks to the presence of a small community that shares its main water source with the local villagers. In 2005, an initiative to create a formal buffer zone for these dozen or so chimpanzees was undertaken by the local

Bindia family with the assistance of an NGO called Friends of Animals. Aside from being a real draw for travellers, this project is of great ecological significance, given that the total chimp population of Senegal stands at around 300. Sightings are most likely towards the end of the dry season, ie April to June, which coincides with the annual initiation ceremony held in the village. A basic but clean camp is operated by a local Bassari family in Ethiolo.

Roughly 20 miles (30km) south of Kédougou, the Peul village of **Dindéfelo** ❽ has an attractive sub-montane location (the name literally means "Foot of the Mountain"), and also offers accommodation in a small camp.

The main attraction in this area are the **Chutes de Dindéfelo**, which lie about 30 minutes' walk from the village. Measuring 100 metres (320ft) from top to bottom, this sacred site is the tallest waterfall in Senegal and one of the most impressive anywhere in West Africa, especially during the rainy season. It's possible to swim in the deep pool at the base of the cascade. Sunday is market day in Dindéfelo, and the most interesting time to visit, as well as being the only day when public transport runs there from Kédougou.

About 25km (15 miles) southeast of Kédougou, **Fongolembi** ❾ lies at the base of the Fouta Djalon mountains and makes an interesting base for excursions into the Guinea-Bissau border region. It is inhabited by the Diallonké people, whose traditional way of life persists almost unmodified by Western influence, at such villages as **Sintiou**, **Wallam**, **Toumanéa** and **Niagalankomé**. In the same region, it is possible to meet gold prospectors in local villages such as **Binbou**, **Saraya** and **Ilimalo**. A few kilometres from Ilimalo there is an important site for pilgrimages and a centre for traditional religious ceremonies. Called **Kourouniengouniengou**, this sacred place is overlooked by a massive rock balancing on a cliff edge high above the valley floor – one of the most spectacular geological formations in Senegal. ☐

RESTAURANTS AND BARS

Restaurants

Prices for a main course per person:
$ = under US$8 (CFA3,200)
$$ = US$8–15 (CFA3,200–6,000)
$$$ = over US$15 (CFA6,000)

Tambacounda

Best Burger
Boulevard Demba-Diop
Tel: 33 981 3203 **$**
This greasy fast-food joint does pretty decent *shwarmas*, burgers, sandwiches and other budget-friendly filling snacks. No alcohol. Open 10am–midnight.

Hôtel Niji
Off Avenue Léopold-Senghor
Tel: 33 881 1250 **$$–$$$**

This smart multi-storey hotel serves a good albeit predictable selection of mostly meat-based Franco-Senegalese dishes. The *menu du jour* isn't cheap, but it is the undoubted culinary highlight of Tambacounda.

Le Relais du Rail
$
Situated off Boulevard Demba Diop alongside the railway line, this cosy restaurant serves meat brochettes and fish stew on an enclosed balcony. Open lunch and dinner.

Parc National de Niokolo-Koba

Hôtel Simenti
Tel: 33 982 3650
$$$

The only lodge in the park has something of a monopoly when it comes to eating, too, and it certainly knows it. The three-course dinners are mediocre and overpriced, portions are less than generous, and the drink prices are plain silly. If you have any autonomy, bring a stock of snacks and drinking water from Tambacounda! Breakfast, lunch and dinner served.

Kédougou

Chez Diao
Route de Saréa
Tel: 33 937 9607 **$**
The food at this popular camp is nothing out of the ordinary, but it's a good place to head for inexpensive local stews

or chicken and chips, ideally ordered a few hours ahead. Open for lunch and dinner.

Le Bedik
Quartier Gomba
Tel: 33 985 1000
The smartest hotel in town has a stylish bistro restaurant on the hillside offering panoramic views down to the river. It's the best bet in town for international cuisine.

Le Niekero
Quartier Tagora
Tel: 33 985 1459 **$$**
With its large thatch roof and leafy gardens, this is one of the most comfortable eating-out options in Kédougou. Open 6.30am–2pm and 7–9pm.

BELOW: essential ingredients for a Senegalese stew.

THE CASAMANCE

Arguably the most beautiful region in the whole of Senegal, the tourists are coming back to the Casamance after it was plagued by a conflict lasting over 20 years, to discover pristine white beaches, lush tropical landscapes and the extraordinary Diola culture

A narrow sliver of land sandwiched between The Gambia and Guinea-Bissau, the Casamance ranks among the more improbable legacies of the 1886 Berlin Conference, a serpentine southern appendage to Senegal that shares few cultural affinities with the rest of the country. Geographically, this moist and low-lying region is dominated by the 320km (200-mile) Casamance River, whose tributaries include the Diouloulou, Kamobeul and Soungrougrou, while its Atlantic coastline boasts some of the most beautiful beach resorts in West Africa. Its Diola (Jola) inhabitants are known for their relaxed and friendly demeanour, a reputation that was undermined during the 1982–2004 civil war, when much of the region was unsafe for travel. Tourism has undergone a significant recovery since the signing of the 2004 Peace Accord, and the people of the Casamance remain as welcoming as ever, but driving after dark remains inadvisable, and cautious travellers should seek current safety advice before visiting.

Copy of the Camargue

The French liken the swampy Casamance to the Camargue, whose lagoons and marshes harbour spectacular bird and animal life. Certainly, the flat areas of wide waters reflecting the sky-blue heavens are reminiscent of that part of France. The further upriver one travels, however, the more arid and harsh conditions become, with temperatures often soaring above 38°C (100°F) in the far east. Bordering the Guinean forest belt, the Casamance is far and away the wettest part of Senegal, and the coastal districts receive in excess of 1,000mm (40ins) of rain annually. However, this seldom falls between mid-November and early May, and – like the rest of Senegal – the Casamance can look very bleak and arid towards the end of this long annual drought.

When the clouds break in late May or June, the ensuing storms are thrillingly violent (and occasionally destructive). Floodplains that looked terminally lifeless a month before sprout fresh green-

Main attractions
ZIGUINCHOR
CATHÉDRALE DE SAINT-ANTOINE-DE-PADOUE
CAP SKIRRING
DIEMBÉRING
RÉSERVE ORNITHOLOGIQUE DE KALISSAYE

LEFT: a Cap Skirring fisherman washes his waterproofs.
BELOW: exotic flora.

An artist displays his colourful canvas in Ziguinchor.

ery, and the villages that cling to the life-giving margins of the Casamance take the opportunity to plant rice, millet, sorghum, maize and other crops. The first harvests, usually in September, are cause for great celebration, and colourful festivals – involving bright costumes, some agile dancing and traditional Diola wrestling competitions – are still held in a large number of rural areas. Between harvests, most villagers depend on the river for sustenance.

Perch and catfish, waterline oysters and crabs, prawns and crayfish provide a nourishing and varied diet balanced by wildfowl like goose, duck and teal. Living in tune with the river, the people of the Casamance are great boatmen, and their pride in river skills shows in the elaborate designs of their pirogues.

Some history

The name Casamance, a corruption of *Kassa Mansa* (King of Kassa), dates back to 1455, when Alvise Cadamosto, a Venetian merchant sailor in the employ of Henry the Navigator, became the first European to explore this part of the West African coast. The area would later be plundered for slaves by the Portuguese, who established the town of Ziguinchor in 1645. The French took a foothold in the Casamance with the purchase of land at Karabane and Sédhiou to establish trading posts in the 1830s. Portugal relinquished its interest in the Casamance following the negotiation of the border with Portuguese Guinea (Guinea-Bissau) at the Berlin Conference of 1886, but Kriol (Portuguese Creole, the lingua franca of Guinea-Bissau) is still spoken by minorities in both Ziguinchor and Kolda.

The Diola of the Casamance have a long history of resistance to outside rule. Local uprisings led by traditional rulers and priests occurred regularly throughout the colonial era, culminating in the 1942 rebellion led by the Aline Sitoé Diatta. Modern resistance commenced in 1947 with the formation of the Mouvement des Forces Démocratiques de Casamance (MFDC), which demanded complete independence. In 1960, when Senegal became an independent state, the MFDC adopted a policy of separatism, leading to several low-key conflicts over the next two decades. The situation

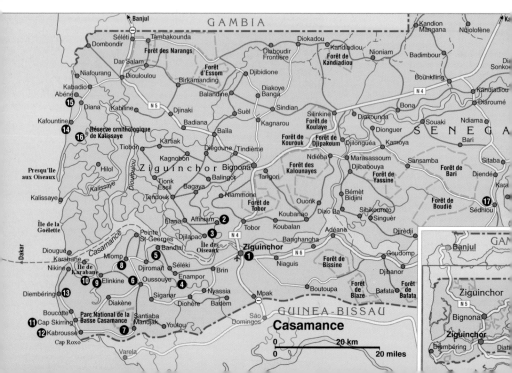

Recommended Restaurants and Bars on pages 286–7

deteriorated after 1983, when an MFDC rally in Ziguinchor led to a clash with the police and the death of 25 demonstrators. In 1990, the MFDC launched a formal armed struggle for independence, a conflict that claimed at least 3,000 victims prior to December 2004, when the MFDC signed a peace treaty with the government and calm was restored.

Orientation and arrival

The Casamance is split across the administrative regions of Ziguinchor and Kolda, both named after their administrative capitals. Conventionally referred to as Basse (Lower) Casamance, Ziguinchor is the smaller and less populous region, but it's also the main centre of tourist development, incorporating the entire coastline between The Gambia and Guinea-Bissau. By contrast, the Haute (Upper) Casamance of Kolda has never featured on the Senegalese tourist map, and is likely to be visited only by travellers en route to and from Tambacounda and localities further east.

At least one flight connects Dakar to Ziguinchor daily, taking about one hour, and landing at the airport 3km (2 miles) south of the town centre. There are also a few flights weekly between Dakar and Cap Skirring. As of January 2008, the MV *Aline Sitoé Diatta*, a German-made ferry with air-conditioned cabins, a restaurant, and a capacity of 500 people and 15 vehicles, does regular overnight runs between Dakar and Ziguinchor. The best road route from Dakar to Ziguinchor is the Trans-Gambia Highway (RN4), a 450km (250-mile) trip that can be covered in one day, crossing the Gambia River at Farafenni. The alternative is the RN5 from Kaolack to Banjul, crossing the Gambia River at Barra. Ziguinchor can also be approached from the east, via Tambacounda, Vélingara and Kolda.

A boatman preparing to sail in his brightly painted pirogue.

Ziguinchor

The relaxed river port of **Ziguinchor** ❶, capital of the eponymous administrative region, is the largest town in the Casamance, with a population of 225,000. It lies on the south bank of the river some 70km (45 miles) from the Atlantic coast, and is connected to the north bank – and hence to Banjul and Dakar – by the only bridge downstream of Kolda. Established by the Portuguese trader Gonçalo Ayala in 1645, Ziguinchor soon established itself as a key slave-trading centre, as alluded to in the Portuguese phrase *"Cheguei eles choravam"* (I arrived and they cried) from which its name probably derives. It experienced an economic slump in the mid-19th century, following the abolition of the slave trade and the establishment of a rival French outpost at Karabane, but its fortunes revived after France took it over

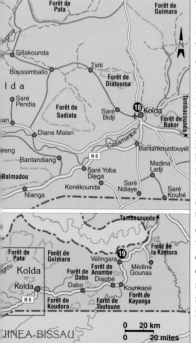

The candy-pink-and-white Cathédrale de Saint-Antoine-de-Padoue in Ziguinchor.

BELOW: getting to grips at a wrestling tournament.

Bureau de Poste, one block back Rue du Général-de-Gaulle. Of t town's more venerable buildings, no has been maintained with quite much conviction as the **Cathédrale Saint-Antoine-de-Padoue**, a gleami white apparition with candy-pink ma gins set on the west side of Rond-Poi Jean-Paul-II (which, aptly enoug commemorates Pope John Paul I visit to Ziguinchor in 1992).

Ziguinchor has better tourist faciliti than most Senegalese towns. Half dozen hotels can be found in the tov centre, including the popular **Le Flan boyant** on Rue de France, whose helpf French managers are a mine of loc travel information and will help set excursions, and the slickly upmark **Hôtel Kadiandoumagne** and mo earthy **Le Perroquet**, which flank t pirogue jetty on the western end of R du Commerce. In addition, there a many stand-alone restaurants, whi lively nightclubs include **Le Bombolor** on Rue du Commerce and **Le Rubis** Rue de Santhiaba. There are also a fe travel agencies, bookshops and intern cafés, and two banks with ATMs.

in the aftermath of the 1886 Berlin Conference. Ziguinchor replaced Karabane as regional capital in 1904.

Ziguinchor today is an attractive town whose wide palm-lined boulevards exude a likeably sleepy tropical ambience. The compact **town centre** is scattered with elegant French colonial buildings in varying states of disrepair. Landmarks include the covered **Marché Escale**, situated opposite the ferry port on **Rue du Commerce** (the main waterfront road through the town centre), and the **Gouvernance de Ziguinchor** and

The Casamance River, Ziguinchor's *raison d'être*, isn't quite the dominating presence one might expect or hope for, largely because a row of double-storey buildings separates it from Rue du Commerce for much of its length. However, the paved western extension of Rue du Commerce running past the pirogue jetty leads to a busy pirogue harbour whose muddy shore is crowded with hundreds of colourful boats and offers clear views across the wide river to the mangrove-lined northern bank. Breezy riverfront views can also be enjoyed from the restaurants at the **Hôtel Kadiandou-nagne** and **Le Perroquet** or the more affordable **Le Érobon**, a casual open-air bar-restaurant set at the far end of the pirogue harbour on Rue du Commerce.

The most poignant feature on Ziguinchor's waterfront, situated opposite the Marché Escale, is a modest memorial to the victims of **MV *Le Joola***, the government ferry that capsized off the Gambian coast whilst travelling from Ziguinchor to Dakar on 26 September 2002. Although the direct cause of this tragedy was a vicious storm that caused the boat to sink within five minutes, *Le Joola* was estimated to be carrying at least 1,860 passengers when it left Ziguinchor, in flagrant disregard of the official carrying capacity of 580 passengers and crew. In terms of fatalities, the loss of *Le Joola* ranks as the second-worst non-military maritime disaster in global history, after the collision of the MV *Doña Paz* with an oil tanker in the Tablas Strait in 1987, which claimed an estimated 4,000 lives. The precise death toll of the Senegalese disaster remains open to conjecture, but it is known that only 64 people survived, meaning that *Le Joola* claimed a greater number of lives than the 1,503 victims of the *Titanic* in 1912.

Ten minutes' walk from the town centre, the **Marché Saint-Maur-des-Fossés** is named after the French town with which Ziguinchor is twinned. This sprawling market, reached by following Avenue de l'Aviation south from the Rond-Point Jean-Paul-II, boasts a tall entrance gate that evidently aspires to combine Art Deco with traditional African architecture, with a result that does neither any favours. Traders from all over Senegal, as well as Guinea-Bissau

The memorial to the victims of MV Le Joola.

BELOW:
the decorative
case à impluvium
inside the Alliance
Franco-Sénégalaise
building.

Traditional Architecture

The Casamance region is known for its unusual traditional architecture. Unique to the area is the ingenious *case à impluvium*, a large circular house whose double roof forms a funnel to feed a central reservoir where rainwater is collected and kept for the dry season. Less unusual but more striking from the outside is the *maison à étage*, a double-storey adobe house whose organic appearance and curvaceous lines recall the architecture of Dogon Country in Mali. The *case à impluvium* forms the architectural basis of a large number of the community-managed *campements villageois* that dot the Casamance, notably in Affiniam and Enampor. The best surviving examples of original *maisons à étage* are to be found in Djilapao and Mlomp

If you want to go off the beaten track and explore the quieter areas then a local guide is recommended. Enquire at your hotel. Rates are approximately CFA5,000 a day.

and Mauritania, haggle here over fish, fruit, vegetables, groundnuts, cotton, rice, spices and palm products – as well as an Aladdin's cave of manufactured and imported goods. The adjacent **Marché Artisanal** supports more than 100 crafts-people, and items on sale include beautiful Diola sculptures.

Another five minutes' walking along Avenue de l'Aviation brings you to the **Alliance Franco-Sénégalaise** (tel: 33 991 2823; www.ziguinchor.af-senegal.org; Mon–Sat 9am–noon and 3–7pm; donation expected), an impressive circular thatched building constructed in the style of a traditional *case à impluvium* and decorated in bright colours. The alliance often hosts exhibitions of local art, there's a pleasant bar-restaurant, and the main hall holds at least one evening performance per week, be it live music, theatre or dance – details are posted on the website. For those interested in local arts and performance, the best time to visit is in February, when the **Ziguinchor Carnival** is held.

A popular day trip from Ziguinchor entails taking a pirogue downriver to **Île des Oiseaux** (Bird Island), which

often hosts large numbers of pelican, herons, waders and other water-associate birds. This can be combined with visi to the north-bank villages of **Affiniam** and **Djilapao** ❸, the former known f its spectacularly restored *case à implu vium*, and the latter for several exam ples of traditional *maisons à étag (double-storey houses)*. Boat trips ca be arranged through any hotel or wi the many private piroguers that har around the jetty on Rue du Commerc More adventurously, Affiniam is co nected to Ziguinchor by a daily ferr leaving from the same jetty in the mi afternoon and returning the followin morning, and accommodation is avai able at the rustic but attractive *camp ment villageois*.

Another interesting trip that can I accomplished as a day or overnight excu sion from Ziguinchor leads to the famou *cases à impluvium* at **Enampor** ❹ ar **Bandial** ❺. Most easily reached in a pr vate vehicle, Enampor lies 35km (2 miles) west of Ziguinchor via Brin, whi Bandial lies another 20km (12 miles) fu ther north along a relatively rough trac Protected as Historic Monuments, the

are among the finest examples of traditional architecture in the region, and the one at Enampor also houses a photographic exhibition about Diola initiation. En route to Brin, about 4km (2 miles) out of Ziguinchor, the **Ferme de Djibelor** (tel: 33 991 1701; daily 9am–6pm; charge) is essentially a large tropical fruit farm, but the birdlife in the gardens can be very rewarding, and there's also a crocodile hatchery on the property.

Oussouye and surrounds

Some 40km (25 miles) southwest of Ziguinchor, **Oussouye** ❻ is the largest town and most important route focus along the main surfaced road to Cap Skirring. On first inspection, it looks like a typically undistinguished and scruffy junction town, especially upon disembarking from public transport at the busy *gare routière*. In fact, Oussouye sits at the heart of the ancient Kassa kingdom, and it remains the seat of its Mane (king), a title that dates to before the 15th-century arrival of the Portuguese, and from which the name Casamance derives. The incumbent King Sybilumbaye, crowned in January 2000 some 15

years after the death of his predecessor Sybacuyane, wears a distinctive red robe for ceremonial occasions. Despite a strong missionary presence, Oussouye retains a strong animist tradition, culminating in the annual **Humabeul Festival**, which is held over 15 days in mid- to late September, the end of the harvesting season, and attracts the participation of a dozen other villages. At other times of year, Oussouye is worth visiting for its memorable **Campement Villageois**, which was built in the *banco* style of a traditional *maison à étage* and first opened to tourists in 1982. Forced to close in 1997 due to local political instability, it was subsequently restored with GTZ assistance and reopened in 2002. The camp makes a great base for exploring the forests around Oussouye, and guides with a deep knowledge of the area are available.

One of the most important reserves in Senegal, the **Parc National de la Basse Casamance** ❼ was established in 1970 to protect a mosaic of mangroves, tidal flats, open water, wooded savannah and rainforest extending over some 50 sq km (20 sq miles) north of the Guinean border

The bright blooms of the yellow hibiscus.

BELOW: drinking coconut milk.

With private transport, it's possible to bump along a track leading north from Mlomp to Pointe Saint-Georges, which lies on the bend in the Casamance River where the estuary is at its widest. Local piroguers can take you out onto the water at this beautiful spot, where dolphins and various marine birds are regularly encountered.

BELOW:
cows on the beach
at Cap Skirring.

some 10km (6 miles) south of Oussouye. The park incorporates Senegal's last remaining patch of Guinea-Congo rainforest, and is of special interest to birdwatchers as the only place in Senegal or The Gambia where several localised forest species can be seen, among them piping and yellow-casqued hornbill, hairy-breasted barbet, rufous-winged illadopsis and four types of greenbul. Primates are numerous, with relatively widespread species such as red colobus and green monkey present alongside the only Senegalese population of the handsome Campbell's mona monkey, and other mammals that might still persist include buffalo, leopard and various forest antelope. Once a favourite day trip from Ziguinchor or Cap Skirring, the national park closed in the 1990s as a result of military activity, and it has yet to reopen due to the probable presence of suspected unexploded landmines, but this is bound to change if the Casamance's newfound stability proves enduring.

Several interesting spots can be visited on the small area of mainland north of Oussouye. The village of **Mlomp** ❽, which straddles the more northerly of two rough roads that connect Oussouye to the small port of Elinkine, is named after the obscure Mlomp language spoken by around 5,000 people living in the village and its immediate surrounds. There are three main attractions here. The first is a mighty buttressed kapok tree held sacred by the local villagers and claimed to be at least four centuries old. The second is a cluster of beautifully maintained *maisons à étage* built in the late 19th or early 20th century and now listed as Historic Monuments.

Three of these striking houses can be seen on the main road near the enormous sacred kapok, but the finest examples are tucked away on nearby side roads. Finally, a small private museum (no fixed hours; charge) contains fetish skulls and other items relating to the animist traditions practised by many Diola.

Using public transport, a more obvious goal a few kilometres west of Mlomp is **Elinkine** ❾, whose small harbour is the best place to pick up boat transport to Île de Karabane. Unexpectedly busy for a remote dead-end village of 350 people, Elinkine has a reputation for illicit goings-on, including the smug-

ling of refugees to the Cape Verde Islands and Europe, and the illegal capture of hammerhead and other shark fins for the Asian market – none of which should be an obstacle to settling into the harbourfront **Campement le Fromager**, whose friendly staff will direct you to footpaths past winding *bolongs* lined with tall palms and thick mangroves, and narrow waterways alive with an extraordinary variety of sea and river birds. Look out, too, for a sacred well associated with a famed local marabout called El Hadj Omar.

Île de Karabane

Arguably the most compelling of the Casamance's array of small villages, the 57-sq km (22-sq mile) island of Karabane ⑩ (or Carabane) lies a mere 5 km (3 miles) upstream of the wide river mouth. The island's principal settlement, also called Karabane, is some 30 minutes distant from Elinkine by motorised pirogue, and it stretches for about 1km (½ mile) along a sandy beach on the southern bank of the estuary, which is otherwise lined with mangroves and tidal sand flats. You would scarcely believe it today, but this unassuming port was the most significant trigonal trade centre for much of the 19th century, and it served as French capital of the Casamance until 1904.

The early history of Karabane is somewhat obscure. It may well have been a Portuguese trade outpost in the early days of the slave trade, but the first outsider known to settle there, *c.*1825, was Pierre Baudin, a trader from Gorée. In 1836, a local Diola chief ceded the island to France in exchange for a small annual pension. The most significant figure in the economic development of Karabane was Emmanuel Bertrand-Bocandé, who governed it from 1849 to 1857, and was responsible for the development of cotton as an export crop, as well as for the construction of a trade factory, small railway line, and a 116-metre (370ft) wharf then considered to be the longest in West Africa. A Catholic Mission was founded in 1880, and Karabane prospered until the end of the century, when its population peaked at 3,000. It fell into rapid decline after 1904, and was practically abandoned by outside traders in the aftermath of a devastating fire in 1913.

EAT

For simple seafood fare on Île de Karabane, head to **Kaaty** (open 6am–midnight).

LEFT: the sacred *fromager* tree.

The Kapok

One of the most impressive trees of the Casamance is the kapok *Ceiba pentandra*. Superficially similar to the baobab, which it often grows alongside, the kapok can be distinguished by its luxuriant canopy and labyrinthine buttressed base. It is indigenous both to equatorial America, where it was held sacred by the ancient Maya people, and to West Africa, where older trees are often the subject of animist fetishes. The kapok can live for hundreds of years, attains heights of

up to 70 metres (230ft), and the trunk of a large specimen might have a diameter of 3–4 metres (10–13ft). A large tree will produce hundreds of pods the size of a small coconut, which break open to emit a fluffy off-white fibre towards the end of the dry season. Used as a filling for mattresses and pillows, this fibre is also known as kapok, and is the source of the alternative name of silk cotton tree. Somewhat more oddly, the tree is referred to throughout Senegal as the *fromager* – French for cheese-maker – which may have something to with the smell of the ripe pod, or may be because it was once used to make cheese containers.

In several respects, Karabane today comes across as the archetypal West African backwater. There's no electricity, no telephonic land line, no cars, and the population of a few hundred souls was largely dependent on drinking water ferried across from Elinkine until USAID installed a deep water pump in 2005. Yet the old harbourfront is strung with low-key camps and restaurants that cater mainly to dedicated anglers and lunching day trippers from Cap Skirring, but which also provide an alluring base for travellers seeking a remote chill-out venue for a few days. Foremost among these is the long-serving **Campement le Barracuda**, with its smart en suite rooms and shady waterfront restaurant at the northern end of town, but there are several other good options, and all offer a range of fishing, birdwatching and other day excursions. A recent develop-

ment, inaugurated in 2007 and likely to be held every April, the three-day **Festival des Arts et Cultures de Carabane** (tel: 77 424 7369 or 77 542 3952) showcases a variety of Senegalese music and other performance arts.

The small village is fun to explore, with its scattering of simple mud-and-thatch Diola homesteads set somewhat incongruously between the crumbling relics of the town's late 19th-century pomp. The **Hôtel Carabane**, with a harbourfront location alongside the Campement le Barracuda, has been converted from the old Governor's Residence and Catholic Mission, both of which date to the 1880s. Behind this, surrounding a brackish well, stand the tall buttressed fortifications that locals refer to as the **Maison des Esclaves** (Slave House). A penitentiary and *école spéciale* for young criminal offenders between 1927 and 1953, this building was established as a French fortress in the late 19th century, too recently for it to have been likely to have been used as a slave hold.

The most striking building in the town centre, the handsome **Église Bretonne** (Breton Church) built of red-brick and

A vulture has lunch on the beach.

BELOW: fishing boats line the beach at Cap Skirring.

sandstone in 1897, has fallen into disuse but still looks structurally sound, despite the overgrown tiled roof and bat colony in the bell tower. On the western outskirts of the village, the old **Cimetière catholique**, set in a lush thicket teeming with birdlife, is the site of the whitewashed triangular grave of the French naval officer Capitaine Aristide Protet (not to be confused with Auguste-Léopold Protet, the founder of Dakar). Killed by a poisoned arrow during a French reconnaissance of the area in 1836, Protet, according to his own wishes, was buried standing up and facing the sea, together with his dog.

Cap Skirring and the south coast

Cap Skirring ⓫ is one of Senegal's most famous resorts, every bit as beautiful as the Petite Côte further north, but with a more unspoilt feel. It is situated about 70km (50 miles) from Ziguinchor, driving southwest along a well-surfaced road via Oussouye, and is also accessible from Dakar by regular flights. Coming from the fascinating but often climatically stifling interior, the fresh sea

breezes that caress this lovely stretch of coast are a delight, while those who fly in from northern Senegal will be struck by the moister climate and lush vegetation. This beautiful stretch of coast is punctuated with white sandy beaches and rocky outcrops, while tracks lead from behind the shoreline to palm-shaded fishing villages surrounded by rice fields.

The focal point of tourism here is the main drag through Cap Skirring, a village whose resident population of around 2,000 is boosted by a comparable number of outsiders – tourists, expatriates and other Senegalese – in season. Tourist development here started in the 1960s and hit full throttle in the mid-1970s, with the construction of the 205-room **Club Méditerranée** on a prime beachfront site, and the creation of an airport immediately northwest of the village. Cap Skirring was little affected by the unrest that plagued the rest of the Casamance in recent decades, and it managed to attract viable tourist volumes throughout the lean times. As a result, the local tourist industry comes across as very stable and settled, and facilities tend to surpass expectations.

Returning with the day's catch.

*Pouring tea,
Senegalese-style.*

BELOW: the pool
at Hôtel Kabrousse.

The Club Med complex is still there today, offering international-style accommodation in 80-hectare (200-acre) grounds with a pool, restaurants and a nightclub, but it caters to the all-inclusive package market rather than independent travellers. Several smaller hotels, ranging from the smart and stylish **Les Palétuviers** to the more homely **Auberge le Palmier**, are also dotted around the town centre. The main surfaced road through town is lined with a good choice of restaurants – French and Senegalese seafood dishes dominate, but most culinary bases are covered – and a selection of bars and nightclubs reinforces Cap Skirring's reputation as party town. There's internet access too, and those requiring retail therapy will find no shortage of clothes and craft shops to browse at the busy *village artisanal* (craft market). By contrast, the central market in Cap Skirring remains defiantly African in mood, as does the chaotic *gare routière* on the main intersection.

A second centre of tourist development lies about 1km (½ mile) south of Cap Skirring along the beach (but more like 3km/2 miles by road) at **Cap Ran-doulène**. Here, half a dozen small hotels and camps are set in lush bougainvillea-draped gardens that run down from a dusty side road to the spectacular beach. Typical is the long-serving and budget-friendly **Chez M'Ballo**, which offers very reasonable full-board packages, but there are also a few smarter options, of which the **Villa des Pêcheurs** is an obvious stand-out. Relative to central Cap Skirring, Cap Randoulène lacks options when it comes to shopping and eating out, and its remote location might inconvenience partygoers without private transport, but it will definitely appeal to those seeking a natural and down-to-earth setting.

Some 6km (4 miles) further south, the asphalt ends – as, to all intents and purposes, does Senegal – at **Kabrousse** ⑫ (or Cabrousse), the birthplace of Aline Sitoé Diatta, the princess who masterminded and led the 1942 Diola Uprising in protest against the taxation of groundnut crops and the seizure of cattle and rice for export to war-torn France. Remembered as a national hero and often referred to as the Senegalese Joan of Arc, Aline Sitoé-Diatta was deported to Tim-

buktu in 1943, and died in jail there a year later, aged 24. Kabrousse today is an unremarkable town of around 1,300 inhabitants, distinguished only by its position tucked right against the Guinean border. That said, the rustic kapok-shaded dirt roads couldn't offer more of a contrast to Cap Skirring when it comes to tourist development, and the tiny fishing village of Boujegets, situated on a wide *bolong* about 4km (2 miles) out of town, is a worthwhile goal for a stroll, and it has a small camp if you feel like a really remote night out.

Another worthwhile rustic getaway within easy day tripping of Cap Skirring, **Diembéring** ⑬ lies about 12km (7 miles) further north, near the Casamance mouth. Dominated by traditional Diola dwellings, this friendly village is notable for its numerous buttressed kapok trees – an especially majestic example shades the market and *gare routière* – and equally splendid baobabs. A tall dune at the north end of the village is the site of a disused camp and offers fantastic views over the watery surrounds. Coconut palms fringe the white sandy beaches, and behind the shoreline little tracks lead through palm forest rice fields to palm-thatched villages.

The **Musée de Sangawatt** (daily 9am–6pm; charge), an open-air museum with artefacts dedicated to Diola culture, lies about 1km (½ mile) along the road back to Cap Skirring. For accommodation or food, the attractive beachfront **Oasis Boucotte** lies in the eponymous village about halfway between Diembéring and Cap Skirring.

North Casamance

The surfaced 100km (60-mile) stretch of the Trans-Gambia Highway (RN4) between Ziguinchor and The Gambia can easily be covered in an hour or so. There's little to distract along the way. The junction town of **Bignona** is the second-largest settlement in Basse Casamance, with a population of 27,000, and although it lacks for inherent interest, those with 4x4 transport could explore the nearby **Forêt des Kalounayes** or the fishing settlement of **Marasassoum** on the Soungrougrou River.

The countryside further north tends to be much drier. The most important settlement en route, 12km (7 miles) before

Fruit comes in all shapes and sizes.

LEFT: keeping up appearances.
BELOW: hitching a ride home to Diembéring.

Fresh fish are auctioned daily at the market.

BELOW: wearing a traditional *boubou*.

Here one can witness every facet of the fishing industry in action, whether it's the covered market where the finest fresh fish are auctioned to Gambian businessmen, or the expansive drying and smoking complexes a bit further back from the beach.

Running north from central Kafountine, a much cleaner and quieter beach offers favourable swimming conditions and a selection of around a dozen camps and resorts, which tend to be more rustic and organic in character than their counterparts at Cap Skirring. Reggae music, *djembé* drumming and clouds of deeply inhaled smoke are integral to the camp scene close to town, with the **Campement le Paradise** being the established pick of these Rasta-styled hangouts. The mood is very different further down the beach, where the determinedly rustic Dutch-owned **Le Kelediang** and unexpectedly stylish **Esperanto** both offer a wonderfully serene getaway in lush overgrown gardens running down to the idyllic beach. Accommodation aside, for a village of 4,000 people Kafountine has excellent facilities, including a small cybercafé.

the **Séléti** border, is **Diouloulou**, the junction town for the coastal villages of Abéné and Kafountine.

Kafountine ⓴, 25km (15 miles) southwest of Diouloulou, is the most popular resort in the Casamance after Cap Skirring, though the two could scarcely be more different in character. A bustling, overgrown fishing village that sprawls inland from its idyllic sandy beachfront, Kafountine hosts one of the largest **fishing markets** in Senegal, and the beach running south of the town centre, lined with hundreds of colourful pirogues, is an incredible (albeit rather smelly) hive of activity as the tide rises and boats return with the day's catch.

Recommended Restaurants and Bars on pages 286–7

wo well-stocked supermarkets, a verita-
le army of willing taxis, and several
ars and restaurants.

Only 5km (3 miles) from Kafountine
long the road back towards Diouloulou,
he smaller village of **Abéné** 🅖 lies
bout 1.5km (1 mile) from an attractive
each whose fishing market is shaded by
ll casuarinas. A couple of inexpensive
amps can be found in the village centre,
hich is famed for a multiple-trunked
acred kapok tree, but the village can
lso easily be visited as a day trip from
Kafountine. Every year around Decem-
er, the festive season of harvesting, the
béné folklore festival attracts large
udiences from around the region to
atch theatre, music, dance and sport.

The maze of creeks and lagoons are a
magnet for bird-lovers. There are several
odgings that will organise trips to bird-
atching sites. Another important local
ttraction, best visited in a motorised
irogue, the **Réserve ornithologique de
Kalissaye** 🅖 (Kalissaye Avifaunal
eserve) protects the river mouth 20km
12 miles) south of Kafountine and
ttracts high seasonal concentrations of
reat white pelican, Caspian tern and
estern reef egret, as well as two species
f marine turtle.

Upriver exploration

ast of Ziguinchor, the Casamance River
idens dramatically, becoming almost
n inland lake, but narrowing again after
iattakounda, past the confluence with
e Soungrougou. About 70km (40 miles)
pstream of Ziguinchor, the regional
dministrative centre of **Sédhiou** 🅖
lso known as Seju) comes into sight on
e north bank. Founded by French
aders in 1836, Sedhiou is more village
an town, and as the colourful pirogues
at line the bank suggest, its inhabitants
epend for their livelihood on the river,
hich is still more than a kilometre (½
ile) wide at this point.

Sédhiou boasts a few interesting archi-
ectural relics, notably the fortress built
y Governor Pinet-Laprade and the old
réfecture. Devil's Island, a few kilo-
etres upriver, hosts a varied selection

of birds. Although the most attractive way
to reach Sédhiou would be to charter a
pirogue from Ziguinchor, the more expe-
dient approach is by road via Bignona.

The river narrows considerably as it
winds east towards **Kolda** 🅖, which lies
about 190km (115 miles) east of Ziguinchor along the surfaced RN6 towards
Tambacounda. In its heyday as capital
of the 19th-century Fouladou kingdom,
Kolda was a renowned crossroads town
and trade centre. There's not much to
see there today, but good facilities –
several hotels, restaurants, cybercafés
and banks – make this city of 70,000 the
obvious place for eastbound travellers
to break the journey. Heading on east,
Vélingara 🅖 is the next major town,
about 120km (70 miles) further along the
RN6, but if you are travelling on
Wednesday it's worth stopping en route
for the large, bustling, weekly market
held at Diaobé, 40km (24 miles) closer to
Kolda. Vélingara, which you also pass
through when crossing into Senegal from
Basse Santa Su (The Gambia), is only
95km (57 miles) southwest of Tambacounda, and the open, dry scenery here is
more typical of southeast Senegal. ❏

A wooden-handled chopper.

BELOW:
preparing to bring
a boat ashore.

RESTAURANTS AND BARS

Restaurants

Prices for a main course per person:
$ = under US$8 (CFA3,200)
$$ = US$8–15 (CFA 3,200–6,000)
$$$ = over US$15 (CFA6,000)

Ziguinchor
Hôtel Tourisme
Rue de France
Tel: 33 991 2223 **$$**
Attached to the popular Le Flamboyant hotel, this small restaurant serves steak and pasta dishes, but is rather lacking in ambience compared to its waterfront rivals.

Le Bombolong
Rue Fargues
Tel: 33 938 8001

Under the same management as the upmarket Hôtel Le Kadiandou-magne, this long-serving nightclub has plenty of character and the Franco-Senegalese food is excellent. Kitchen open noon–3pm and 7–11pm.

Le Érobon
Rue du Commerce
Tel: 33 991 2788 **$**
The most informal eatery in Ziguinchor, this water-front bar and eatery lies in spacious green grounds a few hundreds metres from the town centre. The speciality here is deliciously marin-ated fish, grilled over an open fire and served with chips or rice. Superb value. Open 10am–late.

Le Kassa
Rond-Point Jean-Paul-II
Tel: 33 936 8300 **$**
With more character than its setting alongside a filling station might sug-gest, this is a pleasant spot for a cold beer, and the tasty Senegalese food is good value too. Open 8am–late.

Le Perroquet
Rue du Commerce
Tel: 33 991 2329 **$$**
With its unbeatable view over the Casamance River and main pirogue jetty, this would be the obvious place to eat in Ziguinchor even if it weren't for the excellent fish and prawn bro-chettes, the pick of a great seafood menu.

Oussouye
Le Kassa
$
The key junction town in the Basse Casamance is stronger on camps (all of which serve food) than stand-alone eateries, but this small local restau-rant about 100 metres/yds from the *gare routière* is worth a try for its tasty chicken and chips – assuming that you're not too rushed.

Elinkine
Campement
Le Fromager
Tel: 33 525 6401 **$**
Set below a shady kapok overlooking the pirogue harbour, this small but friendly camp can serve up acceptable fish and

BELOW: it's best to stay cool in the kitchen.

rice at short notice, and slightly more varied and elaborate fare with a little advance warning.

Karabane
Campement le Barracuda
Tel: 33 659 6001 **$$**
The most popular waterfront camp on the island is also the best place to eat, though you need to order a couple of hours in advance.

Bar-Resto La Plume
Situated a few hundred metres further along the waterfront, this small, down-to-earth restaurant is a pleasant spot for a breezy riverside drink, and the staff will rustle up a decent fish meal with a few hours' notice.

Cap Skirring
La Carpe Rouge
Tel: 77 651 2460 **$**
The combination of excellent but reasonably

priced seafood and the unpretentious and welcoming atmosphere make this one of the most popular eateries on the main drag through Cap Skirring. Open 8am–midnight.

La Case Bambou
Tel: 33 993 5178 **$$**
Long regarded to be the most chic nightclub in Cap Skirring, La Case Bambou also serves very good Franco-Senegalese food, with the emphasis, as usual, on seafood. Kitchen open noon–3pm and 7–11pm.

La Maison Bleue
Cap Skirring Beach
Tel: 33 993 5161 **$$$**
Attached to the eponymous beach hotel, La Maison Bleue is arguably the finest seafood restaurant in the Casamance, with a great beachfront location and stylish modern

decor. For a real treat, visit on Friday or Saturday night to enjoy the seafood buffet. Open 7am–11pm.

La Terrazza
Route de Cabrousse
Tel: 33 993 5110 **$$**
This homely outdoor Italian restaurant serves a varied selection of seafood and meat grills, home-made pasta and miniature pizzas. The freshly prepared coffee is excellent. Open daily 7am–1pm and 4–11pm.

Kafountine
Esperanto Lodge
Kafountine Beach
Tel: 33 936 9519
$$–$$$
The most stylish lodge in Kafountine, set alongside the beach about 2km (1 mile) north of the town centre, serving a varied menu of international dishes – ranging from Italian to Mexican – and

superb seafood on the breezy and earthily decorated veranda.

Le Paradise
Kafountine Beach
Tel: 33 936 9492 **$**
Inexpensive burgers, sandwiches and grills with chips or rice are on the menu at this relaxed beachfront camp about 10 minutes' walk from the town centre in the direction of the main fishing beach.

Abéné
Chez Véro
Tel: 33 617 1714 **$**
Easily recognisable on the left-hand side of the main road between the village centre and the beach, this friendly, locally run restaurant has been popular with travellers for years for its tasty but inexpensive lunches and dinners, which are usually eaten communally on the veranda.

BELOW: delicious grilled giant prawns served with fresh lime.

INSIGHT GUIDES

TRAVEL TIPS

THE GAMBIA

TRAVEL TIPS

TRANSPORT

GETTING THERE
AND GETTING AROUND

GETTING THERE

By Air

Banjul International Airport is at Yundum, about 20km (12 miles) inland of the main strip of coastal hotels and some 30km (18 miles) outside Banjul itself. Flights from Europe take about six hours and, depending on where you are coming from, the time difference will be no more than two hours, so jet lag isn't a concern. In the terminal, facilities include a foreign exchange bureau, a few shops, a bar and cafeteria, a tourist information desk and luggage trolleys (porters optional).

Coming from the UK, the most direct and cheapest option is a twice-weekly flight between London Gatwick (and four other British airports) and Banjul operated by

The Gambia Experience (tel: 0845 330 2060; www.gambia.co.uk). These flights run all year long and can be booked in isolation or as part of a package including accommodation in The Gambia. Several other tour operators run charter flights to Banjul in the high season, but the only mainstream carrier routing between Europe and The Gambia is SN Brussels (www.brusselsairlines.com).

Coming from the US, you could fly via Europe, or land at Dakar (Senegal), which is the stopover for twice-daily South African Airways (www.flysaa.com) flights between Johannesburg and the US. From Dakar, there are good road links to Banjul, as well as daily flights operated by Air Sénégal International (www.air-senegal-international.com). From other African countries, routing through Dakar may also be the best option.

All visitors must pay a tourist tax equivalent to around US$10.

By Rail

There are no rail links into or within The Gambia.

By Road

The Gambia shares all its land borders with Senegal, and road connections between the two countries are reasonably efficient. The most direct route for travellers bound for Banjul runs from Dakar via Kaolack and Toubacouta to Barra on the north bank of the Gambia River opposite Banjul. The driving time for this route is about 4 hours, but you should allow 30 minutes for border formalities, another 1–2 hours' wait for the ferry to Banjul, and 45–60 minutes for the actual ferry crossing.

The second main route between Senegal and The Gambia is the Trans-Gambia Highway through Farafenni and Soma. This is the best route for travellers heading between northern Senegal and the Casamance, and the ferry crossing is generally less time-consuming than the Barra–Banjul ferry, but it's a more circuitous route for Banjul-bound travellers, especially as the south-bank road between Soma and Banjul is erratically surfaced.

Other regularly used land routes between the two countries are the surfaced road running south from Brikama to Ziguinchor (Casamance) via Bignona, and the sandy track that links Basse Santa Su to Vélingara, the best route for those heading between The Gambia and Niokolo-Koba.

Bush taxis and minibuses ply all of these routes, though the route between Dakar and Banjul via Kaolack involves several changes of vehicle, and the ferry itself must be

BELOW: bush taxi waiting for fares.

ABOVE: traffic congestion in Banjul.

taken as a foot passenger unless you're in a private vehicle. Public transport between Basse Santa Su and Vélingara is sparse, so an early start is recommended. All border crossings involve passing through customs and immigration for both countries, which is a straightforward process but usually takes up at least 30 minutes. Self-drive visitors will need to register their vehicle and to verify that their car insurance is good for both countries.

GETTING AROUND

Orientation

Signposts and street signs are sparse in The Gambia, but the country is tiny and has a small, uncomplicated road system. Major directions on the few roads inland are signposted. In Banjul, roads are easy to find, but individual buildings not always so, as numbering may be erratic or non-existent.

Airport/City Links

On arrival at Banjul International Airport, tourists on a package deal and those with reservations at the major hotels can expect to find shuttle buses waiting for them. There are no public buses into town, but taxis are available at a set price. The only alternative is to walk to the main

road (about 2km/1 mile) and pick up a shared bush taxi to Serekunda, from where bush taxis abound, but will not drop you at your hotel door. Visitors on package tours will also have their own bus provided for departure. If you are travelling independently, you will have to make your way to the airport by private car or taxi. Bush taxis only run as far as the airport entrance, leaving you with a 20-minute walk, carrying your bags, to the terminal.

Public Transport

Buses and Bush Taxis

The deterioration of The Gambia's roads is generally held responsible for the decline of the once highly regarded Gambia Public Transport Corporation (GPTC). Technically, this holds the monopoly on public bus transport, which in practice means that there is no longer an intercity bus network to speak of in The Gambia. Instead, the main mode of public transport is bush taxis – large saloon cars or minibuses licensed to carry passengers.

In Greater Banjul, as far inland as Brikama, main roads are plied by a steady stream of bush taxis, and you'll seldom wait more than a few minutes for one. East of Brikama, bush taxis between towns are fewer in number, and seats tend to fill up before the vehicle departs, so it's best to go to the taxi park rather than wait on the roadside. Fares are fixed

and overcharging tourists is not common practice, but you may be expected to pay over-the-odds rates for baggage.

Tourist Taxis

Official tourist taxis are easily recognisable: they are green with white diamonds on the doors. They can be found waiting in dedicated ranks outside most hotels and other tourist hotspots in the Greater Banjul area. They have no meters, but fixed

BELOW: a cheap mode of transport.

ABOVE: driving along the baobab-lined roads.

prices are advertised on a board at the taxi rank, covering every conceivable trip between hotels and other destinations, and inclusive of waiting times where appropriate. Tourist taxis are better-maintained than ordinary taxis, and are generally more sedately driven, but fares are usually 2–3 times higher, and there is little room for negotiation. If you want to go somewhere further afield or even cross into Senegal, negotiate a firm price with the driver beforehand. You should only pay at the end of the trip, though you may have to forward a proportion of the fare before departure so the driver can buy fuel.

Local Taxis

The most prolific vehicles around Banjul are yellow-and-green local taxis, which function as an urban equivalent to bush taxis, following prescribed routes and taking up to four passengers at a time. These vehicles are sometimes referred to as "five-fives" in reference to the standard 5 dalasi fare charged along many short routes in the Greater Banjul area. The drivers are usually happy to negotiate a fare for a private charter – referred to as a "town trip" – and this is usually a lot cheaper than a tourist taxi, though you may need to bargain to get a fair price.

Bicycles

Bikes may be hired by the hour, the half-day or the full day from outside the main hotels and are a relatively cheap and enjoyable way of getting around and seeing places off the main roads. There are no hills to contend with, and there is often a cooling breeze. But be careful as drivers (especially taxi drivers) tend

BELOW: no taxis here.

to drive very close to you and can cut you up. Some of the roads are badly maintained and full of potholes, so take care. Rates vary with season and are written up on a board nearby (about US$10–15 for half a day). Prices should still be confirmed beforehand. Check brakes and request a lock and chain with key.

Ferries

Remarkably, there is no bridge across the Gambia River anywhere west of the border with Senegal, so the only way to cross between the north bank and south bank of the river is by ferry. The main ferry services, starting in the west, are as follows:
Banjul–Barra Ferry
This runs every 1–2 hours in either direction, with the first crossing from Banjul at 7am and the first from Barra at 8am, and the last ferry running at around 7pm. The crossing time is about 40 minutes but may be longer, say more than an hour, depending on tides. A nominal fare is charged to foot passengers, but the fare for vehicles is around US$5 one way (more for foreign vehicles). In some parts of the country the ferries only run when they are full, so you may end up waiting a long time to cross the river. You will be surprised at just how many people and vehicles can fit onto one ferry.

On the Barra side, vehicle tickets are bought from an inconspicuous ticket shed a few kilometres north of the ferry itself, but foot-passenger tickets can be bought at the jetty.
Yelitenda–Bambatenda Ferry
Situated between Soma and Farafenni on the Trans-Gambia Highway, it takes about 15 minutes to cross, and runs every 30 minutes or so between 7am and 6.30pm, though long queues often result in longer waits. Coming from Soma, vehicles must buy tickets at a roadside weighbridge about 2km (1 mile) south of Yelitenda, while vehicles coming from the north will find the ticket office a few hundred metres before Bambatenda.
Janjanbureh Island
Small vehicle ferries connect this island to both the north and south bank throughout daylight hours. The crossings only take a few minutes, but if you are unlucky you might wait up to an hour for the ferry to leave.

Pirogues

If you don't want to brave the overcrowded ferries then taking a trip by pirogue (traditional-style,

On Departure

Confirmation of return flight: this is not necessary for visitors on full package tours, but flight-only charter travellers, and those on scheduled flights, should confirm 48 hours in advance with the representatives of their tour companies. Departure taxes are now normally included in the ticket fare, so don't need to be paid in person at the airport.

ABOVE: a pirogue sailing down Oyster Creek.

brightly painted wooden boats) is a good way of seeing life along the mangrove-lined banks of The Gambia. The size of the boats varies from 3 metres to 10 metres (10–33ft), and some even larger. You can explore the quiet waterways of Oyster Creek, a popular destination for anglers and birdwatchers. Contact:
Gambia Tours
PO Box 217
Banjul, The Gambia
Tel: 446 2601/2
Fax: 446 2603
Email: info@gambiatours.gm
www.gambiatours.gm

Private Transport

Car hire is not really worth it, in spite of the high cost of taxis. The new roads are smooth and straight, but

in general the road network is skeletal and many roads are in poor condition. Driving at night should also be avoided because of the poor state of some roads and the lack of street lights. For pottering around the coastal strip, bicycles are the best option, and for trips further afield it is best to hire a Land Rover complete with driver or charter a taxi. If you do hire a self-drive vehicle, be sure hire includes full insurance and that the vehicle is roadworthy. A valid International Driving Licence is required in The Gambia. Driving is on the right.

Remember that breakdown services are non-existent. If you can get access to a telephone, a call to your car-hire agent will perhaps get them to come out to you. Otherwise you must have the car mended

locally if at all possible (mechanics are far from plentiful) and charge the firm on return.

Recommended car-rental companies are as follows:
AB Rent a Car
Office next to Senegambia Beach Hotel, Kololi
Tel: 446 0926
www.ab.gm
Avis
Office at Kairaba Hotel, Kololi
Tel: 446 5881
Email: maboum@cfao.com

On Foot and Hitchhiking

The heat and distances are not conducive to walking tours in The Gambia, and hitchhiking is not common. If you try to hitch and someone stops for you, you may well be asked to pay for your ride.

BELOW: the yellow-and-green local taxis are easy to spot.

A CCOMMODATION

HOTELS, YOUTH HOSTELS & LODGES

Hotels

Visitors to The Gambia are increasingly well served by a selection of hotels to suit most tastes and budgets. The mainstay of the country's hotel industry is large (50- to 350-room) package-oriented resorts and hotels, most of which offer good value by international standards, especially when booked as part of an fly-in package with British or European operators, which get very advantageous prices for block bookings. Recent years have also seen the larger package hotels supplemented by a selection of smaller boutique hotels, many of which – for instance, Coconut Residence, Ngala Lodge and Mandina River Lodge – are simply world-class in terms of accommodation, service and cuisine. As with the package hotels, these more exclusive lodges are often bookable at substantial discounts through international tour operators as part of a fly-in package. Most package and boutique hotels will accept major credit cards (most commonly Visa and MasterCard, less often American Express).

Although they vary greatly in standard and price, all Gambian package and boutique hotels are to some extent self-contained little worlds, set in landscaped gardens of colourful tropical trees and flowers, with their own swimming pools, bars, restaurants, shops, sports facilities, entertainment and access to the beach. Most have air-conditioning, which isn't really essential during the dry (tourist) season, but is recommended at other times of the year. Package-hotel rooms are practically always

ABOVE: attention is in the detail at Mandina River Lodge.

en suite (in other words, they contain a private shower and toilet), and the smarter hotels will usually also have a safe, TV and possibly fridge in all rooms. Although several dozen package and boutique hotels exist in The Gambia, the vast majority are concentrated along the short stretch of coast between Bakau and Kololi.

Elsewhere in the country, accommodation options tend to be somewhat limited, and more rustic and downmarket. Banjul, the Gambian capital, only boasts one proper tourist hotel, the venerable (and highly commendable) Corinthia Atlantic, and there is no such establishment anywhere on the north bank. On the coast south of Kololi, surfacing of the road to Kartung has led to a quiet

blossoming of quality establishments, ranging from the new Sheraton at Brufut to a clutch of low-key eco-lodges around Gunjur and Kartung, the latter particularly recommended for those who want to escape the package-hotel scene further north. Further inland, the only accommodation of international quality can be found at Mandina River Lodge, Sindola Safari Lodge and Badi Mayo tented camp, though the more rustic likes of Tendaba Lodge and Bird Safari Camp will be adequate for reasonably flexible visitors. Otherwise, most hotels outside of the Bakau-Kololi area are simply local set-ups that offer unpretentious accommodation at very reasonable prices, but can only be recommended to those prepared to experience The Gambia on its own terms.

BANJUL AND THE NORTH BANK

Banjul

Carlton Hotel
Independence Drive
Tel: 422 8670
This agreeable, albeit slightly run-down, five-storey block is conveniently located below Arch 22, close to several restaurants. The reasonably priced rooms are all en suite but not all have air-con. A relaxed courtyard bar serves inexpensive food. **$$**

Corinthia Atlantic Hotel
Marina Parade
Tel: 422 8601
www.corinthiahotels.com
The oldest hotel in The Gambia, the 204-room Atlantic has a great beach-front location in the heart of historic Banjul. It is ideal for business travellers but also has plenty of appeal for tourists, with an excellent restaurant, leafy grounds that include a bird garden

and large swimming pool, and good water-sport facilities. Its isolation from other hotels and proximity to the city centre make it feel less superficially resort-like than its counterparts south of Bakau. **$$$$**

Princess Diana Hotel
Independence Drive
Tel: 422 8715
Also known as the Cantora, this long-serving budget travellers' haunt is the cheapest acceptable option in the city centre. Conveniently located, its dozen en suite rooms are clean and most have air-con. **$**

Barra

Barra Hotel
About 50 metres/yards from the ferry jetty
Tel: 779 5134
The run-down multi-storey hotel is worth knowing about if the ferry to Banjul

leaves you stranded on the north bank, but it's a bit too grotty to recommend otherwise. **$**

Juffureh

Juffureh Resthouse
Next to the National Museum of the North Bank
Tel: 705 4419
Consisting of 13 very basic but adequately clean rondavels (round huts) in a rustic bougainvillea-draped compound, this is the only viable overnight option in the Juffureh area. It's a friendly set-up, but aimed mainly at backpackers, with common showers and no facilities more elaborate than mosquito nets. Very cheap. **$**

Niumi National Park

Madiyana Safari Lodge
Tel: 449 4088
www.paradiseisland-gambia.com

By far the most alluring accommodation option on the north bank, Madiyana is one of the most attractively situated and laid-back lodges in The Gambia, provided you are looking for down-to-earth rusticity rather than resort-like glitz. Accessible by 4x4 or boat, it has no generator. The simple lamp-lit reed huts lie on the beach and use common showers. The seafood dinners are usually good, but with advance notice vegans and vegetarians can also be catered for. A great place to get away from it all. **$$**

SEREKUNDA AND THE COAST

Bakau

African Village Hotel
Atlantic Road
Tel: 449 5307
Email: africanvillagehotel@yahoo.com
One of the longer-serving package hotels in The Gambia, this is a good-value mid-range set-up with 73 air-conditioned rooms, compact leafy gardens centred on a swimming pool, a great location for exploring the myriad of shops and

PRICE CATEGORIES

Price categories are for a double room:
$ = under US$25 (D500)
$$ = US$25–50 (D500–1,000)
$$$ = US$50–120 (D1,000–2,400)
$$$$ = over US$120 (D2,400)

eateries in central Bakau, and a clifftop setting above a small private swimming beach. Fussy visitors might feel it's looking a bit frayed at the edges, but it remains a justifiably popular choice in this price bracket. **$$$**

Bakau Guesthouse
Atlantic Road
Tel: 449 5059
This recently renovated three-storey lodge has a great setting overlooking the fishing beach and jetty at Bakau, and the large en suite rooms with fridge, netting, TV, air-con or fan, tiled floor and sea-facing balconies are very reasonably priced. The La Mer Restaurant on the ground floor is less notable for its (very good) seafood than the kitsch of the bombastic Afro-Asian fusion decor. Not to everybody's taste, but this flamboyant guesthouse

scores highly on the character and value-for-money fronts. **$–$$**

Ocean Bay Hotel
Kofi Annan Street
Tel: 449 4265
www.oceanbayhotel.com
Situated almost alongside the Sunbeach Hotel and very similar in standard, the five-star Ocean Bay has 195 rooms, all with air-con, balcony with sea or garden view, safe and satellite TV. The earthy colours give it an attractive Mediterranean feel, and the green gardens with swimming pool run down to an idyllic swimming beach on Cape Point. A good range of sports facilities and excursions is on offer. **$$$$**

Roc Heights Lodge
Samba Breku Road
Tel: 449 5428
www.rocheightslodge.com
Set back one block from

the beach (the penthouse has a sea view), this classy boutique hotel consists of just 14 rooms and suites boasting an airy contemporary decor blending local and European influences. There's a top-notch restaurant and a swimming pool. Highly recommended for those seeking quality non-resort accommodation close to the beach. **$$$**

Sunbeach Hotel & Resort
Kofi Annan Street
Tel: 449 7190
www.sunbeachhotel.com
Formerly the Sun Wing, this

sumptuously renovated five-star resort overlooks the magnificent Cape Point at the juncture of the Atlantic Ocean and Gambia River. One of the smartest and most slickly managed resort hotels in The Gambia, it has 184 rooms and suites, all with air-con, satellite TV, safe, and shaded patio offering a view over the gardens to the beach. Other facilities include two swimming pools, children's playground, wellness centre, internet café, a huge variety of water and other sports, and three restaurants – with several other restaurants lying within a few minutes' walk of the front gate. $$$$

Fajara

Francisco's Hotel
Cnr Atlantic Road and
Kairaba Avenue
Tel: 449 5332
Email: franciscoshotel@yahoo.co.uk
Set in leafy gardens at the heart of Fajara, within easy walking distance of the beach, this English-owned hotel is a commendably unpretentious set-up of 11 double rooms in a garden setting, all with en suite facilities and ceiling fans. The bar-restaurant has a pleasant outdoor ambience and is very reasonably priced. Rooms were looking a bit frayed at the time of research, but renovations should be complete by 2009. No swimming pool, but clients can use the one at Fajara Golf Club nearby. Rates include a full English breakfast. $$

Ngala Lodge
Atlantic Road
Tel: 449 4045
www.ngalalodge.com
Converted from a former ambassadorial residence perched on a low cliff overlooking a small private swimming beach, this stylish boutique hotel consists of 22 air-conditioned suites, all different in shape and individually decorated with a combination of African and international influences. One of the most prestigious addresses in The Gambia, Ngala offers a winning

combination of luxury and personality, and comes complete with one of the finest seafood restaurants in the country. $$$$

Safari Gardens Hotel
Fajara
Tel: 449 5887
www.gamspirit.com
Set in the dusty back-streets of Fajara, this very agreeable and friendly hotel attracts a younger and trendier clientele than the larger resorts. The 18 spacious rooms are decorated in a contemporary style, with tiled floor and a combination of wooden and wrought-iron furniture. A leafy courtyard contains a swimming pool and restaurant serving an Asian-influenced menu that will please meat-eaters and vegetarians alike. $$$

Sissoho Guesthouse
Kairaba Avenue
Tel: 449 7858
Email: sissohoguesthouse@yahoo.com
Opened in 2006, this funky little guesthouse has a dozen large, clean rooms with air-con, TV, fan and fridge. It is well placed for eating out and lies about 10 minutes' walk from the beach. There's a good restaurant and free internet access for residents. Discounts are offered for long stays. $$$

Kotu

Badala Park Hotel
Kotu Stream Road
Tel: 446 0400
www.badalaparkhotel.gm

This recently refurbished hotel sprawls across large green grounds a few minutes' walk through the rice fields from Kotu Beach. One of the better-priced resorts on the coast, it has a swimming pool, restaurant and beach bar. Good value. $$$

Bakotu Hotel
Kotu Stream Road
Tel: 446 5555
www.bakotuhotel.com
Set in tropical gardens only 100 metres/yards from Kotu Beach, this well-run 96-room hotel has been going for 30 years and remains one of the best deals on the coast. Wildlife enthusiasts enjoy it for the birds, monkeys and lizards that inhabit the gardens and the proximity of Kotu Stream. Facilities include two restaurants, a swimming pool and a travel desk. The brightly decorated rooms aren't huge, but they all have a private patio. Self-catering apartments are also available. $$$

Bungalow Beach Hotel
Kotu Beach
Tel: 446 5288
www.bbhotel.gm
This good-value hotel offers self-catering accommodation next door to Kombo Beach Hotel. There are 110 air-conditioned apartments with kitchenettes and 12 de luxe apartments with TV. Facilities include a swimming pool, children's pool and play-ground, restaurant, beach bar and internet café. $$$

Kombo Beach Hotel
Kotu Beach
Tel: 446 5466
www.kombobeachhotel.gm
This comfortable and friendly hotel is one of the best options on the Gambian coast, with stylish contemporary decor and well-tended gardens running down to a superb beach studded with shady thatch umbrellas. The open-air bar hosts some kind of enter-tainment every evening, and an excellent sports team organises games through the day. There are 258 airy and brightly decorated rooms, most with air-con and TV, and the hotel has a swimming pool and seven bars and restaurants. $$$$

Sunset Beach Hotel
Kotu Beach
Tel: 446 6397
www.sunsetbeachhotel.gm
This three-star hotel has excellent facilities and a great location, but the grounds are rather cramped. The 97 rooms and suites all have air-con, satellite TV and internet access, and the suites also have self-catering facilities. Adequate but overpriced. $$$$

Kololi

Bijilo Beach Hotel
Opposite Bijilo Forest Park
Tel: 446 2701
www.bijilobeachjotel.com
In contrast to the large package hotels dominating the Kololi area, this pleas-antly low-key hotel consists

BELOW: Sunset Beach Hotel.

ABOVE: Mandina River Lodge.

of just 22 rooms and apartments in large, quiet beachfront grounds only 10 minutes' walk from the main tourist action at Kololi. Though a little sombrely decorated, the rooms are large and comfortable, with air-con, safe, fridge, TV, internet access and balcony, and the swimming pool area and beach are fabulous. Good value, too! **$$$**

Coconut Residence
Kerr Serign
Tel: 446 3377
www.coconutresidence.com

This five-star boutique hotel is the last word in tropical elegance, boasting a fusion of colonial, African and even Asiatic elements in its imaginative architecture and decor. Facilities include two swimming pools, one of the top restaurants in the Greater Banjul area, wireless internet and a business centre. The airy and stylish rooms have large balconies overlooking the lush gardens. Situated on the main road about 1km (½ mile) from Kololi, this hotel's one drawback is the lack of beach frontage, but it does offer free transfers to and from Kololi or Kotu Beach. **$$$$**

Coco Ocean Resort & Spa
1 Bamboo Drive
Tel: 446 6500
www.cocooceanresort.com

Opened in 2008, this beachfront sister to

Coconut Residence seems set to take over from it as the leading boutique hotel in The Gambia. It lies among swaying coconut palms on the south end of Kololi Beach, adjacent to Bijilo Forest Park, and boasts three restaurants, a world-class spa and three-tier swimming pool. The architecture has an Arabic touch, with its whitewashed exterior and multiple domes and arches, while the rooms are airy and spacious, and come with all the facilities you would expect of a top five-star property. **$$$$**

Kairaba
Kololi Beach
Tel: 446 2940/1/2
www.kairabahotel.com

The most luxurious package hotel in The Gambia, the five-star Kairaba has 150 attractively furnished and well-equipped rooms and suites, all with private terraces overlooking lush gardens running down to Kololi Beach. More formal and sedate than most other package hotels (shorts are not permitted in the bar and restaurant), it eschews organised "entertainment", has its own observatory for star-gazing, and shares sports facilities with the neighbouring Senegambia Hotel. Four restaurants and five bars offer a wide selection of dining and

drinking experiences, and there's plenty more choice within 200 metres/yards of the hotel entrance. **$$$$**

Luigi's
Badala Parkway
Tel: 446 0280
www.luigis.gm

Only 50 metres/yards from Palma Rima Beach, this modern complex of en suite rooms and self-catering apartments, centred around a courtyard garden and swimming pool, is a little deficient in terms of character, but it's clean, calm, conveniently located and very good value. Facilities include a wellness centre, wireless internet access, and a great restaurant whose lengthy menu reflects the nationality of the Italian owner. **$$$**

Palma Rima Hotel
Badala Parkway
Tel: 446 3380/1
Email: palmarimahotel@hotmail.com

This 152-room hotel has large shady grounds and a wonderful swimming pool area, but the rooms and public areas are rather poky and poorly maintained, and the overall impression is slightly depressing. Still, it's perennially popular with a mostly English clientele looking for a good-value all-inclusive package less than five minutes' walk from one of the country's best beaches, and it does look a lot less shabby after dark, when the popular nightclub kicks into action. **$$$**

Sarge's Hotel
Kololi Beach
Tel: 446 0311
www.sargeshotel.gm

Set close to the Senegambia Hotel, this well-run three-storey hotel, formerly the Tafbel, is another place offering minimal character and good amenities at very competitive rates. The 98 en suite rooms come with air-con and satellite TV, there's a nice swimming pool and restaurant, and it's convenient for eating out or enjoying the Kololi nightlife scene. Good value. **$$$**

Senegambia Hotel
Kololi Beach
Tel: 446 2717/8/9
www.senegambiahotel.com

Such is the iconic status of this long-serving four-star hotel that most locals now refer to the surrounding part of Kololi as Senegambia. It is one of the country's best and most convenient package hotels, and a total of 328 rooms and suites also makes it the largest, though the lush green grounds – teeming with birds and monkeys – ensure that it doesn't feel at all cramped. The rooms are comfortable, decorated in an understated but rather old-fashioned manner, and have air-con and private balconies. Suites with a separate lounge and kitchenette will suit families. A wide range of sporting and other activities and excursions is offered. **$$$$**

Serekunda

Camping Sukuta
Main road between Serekunda and Kololi
Tel: 991 7786
www.campingsukuta.com

A stalwart of the West African overland scene, this relaxed campsite has simple but clean accommodation and a laid-back restaurant. It's great value, and despite the distance from the beach, a good place to meet overlanders and backpackers. **$**

Brikama and surrounds

Mandina River Lodge
About 15 minutes east of Brikama
www.makasutu.com

This exclusive eco-lodge lies on the mangrove-fringed banks of Mandina Bolong within the 500-hectare (1,250-acre) Makasutu Cultural Forest, less than an hour from the

TRANSPORT

ACCOMMODATION

ACTIVITIES

A – Z

LANGUAGE

coastal resorts and a few minutes' drive from Banjul International Airport. The eight accommodation units are split between floating or stilted solar-powered river lodges and newer jungle lodges set back from the river. The imaginative architecture and decor are complemented by the large forested-shaded swimming pool, the fine international cuisine, the peaceful bush atmosphere, and a wide range of activities including canoe trips through the mangroves and relaxed walks through the forest. **$$$$**

Brufut

Sheraton Gambia Resort
AU Highway
Tel: 441 0889
www.starwoodhotels.com
Boasting an isolated location on a pristine beach lined with baobabs and palms, the recently opened five-star Sheraton is an unexpectedly low-rise affair, making imaginative use of African and Arabic influences in the attractive mock adobe architecture. The 195 rooms and suites come with all mod cons, including air-con, mini-bar, satellite TV and high-speed internet access, and several have great

beachfront views. Sunbathers can choose between the beach and swimming pool, and there are four different restaurants on site. **$$$$**

Tanji

Kairoh Gardens Guesthouse
Tanji Village
Tel: 990 3526
www.kairohgarden.com
This long-serving budget retreat in the heart of Tanji Village has clean rooms, some of which are en suite, and a good restaurant serving decent Gambian and international fare. **$–$$**

Gunjur

Footsteps Eco-lodge
Gunjur Beach
Tel: 770 0125 or 741 1609
www.footstepsgambia.com
Rebuilt after the original was destroyed by a bushfire in 2006, this eco-friendly owner-managed lodge relies entirely on solar energy to power the swimming-pool pumps and the nine rondavels (round huts), which use compost toilets. Accommodation is comfortable rather than luxurious, but the main draw is the isolated location within easy walking distance of a spectacular and practically unspoilt beach. **$$$–$$$$**

Gecko Lodge
Gunjur Beach
Tel: 777 8551
Email: olicz@hotmail.com
Situated approximately 1km (½ mile) from Footsteps *(see below)*, this owner-managed boutique lodge consisted of four bungalows when it opened in early 2008, with more likely to follow, and a lounge and dining area that combine Mediterranean and African elements in the stylish decor and airy architecture. A wonderfully shady and peaceful retreat, it also offers a range of yoga, massage and detox treatments, and there's likely to be occasional live music at the open-air bar and entertainment area. The restaurant specialises in Italian cuisine, but can serve African dishes by request. **$$$$**

Kartung

Boboi Beach Lodge
Kartung Beach
Tel: 777 6736
www.gambia-adventure.com
This unpretentious and very affordable lodge has an unbeatable setting in a coconut grove overlooking the wide arc of white sand that runs northward from Kartung. If you can overlook the garish tiles, the hutted accommodation

is clean, comfortable and comes with mosquito netting, and a good little restaurant serves seafood and snacks. As good value as you'll find anywhere in the country. **$–$$**

Sandele Bay Eco-Retreat
Kartung Beach
Tel: 449 5887
www.sandele.com
Opened in late 2007, this stunning beachfront lodge is notable for its innovative architecture, brightly coloured exteriors, stylish and earthy African decor, and commitment to community development and use of sustainable resources. Ultra-exclusive, it consists of just four suites at present, though another six will follow in 2009, and the rooftop restaurant serves great seafood and other dishes. **$$$$**

Stala Adventures
Kartung Beach
Tel: 991 5604
www.stala-adventures.nl
This rustic, eco-friendly lodge lies along the river that forms the border with the Casamance, and offers excellent opportunities for bird-watching, fishing or just getting away from it all. The basic rooms use local materials, and the menu usually boils down to the catch of the day. **$–$$**

GAMBIA RIVER ROUTE

Bintang

Bintang Bolong Lodge
Tel: 704 3081
www.bintang-bolong.com
About an hour's drive from Banjul, this atmospheric bush lodge is very convenient for an overnight upriver excursion from the coastal resorts. It has a restaurant-bar overlooking the mangrove-lined Bintang Bolong, and half of the 12 rooms are stilted within the mangroves, while the rest lie back on dry land. Good for birdwatching and for boat trips to James Island and the north bank. **$**

Kanilai

Sindola Safari Lodge
Tel: 448 3414
www.kairabahotel.com
Affiliated to the five-star Kairaba on the coast, this 40-room government hotel is the smartest place to stay in the Gambian interior, located in large green gardens with a sparkling swimming pool, tennis court and classy restaurant serving a varied international cuisine. The thatched en suite rooms are very clean and well maintained, and come with air-con and fridge. **$$$**

Tendaba

Tendaba Camp
Tel: 554 1024 or 991 1088
The largest and most popular upriver camp in The Gambia, consisting of 150 rooms sprawled out along riverside grounds some 2–3 hours' drive from Banjul, Tendaba is a very comfortable set-up in its typically low-key and slightly run-down upriver way. Basic but clean rooms, some with en suite facilities, good restaurant and swimming pool. Excellent birding in the mangroves and surrounding woodland. **$–$$**

Soma

Moses Hotel
Tel: 553 1462
This un-signposted local hotel lies behind the behind the Shell garage 300 metres/yards from the taxi park. Its run by a laid-back Gambian

ABOVE: fine views of the Gambia River.

On the northern river bank just opposite Janjanbureh, this is a comfortable base for exploring eastern Gambia. Mud-brick huts with thatched roofs offer twin-bedded accommodation with toilet and shower. No generator, so hurricane lamps light the way at night. Restaurant and bar. Boat trips organised. **$$**

Basse Santa Su

Fulladu Camp
Tel: 990 6781
Situated on the north bank of the river immediately opposite the town, this is easily the best option in Basse, but it's also become increasingly run-down over recent years, and can be recommended only in lieu of anything better. The gardens are attractive, the en suite bungalows are pleasant enough, the pool is only sporadically usable, and the restaurant bar serves adequate meals. **$$**

Jem Hotel
Tel: 984 3658
This long-serving budget hotel has eight rooms, all with private facilities and fans, and friendly management. The best option in the town centre, it also has a restaurant and serves English or continental breakfast. **$**

Traditions Café
Basse Wharf
Tel: 566 8760
This popular waterfront venue was in the process of converting from a café to a hotel in 2008, and early signs are that the accommodation will be on the basic side, though with en suite showers and toilets. **$**

who lived for several years overseas, and the warm reception compensates for the rather run-down state of the rooms, which have fans and showers. **$**

Pakali Nding Trans-Gambia Highway Lodge
Pakali Nding, north of Soma
Tel: 553 1402 or 779 6701
The best accommodation option along the Gambian stretch of the main highway connecting northern and southern Senegal, this consists of 29 rooms and rondavels (round huts) scattered around a dusty compound on the west side of the main road. The rooms are basic but come with fans and en suite showers, and the staff are very welcoming. Meals are available with a couple of hours' notice. **$**

Farafenni

Eddy's Hotel
Tel: 573 5225
Something of an upcountry institution, Eddy's has been popular with budget travellers for years, and it remains a likeable enough set-up, albeit one that has clearly seen better days. The en suite rooms are inexpensive, and come with the choice of fans or air-con, and there's also a decent courtyard bar and restaurant attached. It has a generator that usually kicks in during Farafenni's regular power cuts. **$**

Gambia River National Park and Kuntaur

Badi Mayo
Tel: 449 7554
www.chimprehab.com
This superb tented camp, consisting of four stilted units nestled on a cliff overlooking the forested banks of the Gambia River and its islands, is perhaps the only one of its kind in West Africa to match the top safari camps of East Africa. Rates are inclusive of meals, village visits, and boat trips that come with a near guarantee of seeing chimps at close quarters, as well as hippo, red colobus, and dozens of forest and aquatic birds. An unforgettable experience, and highly recommended! **$$$$**

Kairoh Gardens Guesthouse
Tel: 566 5118 or 983 0134
www.kairohgarden.com
Affiliated to its namesake in Tanji, this unpretentious harbourfront guesthouse, opened in 2007, is another welcome addition to the upriver accommodation options. It has clean bungalows using common showers and a nice open-sided restaurant with a great view of the river. Set within easy walking distance of Wassu, the hotel also arranges boat trips to River Gambia National Park and on to Janjanbureh. **$$**

Kuntaur Agricultural Resthouse
This offers very basic rooms without fans and erratic common showers in Kuntaur, 2km (1 mile) from Wassu. Not for the squeamish, but dirt cheap, and a useful base for exploring this part of the north bank. **$**

Janjanbureh

Alakabung Lodge
Tel: 567 6123
The most central option in town, this basic place lies on Owen Street opposite the Department of Forestry compound, and consists of 10 basic en suite rooms and an adequate restaurant. Cheaper than the out-of-town options, but otherwise far inferior. **$**

Bird Safari Camp
Tel: 994 4140 or 992 1096
www.hiddengambia.com
Set on the western tip of Janjanbureh Island about 30 minutes' walk west of town, this attractive riverside camp has nice en suite accommodation in 10 tented riverfront units and 10 cool thatched huts, and facilities include a good restaurant, a swimming pool, solar-powered lighting, and well-developed grounds teeming with birdlife. Ring first, and they'll arrange a boat transfer from town. Rates are full-board. **$$$**

Janjang-Bureh Camp
North Bank (accessible by pirogue)
Tel: 567 6182

PRICE CATEGORIES

Price categories are for a double room:
$ = under US$25
  (D500)
$$ = US$25–50
  (D500–1,000)
$$$ = US$50–120
  (D1,000–2,400)
$$$$ = over US$120
  (D2,400)

A CTIVITIES

THE ARTS, NIGHTLIFE, FESTIVALS, SHOPPING, PARTICIPANT SPORTS AND NATIONAL PARKS

ARTS AND CULTURE

You wouldn't expect a country as small as The Gambia to be overly rich in museums, opera houses and other cultural institutions, and the truth is that it isn't. The National Museum in Banjul is diverting rather than essential viewing, but it does house an interesting selection of exhibits covering local jewellery, clothes, utensils, housing, customs and rituals, supported with photos, maps and other clear explanations. Other important cultural sites include the Museum of the North Bank at Juffureh, the megalithic stone circles at Ker Batch and Wassu, and Fort Bullen at Barra. For details of all sites protected by the National Centre For Arts and Culture, see www.ncac.gm.

A number of art galleries are dotted around the Greater Banjul area. Among the more interesting are Africa Living Art Centre (Garba Jahumpa Road, Bakau; tel: 449 5131), the African Heritage Gallery (Samba Breco Road, Cape Point; tel: 449 6778) and the Village Gallery (Kololi; tel: 446 3646). Further afield, on the outskirts of Kartung near the Senegalese border, you'll find the excellent Lemonfish Gallery (tel: 772 8621; http://lemonfish.gm), which displays works by several contemporary Gambian artists. None of these places charges an entrance fee.

For more detailed information on one-off musical concerts, film screenings and other cultural events, ask at the reception desk of your hotel and also keep an eye open for posters advertising these events.

NIGHTLIFE

Nightlife is rather limited in The Gambia, to the disappointment of both Gambians and some visitors. The larger tourist hotels have their own nightclubs, open to members of the public as well as to their own guests. Some are open every evening, some only at weekends. The larger hotels stage entertainments for their visitors. This is a good chance to see local dancers, drummers, fire-eaters, acrobats or fashion shows. Occasionally a hotel will put on its own cabaret, drawing talent from its visitors; sometimes an artiste is hired for the six-month season, doing a tour of these hotels. Large concerts occasionally take place in the National Stadium.

These are some of the major nightclubs, all of which charge an entrance fee.

African Queen
The Strip, Kololi
Informal tourist-oriented restaurant-bar with occasional live music.

Bellengo Nightclub
Kombo Beach Hotel
Tel: 446 5466
Lively disco music.

Destiny's
Kotu Beach
Tel: 446 4604
Smart beachfront nightclub with occasional live music.

Dream Park
Bertil Harding Highway, Kololi
Tel: 779 0354
Amusement park with occasional live music, usually advertised well in advance at the entrance gate.

Jokor
Westfield Junction, Serekunda
Tel: 992 2555

ABOVE: the art of the batik.

Busy and popular with tourists and locals alike, wide selection of West African and international dance styles and occasional live music.
Teranga Beach Club
Palma Rima Beach
Tel: 706 7864
Right on the beach, this earthy set-up has live music on Sunday nights and reggae on Thursdays.
Waaw Night Club
The Strip, Kololi
Tel: 446 0668
Large dance floor and balcony, with good mix of dance and reggae music; no entrance fee weekday nights.

FESTIVALS

Public organised festivals for special occasions are rare in The Gambia. There are plenty of celebrations on feast days and for marriage or name-day ceremonies, but they will be in private. You may be lucky enough to get to know a Gambian whose family will be celebrating something while you are on holiday and who will take you with him/her, or you may happen to be passing a compound where dancing or drumming is taking place and be able to watch. On feast days, small groups of young people may dress up as birds, animals or magicians and dance in the road to the music of whistles and drums.

During the Christmas/New Year season, Fanal processions take place in Banjul, Bakau and Serekunda. Intricate ships made from split bamboo and cut-out paper patterns delicately glued together are constructed by clubs in honour of their patron. These are then paraded through the streets every evening in the dark, with candles lit inside them to illuminate the tracery, accompanied by drumming and dancing crowds, until they reach the patron's house. At the end of the season (just after New Year), the ship is given to the patron for him to display. Donations are accepted for the club. If you know where to go, you can watch the processions.

More contemporary festivals are as follows:

Kartong Festival
Held every year over 4–5 days in late March, this drumming- and music-dominated festival features a variety of local and international performers. www.kartongfestival.org

Bakau Festival
Held in early January, this festival in the heart of The Gambia's main resort area showcases traditional Gambian music as well as styles from elsewhere in West Africa.

International Roots Festival
Held every other June (next one due 2010) this moving festival is a "homecoming" celebration aimed at American, Caribbean and other descendants of the Diaspora caused by the transatlantic slave trade. www.rootsgambia.gm

GAMBLING

Kololi Casino, Kololi, tel: 446 0223. Blackjack, roulette, etc. Saturday is the liveliest night to come and play.

SHOPPING

There are two sorts of buying transactions in West Africa, one representing a modern European influence and the other more in line with informal African traditions. The first is the familiar system of fixed prices used in modern shops and supermarkets where customers

simply pay the displayed price. The second system, which still applies in markets, smaller shops and stalls (as well as dealings with guides, taxi drivers et al), involves bargaining and is therefore not so simple for Westerners to adjust to.

There are no fixed rules when it comes to bargaining, but in most transactions it would be seen as madness to agree to the first price requested by a vendor, as it might be two to three times the going rate. To reach a more realistic price, you must play a leisurely game in which it is perfectly acceptable to feign slight impatience, walk off, pause, turn back, think, discuss details of the goods, etc. The vendor will not understand at all the idea that you might be in a hurry. The best method is probably to start at around one-third of the asking price, so that you can be seen to increase your offer at least once.

While most shops adhere to strict opening hours, the informal sector is very flexible, and no market vendor will turn away a prospective client just because he has half-finished packing up his wares.

The coastal resorts of The Gambia offer limitless opportunities for souvenir-shopping, and the best place to start is usually one of the main craft markets, which can be found in Kololi (at Senegambia Junction), Bakau (corner of Cape Point and Atlantic roads) and within the larger goods markets in Banjul (Albert Market) and Serekunda. Most hotels also have good gift shops, but these tend to have higher prices and to offer a more limited choice than markets. Worth a special mention, at the Fajara end of Garba Jahumpa Road, Timbooktoo is an excellent double-storey bookshop that stocks a good selection of travel guides and

other local-interest books, as well as novels and other reference works.

Popular purchases include batik cloth, sold in lengths or made up into shirts, shorts, skirts, dresses, trousers, children's clothes or table-cloths. Tailors, machines whirring all day long, will run up anything from a pair of shorts to a man's suit in a matter of one or two days. Wood-carvings are also popular, and these too can be custom-made (simply put down a deposit for the wood, making sure you are dealing with a bona fide craftsman), and most markets have several stalls dedicated to contemporary African paintings and other artworks. Other souvenirs include filigree jewellery, bead necklaces and traditionally dressed dolls. Musical instruments are also for sale.

SPORTS

Wrestling is the traditional national sport in both countries, taking place on a Saturday or Sunday evening (except during Ramadan). The atmosphere and audience reaction are to be enjoyed as much as the wrestling itself. The wrestlers are usually draped in amulets to bring luck and often pour over their bodies and drink "magic" potions to protect themselves. Between bouts, followers of each wrestler dance, drum, blow whistles and flutes, playing to the crowd, whipping up excitement and spurring their hero to flaunt himself and show off his strength. The actual wrestling round lasts no time by comparison. First one down loses. Excursions to wrestling matches are organised from the hotels, but anyone can attend by simply turning up.

BELOW: football on the beach, a popular pastime.

Football is popular as a street game with improvised equipment, but also as a spectator sport, and both countries have major stadiums where matches take place. Senegal in particular has emerged as one of the powerhouses of African football following its quarter-final placing in the 2004 World Cup (whereas The Gambia has yet to qualify for the Africa Nations Cup). To find out about forthcoming matches, check the local press, or just ask around – most West African men are football crazy.

Water Sports

Almost all the package hotels offer a range of water sports and activities, from water polo in the swimming pool to windsurfing, surfing and yachting on the open sea, usually with instructors.

Tennis and Squash

Tennis and/or squash courts are available at several of the better resort hotels, among them the Corinthia Atlantic, Kairaba, Senegambia, Kombo Beach and Sunbeach. Other smaller hotels will usually have table tennis facilities. If you're staying at a hotel that doesn't have tennis or squash courts, your best bet is the Fajara Club at the south end of Atlantic Road (tel: 449 5456), which allows day members to use these facilities.

Golf

The 18-hole course at the Fajara Golf Club, the only one in the country, is notable for its greens (referred to

locally as browns!). In addition to a nominal day membership fee, visitors must pay a green fee equivalent to around US$25 per day (or US$100 per week) and can also rent clubs (US$8 per round) and hire a caddy (US$5). The course is rated par 67 and is busiest over weekends, when tournaments are held and visitors may need to book their round well in advance.

Hunting

The Gambia takes very seriously its duty to conserve wildlife, and hunting in virtually all forms is illegal or heavily discouraged.

Fishing

Sea or river fishing with a line from the beach or bank is popular and needs no particular organisation. Upriver, pirogues may be hired everywhere informally for short excursions. Game fishing for the wide variety of species which abound offshore is organised through the major hotels. There are possibilities for reef and beach fishing throughout the year, but the best months for game fishing in the open water are May to September, while the season for freshwater tigerfish runs over December to May. Companies that specialise in game-fishing excursions are World Sport Fishing in the UK (tel: 01480 403 293; www.worldsport fishing.com) and the locally based African Angler (tel: 772 1228; www.gambiafishing.co.uk) and Hooked on Gambia (tel: 777 4728; www.hookedongambia.co.uk).

GUIDES AND LOCAL TOURS

The favourable rates offered to package operators by the coastal resorts encourage visitors to The Gambia to book into one or other of the resorts for the duration of their stay, and do any further exploration in the form of day or overnight tours organised through the hotel reception or activities desk or a local guide. One of the most popular day excursions from the coastal resorts is a "Roots Tour" to James Island and the other historical sites of the north bank, but other good day trips include Abuko Nature Reserve, Lamin Lodge, Banjul city centre and Tanji fish market. Recommended destinations for overnight tours are Tendaba Camp (for birds) and Badi Mayo (for chimps, monkeys and hippos).

Once the plague of the Gambian coast, the persistent unofficial guides known as bumsters are no longer a major problem, largely thanks to the instigation of a system of ID-bearing Official Tourist Guides (OTG) implemented in 2001. OTGs can be found outside all the major coastal resorts, or arranged through your hotel reception, and they charge fixed rates equivalent to around US$6 per half-day and US$10 for a full day. Visitors with a strong interest in birdwatching should ask for an OTG specialised in birding. Most day tours can be organised directly through OTGs, and this will usually work out more cheaply than a similar tour booked through your hotel, though it also comes with accountability.

Wildlife and Birdwatching

The Gambia offers relatively slim pickings when it comes to safari wildlife. Of the so-called Big Five, for instance, the only one that still occurs there naturally is the leopard, and the odds of actually seeing one are negligible. The country fares somewhat better when it comes to primates, with chimpanzees being the main focus of attention at the River Gambia National Park, which recently opened to visitors, while Guinea baboon, red colobus, green monkey and patas monkey all still occur within greater Banjul, at the likes of Abuko Nature Reserve, Bijilo Forest Park and Makasutu Culture Forest. For other wildlife, Abuko is the place to see smaller antelope such as bushbuck and duiker, and it also supports a healthy population of

crocodiles, while Gambia River National Park has resident hippos, and Kiang West National Park is the one place where larger antelope such as roan and sitatunga still survive, along with relic populations of elusive large carnivores such as leopard and spotted hyena.

The Gambia's main draw in terms of wildlife is its extraordinary variety of birds, with some 560 species recorded in an area slightly smaller than Yorkshire. Key birdwatching sites include all the reserves and forests listed above, as well as the Tanji River Bird Reserve, Bao Bolong Wetland Reserve, Niumi National Park, Kunkilling Forest Park and the Tanbi Wetlands around Banjul. One thing that distinguishes The Gambia from most other African countries with a comparably rich birdlife is

that the tourist industry is extremely well equipped for visiting birdwatchers, who almost certainly comprise the country's most significant "special interest" tourist niche. As a result, most resorts and hotels offer a variety of ornithological excursions, or can put you in touch with specialised local guides.

Good UK contacts for birdwatching trips include Birdfinders (tel: 01258 839 066; www.birdfinders.co.uk) and Hidden Gambia (tel: 01285 861 839; www.hiddengambia.com). The definitive resource for planning an independent birdwatching trip is the website of the Gambia Birding Group (www.gambiabirding.org), which has detailed information about all major birding sites, recommended local guides and much else besides *(see also pages 112–13 & 186–89).*

A HANDY SUMMARY OF PRACTICAL INFORMATION, ARRANGED ALPHABETICALLY

A dmission Charges

Museums and nature reserves all levy an admission fee, but in most cases this is nominal – the local equivalent of US$2–3 per person per day.

B udgeting for Your Trip

Day-to-day budgets will depend greatly on what aspects of the trip have been pre-booked, what parts of the country you visit and whether you travel independently. Taking food as an example, a filled baguette at a street stall will cost les than US$1, whereas a light snack in a mid-range eatery might work out at around US$10 and a steak or shellfish dish at a top restaurant could cost US$20–30, which means that you can to some extent tailor your expenditure to almost any reasonable budget.

One way to keep your local spending to a minimum is to book an all-inclusive package that covers flights, accommodation, activities and meals, though this sort of package is increasingly uncommon

and it limits you to eating at your hotel every night. Allowing for a more adventurous approach in terms of where you eat and drink, a pre-booked B&B package to a coastal resort would probably leave you needing to budget another US$25–30 person per day on food and drink, more if you head for the top restaurants and/or drink wine or spirits (which tend to be costly compared to beer and soft drinks), less if you self-cater or are prepared to make do with a DIY sandwich or street food at lunch.

Independent travellers tend to find The Gambia cheap in comparison with Europe or the US, but items and services aimed at tourists can be expensive compared to other developing countries. On the coast, it would be difficult to get away with less than US$50–60 per person daily to cover accommodation, food, drink and getting around. These things tend to be cheaper further upriver, and even on the coast you can save a lot of money by avoiding services (private taxis, upmarket restaurants, etc) that cater almost exclusively to tourists.

C hildren

The Gambia has few activities or attractions geared specifically to children, but the coastal resorts are all reasonably child-friendly, and most arrange a wide variety of activities suited to youngsters. There are no zoos or game reserves along the Gambian coast, but most children will enjoy the semi-habituated monkeys at Bijilo, and it would also be possible to cross into Senegal to look for rhinos and giraffes in the Réserve de Fathala. Opened in early 2006, Dream Park (Bertil Harding Highway between Palma Rima and Senegambia; tel: 793 0354; Mon–Fri 5pm–midnight, Sat–Sun 3pm–midnight; charge) is an amusement park with dodgems, carousels and a selection of other rides suitable to children.

Climate

The entire region has an agreeable subtropical climate. The dry season, which runs from November to May, is characterised by long hours of sunshine, an average temperature of

CLIMATE CHART

Banjul

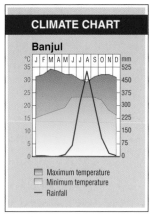

☐ Maximum temperature
☐ Minimum temperature
— Rainfall

24–26°C (72–74°F) and a cool breeze blowing off the sea. In the eastern interior of Senegal, however, temperatures can reach considerably higher, into the 30s or even 40°C (85–105°F). Nonetheless, it can be chilly enough in the evenings for a light jacket or cardigan, or a blanket on the bed, especially inland. It will not rain, except for a freak storm. The dry Harmattan wind, coming from the desert, often blows in January and February, bringing with it thick red dust that settles everywhere very suddenly and can even prevent planes landing and taking off. Throat lozenges are a relief at this time. The dust will disappear as suddenly as it arrived. Upriver, the cool season is shorter, ending in February/March.

During the wet season (June to September), humidity rises drastically (80 percent or more), which makes the temperature (average 28°C/84°F) seem even hotter. Rain falls in torrential downpours with high winds, lasting a few hours at most, giving way to clear skies and a brief cool respite before the sun and humidity take over again.

The hottest months are between the two seasons: May/June and October on the coast, March/June and October inland.

Crime and Safety

The Gambia is one of the safest countries in West Africa in terms of crime, and the risk of mugging or other violent assaults anywhere in the country is negligible. As is the case almost anywhere in Africa, however, Westerners are (accurately) perceived to be rich in comparison with locals, and a certain amount of opportunistic theft does exist, especially in markets, bus stations and other busy areas. When you visit such places, leave your watch and jewellery behind, keep your

handbag fastened up in front of you, and don't carry more cash than you are likely to need for the excursion. When birdwatching in an isolated area, it is best to go in a group without money or valuables (binoculars are not what thieves are after).

All the larger hotels have safes, and you are advised to use them for valuables and documents. If you do lose anything valuable, report it to your hotel, to the local police station and to your tour operator, but don't be surprised if not much happens. In the case of a lost passport, notify your country's High Commission, embassy or consulate and ask for a certificate of loss and a temporary passport.

Lost travellers' cheques, credit cards or chequebooks should be reported immediately to the local banks as well as to your issuing bank at home by phone. The "Tourist Police", who deal solely with problems relating to tourists, routinely patrol all the main tourist areas and have stations in Bakau, Serekunda, Banjul and at the junction of the Kombo and Senegambia roads.

More of a hassle than a genuine threat are the persistent guides and touts that lurk around popular tourist areas such as Kololi, Bakau, Kotu and even downtown Banjul, and attempt to engage any passing tourist in conversation in the hope it will lead to an opportunity to manipulate them into parting with money. Known locally as bumsters, these aspirant guides and hangers-on are far less widespread than they were a few years back thanks to a strict government crackdown, but unless you never leave your hotel, you're bound to come across the phenomenon at some point. Typical opening gambits include asking which hotel you are staying at, then claiming to work there, or asking "Do you remember me?" then looking deeply hurt when you say you don't, or just rattling away inanely, impervious to any attempt at deflection. In most cases, your new chum will quickly lose interest in palling up when he realises you're not open to it, but if anybody becomes too persistent, a threat to report him to the Tourist Police will usually do the trick.

Customs Regulations

Personal belongings (including cameras, binoculars and video cameras which are not for resale) are admitted duty-free. Also duty-free are 200 cigarettes or 50 cigars or 250g tobacco, 1 litre of spirits or wine and 250ml of perfume or eau de toilette. There are no restrictions on the importation of currency.

D isabled Travellers

Virtually no special facilities for disabled people exist in either country, but upmarket hotels are generally low-rise and staff are very willing to assist.

The only Gambian coastal resort with rooms specifically designed for disabled travellers is the Sunbeach Hotel (Bakau), which has four rooms with grab handles and waterproof seats in the showers, and raised sinks in the bathrooms.

E mbassies

Gambian Embassies Abroad

Belgium, 226 Avenue Franklin Roosevelt, 11050 Brussels; tel: 02 640 1049; www.gambiaembassy.be
France, 117 Rue Saint-Lazare, 4th Floor, 75008 Paris; tel: 01 42 94 09 30
Senegal, 11 Rue De Thiong, Dakar; tel: 33 821 4476
UK, 57 Kensington Court, London W8 5DG; tel: 020 7937 6316/7; email: ukgta@ukonline.co.uk
US, 1424 K Street, NW Suite 600, Washington DC 20005; tel: 202 785 1399; www.gambiaembassy.us

Diplomatic Missions in The Gambia

British High Commission, 48 Atlantic Road, Fajara; tel: 449 7590; www.britishhighcommission.gov.uk/thegambia
Senegal High Commission, Kairaba Avenue; tel: 437 3752
US Embassy, Kairaba Avenue, Fajara; tel: 439 2856; http://banjul.usembassy.gov

BELOW: traditional dress.

Emergency Numbers

In The Gambia, the emergency telephone number for the police is 17 (ambulance is 16 and fire 18).

Entry Requirements

A full passport (valid for at least six months after your return from the Gambia) is required. Visas are not required by holders of UK, EU or most ECOWAS and Commonwealth passports for visits of up to 90 days in duration. Citizens of the US and other countries that do require an entry visa must have at least one blank page on their passport for the stamp, which should ideally be obtained in advance at any Gambian Embassy or High Commission (see page 306). Upon arrival, immigration will usually stamp your passport for 15–21 days, or up to 28 days by special request. For a nominal fee, this can be extended on a monthly basis for a maximum of three months at the Immigration Office OAU Avenue in Banjul (tel: 422 7249). Should you be coming from a yellow-fever-infected zone, you may be asked to produce an appropriate certificate of vaccination.

Gay Travellers

Islamic doctrine and the social and moral background of the region are both strongly against homosexuality. Senegal is relatively relaxed and cosmopolitan by comparison with The Gambia, where homosexual acts are illegal. In both places, however, overtly homosexual behaviour may arouse hostility, and might lead to arrest. This is not to say that discreet homosexual activity never takes place – merely that it is not publicly acceptable or legally condoned to the extent it is in Europe and America.

Health and Medical Care

Comprehensive medical insurance should be taken out before you leave your home country. Obtain details from your travel agent, insurance company or bank. Although free emergency medical treatment is theoretically available in both countries, it is likely to be unreliable or non-existent (the latter obviously in remote areas), and full medical insurance to cover all eventualities is therefore necessary.

Immunisations

The one mandatory jab is yellow fever, which is valid for 10 years and

Electricity

The country's mains power can be erratic, with frequent power cuts, though many hotels get around this by having a generator on standby to kick in the moment the mains go down. Supermarkets, banks and restaurants also usually have their own generators, so food and drink are kept fresh and cold and air-conditioners working. The current is 220–230V, but the constant fluctuation of power can damage hi-tech

may be checked upon arrival. Other vaccinations worth considering are as follows:
Typhoid – a gastric fever caught from infected or dirty food. Valid 2–3 years. Oral capsules also available.
Hepatitis A/B – both vaccines are valid for 10 years provided you have boosters within 12 months.
Polio – booster required every 10 years.
Meningitis – valid for 3 years.
Tetanus – booster required every 10 years.
Rabies – recommended to anybody who will be handling animals in The Gambia.
These immunisations are all optional, and it's advisable to contact a doctor for further advice. Also check with your doctor the best time to have them done – some can be given on the same day as yellow fever – otherwise you may have to wait a week or two between injections and thus delay your departure.

Malaria

Anti-malarial drugs should be taken by visitors (and residents) in both countries as this disease, carried by the anopheles mosquito, is prevalent everywhere and can strike anyone at any time. Several prophylactic drugs are available, and it is best to obtain current advice from a doctor or travel clinic. Pregnant women, epileptics or people with a history of depression or mental illness should inform their doctor of their condition as it will affect the recommended drug. Although highly effective, prophylactics are not foolproof, so if you experience malarial symptoms after you return home – typically a high temperature, wracking headache and alternate bouts of the shivers and hot fevers – it is imperative you get to a doctor immediately and inform them you may have been exposed to malaria.
There are fewer mosquitoes around in the dry (tourist) season

equipment, freezers, etc. Private citizens often bring stabilisers. Street lighting is minimal.
Upcountry towns (Basse, Mansa Konko, Farafenni, Bansang and the larger villages) normally have electricity in the evening and for some period during the day, but power should not be relied on. Battery-operated radios, shavers and torches are essential, and chilled drinks will often be unobtainable.

(November to May) than in the wet season. Hotel rooms usually have mosquito-proofed windows, and an air-conditioner and/or fan (if you have electricity) will help keep them away. Upcountry, where there is little or no electricity, a mosquito net or strong anti-mosquito spray is necessary, or you can burn anti-mosquito coils which give off a scented smoke obnoxious to mosquitoes but tolerable for humans. One coil lasts about eight hours. Bring a good supply of insect repellent as a back-up.

Aids

It is prevalent in the region, although figures are unreliable. Considering both Senegal and The Gambia are mainly Muslim, the population is promiscuous, with prostitution fairly common. Billboards warn of the dangers of unprotected sex. In West Africa, the HIV virus is transmitted mainly by heterosexual contact, and also by contaminated needles and blood-transfusion equipment. Emergency medical packs containing sterilised needles and plasma are now available in developed countries for visitors to take with them.

Drinking Water

Bottled water is widely available and should be used in both countries. The extent of other precautions to avoid stomach upsets will vary depending on how much restriction of food choice you are prepared to put up with. It is sensible to peel all fruit, whether washed or not, before eating. Some people will wish to avoid salads and other uncooked, washed foods, as well as ice cream and ice in drinks. Others will resign themselves to the occasional bug and eat whatever is going.
In general, standards of hygiene in both countries in most commercial establishments are well controlled.

Medical Services

Most hotels have a nurse or doctor on call for emergencies and will treat minor irritating infections that occur such as stomach upsets, cuts, sore throats, coughs, etc, at the hotel "clinic". In emergencies, the nearest hospital will be called. If you are on your own and are taken ill, you must make your own way to the doctor or hospital; ambulances are rare, although there is theoretically an emergency ambulance service. The Royal Victoria Hospital in Banjul has good doctors and operating facilities, as has the Westfield Clinic in Serekunda. A recommended dentist is the Swedent (Swedish Dental) Clinic on Bertil Harding Highway in Kololi (tel: 446 1212; www.swedent.gm). For more socialised requirements or emergency treatment, ask your hotel to put you in touch with a recommended local practitioner.

Internet

Inexpensive internet cafés are scattered all around Banjul, Serekunda, Brikama and the main coastal resorts. Connections aren't as fast as is the case in Europe or the US (or even in Senegal for that matter), and the line tends to drop with some frequency, but overall the service is quite reliable. Elsewhere in the country, internet facilities, where they exist, are slow and unreliable.

Maps

Macmillan produces the most up-to-date and comprehensive map of The Gambia. It's usually stocked at Timbooktoo Bookshop in Fajara, and may also be available in some hotel gift shops, but it is perhaps safer to buy it before you leave for The Gambia.

Media

Newspapers and Magazines

Press freedom has deteriorated greatly in the years following the 2001 presidential election. Several reputable journalists have been placed under temporary arrest during this period, newspaper offices and radio stations have been subjected to arson attacks, and the forthright editor Deyda Hydara was assassinated in December 2004 following his criticisms of new laws curtailing the freedom of the press. Under the circumstances, the level of press debate in The Gambia remains surprisingly lively, though you would scarcely think so by reading the prominent *Daily Observer* (www.observer.gm) which toes an overtly pro-government line. Far better are *The Point* (http://thepoint.gm) and *The Gambia Echo* (www.thegambiaecho.com), both of which publish good online editions. Very few foreign publications are available, though Timbooktoo does stock some international magazines.

Radio

Radio Gambia is a government-controlled station with programmes in all the main Gambian languages and in English, with regular news bulletins, schools' broadcasts and general programmes on education, culture, religion and music. Transmission is on 648 kHz.

BBC World Service is easily picked up on several short-wave frequencies, depending on the time of day. Check www.bbc.co.uk/worldservice for frequencies and details of programming.

Television

The Gambia has one official television channel, which focuses mainly on local news, international football and light entertainment. Upmarket hotels generally supplement this uninspired fare with a satellite bouquet of news, sport and movie channels.

Money

Currency

You can take as much money into The Gambia as you wish, either in travellers' cheques or in hard currency, but you may not take out more than you brought in. The local currency is the dalasi, made up of 100 bututs. Notes are in denominations of D100, D50, D25, D10 and D5. Coins are in denominations of D1 (heptagonal), 50, 25, 10 and 5 bututs. Recent exchange rates have fluctuated around £1 = D40 or US$1 = D20.

Banks will exchange US dollar, euro and pound sterling travellers' cheques and cash at the official rates posted up daily in the banks. Take your passport with you when you go to the bank. All major hotels have foreign exchange facilities at their reception desks, but commissions here will be greater and rates will be poorer than at banks. For the best rates, private foreign currency bureaux are dotted all around Greater Banjul, but they usually accept cash only. A limited black market still exists, but it buys little in terms of a better exchange rate, and carries a small but real risk of being arrested or defrauded.

Visa and to a lesser extent MasterCard is accepted by the larger hotels and by some car-hire companies, but you may have to pay a surcharge. Diners Club and American Express are very seldom accepted. In the Greater Banjul area, several branches of the Standard Chartered Bank (including the ones in Kololi and Fajara) have 24-hour ATMs where local currency can be drawn using any PIN-coded Visa card. ATMs are not available anywhere on the coast south of Kololi, upriver of Serekunda, or on the north bank.

Banking hours are normally from 8am–midnight or 1am (Monday to Saturday) and some banks also open from 4–6.30pm (Monday to Friday only). The most efficient bank is usually Standard Chartered, which has branches in Banjul, Serekunda, Kololi, Bakau and Basse Santa Su. Private foreign exchange bureaux tend to keep longer hours, especially in the main resort areas.

Opening Hours

Government offices usually open from 8am–4pm Mon–Fri, while business hours are normally 9am–5pm, though

BELOW: top-up cards for mobile phones can be purchased at corner shops.

TRANSPORT

many shops and other tourist-oriented facilities such as internet cafés or beauty salons keep significantly longer hours, while other places often close for a long lunch. Banking hours vary but typically run from 8am–noon and 4–6.30pm Mon–Fri and some banks also open from 9am–1pm Sat. On Sunday, all offices and some shops are closed.

P hotography

Both countries are very open with regard to photography, but many individuals do not like having their picture taken by tourists, or will expect to be paid to pose. If you do want to photograph people, you must get their permission first and accept gracefully if you are refused. Street scenes can be shot discreetly from a passing car, but using a high-magnification lens from across the street is likely to produce better results. With film being largely obsolete these days, don't expect to be able to buy it locally – if you still use a film camera, bring all the supplies you'll need with you.

Postal Services

Mail between The Gambia and Europe is cheap but unlikely to arrive within a week of being posted. The main post office is in Banjul, next to Albert Market, and there are branches in Bakau (off the road

opposite the African Village Hotel), Kairaba Avenue, and in all of the larger upcountry towns. Opening hours are generally 8.30am–noon and 2–4pm (Monday to Friday) and 8.30am–noon (Saturday). Most hotels will sell you stamps provided you buy the postcards there as well. They also have their own post boxes, which are regularly emptied in time to catch the flights out of the region. It is not advisable to entrust valuables to the ordinary postal service; use a courier company like DHL or FedEx.

R eligious Services

The majority of Gambians are Islamic but many are Christian, and there is complete freedom of religious worship. Visitors are welcome to join local religious services. Anglican and other protestant churches include the Cathedral of St Mary (Independence Drive, Banjul), St Paul's Church (Fajara), Christ Church (Serekunda), the Church of the African Martyrs (Farafenni) and St Cuthbert's Church (Basse Santa Su). Roman Catholic churches include the Cathedral of Our Lady of the Assumption (Banjul), Church of the Holy Spirit (Banjul) and Star of the Sea Church (Bakau). Methodists are catered for at the historic Wesley Church in Banjul, as well as the Methodist Church in Atlantic Road, Bakau.

T elecommunications

Telephones

GAMTEL, Gambia's telecommunications service, is excellent. You can call internationally as easily as you would from home. Phone-card booths are a very affordable way of making a call, and the cards can be bought at the GAMTEL offices in Bakau (Atlantic Road, opposite African Village Hotel), Kotu Beach, Westfield Junction in Serekunda, Banjul (next to Albert Market) and Banjul International Airport. By contrast, most tourist hotels charge extortionate rates for international phone calls.

Mobile phones have caught on in a big way. If you'll be in The Gambia for a while or expect to make lots of phone calls, it's worth replacing your home SIM card with a local one – this effectively costs nothing, as the SIM card comes with airtime units equivalent to the price – and international or local calls or text messages made from local Gambian numbers work out far more cheaply than international roaming. Reception

ABOVE: ladies only.

is good in the coastal resort areas, but there are a few blank spots further upriver.

Time Zone

Both The Gambia and Senegal stick to Greenwich Mean Time all year round.

Tipping

Gambians seldom tip waiters and other restaurant staff, but tipping is more normal at places that cater mainly to tourists, usually around 10 percent of the bill depending on the quality of service. It is also customary to tip guides and drivers employed by companies, but not those with whom you negotiate a direct fee for private services. Most hotels have tip boxes and encourage you to leave a sum to be divided among the entire staff instead of just those individuals who serve you directly.

Toilets

Tourist-oriented hotels and restaurants almost invariably have clean flush toilets with toilet paper supplied. That's not quite so true of places geared more towards a local clientele, though standards are generally acceptable. If you are caught short in a public place, any bank, restaurant, bar, petrol station or hotels will most likely allow you make use of the toilet facilities if you ask politely.

Public Holidays

Senegal and The Gambia both celebrate the feast days of the Muslim Calendar. These are movable feasts that depend upon sightings of the new moon and may not be known until very shortly beforehand.
● Korité (known in Arabic as Aid el Fitr, the end of the month-long fast of Ramadan)
● Tabaski (in Arabic, Aid el Kebir or Aid el Adha, the feast of Ibrahim's sacrifice of the sheep)
● Tamharit (the Islamic New Year)
● Mouloud (the Prophet Mohammed's birthday)

In addition, The Gambia has the following public holidays:
● 1 January: New Year's Day
● 18 February: Independence Day
● March/April (variable): Good Friday
● 1 May: May Day
● 22 July: Revolution Day
● 15 August: Assumption Day
● 25 December: Christmas Day

ACCOMMODATION

ACTIVITIES

A – Z

LANGUAGE

ABOVE: flying the flag for The Gambia.

Tourist Information

The official custodian of tourism to The Gambia is the Gambia Tourist Authority, which has a very useful website, http://visitthegambia.gm. Tel: 446 2491/3/4.

Outside The Gambia

Gambia National Tourist Office, 57 Kensington Court, London W8 5DG, England, tel: 020 7376 0093. Mon–Thur 9.30am–5pm, Fri 9.30am–1pm.

Tour Operators

The Gambia Experience
Tel (UK): 0845 330 2060
www.gambia.co.uk
This is the UK's busiest and most knowledgeable operator to The Gambia. In addition to running its own twice-weekly flights and acting as a booking agent for all the leading hotels, it often has a great selection of special offers, especially for those travelling at short notice.
Hidden Gambia
Tel (UK): 01285 861 839
www.hiddengambia.com
This knowledgeable operator specialises in natural history trips, and is recommended highly for keen bird-watchers and wildlife-lovers. It runs excellent one- to two-week trips for small groups, taking in several days at the coast with a leisurely cruise upriver to Janjanbureh or Basse Santa Su.
Discovery Tours
10 Atlantic Road, Fajara
Tel: 449 5551; www.discoverytours.gm
One of the best ground operators in The Gambia, offering a good selection of package and bespoke trips on the coast and upriver.
Gambia Tours
Tel: 446 2601/2; www.gambiatours.gm
This is a solid family-run local operator with more than 20 years' experience in running trips around The Gambia.
West African Tours
Tel: 449 5258; www.westafricantours.com
Another vastly experienced operator, under the same management since it was first established in 1987, this offers a varied selection of general and special interest tours, within Gambia and further afield to Ghana, Senegal and Mali.

Websites

http://thepoint.gm – news and current affairs from the country's top newspaper.
http://visitthegambia.gm – official website of the Gambia Tourist Authority.
www.accessgambia.com – details information about attractions and services in The Gambia.
www.gambia.co.uk – information-packed website of the UK's top tour operator to The Gambia.
www.gambia.dk – useful background to Gambian culture.
www.gambia.gm – official government website.
www.gambiabirding.org – everything birdwatchers need to know before they visit The Gambia.
www.gambiaguide.co.uk – useful birdwatching information.
www.gambiatouristsupport.com – good practical information for tourists.
www.ncac.gm – website of the National Centre for Arts and Culture.
www.thegambiaecho.com – a good source of current information and political commentary.

What to Bring

From the chemist: high-protection suntan lotion; plenty of insect repellent; antihistamine or sting-relief cream; anti-stomach upset medicine; indigestion tablets; water-sterilising tablets if you are travelling upcountry; throat lozenges; anti-malaria prophylactics *(see page 307)* and cures (ask your doctor); basic first aid equipment including sticking plasters, antiseptic cream, cotton wool; headache tablets; tampons; deodorants, etc. A small selection of such items is available in super-markets and hotel shops, but they tend to be expensive.

Weights and Measures

The metric system is used in The Gambia.

Miscellaneous: a beach towel (some hotels don't like you using theirs); a torch (in case of power cuts); a knife for dissecting mangoes, etc; binoculars for birdwatching.

What to Wear

From November to May, the region has a very pleasant subtropical climate, warm, dry and sunny during the day but with an unexpectedly cool breeze in the evenings. Trousers are necessary in the evenings (against mosquitoes and the chilly breeze) and on expeditions into the bush. A hat is useful on the beach and on excursions (locally made bush hats are cheap, cool and readily available).

In the wet season, an umbrella, lightweight raincoat and shoes that can get wet without spoiling should be brought. Both men and women need open sandals or flip-flops for beach, hotel and street. Roads are exceptionally sandy, so shoes should be strong enough to resist the pressure and open enough to be able to shake out the sand. Stouter shoes such as trainers (with socks) are recommended for excursions into the bush.

In public, visitors should respect Islamic customs: women should try to wear knee-length skirts, trousers or a wraparound piece of cloth and shirt; men are tolerated in shirt and shorts.

Hotels provide a laundry service.

Women Travellers

There's no particular obstacle preventing women from travelling solo in The Gambia, and the associated risks are not significantly greater than for men travelling on their own. That said, single women travellers do attract plenty of attention from local men, some of it bordering on harassment, and although no harm is intended, the regular stream of implicit sexual proposals can become exhausting. To some extent, this situation is a by-product of the sex tourism that attracts many European women to The Gambia, and if you make it clear that you're not interested, things are unlikely to go beyond unwanted banter. Away from the beach resorts, female travellers are advised to dress modestly, especially if they are alone. Some single women reckon that wearing a wedding ring does much to limit the unwanted attention, and many experienced female travellers will respond to an uncomfortable line of questioning by inventing a waiting husband or boyfriend.

LANGUAGE

UNDERSTANDING THE LANGUAGE

General

English is the official language of The Gambia and is almost universally spoken. In addition, the region has more than 10 indigenous languages. The most widespread is Wolof.

Useful Words and Phrases

Hello *Sala maleikum* (this is, in fact, Arabic)
Good morning *Jamm ga fanan*
Goodnight *Fanan jamm*
How are you? *Nanga def?*
I am well *Magni fi rek; Jamba rek* (used in The Gambia)
How is your family? *Ana waa keur ge?*
They are well *Nyunge fe*
Are you well? *Ba dara metee wula?*
Thank you *Jerejef*
Yes *Waow*
No *Deedeet*
Come *Kai*
Come here *Kai fi*
I would like/I want *Dama buga*
I want to eat *Dama buga lek*
To eat *Lek*
To drink *Naan*
Breakfast *Ndeki*
Lunch *Agn*
Dinner *Rer*
To go *Dem*
To come *Nyo*
I am going (= Goodbye) *Mangi dem*
I shall come back *Dina nyo at; dina delussi at*
Day *Betiek*
Night *Gudi*
Now *Leegi*
Today *Tey*
Yesterday *Demb*
Tomorrow *Elek; Souba*
See you tomorrow *Be soube*
Until next time *Be beneen yon*
Bread *Mburu*
Water *Ndoh*

Meat *Yap*
Fish *Jen*
Just a little *Tutti rek*
I am hot *Dama tange*
I am cold *Dama sedde*
I am thirsty *Dama maar*
I am tired *Dama sonne*
It is hot *Dafa tange*
It is cold *Dafa tsedde*
Where? *Ana?*
Here *Fi la*
There *Fale la*
Here *Fi*
There *Fofu*
Where is the market/hotel?
Ana marsé/hotel?
Do you speak English?
Degg nge Anglais (or *English*)?
I don't speak Wolof *Degguma Wolof*
I don't understand *Degguma*
How much? *Nyata?*
How much is this? *Bi, nyata le?*
It is too expensive *Dafa jafé*
Lower the price, please *Wanyi ko*
Good (It's good) *Baakhne*
It's bad (No good) *Baahul*
Wait! *Haaral!*
Go straight on *Talal*
Where is the restaurant?
Ana restaurant bi?
I want to get down here *Fi laay wach*
I have had enough to eat, thanks *Suur naa*
She (it) is pretty *Rafet ne*
It is good (of food) *Neehne*
My friend *Suma harit*
Give me *Joh me*
Sell me *Jai me*
Put it here *Bai ko fi*
Bring it *Indi ko*
Bring me a beer
Indi me beer (or *bière* in French)
Take this *Amm*
Excuse me *Baal me*
I am going to rest *Damai dem nopelu*
My wife *Suma jigeen*
My husband *Suma jekeur*

Tea (Senegalese-style) *Attaya*
Money *Halis*
I haven't any money *Anuma halis*
I have a headache *Suma bop dey meti*
I have a stomach ache *Sume biir dey meti*
Charity has already been made (a useful phrase to get rid of beggars) *Sarak be ague na*

Numbers

1	*Benn*
2	*nyar*
3	*nyet*
4	*nyent*
5	*juroom*
6	*juroom (ak) benn*
7	*juroom (ak) nyar*
8	*juroom (ak) nyet*
9	*juroom (ak) nyent*
10	*Fouk*
20	*nyar four*
30	*fan wer*
40	*nyent fouk*
50	*juroom fouk*
100	*teemeer*

BELOW: the school motto.

INSIGHT GUIDES
TRAVEL TIPS
SENEGAL

TRAVEL TIPS

TRANSPORT

ACCOMMODATION

ACTIVITIES

A – Z

LANGUAGE

T RANSPORT

GETTING THERE AND GETTING AROUND

GETTING THERE

By Air

Senegal is well connected to Europe, America and African countries. Dakar's Aéroport International Léopold Sédar-Senghor, 15km (10 miles) north of Dakar, is one of West Africa's main transportation hubs. There are several daily flights between Dakar and Paris, and frequent (often daily) direct connections to Belgium, Spain, Portugal, the US (New York), Brazil, Nigeria, Ethiopia, Kenya, South Africa, Morocco, Algeria, Guinea, Mali, Ivory Coast and other countries. Flights to the UK require a stopover in another city (usually Paris, Brussels, Casablanca, Madrid or Lisbon, depending on the airline).

The main airlines operating scheduled flights into Dakar include

BELOW: welcome aboard.

SN Brussels, Air France, Royal Air Maroc, TAP Portugal, Iberia, South African Airways and Air Sénégal. Several French tour operators run charter flights to Dakar, and often have very competitive offers. The largest one is Nouvelles Frontières. Visitors from Britain could buy a charter flight into The Gambia and continue to Dakar via Air Sénégal, though the small savings you'll make might not always justify the efforts to organise such a trip.

By Sea

If you wish to reduce your carbon footprint and have plenty of time, sea travel might be an option. Allow 8 to 10 days for this journey, and be ready for surprised faces – it's not a particularly popular way of travelling. Accommodation is on cargo boats from Liverpool, London or other European ports, which call

ABOVE: Dakar station façade.

at other ports en route and may even leave out a port if there is no reason to stop there for cargo. Not all ships allow passengers, so make your enquiries in good time. It is even less common for ships returning to Europe to take passengers, so you cannot count on obtaining a return ticket.

For details of European lines serving Dakar, contact the nearest Senegalese diplomatic or tourist representative well in advance of your intended departure date.

By Rail

The train journey from Dakar to Bamako (Mali) is something of a classic among adventure-seeking travellers, and the hype surrounding the trip seems to grow as the service deteriorates. In theory, there is one train a week ploughing the distance between Bamako and Dakar. However, the official schedule is ignored with astonishing consistency, and trains leave a day or two after whenever they've arrived. Delays (often of several days), cancellations and derailments are frequent. You need to check information on the ground, best by visiting the railway office at Dakar's stunning central train station near the port, or by calling the Dakar–Bamako Express train operators on 33 849 4646 and hoping that someone is going to answer the phone.

The journey takes around 48 hours if all goes well, though unlucky travellers have spent days on the train. A first-class sleeper seat costs around CFA52,000. Make sure you check current prices before travelling, as there's a strong chance they may have increased.

For relative comfort, make sure you buy a "first-class" ticket, take plenty of water, food and any comfort items you may need. Beware of your personal belongings – the train is a known working ground for pickpockets.

ABOVE: the road to Kafountine.

By Road

The famous Paris–Dakar rally may have found a new home, but for "ordinary travellers", the desert trip from North Africa and the Mediterranean to Senegal is becoming increasingly popular. The long and complex journey requires considerable equipment and planning and should only be attempted by groups in rugged 4x4 vehicles, preferably with an experienced guide. The shortest route passes through southern Morocco and Mauritania to the border at Saint-Louis. There are other routes via Algeria and Mali, though they are often closed due to rebel activity in Algeria and northern Mali.

In the south, a perfectly serviceable road connects Senegal with Guinea-Bissau, crossing from Fatim, in Guinea-Bissau, into Tanaf (Senegal). It is also possible to enter from Guinea; the crossing point is from Koundara (Guinea) into Vélingara (Senegal).

Overland connections between Senegal and The Gambia are reasonably efficient. The roads from Dakar via Kaolack to Barra (4 hours' drive) on the mouth of the Gambia River are manageable. The most popular connection with traders is the Trans-Gambia Highway that links Dakar and Farafenni. The journey takes around 5 hours. At Farafenni, a 15- to 20-minute car-ferry crossing takes you once every hour to Mansa Konko, from where a tarmac road with a reasonable surface goes east to Basse, west to Banjul (3 hours) or

south on to Ziguinchor in Senegal. Be prepared for a longish wait in the queue to get on the ferry.

If you cross the Gambia River at Barra, a ferry delivers you straight to Banjul. Customs and Immigration controls are at Karang on the Senegalese side and at Amdalai on the Gambian side. Make sure that your car insurance covers you in The Gambia. Cars insured in Senegal need extra cover for The Gambia.

To go to Barra from Kaolack, turn sharp right off the Trans-Gambia Highway after crossing the mud/salt flats, at a tumble-down signpost marked "To Karang".

Coming from the south, the Trans-Gambia Highway goes from Ziguinchor to Mansa Konko. At Bignona, there is a left turn to The Gambia via Diouloulou, which takes you to Banjul (2 hours). This route doesn't involve any ferry crossings, just the completion of customs and Immigration procedures on the Senegalese and Gambian sides of the border.

Taxis and minibuses ply all these routes. You usually have to change vehicles at the border, sometimes even twice – once to cross the border, then again just after arriving in Senegal/Gambia. This is usually straightforward, and other passengers or the taxi drivers will indicate to you the vehicles to take.

On Departure

For scheduled flights, you should confirm your flight 72 hours in advance with the airline in question or a travel agent. Most hotels will be

able to confirm tickets for you. Airport taxes are normally included in ticket prices. Airport Léopold Sédar-Senghor is well organised, and it's usually sufficient to arrive two hours before departure time.

GETTING AROUND

On Arrival

Once you step out of Dakar Airport, you will find yourself quickly surrounded by youngsters asking to carry your luggage, change money, find you a taxi and offering all sorts of unwanted services. Though these guys aren't usually dangerous, they can be hard to shake off, and quite frankly make for an unpleasant start to your Dakar adventure. If you do take up their services, CFA1,000 should normally be sufficient as a tip. You can change money at the airport, make calls, hire a car and make use of a variety of other services.

Airport/City Links

It's best to arrange for someone to meet you at the airport. Most hotels have courtesy minibuses to pick up guests that have reserved in advance. If you can't arrange pick-up, you can get a taxi. You will find rows of typical yellow-black taxis just outside the airport, on the right-hand side. The journey from the airport into town should cost CFA4,000, though drivers will inevitably try to get more. If you have a lot of luggage, you should leave an extra CFA1,000 as a sort of "baggage fee". Always make sure you negotiate the price clearly with the driver in advance in order to avoid complications later.

Public Transport

Buses

Dakar and its immediate surroundings are served by the reliable DDD (Dakar Demm Dikk) bus company, which covers all major routes around the city. Its website (www.demdikk.com) provides information on routes and fares. A typical bus journey is cheap at CFA150 per trip. This service is fairly reliable and comfortable, as long as you avoid rush hour (8–10am and 4–6pm). You buy your ticket at the conductor's booth when you board the bus.

Bus connections between Senegalese cities, including Kaolack, Tambacounda, Saint-Louis, Touba and Thiès, are provided by the *cars mourides* that are owned and run by Senegal's religious Mouride community. In Dakar, they leave from the bus station Pompiers, usually around midnight or 1am. You need to book a seat in advance by going to Pompiers, where you'll be directed to the ticket salesman.

The buses follow an organised schedule, but only leave once full, so be prepared for a late-night wait at the bus station. Upcountry bus journeys can also be extremely tiring. The vehicles are often packed and don't usually have air-conditioning or toilets, all making for a rather uncomfortable journey.

Minibuses and Cars Rapides

Various small minibuses provide public transport on the streets of Dakar. The white TATA vehicles are clean and reliable, though infrequent and limited in the number of routes they cover.

Dakar's iconic *cars rapides*, brightly painted blue-and-white minibuses in various states of decay, are not only battered and crammed, but also follow a network of routes no outsider can easily understand. Still, they're symbols of the city, and a journey in them is something of a classic, though rough, Dakar experience. You stop the bus by waving from the roadside and will be ushered into the bus, probably tear your clothes, and spend the journey squeezed between an astonishing number of people, bags of rice and quite possibly a couple of chickens. Most short *car rapide* journeys cost less than CFA100.

Taxis

Government-licensed and regulated taxis are painted yellow and black and circulate in the streets of Dakar. Though many of them are equipped with meters, those are invariably broken, and prices have to be negotiated before travel. If you don't know the approximate cost of a trip, aiming for half the initial amount proposed by the driver is usually a good guide to get to a reasonable rate. Short trips in the inner city should cost around CFA700, trips from Dakar plateau to neighbourhoods such as Point E around CFA1,500 to 2,000. Rising petrol costs immediately result in higher taxi rates, so these may well have changed by the time you read this.

Outside Dakar's main hotels you can also catch the so-called Sister Taxis, tiny yellow vehicles driven exclusively by women as part of a governmental campaign for women's equality. They may be slightly more expensive than regular cabs, but are often in a better state and less hard to negotiate than regular taxis.

Sister Taxis
Tel: 33 849 5949

Bush Taxis

Also known as *sept-places*, these are typically Peugeot estates carrying up to seven passengers, which ply the routes between Senegal's towns and villages. Every town has its garage *(gare routière)* from which the taxis leave. There are no schedules – taxis leave when they're full. It's therefore best to get to the *gare routière* early, around 8am, as most Senegalese tend to travel early, and chances for a quick departure are therefore better. If you have enough money and no time to wait, you can always offer to pay for empty seats, thus leaving earlier and even having more seating space in the usually packed vehicles.

Enquire at the *gare routière* for current fares. Long-distance rates are prescribed and therefore non-negotiable. If you have a lot of luggage, be prepared to pay a small additional baggage fee (usually about CFA100 per item).

Bicycles

The extreme heat, desolate state of the road system and "don't-care attitude" of drivers make bicycle tours dangerous and uncomfortable. Especially in the cities, the risk of accidents is great, as most drivers aren't used to watching out for two-wheeled vehicles and traffic is generally ruled by the law of strongest. Still, the country's flat lands invite keen cyclists for cross-country tours. Bicycle hire is rare in Senegal and more common with the hotels in southern Senegal and Saint-Louis than the hotels of Dakar.

Water Transport

The main sea journey within Senegal is the 12-hour trip from Dakar to Ziguinchor by the modern new boat MV *Aline Sitoé Diatta*. The boat leaves the port of Dakar every Tuesday and Friday. Boarding time is 2.30–5.30pm. Tickets should be bought in advance. You can book seats (CFA15,500) or beds in sleeper cabins of different sizes (CFA18,500–30,500). It is possible to transport cars (CFA63,000) and motorcycles (CFA30,000). There is an on-board restaurant.

BELOW: a journey in a *car rapide* is always an interesting experience.

ABOVE: the ferry bound for Gorée Island.

In the north of the country, the Senegal River is another navigable waterway. The Saint-Louis-based company Sahel Découverte organises picturesque cruise tours along the river with the classic boat *Bou el-Mogdad* from Saint-Louis to Podor.

The river is also crossed by the ferry to Rosso in Mauritania, one of the principal ways of entering Mauritania. Visas can be bought at the border.

A frequent ferry service connects Dakar and Gorée Island. Ferries leave every 1½ hours from the *embarcadère* near the port of Dakar. The journey takes 20 minutes; tickets (CFA5,000) can be bought right before the journey at the counter.

Aline Sitoé Diatta
Tel: 33 991 7200 (Ziguinchor)
Tel: 33 849 48 93 (Dakar)
Gorée Ferry
Tel: 33 849 7961
Fax: 33 823 8051
www.dakar-goree.com
Sahel Découverte
Tel: 33 961 5689
Fax: 33 961 8320
www.compagniedufleuve.com

Trains

The train service to Bamako also connects Dakar to Thiès, Diourbel and Tambacounda twice a week. As mentioned above, this train service is far from reliable, and all three towns are more easily reached by bush taxi. Still, the train is a good choice if you are up for an adventure.

Make sure you obtain information either at Dakar's central train station, a beautiful turn-of-the-century building near the port, or by phoning 33 849 4646.

Internal Flights

Air Sénégal International connects Dakar to Tambacounda, Saint-Louis, Ziguinchor and Cap Skirring. However, internal flights do not always adhere to schedule. The most reliable line is the Ziguinchor–Cap Skirring one. It only operates in high tourist season (November to April).

Air Sénégal International
Tel: 81 804 0404 (Senegal)
Tel: +33 8 20 20 21 23 (Europe)
www.air-senegal-international.com

Private Transport

There are several car-hire companies in Dakar, including Hertz, Avis and Budget. Hire tends to be expensive, especially when you are planning to take a car upcountry. Rates can be as high as CFA100,000 a day for a 4x4 vehicle – and that's excluding petrol and food/accommodation for the driver. Driving yourself is only an option if you are confident in negotiating dirt roads and potholes. If you do hire a self-drive vehicle, make sure hire includes full insurance and that the vehicle is roadworthy. A valid International Driving Licence is required to drive in Senegal. Driving is on the right.

Breakdown services are non-existent. If you can get access to a telephone, a call to your car-hire

agent will perhaps get them to come out to you. Otherwise you must have the car mended locally at one of the makeshift welding spots that serve as mechanics' workshops upcountry.

AVIS
Km 2.5 Boulevard du Centenaire-de-la-Commune-de-Dakar
Tel: 33 849 7757/7777
Fax: 33 849 7756
Budget
Avenue Lamine-Guèye
Tel: 33 889 7676
Fax: 33 822 2506
Hertz
64 Rue Joseph-Gomis
Tel: 33 822 2016/33 821 5623
Fax: 33 821 1721
www.hertz.sn
Sénécartours
64 Rue Carnot
Tel: 33 889 7777/33 869 5007
Fax: 33 820 4803
www.senecartours.sn

On Foot

The heat and distances are not conducive to walking tours in Senegal. The only area where hiking tours are common is the south-eastern corner of the country, near Kédougou. It's only here that the flat Senegalese landscape is made a bit more interesting by a few hills. Most hotels here can find you a local guide who can arrange and take you on exciting hiking expeditions. Some of the most reliable guides are found at the Hôtel Bédik (tel: 33 985 1000) and the Relais · de Tamba (tel: 33 981 1000).

A CCOMMODATION

HOTELS, HOSTELS AND *CAMPEMENTS*

Hotels

As a much larger and more varied country than The Gambia, Senegal has a wide range of accommodation, from the most basic of overnight facilities to luxurious modern 300-room hotels exactly as you would expect to find in Europe or the United States. Unlike The Gambia, where the vast majority of hotels are recently built and designed for tourism, Senegal also contains many small hotels in towns built from any time over the past century and which cater for travellers of all descriptions.

The general cultural background of the hotel industry in Senegal is predominantly French, and a number of small establishments run by French proprietors offer a service not dissimilar to that of French country inns.

It is impossible to list all hotels, hostels and travel lodges and campsites here, but a selection of the more prominent places follows. See also the text in the Places section for hints on accommodation. Note that, in some cases, a telephone number is unavailable; in others, a complete address is not given where a town is too small to warrant it.

The Senegalese Ministry of Tourism grades hotels on a scale of 0 to 4 stars, although the actual top category is 4 stars plus the letter L for luxury. This category would be occupied by large modern air-conditioned hotels with sizeable, well-decorated rooms with bath and toilet en suite. The lowest category would be a campsite or extremely basic small hotel without any of these facilities.

Where to Stay

In addition, the Casamance region is the centre for the project of village *campements*, a way of offering low-rent accommodation to travellers who are interested in experiencing village life at close quarters. The *campements* are run cooperatively by villagers and consist of huts exactly like the others in the village, furnished with between two and four simple beds equipped with foam mattresses and mosquito nets. Lighting is usually by paraffin lamp, and there will be simple separate WCs and showers. Basic meals will be offered, as well as the chance to participate in any activities that may be scheduled. *Campements* are situated in the following villages in the region: Elinkine, Enampor, Baila, Koubalan, Thionck Essyl, Affiniam, Abéné, Oussouye, Palmarin.

BELOW: Savannah hotel, Dakar.

ACCOMMODATION LISTINGS

DAKAR AND THE CAP VERT

ABOVE: sea views from Hôtel Lagon 2.

Dakar

Al Afifa
46 Rue Jules-Ferry
Tel: 33 889 9090
www.alafifa.com
It has something of a 1950s charm, this humble, wood-panelled place in the centre of town. Yet beyond the front door and the lobby lie pretty rooms and a leafy restaurant overlooking a pool. And with a slight effort, you can imagine that you're staying in one of Dakar's really classy hotels. **$$**

Auberge Good Rade
Sacré-Cœur 3 Extension, VDN
Tel: 33 860 6030/6090
Fax: 33 860 6040
It's named after a tyre and grown from a nightclub – none of which sounds particularly encouraging. But this hostel is good value for money. Accommodation is in clean, bright rooms or apartments, the rates are decent, and the location (halfway between the beach and the city) means that you're nowhere really, but everywhere quickly. **$**

Auberge Marie-Lucienne
Rue A, junction with Rue 2, Point-E
Tel: 33 869 0090
Fax: 33 869 0115
This simple hostel is in an excellent location – the neighbourhood Point-E is a safe, affluent residential area, with plenty of little shops and some excellent live music places. The hotel itself is a little run-down, but the rooms are more than adequate and wifi is free. A great option for the travellers lucky enough to get a room – it's usually full. **$**

Ganalé
38 Rue Amadou-Assane-Ndoye
Tel: 33 889 4444
Fax: 33 822 3430
Ganalé has gradually forged a solid reputation among independent travellers. There's nothing particularly exciting about this place – except the quirky bar – but it does the accommodating job really well, and at very decent rates. **$$**

Hôtel du Phare
36 Cité des Magistrats,
Les Mamelles
Tel: 33 860 3000
www.lesmamelles.com
Les Mamelles is an upcoming area close to the famous lighthouse, still cheap enough, but also quiet and residential. The Hôtel du Phare is just like that – a quiet, pretty, no-frills place that's affordable to those on a small budget and doesn't have the rough edges that define some of the low-price hostels. Phone to book, as they only have a handful of rooms. **$**

Hôtel Lagon 2
Route de la Corniche Est
Tel: 33 889 2525
www.lagon.sn
Adjacent to one of Dakar's best fish restaurants sits this newly refurbished, gleaming palace. Rooms aren't big – but the view is, and the whole place is done up in style. Service can be a bit rusty, but you can always hide in your smart sea-view parlour or on the hotel's private beach to get away. A good location for deep-sea fishing. **$$$**

Résidence Les Arcades
8 Avenue Djily-Mbaye
Tel: 33 849 1500
Fax: 33 849 1502
www.arcades.sn
Strictly not your average hotel, the Arcades seduces with prime apartments in the centre of town. A great choice for self-caterers, families and all those more comfortable in a home than a bland hotel. Rooms are large, well equipped and cared for, and there is a daily cleaning service. **$$**

Saint-Louis Sun
68 Rue Félix-Faure
Tel: 33 822 2570
Fax: 33 822 4651
This bright, leafy hotel in the heart of Dakar's busiest area is a favourite with independent travellers, and for good reason. It's safe, clean, pretty, offers free wifi, and the centre of town is right outside your doorstep. Rooms are a bit on the small side though. **$$**

Sofitel Teranga
Place de l'Indépendance
Tel: 33 889 2200
Fax: 33 823 5001
If efficiency, reliability and predictability are the things that say "comfort" to you, then the Sofitel is your place. This is your standard, round-the-world, four-star hotel. Great if you're not keen on surprises, probably not exciting enough if you seek thrills in every corner of your holiday. **$$$**

Sokhamon
Boulevard Roosevelt, junction with Avenue Nelson Mandela
Tel: 33 889 7100
Fax: 33 823 5989
www.hotelsokhamon.com
The artistic, quirky architecture of this place lies somewhere between pseudo-Arabic and cartoon castle. The room design is slightly less eccentric, and everything from the woven blankets to the wall paint has a handmade feel. The sea-view rooms get a guaranteed sunset from the balcony, otherwise you can enjoy this from the wooden terrace that leads from the restaurants onto the sea. **$$**

PRICE CATEGORIES

Price categories are for a double room:
$ = under US$50 (CFA25,000)
$$ = US$50–100 (CFA25,00–50,000)
$$$ = over US$100 (CFA50,000)

Gorée

Auberge Keur Beer
1 Rue du Port, Île de Gorée
Tel: 33 821 3801
Fax: 33 821 3801
This friendly, down-to-earth
hostel is one of the
cheapest, most easygoing
addresses on the island.
If there's no space in the
auberge itself, the owners
will usually find you a room
or apartment in one of
Gorée's houses, which
often works out more
comfortable. **$**
**Hostellerie du Chevalier de
Boufflers**
Île de Gorée
Tel: 33 822 5364
Fax: 33 822 5364
One of Gorée's long-standing
tourist ventures, this is a
guesthouse of utterly
reliable quality. It's most
famous for its restaurants,
but has great rustic accommodation spread over a few
old Gorée houses. **$$**

Lac Rose

Bonaba Café
Niaga Peul

Tel: 33 957 1256
Once you've found this
place on the far side of the
lake, you'll find yourself
rewarded with a calm and
relaxing stay in a small,
friendly guesthouse. Take in
the excursions they offer –
including a trip to the horse
stable not far from Bonaba.
$
Chez Salim
Niaga Peul
Tel: 33 836 2466 or 77 638 1019
Fax: 33 836 2053
www.chez-salim.com
This is just one of several
tourist addresses grouped
around Lac Rose. It's a
good one though, with
pretty rooms and a wide
range of excursions
(including beach-buggy
tours and camel
promenades). Beware
the bothersome traders
outside the front gates.
$$

Yoff and N'Gor

Archôtel
Route de N'Gor
Tel: 33 820 4163
Fax: 33 820 4207

It's easy to miss this place.
It's not glamorous and it's
not your cult place. It's
simply a well-run, basic
and surprisingly good little
hotel that seems a bit lost
among all the glamour of
the Almadies neighour-
hood. **$$**
Cap Ouest
Yoff Virage
Tel: 33 820 2469
Fax: 33 860 2307
This small, family-run hotel
may not look like much at
first glance, but is in fact
a bit of a bargain. The
recently refurbished rooms
are equipped with all the
basics you can expect at
this price. **$**
Chez Carla
N'Gor Island
Tel: 33 820 1586
Fax: 33 826 0035
Everybody loves Chez Carla
– N'Gor's longstanding,
homely place, that
encourages you to prolong
your beach day to include
both sunset and sunrise.
It's small, it's friendly, it's
rootsy – just like a home-
style guesthouse on a tiny
island should be. **$**

La Madrague
Plage de N'Gor
Tel: 33 820 0223
Fax: 33 820 0223
This hotel sits right on
Dakar's busy Plage de
N'Gor, where everything
from surfing to swimming
and diving is organised
within five steps' walking
distance. You're right in
the middle of the sun and
sea crowds here – on the
hotel's private stretch of
beach – so the place can
get noisy. **$$**
Méridien Président
Route des Almadies
Tel: 33 820 4704
Fax: 33 820 3956
Its reputation as Dakar's
top hotel is only now being
threatened, as new luxury
hotels emerge on the
Corniche. The Méridien has
all the conveniences you'd
expect at around US$300
a night, including a large
pool, several high-quality
restaurants and plenty of
shiny chrome everywhere.
Rooms are a bit of a let-
down though – pretty
enough, but lacking that
special touch. **$$$**

PETITE CÔTE AND SALY

Toubab Dialaw, Popenguine and Ndayane

Espace Sobo Badé
Toubab Dialaw (55km/35 miles
from Dakar)
Tel: 33 836 0356 or 77 573 1129
Fax: 33 836 0356
www.espacesobobade.com
Something of a cult address
among independent
tourists, Sobo Badé is
equally as renowned for its
quirky, seashell decor as its
excellent range of courses.
Activities include African
drumming and dance as
well as horse riding and
other sports. Tends to
attract young travellers
and backpackers. **$**
Iris Hotel
Toubab Dialaw
(55km/35 miles from Dakar)
Tel: 33 836 2969
Fax: 33 836 2991

Toubab Dialaw's largest
hotel is beautifully located
on the ocean. The place
looks slightly weather-
beaten, though rooms are
perfectly adequate, and the
apartments a particularly
good deal for families. Be
sure to book in advance, as
this is a favourite with
Senegalese conference
attendees. **$$**
Keur de Sable
Popenguine Beach, Popenguine
(70km/45 miles from Dakar)
Tel: 33 957 7164

LEFT: a bungalow in La Teranga Saly, in Mbour.

Fax: 33 957 7164
Run by a cultural association, this hotel sits right at the end of the dust road that runs parallel to the beach away from the village centre. It's a great place for anyone who prefers a rootsy experience over comfort. Accommodation is basic, but the young management are usually able to cook up some music or dance feat at short notice. **$**

La Pierre de Lisse
Ndayane
(55km/35 miles from Dakar)
Tel: 33 957 7148 or 77 547 7100
www.itinerairelisse.net
Places like this are hard to find – quite literally, as you need careful guidance along the signs on the dirt tracks to get there. Accommodation is in welcoming huts spread across a spacious terrain, and the management can't be beaten for its helpful attitude. Advance booking is essential – this *campement*'s reputation is spreading fast. **$**

La Somone and Saly

Au Petit Jura
Saly Niakhniakhal
Tel: 33 957 3767
www.aupetitjura.ch
If the mere thought of Saly's crowds and traders exhausts you, the village-like neighbourhood Niakhniakhal may be a better choice. The family-run Petit Jura sits on a fairly secluded part of Saly beach, and offers all the services of a top hotel in a more intimate setting. **$$**

Le Bassari
La Somone
(75km/45 miles from Dakar)
Tel: 33 957 7464 or 76 663 2409
Fax: 33 957 7463
La Somone is the calmer, prettier sister of the busy tourist centre Saly, and Le Bassari one of several pretty hotels. The decor calls the masks and clothes of the southern Senegalese Bassari people to mind, and accommodation is in huts inspired by their traditions. The only real drawback – La Somone's large sand beach is a walk away from the hotel. **$$**

ABOVE: Tama Lodge.

Les Bougainvillées
Place des Bougainvillées
Tel: 33 957 2222/3
Fax: 33 957 2225
In the heart of Saly's tourist centre, this is a popular place both with independent travellers and package tourists. It's simple, but the setting is attractive, and the rooms' small size is made up for by the simple charm of the decor. You'll need to book in advance to make sure of a reservation. **$$**

Club Baobab
La Somone
Tel: 33 957 7402
Fax: 33 957 7404
Club Baobab is easily the best-known place in town. It sits right on the beach, a stone's throw from the stunning lagoon the village is known for, and offers everything in beach-tourist comfort. Phone in advance, as the hotel is often booked up by tour agencies. Low season (May to October) is your best option. **$$**

Espadon
Saly Beach
Tel: 33 957 2066/1949
Fax: 33 957 2000
www.espadon-hotel.com
One of Saly's more luxurious addresses, the Espadon is a well-run, comfortable and attractive place. It's also known for its fish restaurant and fishing excursions that non-residents can also take advantage of. **$$$**

Lamantin Beach Hotel
Saly (northern end)
Tel: 33 957 0777/0696

Fax: 33 957 0697
www.lelamantin.com
This is a rare treat anywhere in Senegal – a truly luxurious, stunning hotel. Rooms are impeccable, and the food divine. The best thing, though, is the Thalasso massage centre. All of that five-star fun has its price of course – but every penny is well spent. **$$$**

La Médina
Saly Village
Terrain de Football
Tel: 33 957 4993 or 76 683 7447
Fax: 33 957 4993
Still an insider tip after years of existence, the Médina is an impressive three-storey building with a leafy patio, vaguely reminiscent of Mediterranean charms. This is not your sea-and-sun resort, but a great place to experience a bit of real village life, still in good proximity to Saly's restaurants, bars and clubs. **$**

Palm Beach
Saly
Tel: 33 939 5999
Fax: 33 957 2094
This is where tourism is big business. This vast hotel is usually booked, and a favourite with Senegal's touring agencies. It's run efficiently, though you might just feel like another tourist beast in a big herd. A no-frills, no-risk place. **$$**

Savana Saly
Tel: 33 939 5800
Fax: 33 939 5827
www.savana.sn

Unlike its Dakar sister, the Savana Saly is a place that's well run and offers great value for money. With two-storey huts arranged on a large garden space, it's great for peace and quiet. Particularly good for families, as there's plenty of space for running and playing, and apartments come with separate rooms. **$$**

Mbour

Tama Lodge
(85km/50 miles from Dakar)
Plage des Cocotiers, Mbour
Tel: 33 957 0040 or 77 569 9411
Fax: 33 957 0718
www.tamalodge.com
Right on a bathing beach, Tama Lodge convinces with the inspired design of its large, stylish huts. Dark wood, natural colours and African sculptures are the theme. The restaurant offers a great selection of imaginative dishes – best consumed in the atmospheric beach restaurant by candlelight. **$$**

La Teranga Saly
BP 14 Mbour
Tel: 33 957 4545
Fax: 33 957 4030
www.terangahotel.com
Thatched, two-storey bungalows are set in lush surroundings of baobab trees and bougainvillea. Facilities include three swimming pools and stylish restaurant. **$$$**

Village Petit Eden
Avenue Seydou Nourou Tall, Mbour
Tel: 33 957 4477
www.petite-eden.de
This friendly, German-run place is quite possibly the best value in town. It's not glamorous, but clean, sweet and cheap, and hotel staff are always ready to help out with organising trips around the country. **$**

TRANSPORT

ACCOMMODATION

ACTIVITIES

A – Z

LANGUAGE

SINÉ-SALOUM

ABOVE: a welcoming, cool interior.

Kaolack

Relais de Kaolack
Plage de Kundam
Tel: 33 941 1000
Fax: 33 941 1002
The busy trade and travel city of Kaolack is hardly holiday wonderland, and the Relais provides some welcome respite from the dust and bustle of this town. It's a clean, well-run hotel with comfortable rooms and a pool. It even sits at a "beach", which means a calm atmosphere and a bit of a view, rather than swimming and snorkelling. **$$**

Ndangane and Mar Lodj

Les Cordons Bleus
Ndangane
Tel: 33 949 9312
Fax: 33 949 9335
www.lescordonsbleus.com
Most people travel to Ndangane to catch the pirogue to the pretty island of Mar Lodj. If you wish to stay a bit longer, the Cordons Bleus is a good choice. It's spacious, with good-quality huts and a calm, relaxing atmosphere. As with Ndangane's other hotels, the owners will be happy to provide

assistance for a trip to Mar Lodj and other excursions. **$$**
Essamaye
Île de Mar Lodj
Tel: 77 555 3667 or 77 544 8918
www.senegalia.com
This simple holiday camp has a warm and welcoming atmosphere and a charming decor. Accommodation is basic, with simple huts providing a comfortable shelter, and there's a lively communal area. Enquire about excursions – the owners will be happy to help. **$**
Le Limboko
Île de Mar Lodj
Tel: 77 429 9908
www.limboko.com
This is one of many Mar Lodj holiday camps – most are equally as good. This one only consists of a few, recently built, spacious huts. Run by people who really know the area, it's also a good address for boat- and birdwatching tours in the waters of Mar Lodj. **$**

Palmarin

Djidjack
Palmarin
Tel: 33 949 9619
www.djidjack.com
Along the long stretch of

villages that form the Palmarin community you will find plenty of great accommodation options. Djidjack is a Swiss-run place that stands out through the huge *case à impluvium* (rain-collection hut) that forms the vast communal area. Accommodation is in pretty huts that sit in a well-tended garden. **$$**
Lodge des Collines de Niassam
Palmarin Ngallou
Tel: 76 669 6343 or 77 639 0639
www.niassam.com
One could suspect that this hotel was built with no one but honeymoon couples in mind – it's that romantic. Spacious huts are built into baobab trees and onto the water, and all get a great view over Palmarin's vast lands. The restaurant is great, and you can even do relaxation courses. Phone in advance – it's often booked up. **$$**
Royal Lodge
Palmarin

Tel: 33 957 6000
Fax: 33 957 6040
www.le-royal-lodge.com
If you've got US$200 or more to spare and a taste for luxury, the Royal Lodge is your place. With individual jacuzzis in each of the rooms, top-quality restaurants, massages on the menu and plenty more, it does its name justice. It's hard to find a more extravagant treat anywhere in Senegal. Phone for special deals in the low season. **$$$**
Le Yokam
Palmarin Ngallou
Tel: 77 567 0113 or 76 284 7072
This *campement* stands out for its friendly, young

BELOW: the restaurant terrace at Les Palétuviers.

ambience. It's one of Palmarin's cheapest places, and still offers simple, good-quality accommodation in straw-covered huts. The friendly, enthusiastic staff make you feel welcome and will help you out with the planning of trips. Clean and comfortable. **$**

Toubacouta

Le Bandiala
Missirah
Tel: 33 948 7735
Far off the beaten track, the Bandiala is the first address for most travellers keen to explore the forest part of the Siné-Saloum National Park. Phone in advance to make travel arrangements – this secluded camp is not easy to get to. Once there, you'll be rewarded with a unique natural atmosphere and plenty of animal sightings. **$**

Keur Bamboung
Toubacouta
Tel: 33 842 4052 or 77 510 8013
www.oceanium.org
There is no place quite like this far-flung, totally secluded, island-set eco-tourism camp. There's nothing but nature around you – specifically a protected sea area with waters, mangrove swamps

and forest to explore. If you love camping you'll adore this space, and you'll do a good thing for the village community that runs the camp, as they will benefit from the profits. Best check with Oceanium in Dakar for travel arrangements there. **$**

Keur Saloum
Toubacouta
Tel: 33 948 7715
Fax: 33 948 7716
www.keursaloum.com

Toubacouta is an unexpected small-scale tourist centre at the edge of a long dirt road. There are plenty of good places to stay. Keur Saloum is one of two large hotels. It provides excellent accommodation in quite secluded huts, has a good restaurant with an excellent river view and offers a good range of excursions. It's not one of Toubacouta's cheapest places, but it's restful and reliable – big hotel-style. **$$**

Les Palétuviers
Toubacouta, Région de Fatick
Tel: 33 948 7776
Fax: 33 948 7777
www.paletuviers.com
On the outskirts of Toubacouta, these thatched-roof bungalows are set amongst spacious grounds with views to the hotel's jetty. All rooms have showers, air-conditioning and mosquito nets. Mangrove tours and guided fishing tours can be organised. **$$**

BELOW: the thatched-roof bungalows at Les Palétuviers.

SAINT-LOUIS AND NORTHERN SENEGAL

Saint-Louis

Auberge La Louisiane
Quartier Pointe Nord
Tel: 33 961 4221/6115
www.aubergelalouisiane.com
For those travelling on a small budget, La Louisiane has been the favourite choice for years. Rooms

PRICE CATEGORIES

Price categories are for a double room:
$ = under US$50
(CFA25,000)
$$ = US$50–100
(CFA25,00–50,000)
$$$ = over US$100
(CFA50,000)

are basic but clean and cute, and you get a spectacular view across the river from the tiny garden restaurant. There's no air-conditioning – you'll have to make do with the ceiling fans. **$**

Hôtel de la Poste
Place de Lille
Tel: 33 961 1118/2313
This historical building greets you right after crossing Pont Faidherbe. It pays homage to Mermoz, the famous French air pioneer, and is also a top-quality hotel with good rooms, service and one of the best fishing clubs in the Saint-Louis region. **$$**

Hôtel de la Résidence
159 Rue Blaise-Diagne
Tel: 33 961 1260
Fax: 33 961 1259
www.hoteldelaresidence.com
One of Saint-Louis's oldest hotels, the Résidence is a classic place to stay, and every piece of colonial memorabilia drives the message of historical importance home. The patio restaurant is fantastic – both for atmosphere and quality of the meals – and management is helpful and knowledgeable when it comes to arranging trips around the region. Rooms are comfortable but a bit on the small side. Best to

book ahead as this is a popular spot. **$$**

Hôtel Sindone
Quai Henry Jay
Tel: 33 961 4244
Fax: 33 961 4286
www.hotelsindone.com
This beautifully restored old-style building not only overlooks the river, it

ABOVE: the colourful exterior of La Maison Rose in the heart of Saint-Louis.

has a lovely terrace restaurant where you can enjoy sumptuous meals right on top of the waters. Decorated in warm, earthen tones, the rooms suggest honeymoon romance. **$$**

La Maison Rose
40 Rue Potin junction
Blaise-Diagne
Tel: 33 938 2222/2220
www.lamaisonrose.net
Respectful restoration and tasteful decoration have turned this place into one of Saint-Louis's most prestigious addresses. Each piece of furniture looks like a rare discovery, hand-selected to match the individualised decor of each room. The suites are particularly beautiful. **$$$**

Sunu Keur
Quai Giraud-Nord
Tel: 33 961 8800 or 77 524 2732
www.sunu-keur.com
This cute hotel only has a handful of rooms, all set around a colourful patio in a classic Saint-Louis house. It's not in the most excitingly vibrant part of town, but the island is small enough for you to reach all places through short walks. With its friendly and helpful owners the place feels as close to a family home as you're going to get on a holiday abroad. **$**

Djoudj

Hôtel Djoudj
Parc du Djoudj
Tel: 33 963 8702
Fax: 33 963 8703
Most people tend to visit the Parc National du Djoudj on a day trip from Saint-Louis. But if you want more time among the crocs and pelicans – and nature-lovers will find plenty here to keep themselves occupied for two days or more – this basic, quite predictable hotel is your place to stay. **$**

Langue de Barbarie

Cap Saint-Louis
Langue de Barbarie
Tel: 33 961 3939
Fax: 33 961 3909
www.hotelcapsaintlouis.com
In close proximity to remote corners of the Parc National de la Langue de Barbarie and the historical charm of Saint-Louis, Cap Saint-Louis is a perfect place for exploring both, while enjoying the luxuries of a perfect beach holiday. With plenty of sports and leisure activities on offer and a vast terrain to explore, it's perfect for a family holiday. **$$**

Océan et Savane
Langue de Barbarie
Tel: 33 961 1260

Fax: 33 961 1259
www.oceanetsavane.com
For a holiday away from it all, you'll hardly find a better place than the Campement Océan et Savane, right on the Langue de Barbarie. Accommodation is in large Mauritanian tents or huts, but you're unlikely to spend much time under your rented roof, as the hotel offers a vast range of activities, ranging from canoeing and kayaking to fishing and birdwatching. Check for their tailor-made holidays. **$**

Zebrabar
Mouit Gandiol (Parc National de la Langue de Barbarie)
Tel: 33 962 0019 or 77 638 1862
Remote, secluded, spacious and friendly, this is the place to let your kids run wild while preparing outings to the Langue de Barbarie by fishing boat or kayak. The Swiss owners are excellent hosts with a vast knowledge of the area – rely on their guidance if you plan birdwatching tours or other specialised activities. **$**

Senegal River Region

Gîte d'Étape du Fleuve
Richard Toll
Tel: 33 963 3240

Fax: 33 963 3240
Richard Toll has a handful of places, and the Gîte d'Étape tends to be the hotel of choice for most northbound travellers. The restaurant is overpriced and overrated, but the rooms are good, clean, comfortable and air-conditioned. Facilities include a pool. **$$**

Maison Guillaume Foy
Quai Boubou Sall, Podor
Tel: 77 526 5200
www.podor-rivegauche.com
Among the run-down hostels, Catholic Mission and rooms above restaurants, the Maison Guillaume Foy is a rare treat. Rooms are located in a beautifully restored 19th-century trading house overlooking the old quay – Podor's best place. It's possible to organise excursions around the river region from here. **$$**

Oasis du Fouta
Ouro Sogui
Tel: 33 966 1294
Fax: 33 966 1296
Ouro Sogui is no beauty, and neither are its hotels. Among the available choices, the Oasis du Fouta is one of the better ones. An adequate and safe place to put down roots while exploring Matam, Bakel and surroundings. **$**

CENTRAL INTERIOR

Thiès

Hôtel Massa Massa
101 Cité Malick-Sy
Tel: 33 952 1244
Fax: 33 952 1244
This small guesthouse is mainly known for its restaurant – try the food here even if you don't spend the night. It has simple, clean rooms with fans or air-con for passing travellers. **$$**

Résidence Lat Dior
Opposite Thiès Stadium
Tel: 33 952 0777
Fax: 33 952 0779
Thiès's most upmarket place, Lat Dior has all the mod cons you would hope for in a hotel. The room decor is as uninspired as the design of the entire town, but the overall standard and service are good. A safe and comfy place that tends to attract conference guests and the odd tourist. **$$**

Touba, Mbacké

Le Baol
Mbacké
Tel: 33 976 5505 or 77 516 0199
Fax: 33 976 7254
There isn't really much choice of accommodation for overnight visitors to Touba: either you stay at the basic, but adequate Baol or you try to get a room in a private home. The holy city itself doesn't have any hotels, so the trip to Mbacké is inevitable for those in search of a roof. The Baol is a simple place, but wholly adequate. **$**

Lompoul

Le Lodge de Lompoul
Tel: 33 957 1256
Fax: 33 957 3811
It's best to get to this desert space in the midst of sand dunes with an

organised tour from Dakar, Thiès or Saint-Louis. You have to come equipped for the desert, as you'll stay in a Mauritanian tent, surrounded only by sand and camels. An unbeatable experience. **$$**

SOUTHEASTERN SENEGAL

Tambacounda

Keur Khoudia
Route Nationale
Tel: 33 981 1102
Fax: 33 981 1102
For a friendly, simple option, Keur Khoudia is one of the recommended places in Tambacounda. The rooms are basic (some have fans only and no air-con), but they're in good shape and are being made to feel well looked after. A good choice for those on a low budget. **$**

Le Relais de Tamba
Route de Kaolack
Tel: 33 981 1000
Fax: 33 981 3111
On the outskirts of dusty Tambacounda, the faintly luxurious and utterly decent Relais is the right place for respite after a long trip from Dakar or Niokolo-Koba Park. The rooms are comfortable, well maintained and air-conditioned, and management able to help out with arrangements for a visit to the National Park. **$$**

Kédougou

Le Bedik
Kédougou
Tel: 33 985 1000
If the rustic *campement* experience is not your thing, the Bedik with its bright, sparkling rooms, swimming pool and creature comforts should be your place of choice. It's Kédougou's most upmarket hotel – the right place to steel yourself before heading further upcountry into Bassari land. **$$**

Chez Diao
Kédougou
Tel: 33 937 9607 or 77 424 1561
Fax: 33 985 1278
Kédougou is such a vast sprawl of huts and alleyways it's hard to tell where the centre of town is. Chez Diao is centrally placed. Like most Kédougou camps, it's fairly basic, with clean, shared toilets and fan-cooled rooms. The young staff are hands-on when it comes to arranging anything from trips to Bassari land to bicycle hire. **$**

Le Nieriko
Kédougou
Tel: 33 985 1459
Kédougou thrives with small camps, usually consisting of a handful of straw-covered huts held together by super-relaxed staff. The Nieriko is no exception. It sits on the outskirts of town and hence feels totally secluded. Like most Kédougou camps, it only has basic amenities but plenty of character. The right place for a camping experience. **$**

Niokolo-Koba

Campement Villageois Dar Salam
Dar Salam
Tel: 33 981 2575 or 76 464 9459
At the entrance to the National Park, this humble, community-run camp is the place to get transport to Simenti from if you haven't arranged it already, get some more information and stock up on water. It really isn't much more than that – but if planning a visit to Senegal's rugged park, this is plenty. **$**

Hôtel Simenti
Simenti,
Parc National de Niokolo-Koba
Tel: 33 982 3650
Fax: 33 981 1102
It's hard to bypass Hôtel Simenti when visiting the Parc National de Niokolo-Koba. It sits right next to the park's prime animal-watching area and is one of the best places in the park to spot lions and other big animals. It's a practical place to stay – you can arrange tours and guides here – but it's not particularly pretty, and certainly not as glamorous

as safari lodges in other countries. **$$**

Bassari Land

Campement de Salemata
Salemata
Tel: 33 985 1400 or 77 654 4935
If you have ventured as deeply into the remote hills of Bassari land as you are likely to take a rest at Salemata, where this well-run camp welcomes you. It's good to know that all your spending goes directly back into the community. Ask the manager about any traditional dancing that might be happening. **$**

PRICE CATEGORIES
Price categories are for a double room:
$ = US$50 (CFA25,000)
$$ = US$50–100 (CFA25,00–50,000)
$$$ = over US$100 (CFA50,000)

TRANSPORT

ACCOMMODATION

ACTIVITIES

A – Z

LANGUAGE

CASAMANCE

Cap Skirring

Les Hibiscus
Plage de Kabrousse
Tel: 33 993 5136
www.hibiscus.sn
A short drive from the town centre and main beach of Cap Skiring, Les Hibiscus is a place for luxurious lounging. You can rent rooms, but the best accommodation is in the small villas, particularly if you're travelling as a family. **$$**

Hôtel Kaloa les Palétuviers
Cap Skirring
Tel: 33 993 5210
Fax: 33 993 5210
www.hotel-kaloa.com
In the centre of Cap Skirring, this large place is great for space, quiet and comfort. It's not on the beach (though not far), but next to a river, and in close proximity to Cap Skirring's restaurants, bars and clubs. Rooms are spacious and beautifully decorated. **$$**

Oudja Hôtel
Boucotte Beach
Tel: 77 228 9439
Fax: 33 991 2981
A short drive from Cap Skirring, this nicely secluded hotel sits steps away from a fantastically wide beach, away from the bustle of the Cap. The rooms are simple – basic roofs over your head for the moments you intend to spend away from the sand and waves. **$**

Le Paradise
Plage du Cap Skirring
Tel: 33 993 5129/5303
Cap Skirring Beach is helpfully lined with a number of small, simple holiday camps. Le Paradise is like many of them – an arrangement of adequate huts (you can choose en suite or really cheap rooms with shared bathrooms) that appeals to shoestring travellers in search of a good time. **$**

Royal Kabrousse Hotel
Plage du Cap

Tel: 33 993 51 26
Fax: 33 993 51 27
www.senegal-hotels.com
Overlooking the vast, sandy beach of Cap Skirring, located in lush tropical gardens, the hotel offers 50 well-appointed rooms. **$$**

Villa des Pêcheurs
Cap Skirring Beach
Tel: 33 993 5253
www.villadespecheurs.com
The Villa des Pêcheurs is one of the more upmarket places on Cap Skirring beach. It's more expensive, but also better-equipped and maintained than some of its neighbours. It's mainly intended for anyone interested in fishing vacations, but other tourists are welcome too. **$$**

Île de Karabane

Barracuda
Île de Karabane
Tel: 33 993 1127
You arrive and you feel as though everybody's been waiting for you. The Barracuda owes much of its reputation to its warm welcome and kind staff. It's also great for fishing excursions – with a bit of luck you may even spot dolphins. Phone in advance, and the hotel can arrange pick-up by boat from the mainland. **$**

Hôtel Carabane
Île de Karabane
Tel: 33 991 2685 or 77 569 0285
Fax: 33 991 2981
This lovingly done-up hotel once used to be a gover-nor's residence – just one of the colonial reminders you'll find on this island. It's one of the pricier places on the island, but also offers good-quality accommodation, fishing and birdwatching excur-sions and a welcoming atmosphere. **$$**

Kafountine and Abéné

A la Nature
Kafountine
Tel: 33 994 8524 or 77 609 3398

In line with Kafountine's dominant vibes, this place is very reggae indeed. The hammocks, colourful painting and drumming sounds indicate it from afar. It's intended to be a camp for chilling, enjoying and not doing much else. And for that it's perfect. **$**

La Belle Danielle
Abéné
Tel: 33 936 9542
It's one of the first places you'll stumble across when entering Abéné village. And though it's not the prettiest, it's quite possibly the most charming. A perfect address for all those keen on arranging tours around the region (you can hire bicycles here), not so good if you wish to be close to the beach. **$**

Esperanto Lodge
Kafountine Beach
Tel: 77 635 0280 or 33 994 2223
www.esperantolodge.com
Overlooking the river and the sea and adorned with plenty of greenery, hammocks and cute huts, this is one of Kafountine's prime locations. Make sure you take up their offers of excursions around the region – they're brilliant – and try the many flavours on the restaurant menu. **$$**

Le Fouta Djalon
Kafountine Beach
Tel: 33 936 9494 or 77 503 9922
Fax: 33 936 9494
Kafountine's wide, sandy beach is only a few steps up the dune from your comfy hut. That's all it should take to persuade anyone to stay here. The Fouta Djalon is all about relaxed beach comfort and does it really well. **$$**

ABOVE: dining by the pool at Les Hibiscus.

Le Kelediang
Kafountine
Tel: 77 542 5385
This rootsy eco-camp consists of several huts on a vast terrain thick with trees. It's right behind the beach, and hence has the best of all the worlds – including good food and company. **$**

Kolda

Hôtel Hobbe
Kolda
Tel: 33 996 1170
Fax: 33 996 1039
Kolda is a place hardly visited by anyone other than hunters and tourists on their way towards the Cap. For both, the Hôtel Hobbe is a good choice. They often arrange for hunting trips, though you'll need to book them in advance, and the oddly decorated rooms provide enough comfort for a passing traveller. **$$**

Village *Campements* Lower Casamance

Campement d'Affiniam
Affiniam
Tel: 33 936 9619
Among all of the stunning village camps, the Campement d'Affiniam ranks among the most impressive. It consists mainly of a large *case à impluvium* – a traditional hut designed to collect rainwater, placed on the edge of a small village in the forest. It's easily reached by boat and road, and there's a whole range

BELOW: Cap Skirring Beach.

of activities (including cooking, traditional dance, experiencing village life) on offer. **$**

Campement de Coubalan
Coubalan (north of Ziguinchor, south of Bignona)
Tel: 33 992 0073 or 77 578 2091
This village-run *campement* sits romantically close to the edge of a small stream. A large, round hut has nine rooms available for rent to people keen to get a taste of village life and give something back to the community. There's no electricity – lighting is secured with oil lamps. **$**

Campement Enampor
Enampor, near Brin
Tel: 33 993 0038 or 77 441 4484
Some 25km (15 miles) of dirt track from Ziguinchor, this enormous *case à impluvium* was the first village camp ever to be created. There is running water but no electricity, and the village surroundings allow for exciting and insightful tours exploring the heritage of the Diola people. Phone to arrange transport to take you there. **$**

Campement Villageois Oussouye
Oussouye
Tel: 33 993 0015
Halfway between Ziguinchor and Cap Skirring, Oussouye is a beautiful, quiet, forest-surrounded village that is worth exploring for a day or two. The village camp is housed in a stunning,

traditional-style mud-brick house *(maison à étage)*, where the air stays naturally cool. Excursions can be arranged by the accommodating staff or the Oussouye-based bike-hire company Casamance VTT. **$**

Ziguinchor

Le Flamboyant
Rue de France, Ziguinchor
Tel: 33 991 2223/3578
Fax: 33 991 2222
www.flamboyant.info
This steadily expanding place is pretty much perfect. Rooms are excellent value – entirely affordable and equipped with all amenities from double beds to satellite TV and air-conditioning. The best thing about it is the helpful staff, though, who are able to give you reliable information (including security updates) about the region and sort out your trips upcountry. **$$**

Le Kadiandoumagne
Embarcadère de Boudady, Ziguinchor
Tel: 33 938 8000
Fax: 33 991 1675
www.hotel-kadiandoumagne.com
One of Ziguinchor's largest hotels, this attracts lots of groups and individual travellers. It's an excellent option for anyone in search of a bit of comfort, and it's entirely wheelchair-accessible. Even if you don't stay here, try the fantastic restaurant. **$$**

ACTIVITIES

THE ARTS, NIGHTLIFE, FESTIVALS, SPORTS, SHOPPING AND NATIONAL PARKS

ACTIVITIES

Most tourists arriving in Senegal choose the beaches of the Petite Côte as their primary destination. From swimming to surfing and fishing, the main tourist resorts offer plenty of activities for beach-lovers. Horse riding and cycling are becoming increasingly attractive. Many independent travellers choose excursions to the remoter areas inland over the populated tourist zones. And if you can't go without the city thrills, Dakar has plenty to offer in terms of nightlife, live music and the arts.

THE ARTS

Senegal is a great place for artistic activity. Dakar in particular has a vibrant music scene as well as several museums and galleries. The main exhibition space is the Musée Théodore Monod d'Art Africain (ex-IFAN), Place de Soweto, which has a collection of masks and musical instruments, as well as a space for contemporary arts. In the north of Dakar, the Village des Arts hosts galleries by many of Senegal's great visual artists. In the centre of town, the Galerie Le Manège, part of the Institut Français, often has great exhibitions by Senegalese and international artists, and the Place du Souvenir on the Corniche has two excellent gallery spaces with changing displays. On Gorée Island, the Musée de la Femme, the Fort and Maison des Esclaves are museums and historical spaces to explore. A visit during the visual arts

ABOVE: the Alliance Franco-Sénégalaise in Zinguichor, Casamance.

festival Dak'Art Biennale is highly recommended. During this time, the city is brought to life by a multitude of formal and informal exhibitions featuring artists from across the continent.

Dakar's Théâtre National Sorano is a great place to see concerts, plays and dance performances. Other live concert venues range from the national stadium, where major international stars perform frequently, to tiny music cafés. The Institut Français features concerts by some of Senegal's greatest performers almost every week.

Musée Théodore Monod d'Art Africain
Place de Soweto, Dakar
Tel: 33 825 0090 or 33 824 4918
Galerie Le Manège
Rue Parchappe
Tel: 33 823 0320
Galerie Atiss
12 Avenue Albert-Sarraut
Tel: 33 823 1877
Galerie Kemboury
Canal 4, Point-E
Tel: 33 825 4843

NIGHTLIFE

Dakar nightlife is vibrant and sexy, with clubs and bars lining much of the inner city and especially the northbound Route des Almadies. In addition, live popular music is available both at large open-air concerts and in clubs. Top Senegalese artists and groups such as Youssou N'Dour and Thione Seck have their own clubs, and often hold residencies at other places.

Nightclubs open late. At midnight they might still be three-quarters empty, and 4am is about the time of maximum activity. Admission is usually around CFA5,000 (ladies often go free). Some addresses are:
Just 4 U
Km 2, 5 Avenue Cheikh-Anta-Diop
Tel: 33 824 3250
Blue Note
Route de N'Gor
Tel: 33 820 4551
Koulgraoul
Route de la Corniche Est

Pen-Art
12 Boulevard du Sud, Point-E
Tel: 33 864 5131
Duplex
Route de N'Gor
K-Club
Route de N'Gor
Sénat
Méridien Palace

FESTIVALS

Senegal has a packed festival
calendar. Every year, new music,
theatre, dance and film festivals
see the light while others disappear.
There are two main festival seasons
– the month of December, when the
dry season is at its cool height, and
May/June, before the rainy months
kick in.
The Dak'Art Biennale (www.dakart.org)
Held every two years in May, this arts
festival showcases the very best in
contemporary African art.
**Festival International du Film de
Quartier** (www.festivaldufilmdequartier.com)
Held in December, this is an annual
screening of Senegal's contemporary
film.
Kaay Fecc Dance Festival
(www.kaayfecc.com) Held in June, this is
one of Africa's most popular dance
festivals featuring traditional and
contemporary dance.
**Saint-Louis International Jazz
Festival** (www.saintlouisjazz.com) This
legendary jazz festival takes place
every May/June.

BELOW: wrestling posters.

SPORTS

Cycling

While cycling in the city of Dakar
can hardly be recommended due
to the huge safety risks, the often
deserted roads and flat lands
upcountry lend themselves to
bicycle excursions. To be safe, best
bring your own helmet. It's best to
go with an experienced guide to
avoid getting lost, getting stuck with
a flat tyre or getting bored having
chosen the wrong routes.
Fédération de Cyclisme
73 Avenue Peytavin, Dakar
Tel: 33 822 5567
Espace Sobo-Badé
Toubab Dialaw
Tel: 33 836 0356 or 77 573 1129
www.espacesobobade.com
Hôtel Cap Saint-Louis
Langue de Barbarie, Saint-Louis
Tel: 33 961 3939
www.hotelcapsaintlouis.com
Hôtel de Wassadou
Village de Wassadou
(near the Parc National de Niokolo-
Koba and Tambacounda)
Tel: 33 982 3602
Casamance VTT
Oussouye, Casamance (on the way
from Ziguinchor to Cap Skirring)
Tel: 33 993 1004
http://casavtt.free.fr
Hôtel Le Fouta Dialon
Kafountine Beach, Casamance
Tel: 33 936 9494 or 77 503 9922

ABOVE: Dak'Art Biennale poster.

Diving

Senegal may not have much in the
way of stunning coral riffs, but diving
is still an exciting activity that draws
a large number of tourists. The
Océanium in Dakar is a place that
combines tourist diving with an
environmental ambition, being an
important centre of environmental
research at the same time.
   Apart from the addresses below,
major hotels in Saly, Palmarin and
the coastal areas of the Casamance
usually offer diving, pirogue rides,
kayaking and other sea sports – and
not only to residents.
Océanium
Route de la Petite Corniche Est,
Dakar
Tel: 33 822 2441
www.oceanium.org
Nautilus Club
Plage de N'Gor
Tel: 77 637 1422
www.nautilus-dakar.com
Atlantic Évasion
Plage de N'Gor, Dakar
Tel: 33 820 7675
www.atlantic-evasion.com
Aqua Passion Plongée
Club Baobab, Hôtel Baobab,
La Somone (near Saly)
Tel: 33 958 5049 or 77 654 3139
www.aqua-passion-plongee.com

Fishing

Fishing is a main branch of Senegal's
economy, and though fish stocks are
dwindling rapidly, the small impact
sports fishing has on those numbers
is not hugely detrimental to the
environment.

From a boat in the *bolongs* off the Casamance and Saloum rivers and their substantial estuaries, a whole range of river and sea fish can be caught. Underwater fishing, for which insurance is obligatory, takes place particularly in the Cap Vert region for larger grouper and barracuda.

In Dakar, the Embarcadère de Gorée and Plage de N'Gor are good starting points for enquiries about and booking of fishing trips. Many of the hotels in Saint-Louis, Saly, Cap Skirring and other coastal places offer fishing activities. Some of the most popular places are listed below.

West African Sport Fishing
Embarcadère de Gorée
Tel: 33 823 2858
Fax: 33 823 4837
Atlantic Évasion
Plage de N'Gor
Tel: 33 820 7675
www.atlantic-evasion.com
Hôtel de la Poste
Saint-Louis
Tel: 33 961 1118
Marlin Club
Saly
Tel: 33 957 2477 or 77 245 0017
Fax: 33 957 2477
Arcandia
Saly
Tel: 33 957 2012 or 33 958 5055
www.arcandiafishing.com
Keur Saloum
Toubacouta
Tel: 33 948 7715
www.keursaloum.com
Villa des Pêcheurs
Cap Skirring

Tel: 33 993 5253
www.villadespecheurs.com
Diattacounda
162 Kabrousse
Tel: 33 993 5400 or 77 452 2133
www.diattacounda.com

Horse Riding

If lazing at the beach loses its excitement, break the rhythm with a beach tour on horseback. Numerous places offer horse-riding excursions and courses for beginners. It's best to bring your own helmet, as they are not always provided – especially if you are planning a tour with your children.
Hann Poney Club
Hann (at Hann Zoo)
Tel: 33 832 0652 or 77 638 9058
www.poneyclubdakar.com
Espace Sobo-Badé
Toubab Dialaw (a 2-hour taxi ride from Dakar)
Tel: 33 836 0356 or 77 573 1129
www.espacesobobade.com
Les Cavaliers de la Savane
Toubab Dialaw
Tel: 77 637 3215 or 77 569 0365
Les Chevaux du Lac
Lac Rose (1 hour from Dakar)
Ndiaga Village
Tel: 77 630 0241 or 77 646 6532

Surfing

Surfing is steadily growing in popularity. The rugged, windy shores that line the north and west of the Cap Vert peninsula make for excellent surfing spots. The sport is not yet supported by a great

infrastructure. The few addresses below can help you get in touch with the people in the know, hire boards and arrange courses.
Tribal Surf Shop
Yoff Virage, Dakar
Tel: 33 820 5400 or 77 646 0914
Surf Camp Chez Omar
N'Gor Village, Dakar
Tel: 77 658 6926
Surf Camp Adventure
Île de N'Gor, Dakar
Tel: 76 687 3467
Ibys Loisirs
Nianing (south of Saly)
Tel: 33 957 2489 or 77 573 6677

Swimming

Dakar may lie at the tip of a peninsula, yet its beaches are quite dire. Many of its safe shores are either polluted or overcrowded, while the wide northern beaches are too dangerous for swimming. The most popular beaches around Dakar are the Plage de N'Gor and the Île de N'Gor opposite, reached via a short pirogue ride (boats leave permanently throughout the day). Another good choice is the beach of Gorée Island, a 20-minute ferry ride from Dakar.

The best areas for swimming are the coastlines along the Petite Côte and Cap Skirring in the Casamance. Saly is the busy tourist centre of the Petite Côte and has great, wide beaches, though you might find the small neighbouring villages such as Toubab Dialaw, Popenguine and Mbodiène calmer and slightly more private.

BELOW: traditional crafts for sale in the Marché Kermel, Dakar.

ABOVE: take a beach tour on horseback.

Cap Skirring is slowly picking up again as a tourist centre. The Cap has everything a centre of beach tourism needs, and most hotels and camps sit directly above the wide, golden sand shore.

If you prefer the safety of a swimming pool, try the Piscine Olympique in Dakar, that also hosts a great sports centre. Otherwise, the pools at Dakar's top hotels can be used by non-residents for a fee (CFA5235–10470/US$10–20). The pools at Sofitel, Meridien and Novotel are particularly good.

Piscine Olympique
Point-E, Dakar
Tel: 33 869 0606
www.pon.sn

SHOPPING

To pick up souvenirs from your Senegal holiday, you can brave the local markets, where fabrics, woodcarvings, recycled-metal toys, sand paintings and batiks coexist peacefully with cheap household items and second-hand clothes. A more relaxed, though less exciting and much more expensive option are souvenir shops and boutiques. On the markets, haggle with determination to get a reasonable rate. Some shops have negotiable prices too, though fixed prices are part of their appeal.

The largest market in Dakar is the sprawling Marché Sandaga, which by now covers much of the inner city with street-side stalls and roaming traders. This is the place to find anything, if you have the patience to squeeze through packed streets, shake off over-eager traders and keep your bag safe from pickpockets. The beautiful Marché Kermel is a short walk or drive from here (off Avenue Hassan II). This covered market sells mainly groceries, meat, fish and flowers, but also has a few stalls trading in tourist items. For cloth, try Marché des HLM, in a slightly poorer part of town. If you wish to have African clothes sewn on-site, simply ask your cloth-seller for a good tailor and take your purchase there to be sewn.

Any taxi driver can take you to those markets. It's useful to go in the company of a local guide you know and trust to help you find your way around and get good deals. Beware of guides offering their services: few of them are serious, and you risk becoming a victim of scams or even being mugged.

For shops, try the Corniche, near the area of Soumbédioune. Before the expansion of the road, this used to be the home of a vibrant crafts market. Today, there are fewer artisans, though you still find a number of stalls across the road. A few other shops and galleries selling original artwork are listed below.

Atiss: 12 Avenue Albert-Sarraut
Tel: 33 823 1877
A cross between a furniture shop and art gallery, this place offers a tasteful selection of beautifully designed items. In a side street not far from the main shop, you will also find sandals and handbags made from woven cloth.

Cocktail du Sénégal: 108 Rue Moussé-Diop
Tel: 33 823 53 15
This shop has one of the largest and most original selections of souvenirs in the country. Great for batik items, glass paintings and woodcarvings.

Galerie Arte: 5 Rue Victor-Hugo
Tel: 33 821 9556
www.arte.sn
A great place to buy originals by contemporary artists as well as precious pieces of traditional art.

Galerie Antenna: 9 Rue Félix-Faure
Tel: 33 822 1751
Far from a souvenir shop, this gallery features an exclusive selection of contemporary and classic pieces of art – sold exactly at the high rates the items are worth.

NATIONAL PARKS

Senegal has a large number of National Parks. You won't find the Big Five here, but plenty in the way of birds. In December and January, European migrants join the bird populations of Senegal – a feast for bird-lovers. Other animals frequently seen in Senegal's parks include several kinds of antelopes, monkey species, gazelles and crocodiles. The Parc National de Niokolo-Koba in the southeast of Senegal is at 73,000 hectares (180,000 acres) one of the largest big mammalian reserves in West Africa. This is the only place in Senegal where you have a chance of spotting elephants and lions. The park is well equipped with hotels and camps, though the infrastructures are not as advanced as in the parks of eastern and southern Africa.

Parc National des Oiseaux du Djoudj
In the northeast, not far from the mouth of the River Senegal, 60km (40 miles) from Saint-Louis by good sand road. This is the gathering place for millions of migrating birds. The best time to visit is between November and March.

Parc National du Delta du Saloum
Eighty km (50 miles) west of Kaolack. The park is dotted with small islands, mangrove swamps, sand dunes and stunning lagoons. You will find pink flamingos, storks and many other birds here. Some of the best holiday camps and hotels are found in Palmarin and Toubakouta.

Parc National de la Langue de Barbarie
A refuge for birds and turtles, this park is a narrow strip of sandy land between the Atlantic Ocean and the Senegal River. Easily reached from Saint-Louis, this is a great place for birdwatching and pirogue tours.

Parc des Îles de la Madeleine
Just off the Corniche in Dakar, this tiny, rocky island is great for nature-lovers and birdwatchers. It is reached by canoe from the Corniche.

For more information on game- and birdwatching, see page 304.

For more information on game- and birdwatching, see page 304.

A – Z

A HANDY SUMMARY OF PRACTICAL INFORMATION, ARRANGED ALPHABETICALLY

A dmission Charges

This is an approximate guide to admission fees in Dakar. Outside the capital and the tourist centre Saly, everything is much cheaper, and entry fees rarely reach the equivalent of CFA5,235 (US$10).
Nightclub (weekend): CFA5,235–1,3088 (US$10–25).
Live Concert Théâtre Sorano: CFA1,3088–2,6175 (US$25–50).
Live concerts: free to CFA7,853 (US$15).
Museums: free to CFA2,618 (US$5).

B udgeting for Your Trip

Senegal is not a cheap place compared to other West African nations. Especially in Dakar, you might find your travel budget shrink fast, and global price rises for petrol and food have caused steep price hikes in Senegal too. If you plan to self-cater, be aware that imported foods in supermarket cost twice to three times the amount you'd pay in Europe or the US. Please note that the prices quoted

below are likely to increase rapidly in line with global developments.
Airport Transfers: The official taxi rate is CFA4,000 (US$10), though you have to bargain hard to get this rate, and you will usually be charged more, especially if you have a lot of luggage. Don't pay more than CFA6,000 (US$14).

BELOW: supermarket in Saly.

Car Hire (see also Transport chapter): Rates start from around US$60 for a small car to be used in Dakar and quickly go up to US$175 and more if you're after a rugged 4x4 to take you to remote areas.
Hotels: Dakar hotels are invariably pricey. You have to be lucky to find basic accommodation for less than CFA30,000 (US$70). The city's top hotels charge up to CFA150,000 (US$350) per night. Prices are much cheaper anywhere outside Dakar, where you may find simple rooms from CFA10,000 (US$23) upwards.
Restaurants: For a plate of rice and sauce in a simple, local eatery, you'll pay around CFA2,000 (US$5). Shawarmas, burgers and other fast food also start at US$5. Lunch or dinner in a Dakar restaurant starts at around CFA4,000 (US$9), excluding drinks.
Taxis: Taxis have no meters, and fares in Dakar need to be negotiated. Short journeys in Dakar start at around US$5. Dakar to N'Gor

should cost around US$7 one way. Hiring a taxi for a whole day costs around US$80. Prices of regular bush-taxi rides are fixed, but are rising quickly due to the increasing cost of fuel. Check at the garage before travelling.

Business Travellers

Dakar has become quite a hub of business travel. Most major hotels cater for business travellers with conference rooms of different sizes, business centres and wireless internet (often free of charge).

Children

There isn't much in terms of specific children's activities in Senegal, though children are welcome almost everywhere, and most hotels and restaurants are keen to "improvise" if necessary to make kids and parents more comfortable. Child-friendly restaurants include LGM (tel: 33 825 5554), which has a small playground and does fantastic pancakes, the Institut Léopold Sédar-Senghor (tel: 33 823 0320), where kids can try their hand at reverse-glass painting after a great meal at the friendly café. La Gondole (tel: 33 823 9958) is best for ice cream.

Magic Land (Route de la Corniche Ouest; Tue and Thur 5–10pm, Wed and Fri 4–10pm, Sat and Sun 2–10pm; entrance charge; tel: 33 842 7307) is a theme park complete with Ferris wheels, merry-go-rounds and other sttractions, though relatively steep admission fees (CFA2,500/US$6) mean that it's often strangely empty.

A 65km (40-mile) ride from Dakar, children will enjoy the Réserve de Bandia (tel: 33 958 2024; www.reserve debandia.com) with its imported rhinos, buffalos, giraffes and other animals, and love spotting pelicans, croco-diles and flamingos at the vast Parc National des Oiseaux du Djoudj near Saint-Louis *(see also Senegal River chapter).*

Difficult travel conditions and rudimentary health services in the rural regions render travel around the country with very young children difficult. If you do feel up to the challenge, make sure that you have ensured health coverage (including malaria prophylaxis) and carry any special baby food and other items you may need. Nappies and infant milk are easy to get hold of in urban centres such as Saint-Louis, Thiès and Dakar, but may not be available in small towns.

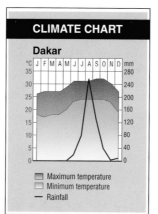

CLIMATE CHART

Dakar

- Maximum temperature
- Minimum temperature
- Rainfall

Climate

Senegal has a subtropical climate. Thanks to its coastal position, Dakar is relatively "cool" compared to the regions inland, meaning that temperatures rarely exceed 35°C (95°F), as they do in places such as Tambacounda or Podor.

The dry season runs from November to April/May with sunshine, an average temperature of 72–74°F (24–26°C) and a cool breeze blowing off the sea. In the eastern interior of Senegal, however, temperatures can reach considerably higher, into the 30°C or even 40°C (85–105°F) bracket. During those months, it can get chilly enough in the evenings for long sleeves and jackets. Except for very rare freak storms, it won't rain.

From January to March, the desert wind Harmattan brings thick red dust with it that settles everywhere and can cause health problems for asthma sufferers.

During the wet season (June to September), humidity rises drastically (80 percent or more), which makes the high temperatures (average 84°F or 28°C) seem even hotter. Rain falls in

torrential downpours with high winds, lasting a few hours at most, giving way to clear skies and a brief cool respite before the sun and humidity take over again. In Dakar, rains are fairly infrequent, while the Casamance sees almost daily rainstorms during that season. The hottest months are May/June and September on the coast, March/June and October inland.

Crime and Safety

Senegal is a fairly safe country with a relatively low crime rate. It is generally safe to walk around, even after dark, as long as you don't take any unnecessary risks and avoid certain areas, such as the Petite Corniche (the hill rise along the coast starting behind the Sofitel), deserted beaches and lonely side streets.

The greatest worry in Dakar is street crime, including muggings and scams. When walking around the inner city you will invariably be approached by street vendors, trying to sell you all sorts of souvenirs. Not only can they be extremely hard to shake off, they are also often pick-pockets, distracting you with their wares to get hold of your wallet.

Avoid using your mobile phone in the street, and take care of your belongings in public places. Dakar's markets and beaches are the main working grounds for pickpockets, so avoid carrying large bags and valuables with you.

All the larger hotels have safes, and you are advised to use them for valuables and documents. In the case of a lost passport, notify your country's High Commission, embassy or consulate and ask for a certificate of loss and a temporary passport. Lost travellers' cheques, credit cards or chequebooks should be reported immediately to the local banks as well as to your issuing bank at home by phone.

BELOW: colourful inflatable toys for sale.

ABOVE: a pharmacy in Dakar.

Customs Regulations

Senegalese duty-free allowance consists of: two cameras, a cine camera, a portable radio receiver, a portable record player, a laptop, personal jewellery, 200 cigarettes, 50 cigars, 250g of tobacco and your personal clothing.

D isabled Travellers

Facilities for disabled travellers are very rare and usually restricted to the top hotels (eg Novotel, Méridien). Many restaurants are wheelchair-accessible, but the roads are very hard to negotiate for wheelchair users. Travellers with particular needs should contact their hotel before setting out to see what kinds of services are available. Staff are usually more than happy to assist.

E mbassies

Senegalese Diplomatic Representation Abroad

Belgium
196 Avenue Franklin-Roosevelt,
1050 Bruxelles
Tel: 02 673 0097
Email: ambassade.senegal@coditel.net
France
14 Avenue Robert-Schumann,
75007 Paris
Tel: 01 47 05 39 45
www.amb-senegal.fr
Germany
Dessauerstr 28/29,
10963 Berlin
Tel: 030 85 62 19-0
Fax: 030 85 62 19-21
www.botschaft-senegal.de

Italy
Via Giulia 66, 00186 Rome
Tel: 06 687 2381/06 687 2353/
06 686 5212
Fax: 06 6821 9294
Email: ambasenequiri@tiscali.it
Sweden
8 Skeppsbron, 1st Floor, Box 2036,
Stockholm
Tel: 08 411 7160
UK
39 Marloes Road, London W8 6LA
Tel: 020 7938 4048 or 020 7937
7237
Fax: 020 7938 2546
www.senegalembassy.co.uk
US
2112 Wyoming Avenue, Washington
DC 2000
Tel: 212 279 1953

Embassies in Dakar

Austria
26 Boulevard Pinet-Laprade
Tel: 33 849 4000
Belgium
Route de la Corniche Est
Tel: 33 821 2524
Canada
45 Boulevard de la République,
4th Floor
Tel: 33 889 4700
Cape Verde Islands
1 Rue de Denain
Tel: 33 821 1873
France
1 Rue Elhadji Amadou-Assane-Ndoye

Electricity

The major towns are all well supplied with reliable mains electricity. The voltage is 220V. Two-pin plugs are standard.

Tel: 33 839 5100
www.ambafrance-sn.org
Guinea
Km 4/5, Route de Ouakam
Tel: 33 824 8606
Guinea-Bissau
Point-E, Rue 6
Tel: 33 824 5922
Italy
Rue Elhadji Seydou Nourou Tall
Tel: 33 822 0076
Ivory Coast
2 Avenue Albert-Sarraut, 3rd Floor
Tel: 33 869 0270
Mauritania
37 Avenue du Général-de-Gaulle
Tel: 33 823 5344
Netherlands
37 Rue Kléber
Tel: 33 849 3060
Portugal
5 Avenue Carde
Tel: 33 864 30 17
Spain
18–20 Avenue Nelson-Mandela
Tel: 33 821 3081 or 33 823 9137
Email: emb.dakar@mae.es
UK
20 Rue du Dr-Gillet
Tel: 33 823 7392
www.britishembassy.gov.uk
US
Avenue Jean-XXIII
Tel: 33 823 3424 or 33 825 3681

Entry Requirements

Full valid passports are required for anyone entering the country. Citizens of EU and UMEOA countries, the US, Canada and South Africa do not need a visa to enter Senegal. Nationals of all other countries require a visa and need to obtain it before entering the country. It is not possible to purchase visas on arrival.

Extension of Stay

To obtain a visa extension, you need to get a letter of approval from the Ministry of the Interior, Dakar (tel: 33 821 0089; Boulevard de la République), which you then take to the Ministry of Foreign Affairs to get your passport stamped. The procedure is normally uncomplicated, though it can take a couple of weeks and several trips to the ministries to speed up the process. An easier option chosen by many travellers is to take a quick trip to The Gambia or Mauritania and obtain another three months upon return to Senegal.

G ay Travellers

Senegal is not a country that is tolerant towards homosexuality. Islamic belief and the general cultural environment of the West African region are usually cited as reasons. Senegal's gay scene (mainly concentrated in Dakar and Saly) remains therefore largely underground. Public expressions of affection are generally disapproved of, and provoke aggressive and even violent reactions if expressed by homosexuals.

H ealth and Medical Care

Comprehensive medical insurance should be taken out before you leave your home country. If you are entering Senegal from a yellow-fever-risk area (such as The Gambia), you may be required to show proof of vaccination at the border. Regulations are strict, and if you can't present the required certificate at the border upon request you will either be refused entry or vaccinated there and then. Other optional but recommended vaccinations include:

Typhoid – a gastric fever caught from infected or dirty food. Valid three years.

Hepatitis A – caught from infected water or food. Valid 10 years provided you have a booster within six months.

Cholera – diarrhoea, vomiting, dehydration. Valid six months.

Polio – valid two years.

Meningitis – valid 10 years.

Always consult a travel clinic before heading off to a tropical region, and present yourself at a clinic for check-up once you've returned home.

Malaria

Malaria is a risk throughout the year, though the rainy season is particularly dangerous. Short-term travellers should always take malaria prophylaxis. As parasites become increasingly resistant to available vaccines, you should consult a travel clinic before setting out for the latest

advice. Lariam and Malarone are among the most recommended drugs, though you need to seek a doctor's advice to ensure they are suitable for you.

You should avoid getting bitten by wearing light, long-sleeved clothing and long trousers, especially around dawn and dusk. Avoid wearing dark colours as they attract mosquitoes. Top hotels spray their grounds regularly and have air-conditioning, which helps to keep mosquitoes away. If you don't have that luxury, make sure you sleep under a mosquito net. If you fail to bring one, you can purchase one at any Senegalese pharmacy.

The most effective mosquito sprays contain around 50 percent deet.

Aids

Compared to other African countries, HIV/Aids rates are low, with official rates currently at 0.8 percent. Blood for transfusion is scanned, and hospitals reliably use clean, non-infected needles.

Particularly in the tourist zones, prostitution is common, and HIV infection hence a greater risk. As anywhere else, it's important to avoid infection by avoiding unprotected intercourse. Condoms can be bought at any pharmacy.

Drinking Water

Stomach bugs are easily caught by the newly arrived traveller. Drinking bottled water goes a long way in protecting you from the unpleasant effects of "tourista", as diarrhoea is "lovingly" called. The locally produced types of bottled water are Kirène and Fontaine, and they are widely available throughout the country. In some places bottles are refilled with tap water, so make sure you check the seal before purchase.

ABOVE: graffiti warning against Aids.

It is also sensible to peel all fruit before eating and avoid eating salads, ice cubes and ice cream sold on the streets. It's possible that it may have melted and then been refrozen.

Medical Services

Dakar's medical services are comparatively good. There are a number of private clinics and emergency services that offer a good service. Public hospitals, by contrast, are notoriously understaffed and under-equipped. Upcountry, medical services are poor to barely existent. Anyone with special medical requirements should make sure to have any medication needed with them.

Emergency Services

SUMA
Km 5, Avenue Cheikh-Anta-Diop, Dakar Fann
Tel: 33 824 2418 or 33 824 6030
www.sumassistance.com
SOS Médecins
Tel: 33 889 1515
Email: sosmeddk@sentoo.sn

Hospitals

Hôpital Principal
Avenue Nelson-Mandela, Dakar
Tel: 33 839 5050
Hôpital Le Dantec
Avenue Pasteur, Dakar
Tel: 33 822 2420
Clinique de la Madeleine
18 Avenue des Diambars
Tel: 33 821 9470

Dentists

Dr Abdel Kader Bengeloume
Imm. Mbacké Anta, Sacré Cœur 2 x
Rond-Point Liberté 6
Tel: 33 864 6342
Emergency number: 76 665 0000
mail: sosdentiste@sentoo.sn

BELOW: hospital entrance in Dakar.

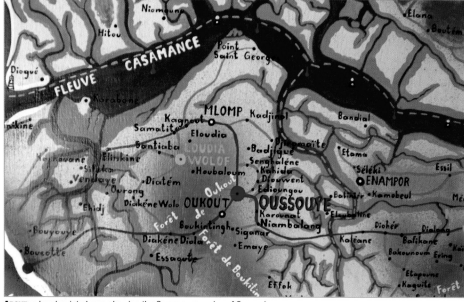

ABOVE: a hand-painted map showing the Casamance region of Senegal.

Internet

Senegal has very good and fast internet connections. Dakar is particularly well served, though other regional centres and even small towns are equipped with a few internet cafés. In Dakar, many hotels and clubs now offer wifi, often free of charge (eg Novotel, Cap Ouest, Pen'Art). If you don't have your own laptop, try the business centres in the hotel or the many internet cafés (cybercafés) around Senegal's major towns. Internet cafés come and go frequently. You'll easily find one by walking around the centre of any town you're in and by asking the locals. You can also try to phone the main office of the internet and telephone provider Orange for advice.

Agence Orange
46 Boulevard de la République, Dakar
Tel: 33 839 2100

Lost Property

Always protect your valuables by leaving them in a secure place, preferably a hotel safe. Should you lose or be robbed of any valuables, visit the nearest police station on the off-chance that your belongings have been handed in and to file a complaint.

Police Plateaux Dakar
Rue Félix-Faure, Dakar
Tel: 33 821 0394

Police Saint-Louis
Nord Saint-Louis
Tel: 33 961 1025
Police Ziguinchor
Escale Ziguinchor
Tel: 33 991 1013

Maps

Among the most recently updated maps to Senegal and The Gambia are those by International Travel Maps (2006) and Freytag-Berndt & Artaria KG (2005). Check before setting out though, as other publishers may well have appeared on the scene.

In Dakar, a good city map is useful. Many hotels and bookshops distribute free maps that feature several tourist attractions and landmarks. At the time of writing, the most recently updated and most accurate map was that by Laure Kane Editions (US$9; www.editionslaurekane.com).

Media

Newspapers and Magazines

Freedom of press is generally respected in Senegal, and there are a large number of papers and magazines available to the French speaker. National dailies include *Le Soleil* (the most government-prone), *Le Quotidien*, *Sud*, *Le Populaire* and others.

Every month, there seems to be a new glossy magazine on the market, featuring news and gossip about Senegal's rich and mighty, as well as

the latest in fashion and music. For an insight into Dakar nightlife and popular culture, these are real treasures. The main magazines include *Thiof* and *Icône*.

The journal *221* is the leading magazine on cultural information and leisure activities, and free advertising magazines such as *Waaw* often contain listings of restaurants, medical services, etc.

English-language magazines are hard to get hold of. Your best bets are the newspaper stalls near the Place de l'Indépendance.

Radio and Television

The RTS (Radiodiffusion Télévision du Sénégal) is the national government-controlled radio and TV network. The RTS TV channel features mainly political news while 2STV is more devoted to cultural information and series. Most international hotels will offer CNN and BBC World Service, but not usually any other English-language channels.

Radio is a good place to catch up with the latest trends in Senegalese music. Nostalgie is particularly great for music, while RFM and Walfajiri broadcast a mix of news and music. Most programmes are in Wolof.

Money

Senegal belongs to the CFA franc system common to all of France's former West African colonies. CFA stands for Communauté Financière

Africaine. The CFA franc issued by any of these territories is accepted by all of them. The exchange rate of the CFA franc is tied to the euro at 655:1. There are notes of CFA10,000, 5,000, 2,000, 1,000 and 500, as well as coins of CFA500, 100, 50, 25, 10 and 5.

Major hotels have foreign exchange facilities but charge commissions. Otherwise you can change money at banks or foreign exchange bureaus. Rates don't differ much from one place to the next.

ATMs exist across Dakar and in all major towns of the country. The most widely accepted card is Visa, though MasterCard often works as well. Only large supermarkets, shops and car-hire companies accept cards for payment, and there is a fairly high risk of fraud.

Banks in Dakar

Most banks are open from 8–11.30am and 12.45–5pm (Monday to Friday), with slight variations.

Most banks have their main branches at Place de l'Indépendance. They are usually very busy, and you may be in for a long wait if you have to speak to a personal adviser. The largest banks catering to international customers include:

BICIS (Central Branch)
2 Avenue Léopold Sédar-Senghor, Dakar
Tel: 33 839 0390
Open: 7.45am–4.45pm
SGBS (Central Branch)
19 Avenue Léopold Sédar-Senghor, Dakar
Tel: 33 839 5500
Open: 7.30am–6pm
CBAO (Central Branch)
2 Place de l'Indépendance

BELOW: post office sign.

Tel: 33 839 9696
Open: 7.30am–5pm

O pening Hours

Most offices open at 8.30am or 9am and close at 4.30pm or 5pm. Many take a break from 1pm to 2.30pm. Most banks close earlier than shops, at 4pm. On Friday, the main Muslim holiday of the week, many businesses close early, around 12.30pm. Only some open again at 3pm. Shops tend to open at 9am and close at 8pm with lunch from 1 to 2.30pm. Unlike most businesses and banks, shops are often open on Saturdays, at least until around 12.30pm, and corner shops are open until late at night.

P hotography

It's perfectly legal to take pictures, as long as you avoid government, strategic or military buildings. However, people often do not like having their picture taken. Particularly in the city, on markets and in nightclubs you may encounter hostility. Always get people's permission first, and if this is refused don't take the picture. Sometimes you may be asked for a small payment. Street scenes are best shot from a passing car – you are definitely in for trouble if attempting to take pictures at Dakar's inner city markets. Compact Flash and SD cards are easy to get hold of in Dakar, though they are invariably cheaper if bought online.

Take care of your camera when travelling around, as the dust and grit will easily find its way into your lens and camera. It is best to transport your equipment in a sealed camera bag.

ABOVE: happy to be snapped.

Film can be quite expensive, so it is advisable to bring with you what you need.

Postal Services

Mail between Europe and Senegal is reasonably efficient. A letter should not take longer than a week and can take as little as four days. All major towns have post offices and most medium-sized and large hotels will sell stamps and accept letters for posting. For urgent deliveries, DHL is your best choice.

Post Office Central Dakar
Avenue Malick-Sy, Dakar
Tel: 33 849 2163
Post Office Dakar Fann
Rond-Point Fann, Dakar
Tel: 33 865 2000
DHL Dakar
Avenue Hassan II (formerly Avenue Albert-Sarraut)
Tel: 33 823 1393

Public Holidays

Senegal (along with The Gambia) celebrates the feast days of the Muslim calendar (see page 309). In addition, Senegal has the following public holidays:

1 January **New Year's Day**
March (variable) **Easter Monday**
4 April **Independence Day**
1 May **Labour Day**
15 May **Whitsuntide**
15 August **The Assumption**
1 November **All Saints' Day**
25 December **Christmas Day**

Time Zone

Senegal Standard Time is GMT and does not operate Daylight-Saving Time.

R eligious Services

Dakar is a secular country. The majority of the population is Muslim, but there are also several churches, and the climate between different faith groups is harmonic and respectful. The largest Christian communities are found in the south (Casamance) and western Coast (Siné-Saloum) of Senegal. In Dakar, the main places of worship are the following:

Protestant

St Paul's Church, Rue Carnet, Dakar Plateaux

Roman Catholic

Cathédrale du Souvenir Africain, Avenue de la République, Dakar Plateaux

Muslim

Grande Mosquée, Avenue Malick-Sy, Dakar

S tudent Travellers

Senegal doesn't offer any discounts to student travellers. You may want to make contact with the grand university Cheikh Anta Diop in Dakar and encounter fellow students. The university also organises exchange programmes with universities in Africa, Europe and the United States.

Université Cheikh Anta Diop
Avenue Cheikh-Anta-Diop, Dakar
Tel: 33 864 4545

T elecommunications

The International Dialling Code for Senegal is 221. Senegal has an efficient telephone network, operated by the national company Sonatel/Orange. The main mobile phone networks are Orange and Tigo. The best way to make calls is to bring an open mobile phone and purchase a local SIM card (US$5). Top-up cards are sold on every street corner.

For international calls, dial 00 followed by the country code, area code omitting the 0, and number. Fax machines are found in the business centres of the major hotels.

Orange
46 Boulevard de la République, Dakar
Tel: 33 839 2100

Tigo
15 Route de N'gor, Dakar
Tel: 33 869 7420

Dialing Codes

The following is a list of some of the most popular country codes:

Austria	43
Belgium	32
Denmark	45
France	33
Germany	49
Ireland	353
Netherlands	31
Norway	47
Sweden	46
Switzerland	41
UK	44
USA and Canada	1

Important Numbers

Directory Enquiries 12
Police 17
Fire 18

Tipping

As a general rule, anyone who provides you with a "free" service is likely to expect a tip at the end. Small services, such as showing the way (and accompanying you there), helping you make phone calls, shake off traders, etc, can be rewarded with a CFA1,000 note. If you stay

in an upmarket hotel, then tipping is expected.

Tipping taxi drivers defeats the point of negotiating hard for a reasonable fare. You don't need to tip on short drives. However, if you have hired a driver for a day and are happy with the service you might want to give him something for his efforts.

Restaurants will expect the usual 10 percent tip.

Toilets

Public toilets are very rare in Senegal, and even if you find one, you certainly don't want to risk using it. Restaurant toilets range from very clean to rather rotten. Both flush toilets and squat loos are in use – the squat ones are often cleaner. You may not always find toilet paper, as most people use water (and their left hand) to clean their backside. If you don't feel like going quite that local, put some loo roll in your bag before heading out.

Tourist Information

Senegal is very poorly equipped with tourist information services. It's best to read up beforehand and then get in touch with a tour operator. Outside Dakar, the *syndicats d'initiative* are often very good.
Syndicat d'Initiative de Saint-Louis
Opposite Pont Faidherbe
Tel: 33 961 2455
Email: sltourisme@orange.sn
Syndicat d'Initiative de Gorée
Information booth near arrival quay
Tel: 33 823 9177
Email: methiourseye@hotmail.com
Syndicat d'Initiative de Thiès/Saly
Town Centre Mbour
Tel: 33 957 2222
Email: bgvsn@yahoo.fr
Syndicat d'Initiative de Ziguinchor
Tel: 33 993 5151
www.lacasamance.info
Syndicat d'Initiative de Tambacounda
Hôtel Niji
Tel: 33 981 1250
Email: nijihotel@orange.sn

Tour Operators

There are plenty of travel and tour agencies in Senegal. The following is a small selection of agencies that have stood the test of time.
Sahel Découverte
Rue Blaise-Diagne, Saint-Louis
Tel: 33 961 4263
Fax: 33 961 8320
www.saheldecouverte.com
Africa Travel
Route de N'gor, Dakar
Tel: 33 869 7900
www.africatravel-group.com

ABOVE: Joal-Fadiouth mosque.

Nouvelles Frontières
Route des Almadies, Mamelles
Aviation Lot no. 1, Dakar
Tel: 33 859 4447 or 33 859 4445
www.nfsenegal.com
Diatta Tours
3 Rue Charles-de-Gaulle, Ziguinchor
Tel: 33 991 2781
M'boup Voyages
27 Avenue Léopold-Sédar-Senghor,
Dakar
Tel: 33 821 1382
www.mboupvoyages.com

W ebsites

The following is a small selection of
useful websites containing information
on Senegal.
www.au-senegal.com
Exhaustive tourist site containing up-to-
date accommodation, travel, transport
and other information as well as listings of cultural events. Main website in
French, partially translated into English.
www.seneweb.com
Excellent site for news and current
affairs, summarises the main news
items from Dakar's leading papers.
www.saintlouisdusenegal.com
A good source of tourist information
for northern Senegal.
www.casamance.net
Contains reliable information on the
Casamance, including news on safety
as well as tourist activities.

www.senegal-tourism.com
Tourist site listing attractions and
travel tips.
www.sunugaal.com
Tourist and general information site
in English.

What to Bring

It's best to bring all the health
and travel basics you need. This
includes **from the chemist:** high-
protection suntan lotion, plenty of
insect repellent containing deet;
antihistamine or sting-relief cream;
indigestion tablets; water-sterilising
tablets if you are travelling upcountry; throat lozenges; anti-
malaria prophylactics *(see Health)*
and cures (ask your doctor); basic
first aid equipment including
sticking plasters, antiseptic cream,
cotton wool; headache tablets;
tampons; deodorants, etc. Many of
these items are also available in
Dakar's supermarkets and hotel
shops, but they tend to be
comparatively expensive.
Miscellaneous: A torch to help you
through power cuts; a pocket knife;
binoculars for birdwatching; a beach
towel; a sunhat; swimming and
snorkelling gear; a French-English
dictionary; an open mobile phone; a
small tube of washing liquid to hand-
wash your underwear.

You may also want to bring small
gifts for the people you are likely to
visit or as tips.

What to Wear

From November to May, the region
has a very pleasant subtropical
climate. Days are warm, dry and
sunny with an unexpectedly cool
breeze in the evenings. Bring
therefore a couple of sweaters
or cardigans as well as summer
clothes. Pack a few light, long-
sleeved items to protect you from
mosquito bites. In Senegal, people
like dressing smart, especially
when going out to eat or party.
You should therefore bring some
elegant items besides flip-flops
and T-shirts.
    Most Senegalese are Muslim,
and though women rarely go fully
veiled, some basic dress codes
should be respected: men should
wear long trousers and women skirts
below the knee or trousers. T-shirts,
even sleeveless ones, are acceptable.
In nightclubs and bars, even super-
sexy outfits for women are fine, as
long as they are ready to deal with
the ensuing attention.
    Hotels provide laundry services at
reasonable prices.

Women Travellers

Senegal is a fairly safe place
for women travellers, though
not without hassle. Lone female
travellers will invariably be
approached and constantly
pestered by young men, particularly
on the beach and in the inner city.
Though you may well be promised
the world, guys approaching you
in that way in the streets or clubs
are hardly ever serious, however
clever their approach. The best way
to shake them off is by being firm,
confident, or simply ignoring their
advances. Single women wishing
to stay that way may want to
pretend that they are married.
That usually means they will be
given more respect.
    Women should avoid spending
time alone at the beach, particularly
close to nightfall, and not walk
alone through the streets after
dark. It's always a good idea to
register with your embassy when
entering the country in case anything
should happen.

Weights and Measures

The metric system is used
in Senegal.

L ANGUAGE

UNDERSTANDING THE LANGUAGE

Senegal's Languages

The official language of Senegal is French. Wolof, the language spoken by the ethnic group of the same name, is the most widely spoken African language in Senegal. It has become the *lingua franca* for both Senegal and The Gambia and is spoken by more than 90 percent of people in the region as a first or second language. Pulaar is spoken by around one-quarter of the Senegalese population, and around 15 percent of The Gambia's.

Words and Phrases

How much is it? *C'est combien?*
What is your name? *Comment vous appelez-vous?*
My name is… *Je m'appelle…*
Do you speak English? *Parlez-vous anglais?*
I am English/American *Je suis anglais(e)/américain(e)*
I don't understand *Je ne comprends pas*
Please speak more slowly *Parlez plus lentement, s'il vous plaît*
Can you help me? *Pouvez-vous m'aider?*
I'm looking for… *Je cherche…*
Where is…? *Où est…?*
I'm sorry *Excusez-moi/Pardon*
I don't know *Je ne sais pas*
No problem *Pas de problème*
Have a good day! *Bonne journée!*
That's it *C'est ça*
Here is… *Voici…*
There is… *Voilà…*
Let's go *On y va/Allons-y*
See you tomorrow *À demain*
See you soon *À bientôt*
Show me the word in the book *Montrez-moi le mot dans le livre*
yes *oui*
no *non*

please *s'il vous plaît*
thank you (very much) *merci (beaucoup)*
you're welcome *de rien*
excuse me *excusez-moi*
hello *bonjour*
OK *d'accord*
goodbye *au revoir*
good evening *bonsoir*
here *ici*
there *là*
today *aujourd'hui*
yesterday *hier*
tomorrow *demain*
now *maintenant*
later *plus tard*
this morning *ce matin*
this afternoon *cet après-midi*
this evening *ce soir*

On Arrival

I want to get off at… *Je voudrais descendre à…*
What street is this? *Dans quelle rue sommes-nous?*
How far is…? *A quelle distance se trouve…?*
airport *l'aéroport*
train station *la gare*
bus station *la gare routière*
bus *l'autobus, le car*
bus stop *l'arrêt*
platform *le quai*
ticket *le billet*
return ticket *aller-retour*
toilets *les toilettes*
This is the hotel address *C'est l'adresse de l'hôtel*
I'd like a (single/double) room… *Je voudrais une chambre (pour une/deux personnes)…*
…with shower *avec douche*
…with a bath *avec salle de bain*
…with a view *avec vue*
Does that include breakfast? *Le prix comprend-il le petit déjeuner?*

May I see the room? *Je peux voir la chambre?*
washbasin *le lavabo*
bed *le lit*
key *la clé*
lift/elevator *l'ascenseur*
air-conditioned *climatisé*
swimming pool *la piscine*
to book *réserver*

On the Road

Where is the spare wheel? *Où est la roue de secours?*
Where is the nearest garage? *Où est le garage le plus proche?*
Our car has broken down *Notre voiture est en panne*
I want to have my car repaired *Je veux faire réparer ma voiture*
It's not your right of way *Vous n'avez pas la priorité*

Native Language

Pulaar is the language spoken by the Fula people who are found across West Africa. There are many regional dialects which are not always recognisable between groups, but the following phrases should be understood in most parts of Senegal.

Hello *no ngoolu daa*
Goodbye *ñalleen e jamm*
Please *njaafodaa*
Thank you *a jaaraamah*
Sorry *yaafo/achanam hakke*
Yes *eey*
No *alaa*
How are you? *no mbaddaa?*
My name is… *ko … mbiyetee mi*
Where is…? *hoto woni?*
Do you speak English/French? *ada faama engale/faranse?*

I think I must have put diesel in the car by mistake *Je crois que j'ai mis du gasoil dans la voiture par erreur*
the road to... *la route pour...*
left *gauche*
right *droite*
straight on *tout droit*
far *loin*
near *près*
opposite *en face*
beside *à côté de*
car park *parking*
over there *là-bas*
at the end *au bout*
on foot *à pied*
by car *en voiture*
town map *le plan*
road map *la carte*
street *la rue*
square *la place*
give way *céder le passage*
dead end *impasse*
no parking *stationnement interdit*
motorway *l'autoroute*
toll *le péage*
speed limit *la limitation de vitesse*
petrol *l'essence*
unleaded *sans plomb*
diesel *le gasoil*
water/oil *l'eau/l'huile*
puncture *un pneu crevé*
bulb *l'ampoule*
wipers *les essuie-glaces*

Shopping

Where is the nearest bank/post office? *Où est la banque/Poste la plus proche?*
I'd like to buy *Je voudrais acheter*
How much is it? *C'est combien?*
Do you take credit cards? *Est-ce que vous acceptez les cartes de crédit?*
I'm just looking *Je regarde seulement*
Have you got...? *Avez-vous...?*
I'll take it *Je le prends*
I'll take this one/that one *Je prends celui-ci/celui-là*
What size is it? *C'est de quelle taille?*
Anything else? *Avec ça?*
size (clothes) *la taille*
size (shoes) *la pointure*
cheap *bon marché*
expensive *cher*
enough *assez*
too much *trop*
a piece *un morceau de*
each *la pièce* (e.g. *ananas, CFA500 la pièce*)
ripe *mûr*
bill *l'addition*
chemist *la pharmacie*
bakery *la boulangerie*
bookshop *la librairie*
library *la bibliothèque*
delicatessen *la charcuterie*

ABOVE: the French Institute in Dakar.

fishmonger *la poissonnerie*
grocery *l'alimentation/l'épicerie*
tobacconist *tabac* (can also sell stamps and newspapers)
market *le marché*
supermarket *le supermarché*

Sightseeing

town *la ville*
old town *la vieille ville*
abbey *l'abbaye*
cathedral *la cathédrale*
church *l'église*
keep *le donjon*
hospital *l'hôpital*
town hall *l'hôtel de ville/la mairie*
nave *la nef*
stained glass *le vitrail*
staircase *l'escalier*
tower *la tour*
walk *le tour*
museum *le musée*
art gallery *la galerie*
exhibition *l'exposition*
tourist information office *l'office de tourisme/le syndicat d'initiative*
free *gratuit*
open *ouvert*
closed *fermé*
every day *tous les jours*
all year *toute l'année*
all day *toute la journée*

Dining Out

Table d'hôte (the "host's table") is one set menu served at a set price.
Prix fixe is a fixed-price menu.
À la carte means dishes from the menu are charged separately.
breakfast *le petit déjeuner*
lunch *le déjeuner*
dinner *le dîner*
meal *le repas*
first course *l'entrée/les hors d'œuvre*

main course *le plat principal*
made to order *sur commande*
drink included *boisson comprise*
wine list *la carte des vins*
the bill *l'addition*
fork *la fourchette*
knife *le couteau*
spoon *la cuillère*
plate *l'assiette*
glass *le verre*
napkin *la serviette*
ashtray *le cendrier*

Breakfast and Snacks

baguette **long thin loaf**
pain **bread**
petits pains **rolls**
beurre **butter**
poivre **pepper**
sel **salt**
sucre **sugar**
confiture **jam**
œufs **eggs**
...à la coque **boiled eggs**
...au bacon **bacon and eggs**
...au jambon **ham and eggs**
...sur le plat **fried eggs**
...brouillés **scrambled eggs**
tartine **bread with butter**
yaourt **yoghurt**
crêpe **pancake**
croque-monsieur **ham and cheese toasted sandwich**
croque-madame **...with a fried egg on top**
galette **type of pancake**

First Course

An *amuse-bouche, amuse-gueule* or appetiser is something to "amuse the mouth", served before the first course.
anchoïade **sauce of olive oil, anchovies and garlic, served with raw vegetables**
assiette de charcuterie **cold meats**
potage **soup**

La Viande – Meat

saignant/bleu **rare**
à point **medium**
bien cuit **well done**
grillé **grilled**
agneau **lamb**
andouille/andouillette **tripe sausage**
bifteck **steak**
boudin **sausage**
boudin noir **black pudding**
boudin blanc **white pudding**
(chicken or veal)
à la bourguignonne **cooked with red wine, onions and mushrooms**
brochette **kebab**
canard **duck**
contre-filet **cut of sirloin steak**
coq au vin **chicken in red wine**
côte d'agneau **lamb chop**
daube **beef stew with red wine, onions and tomatoes**
dinde **turkey**
entrecôte **beef rib steak**
escargot **snail**
faisan **pheasant**
farci **stuffed**
faux-filet **sirloin**
foie **liver**
foie gras **goose or duck liver**
pâté
cuisses de grenouille **frog's legs**
grillade **grilled meat**
hachis **minced meat**
jambon **ham**
lapin **rabbit**
lardon **small pieces of bacon, often added to salads**
magret de canard **breast of duck**
médaillon **round pieces of meat**
oie **goose**
perdrix **partridge**
pintade **guinea fowl**
porc **pork**
poulet **chicken**
rôti **roast**
sanglier **wild boar**
saucisse **fresh sausage**
saucisson **salami**
veau **veal**

Poissons – Fish

anchois **anchovies**
anguille **eel**
bar (or loup) **sea bass**
Bercy **sauce of fish stock, butter, white wine and shallots**
brandade **salt-cod purée**
cabillaud **cod**
calamar **squid**
coquillage **shellfish**
coquilles Saint-Jacques **scallops**
crevette **shrimp**
daurade **sea bream**
fruits de mer **seafood**
homard **lobster**
huître **oyster**
langoustine **large prawn**
limande **lemon sole**
lotte **monkfish**
moule **mussel**

Telling the Time

The 24-hour clock is frequently used in French when giving times: 8am is huit heures, noon (midi) is douze heures, 8pm is vingt heures, and midnight (minuit) is zéro heure.

moules marinières **mussels in white-wine sauce**
saumon **salmon**
thon **tuna**
truite **trout**

Légumes – Vegetables

ail **garlic**
artichaut **artichoke**
asperge **asparagus**
aubergine **aubergine/eggplant**
avocat **avocado**
bolets **boletus mushrooms**
céleri rémoulade **celeriac served with mayonnaise**
cèpes **cep mushroom**
champignon **mushroom**
chips **potato crisps**
chou **cabbage**
chou-fleur **cauliflower**
concombre **cucumber**
cornichon **gherkin**
courgette **courgette/zucchini**
cru **raw**
crudités **raw vegetables**
épinard **spinach**
frites **chips, French fries**
gratin dauphinois **sliced potatoes baked with cream**
haricot **dried bean**
haricots verts **green beans**
lentilles **lentils**
maïs **corn**
mange-tout **mange-tout/snow pea**
mesclun **mixed-leaf salad**
noix **nut, walnut**
noisette **hazelnut**
oignon **onion**
persil **parsley**
pignon **pine nut**
poireau **leek**
pois **pea**
poivron **bell pepper**
pomme de terre **potato**
riz **rice**
salade Niçoise **egg, tuna, olives, onions and tomato salad**
salade verte **green salad**
truffe **truffle**

Fruits – Fruit

ananas **pineapple**
cerise **cherry**
citron **lemon**
citron vert **lime**
fraise **strawberry**
framboise **raspberry**
mangue **mango**
pamplemousse **grapefruit**
pêche **peach**

poire **pear**
pomme **apple**
prune **plum**
pruneau **prune**
raisin **grape**
raisin sec **raisin**

Puddings – Dessert

Belle Hélène **fruit with ice cream and chocolate sauce**
clafoutis **baked pudding of batter and cherries**
crème anglaise **custard**
crème Chantilly **whipped cream**
fromage **cheese**
(fromage de) chèvre **goat's cheese**
île flottante **whisked egg whites in custard sauce**
tarte tatin **upside-down tart of caramelised apples**

In the Café

drinks **les boissons**
coffee **café**
...with milk/cream au lait/crème
...decaffeinated déca/décaféiné
...black/espresso noir/expresso
...filtered coffee filtre
tea **thé**
...herb infusion tisane
...camomile verveine
hot chocolate **chocolat chaud**
milk **lait**
...full-cream entier
...semi-skimmed demi-écrémé
...skimmed écrémé
mineral water **eau minérale**
fizzy **pétillante/gazeuse**
non-fizzy **plate/non-gazeuse**
fizzy lemonade **limonade**
fresh lemon juice served with sugar **citron pressé**
fresh orange juice **orange pressée**
fresh or cold **frais, fraîche**
beer **bière**
...bottled en bouteille
...on tap pression
pre-dinner drink **apéritif**
white wine with cassis **(blackcurrant liqueur)** kir
kir with champagne kir royal
with ice **avec des glaçons**
neat **sec**
red **rouge**
white **blanc**
rose **rosé**
dry **brut**
sweet **doux**
sparkling wine **crémant**
house wine **vin de maison**
pitcher **carafe/pichet**
...of water/wine d'eau/de vin
cheers! **santé!**
hangover **gueule de bois**

FURTHER READING

General

Very little has been written specifically about Senegal and The Gambia in English and virtually nothing modern is in print, apart from a number of guidebooks which include the country in a wider region, e.g. West Africa as a whole. This is a small selection of recommended reading covering the specific region as well as Africa in general, beginning with a good paperback edition of the 17th-century explorer Mungo Park's excellent account of his perilous journeys.

Travels into the Interior of Africa by Mungo Park, Wordsworth Editions, 2002 Eland, London and Hippocrene. NY, 1983.

Enter Gambia, the Birth of an Improbable Nation by Berkeley Rice, Angus and Robertson, London, 1986.

Ethnic Groups of the Senegambia by Patience Sonko-Goodwin, Book Production Unit, Banjul, 1985.

A Naturalist's Guide to the Gambia by Etienne Edberg, J.G. Sanders, Sweden, 1982.

Roots by Alex Haley, various editions, from 1976.

The Music in My Head by Mark Hudson, Jonathan Cape 1998

Our Grandmother's Drums by Mark Hudson, Vintage 2004

Two Rivers: Travels in West Africa on the Trail of Mungo Park by Peter Hudson, Chapmans Publishers, 1992.

The Scramble for Africa by Thomas Pakenham, Abacus, 1992

Africa: A Biography of the Continent by John Reader, Penguin, 1998

Landlords and Strangers: Ecology, Society & Trade in West Africa, 1000–1630 by George E Brooks, Westview Press 1994.

The Forest Dwellers (with introduction by Jane Goodall) by Stella Brewer, Harper Collins 1979.

Sufism and Religious Brotherhoods in Senegal by Khadim Mbacke, Markus Wiener, 2005.

History of the Gambia: AD1000 to 1965 by Dawda Faal, Edward Francis Press, 1997.

Black, French and African by Janet G. Vaillant, Harvard University Press.

Field Guides

Several field guides are in print covering the mammals of Africa, though many older guides are dated both in terms of nomenclature and modern distribution. Of the more current guides these are recommended, *The Kingdon Field Guide to African Mammals* by Jonathan Kingdon (Academic Press, 1997). The definitive guide to Africa's mammals, both great and small. *Field Guide to the Larger Mammals of Africa* by Chris and Tilde Stuart (Struik Publishers, 1997). Highly informative lightwight guide. Also, indispensable to anybody with an interest in ornithology, the definitive *Field Guide to Birds of The Gambia and Senegal* by Barlow, Wacher and Disley (Pica Press, 1997) is far superior within its geographical limitations to any of the several field guides to West African birds currently in print.

Send Us Your Thoughts

We do our best to ensure the information in our books is as accurate and up-to-date as possible. The books are updated on a regular basis using local contacts, who painstakingly add, amend and correct as required. However, some details (such as telephone numbers and opening times) are liable to change, and we are ultimately reliant on our readers to put us in the picture.

We welcome your feedback, especially your experience of using the book "on the road". Maybe we recommended a hotel that you liked (or another that you didn't), or you came across a great bar or new attraction we missed.

We will acknowledge all contributions, and we'll offer an Insight Guide to the best letters received.

Please write to us at:
   Insight Guides
   PO Box 7910
   London SE1 1WE
Or email us at:
   insight@apaguide.co.uk

Other Insight Guides

The classic Insight Guides series combines in-depth features and an exploration of not-to-be-missed places accompanied by evocative, vibrant photography. Insight Guides that highlight destinations to Africa include :

Insight Guide: East African Wildlife covers the flora and fauna of all the nature reserves; essential reading to complete the African safari experience.

Insight Guide: Kenya is full of information on the country's history, peoples and wildlife parks, with superb photography capturing the very essense of Africa.

Insight Guide: Namibia is a comprehensive guide to this dramatic and beautiful country, **Insight Guide: South Africa** paints a complete portrait of one of the most exciting destinations in the world.

ART AND PHOTO CREDITS

AFP/Getty Images 54R, 56, 204, 208T
AISA 218
akg-images 32T, 34, 37, 38, 39R, 40, 41B, 44, 46, 49R, 50, 230T
The Art Archive 30T, 31T&B, 35, 36R, 48
Art Directors/Ark Religion 153
Authors Images/Photoshot 10BL, 205, 206, 207T&B, 213, 246
Authors Images/TIPS 254T, 265L
Biosphoto/Grospas Jean-Yves/Still Pictures 211, 242T
blickwinkel/Alamy 274
Bonnet/Andia.fr/drr.net 11T
Nic Bothma/epa/Corbis 158, 254
Richard Bowler/Alamy 128T
Francois Brey/GODONG 250
Bridgeman Art Library 38B, 39L
Julien Chatelin/Rapho/Camerapress 55
Bene Christophe/WpN 223, 224, 225, 229, 247T&B, 248T
Shelley Cryan/PhotoShelter 69R, 217, 225T, 226
Mary Evans Picture Library 41, 42, 43, 47
Mark Eveleigh/Alamy 124
Mark Eveleigh/drr.net 208BR
FLPA/Jurgen & Christine Sohns 121T
FLPA/Roger Tidman 9C
Laurent Geslin/naturepl.com 216
Getty Images 52
Getty Images/National Geographic 159, 268T
Globe Photos Inc/Rex Features 69
Amar Grover/John Warburton-Lee Photography 120
Franck Guiziou/hemis.fr 256, 259, 261, 263, 264, 266T&B, 268
James Hawkins/Alamy 240, 241
Jon Hicks/Corbis 87
hiddengambia.com 7CLT, 123T, 262T
Michel Houet/Belpress 236T&B
Michel Houet/Belpress/Andia/drr.net 6BR, 210
Richard Human/Alamy 125BL
Isifa Image Service/Rex Features 119
iStockphoto.com 9BL, 77T, 99T, 122T, 125BR, 193, 241T, 260, 262, 264T, 265R
Alan King engraving/Alamy 46B
David Knowles/fotoLibra 190
Philippe Lissac/GODONG 245
Look/Travel Lounge Images 136
Eamonn McCabe/Redferns 68B
Janis Miglavs/Danita Delimont

Agency/drr.net 9BR, 267
Christine Osborne/Corbis 30B
Aldo Pavan/SIME-4Corners Images 138/139, 208BL, 222, 238/239, 326
Dave Penman/Rex Features 88
photolibrary.com 131BR, 210T, 219, 220, 235
Sylvaine Poitau/APA 1, 2/3, 3B, 4(all), 6/7T, 6CL, 7TR, CLB, CR&BL, 8R, 9TR, 10TL, TR&BR, 11C&B, 12/13, 14/15, 16/17, 18, 19L&R, 20, 21, 22T&C, 23, 24(all), 25, 26, 27, 28/29, 32C&B, 33T&B, 36L, 43B, 45, 51, 57L&R, 58, 59, 60(all), 61C&B, 62C&B, 63L&R, 66, 67, 68, 69L, 70, 71, 72/73, 74/75, 76, 77L, 78, 79, 80, 81T&B, 82T&B, 83T&B, 84(all), 85T&B, 86T&B, 87T, 90T&B, 91T&B, 92, 93, 94, 95(all), 96T&B, 97, 98T&B, 99, 100T&B, 101T&B, 102, 103(all), 104T&B, 105T&B, 106(all), 107T&B, 108, 109, 110/111(all), 115, 116, 117, 118, 121BL&BR, 122, 123, 125T, 127, 132L&R, 133T&B, 137, 140, 141L&R, 144, 145, 147T&B, 148T&B, 149(all), 150T&B, 151T&B, 152T&B, 153T, 154, 155T&B, 156, 157T&B, 159T, 160, 162, 163, 164, 165T&B, 166(all), 167, 168, 169, 171T&B, 174BR, 175T&B, 176T&B, 177T&B, 178(all), 179T&B, 180T&B, 181T&B, 182(all), 183T&B, 184, 185, 191, 193T, 194, 195T&B, 196T&B, 197L&R, 198T&B, 199(all), 200(all), 201T&B, 203, 209, 221T, 223T, 232, 233, 234, 242, 243, 244T&B, 245T, 248, 249, 251T&B, 252T, 253, 255, 257, 259T, 267T, 269, 270, 271, 272, 273, 274T, 275T&B, 276, 277T&B, 278T&B, 279L&R, 280/281(all), 282T&B, 283(all), 284T&B, 285T&B, 286, 287, 288, 292T&B, 293T&B, 294T&B, 295T&B, 296T&C, 298, 299, 301, 302T&C, 303, 305, 306, 308, 309, 310, 311T&B, 312, 316(all), 317, 318, 319, 320T&B, 321, 322, 323, 324T&B, 325, 328, 329T&B, 330T&C, 331T&B, 332, 333, 334T&B, 335, 336, 337T&B, 338, 339T&B, 340, 341, 342, 343
Patrick Robert/Sygma/Corbis 53
Isabelle Rozenbaum/StockFood UK 161
Anup Shah/naturepl.com 8BL

Friedrich Stark/Das Fotoarchiv./Still Pictures 128B
Liba Taylor/Robert Harding 114
Roger Tidman/Corbis 135
David Tipling 126T
Topfoto 31C, 49L
Ami Vitale/Panos 54L
Andrew Woodley/Alamy 120T
Ariadne Van Zandbergen 7BR, 8T, 119T, 129T&B, 131BL, 136T, 172T&B, 173T&B, 174T&BL, 192, 202T&B, 212T&B, 213T, 214, 215, 221, 226T, 227, 228T&B, 230, 231, 237, 238T, 252, 258, 261T
Ariadne Van Zandbergen/African Pictures 6CR, 126
Ariadne Van Zandbergen/Still Pictures 130, 131T

64/65: AFP/Getty Images 64/65T, 65TR; Shelley Cryan/PhotoShelter 64CR; Isifa Image Service/Rex Features 65BR; Sylvaine Poitau/APA 65BL; Finbarr O'Reilly/Reuters 64BC; Sandro Vannini/Corbis 65CL; Ariadne Van Zandbergen/Alamy 64TL

112/113: iStockphoto.com 112/113T, 112BC; Mark Eveleigh/drr.net 113TR; FLPA/Ariadne Van Zandbergen 113BL; Ariadne Van Zandbergen 112BR, 113BR

186/187: Philip van den Berg/African Pictures 187C; K. Hennig/Still Pictures 187BR; Eric Hochstadt 186/187T; Bernard Howden/fotoLibra 187TR; iStockphoto.com 186BL, 187CL; David Knowles/fotoLibra 186BR; Carles Martorell/Superstock 187BC; Ariadne Van Zandbergen 187BL

188/189: FLPA/Roger Tidman 189TR; Michel Houet/Belpress/Andia/drr.net 188/189T; iStockphoto.com 188TL, BL&BR, 189CL; René Mattes/hemis.fr 188CR; Sylvaine Poitau/APA 189B

Map Production: Stephen Ramsay

© 2009 Apa Publications GmbH & Co. Verlag KG (Singapore branch)

Production: Linton Donaldson

INDEX

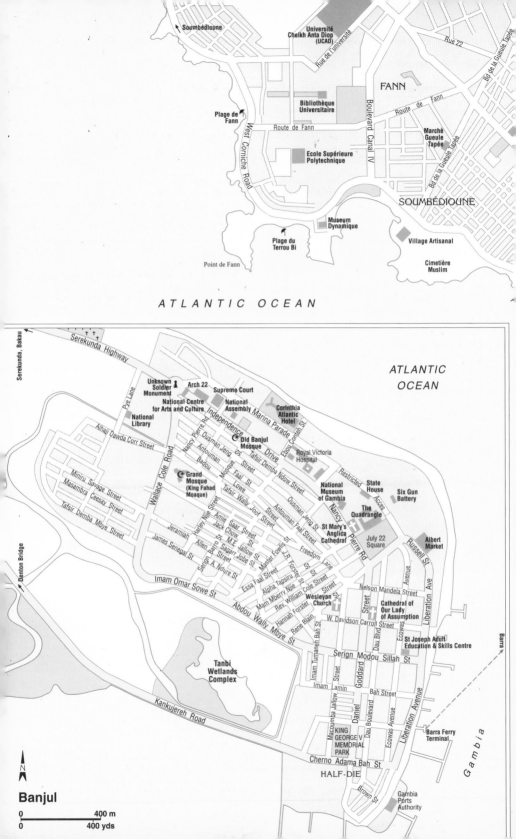

ATLANTIC OCEAN

Soumbédioune

Université
Cheikh Anta Diop
(UCAD)

Rue 22

FANN

Bibliothèque
Universitaire

Route de Fann

Boulevard Canal IV

Bd de la Gueule Tapée

Plage de
Fann

Route de Fann

Marché
Gueule
Tapée

Ecole Supérieure
Polytechnique

SOUMBÉDIOUNE

Museum
Dynamique

Plage du
Terrou Bi

Village Artisanal

Point de Fann

Cimetière
Muslim

West Corniche Road

ATLANTIC OCEAN

Serekunda, Bakau

Serekunda Highway

ATLANTIC
OCEAN

Unknown
Soldier
Monument

Arch 22

Supreme Court

Corinthia
Atlantic
Hotel

Pye Lane

National Centre
for Arts and Culture

National
Assembly

Marina Parade

National
Library

Independence

Old Banjul
Mosque

Ebou Conteh St

Alhaji Dawda Corr Street

Nancy Pierre Rd

Pierre Rd

Ousman Jeng St

Tafsir Demba Ndow Street

Royal Victoria
Hospital

Restricted

Wallace Cole Road

Antouman
Badou

Mosque Faal St

National
Museum
of Gambia

State
House

Six Gun
Battery

Miniru Savage Street

Grand
Mosque
(King Fahad
Moaque)

Tafsir Wally Joof Street

Antouman Faal Street

Ousman Jeng St

The
Quadrangle

Masambra Ceesay Street

Lowe
Street

St Mary's
Anglica
Cathedral

Nancy

Pierre Rd

July 22
Square

Albert
Market

Tafsir Demba Mbye Street

Amie Saar Street

Jack Chow St

M.E. Jallow St

Master Fowls St

J.R. Forster St

Freedom
Lane

Russell St

Liberation Ave

Jeramiah
Barden Nile Street

Allen Barro
Street

Selign A. Noure St

Essa Faal Street

Alpha Tapsiru
St

Master Fowls
St

J.R. Forster
St

James Senegal St

Sagarr Jobe St

Mam Mberry Nile
Rev. William Cole Street

Wesleyan
Church

Cathedral of
Our Lady
of Assumption

Imam Omar Sowe St

Hannah Forster St

Rene Blain

Nelson Mandela Street

W. Davidson Carroll Street

Goddard Street

Dau Blvd

Ecowas

St Joseph Adult
Education & Skills Centre

Barra

Denton Bridge

Abdou Wally Mbye St

Serign Modou Sillah St

Tanbi
Wetlands
Complex

Imam Tumaneh Bah St

Imam Lamin

Bah Street

Liberation Avenue

Barra Ferry
Terminal

Kankujereh Road

Macoumba Jallow

Daniel Goddard

Dau Boulevard

Ecowas Avenue

KING
GEORGE V
MEMORIAL
PARK

Cherno Adama Bah St

HALF-DIE

Brown St

Gambia
Ports
Authority

Gambia

N

Banjul

0   400 m
0   400 yds